ST BASIL THE GREAT

On Christian Ethics

T0326831

ST VLADIMIR'S SEMINARY PRESS
Popular Patristics Series
Number 51

The Popular Patristics Series published by St Vladimir's Seminary Press provides readable and accurate translations of a wide range of early Christian literature to a wide audience—students of Christian history to lay Christians reading for spiritual benefit. Recognized scholars in their fields provide short but comprehensive and clear introductions to the material. The texts include classics of Christian literature, thematic volumes, collections of homilies, letters on spiritual counsel, and poetical works from a variety of geographical contexts and historical backgrounds. The mission of the series is to mine the riches of the early Church and to make these treasures available to all.

Series Editor
BOGDAN BUCUR

Associate Editor
IGNATIUS GREEN

* * *

Series Editor
1999–2020
JOHN BEHR

ST BASIL THE GREAT

On Christian Ethics

Translated by

JACOB N. VAN SICKLE

ST VLADIMIR'S SEMINARY PRESS
YONKERS, NEW YORK

Library of Congress Cataloging-in-Publication Data

Basil, Saint, Bishop of Caesarea, approximately 329–379, author.
[Ethike. English]
On Christian ethics / St. Basil the Great ; translation and introduction by
Jacob Van Sickle.
    pages cm. — (Popular Patristics series, ISSN 1555–5755 ; number 51)
    In Greek and English; English text translated from Greek; introduction and
notes in English.
    Includes bibliographical references.
    ISBN 978–0–88141–493–6 (paper) — ISBN 978–0–88141–494–4 (electronic)
    1. Christian ethics—Early works to 1800. 2. Basil, Saint, Bishop of Caesarea,
approximately 329–379. 3. Basil, Saint, Bishop of Caesarea, approximately
329–379. Ethike. I. Van Sickle, Jacob, translator. II. Clarke, W. K. Lowther
(William Kemp Lowther), 1879–1968, translator. III. Wagner, Monica, 1910–
2006, translator. IV. Basil, Saint, Bishop of Caesarea, approximately 329–379.
Ethike. V. Basil, Saint, Bishop of Caesarea, approximately 329–379. Ethike. VI.
Title.
    BR65.B3E8 2014
    241—dc23

                           201401

COPYRIGHT © 2014 BY
ST VLADIMIR'S SEMINARY PRESS
575 Scarsdale Road, Yonkers, NY 10707
1-800-204-2665
www.svspress.com

Scripture from the Revised Standard Version of the Bible
Copyright © 1946, 1952 and 1971 National Council of the
Churches of Christ in the United States of America.
Used by permission. All rights reserved.

ISBN 978–088141–493–6 (paper)
ISBN 978–088141–494–3 (electronic)
ISSN 1555–5755

For Michael,
John,
and Aaron

Ἀκούσατε, παῖδες, παιδείαν πατρὸς,
καὶ προσέχετε γνῶναι ἔννοιαν.

Hear, O children, a father's instruction, and
be attentive, that you might know how to think.
Prov 4.1

Table of Contents

Acknowledgments

This book was five years in the making. It began as a study of Basil's *Ethics* accompanied by a translation of the rules from that work (not the Scriptures quoted) for a master's thesis submitted to St Vladimir's Seminary in 2010. Then slowly over the next four years, as I pursued my doctoral studies at Saint Louis University, the other pieces were added, the thesis largely rewritten into a suitable introduction, and finishing touches made with the help of excellent editors. It is my joy to report that the list of people whom I have to thank for their assistance in seeing the work through to completion is likewise long. I would first like to thank my teacher of Greek, Professor Michael Kumpf, whose enthusiasm for Greek language and history infected many of us unwary students, felicitously altering the course of our studies and careers. I thank also my undergraduate mentor, Dr. Scott Huelin, who introduced me to the writings of St. Basil and recommended him to me when I was casting about blindly for a senior project. I owe an enormous debt of gratitude to Fr John Behr, from whom I learned the Fathers. He first suggested Basil's *Ethics* as a potentially fruitful topic for a ThM thesis and then encouraged me to continue to work toward this publication. His mentorship from the inception all the way through to the completion of the project as editor has ensured a far better volume than I could have otherwise produced and taught me a great deal about the practice of scholarship.

Thanks are due to Peter Martens, my doktorvater, who initiated me into manuscript studies, paleography, and the tools of research, without all of which this volume would have been poorer. I also

wish to express my thanks to Ron Crown, research librarian at Saint Louis University's Pius Library for help in tracking down resources. For helpful comments on aspects of the work I thank Mark Del-Cogliano, Scott Dermer, Rodney Malone, Alex Giltner, and Blake Hartung. Thanks to Dr. Maria Pantelia, director of the *Thesaurus Linguae Graecae*, for graciously giving me use of digital copies of the Greek texts of *On the Judgment of God* and *On the Faith* from that database. Thanks also to Michael Soroka and Fr Benedict Churchill for negotiating the permission to use the Revised Standard Version of the New Testament, and to Rachel Reinsche of the National Council of Churches for granting it on unprecedented terms. Fr Benedict, general editor of SVS Press, is especially to be thanked for shepherding this book through production and providing many useful suggestions for improving its flow and format. I want to thank my parents, Brian Mark and Victoria Lynn Van Sickle, for inspiring me to make the study and teaching of faith my life's work, for their undying support both material and spiritual, and for their constant example. I thank my father also for combing the manuscript more meticulously than any editor, for making many helpful suggestions for its improvement, and for thinking through with me several of Basil's more profound ideas. To my wife, Jenna Renée Mary Van Sickle, there are no words. Thank you for your love and support through this and every project, for setting me an example of discipline and hard work, and for the many sacrifices you make daily for the flourishing of our family.

Abbreviations

BBV III   Paul Jonathan Fedwick, *Bibliotheca Basiliana Vniversalis: A Study of the Manuscript Tradition, Translations and Editions of the Works of Basil of Caesarea III. The Ascetica, Contra Eunomium 1–3, Ad Amphilochium De Spiritu Sancto, Dubia et Spuria, with Supplements to Volumes I–II.* Turnhout: Brepols, 1997.

Clarke   W. K. Lowther Clarke, tr. *The Ascetic Works of Saint Basil.* Oxford: Society for Promoting Christian Knowledge, 1925.

De Sinner   Gabriel Rudolf Ludwig de Sinner, *Sancti Patris nostri Basilii Caesareae Cappadociae archiepiscopi, opera omnia quae exstant, vel quae sub eius nomine circumferuntur, ad manuscriptos Codices Gallicanos, Vaticanos, Florentinos et Anglicos, nec non ad antiquiores editiones castigata, multis aucta: Nova Interpretatione, criticis Praefationibus, Notis, variis Lectionibus illustrata, nova sancti Doctoris Vita et copiosissimis Indicibus locupletata. Tomus Primus et Secundus: Opera et studio Domni Iuliani Garnier, Presbyteri et Monachi Benedictini, e Congregatione Sancti Mauri. Tomus Tertius: Opera et studio Monachorum Ordinis Sancti Benedicti, et Congregatione Sancti Mauri.* Editio Parisina altera, emendata et aucta. Paris: Gaume Fratres, 1839.

Ep.   *Epistulae* (Letters)

Garnier   Domini Iuliani Garnier, *Sancti Patris nostri Basilii*
               Caesareae Cappadociae Archi-Episcopi Opera omnia
               quae extant, vel qvae ejus nomine circumferuntur, ad
               Mss. codices Gallicanos, Vaticanos, Florentinos, et Angli-
               cos, nec non ad antiqviores Editiones castigata, mul-
               tis aucta: nova Interpretatione, Criticis Praefationibus,
               Notis, variis Lectionibus illustrata, nova Sancti Doctoris
               Vita, et copiosissimis Indicibus locupletata. 3 vols. Paris:
               I. B. Coignard, 1721–1730.

LXX   Septuagint (Greek Old Testament)

ms(s)   manuscript(s)

Orat.   *Orationes* of Gregory of Nazianzus

PG   *Patrologia Cursus Completus: Series Graeca,* ed. J.P.
               Migne.

Introduction

Basil's Life

Basil was born in either 329 or 330 to wealthy Christian parents in the city of Caesarea, Cappadocia, a Roman province which cut a swath through the middle of eastern Asia Minor. He was the fourth of ten children, nine of whom survived infancy: five daughters and four sons. Four of his siblings are known by name. His sister, St Macrina the Younger, was three years his senior. His youngest brothers, St Gregory and St Peter, became bishops of Nyssa and Sebaste respectively. Basil's oldest brother, Naucratius, died tragically in a hunting accident at about the age of twenty-six, leaving Basil the oldest surviving son just as he was coming of age.

Basil's father, Basil the elder, was an established rhetor. His mother's name was Emmelia, and his paternal grandmother, St Macrina the elder, also lived with the family for much of Basil's childhood. The family was known for their pious pedigree. Emmelia's father had been martyred, and Macrina the elder instructed the family with the very words of St Gregory the Wonderworker, the evangelist of Cappadocia by whom she had been catechized. Early in Basil's life the family moved to Annisa in Pontus, a neighboring province on the Black Sea northeast of Cappadocia, to live on the estate of the elder Macrina where they remained until the death of Basil's father in 346. His sister Macrina and their mother would ultimately transform the estate into an ascetic community as the other children grew to maturity and left home.

Basil returned to Caesarea upon his father's death to begin his formal education. It was there that he met St Gregory of Nazianzus,

with whom he would develop what John McGuckin calls "one of the most longstanding, famous, and stormy friendships in Christian history."[1] In 348 or 349 he moved to Constantinople to continue his studies with Libanius, a pagan and the most famous orator of his generation. After a year under Libanius he joined Gregory in Athens, where he spent five or six years completing the finest classical education available. Evidently his intellect was prodigious, for we are told by Gregory that his reputation preceded him to Athens.[2] Among his many illustrious classmates was a certain Julian who would eventually become Emperor and is known to history as the Apostate. According to Gregory, Basil quickly became dissatisfied with Athens, and it was only on account of the pressure of his friend that he remained as long as he did. Gregory recalls that he alone was "able to soothe Basil's disillusionment and set him on the right track of intellectual development."[3] By 355 he had had enough, and he returned to Caesarea where he began teaching rhetoric.

Very soon after his return to Caesarea, Basil had an epiphanic moment, which he describes in *Ep.* 223:

> I had wasted much time on follies and spent nearly all of my youth in vain labors, and devotion to the teachings of a wisdom that God had made foolish. Suddenly, I awoke as out of a deep sleep. I beheld the wonderful light of the Gospel truth, and I recognized the nothingness of the wisdom of the princes of this world.[4]

He set off once again, this time for a different sort of education. He headed south where he made a tour of the renowned monastic communities of Egypt, Syria, and Palestine. Upon his return home

[1]*Saint Gregory of Nazianzus: An Intellectual Biography* (Crestwood, NY: Saint Vladimir's Seminary Press, 2001), 54.

[2]*Orat.* 43.16

[3]*Orat.* 43.18

[4]*Ep.* 223.2. Quoted in Johannes Quasten, *Patrology III: The Golden Age of Greek Patristic Literature* (Allen, TX: Christian Classics, 1995), 205.

sometime in 357, he was baptized by Dianius, the Bishop of Caesarea, and he retired to the family estate in Pontus to practice asceticism according to the manner he had witnessed on his travels. He found there that his mother and sister Macrina were already engaged in a communal form of the ascetic life inspired by their friend Eustathius of Sebaste.[5] It is in this period that Macrina's influence on Basil, which, according to their brother Gregory would prove a lifelong boon,[6] seems to have been well inculcated. Some time in 358 Gregory of Nazianzus joined Basil briefly at Annisa where together they compiled the *Philokalia*, an anthology of excerpts from the writings of Origen juxtaposed and arranged by topic.

Basil had obviously remained in contact with Dianius throughout his time in retreat, for he was invited by the latter to attend the Synod of Constantinople in January of 360 in the capacity of a lay theological spokesman. This was Basil's first real taste of the "discord" that had spread throughout the Churches in the course of the Arian controversy, which became the impetus for his writing the works in this volume. The council affirmed an Homoian[7] creed and resulted in the deposition of a number of Anomoean[8] and Homoiousian[9] bishops. It is this last position that Basil favored at the time; however, Basil appears to have been less distressed over the theological disagreements per se than over the blatantly un-Christian manner in which those engaged in the controversy conducted themselves. To Basil's dismay Dianius signed the Homoian creed, and upon their return from the council, though Dianius had

---

[5]Eustathius is principally remembered for his Arianizing theology, but in his own lifetime he was highly esteemed as an ascetic master, and he had a formative influence on St Basil in this regard. Indeed, Eustathius is perhaps more rightly regarded as the "father" of Cappadocian monasticism, even if Basil refashioned it into its enduring form.

[6]Demonstrating Macrina's impact on Basil seems to have been the primary motivation for Gregory in writing the *Life of Macrina*. See Philip Rousseau, *Basil of Caesarea* (Berkeley: University of California Press, 1994), 9.

[7]That the Son is "like" the Father.

[8]That the Son is "unlike" the Father.

[9]That the Son is "like in essence" to the Father.

just made him a Reader, Basil retired once again to Annisa. Only months later, however, Basil returned to attend Dianius' deathbed where the two reconciled.

Before he could run off again, Basil was ordained a presbyter by the newly-elected Eusebius. Basil's relationship with Eusebius was unsteady from the beginning. Eusebius seems, from an early date, to have felt the pressure of Basil's popularity and great reputation among the people on account of his well-beloved father, his exceptional education and his evident piety. Basil, for his part, did nothing to discourage his following and perhaps also harbored secretly the common belief that he would make the better bishop. History has certainly vindicated him if he did. In any event, a first misunderstanding with Eusebius seems to have been the reason for his quitting the city, again for Annisa, sometime between the end of 363 and the beginning of 365.[10] Late in 365 Eusebius repented of his animosity toward Basil and recalled him to ministry. Relations between the two remained taut, but Basil remained in place until Eusebius' death in 370 when he was promptly, and with much fanfare, elected to replace him.

Even before his election, Basil was from 365 onwards, in the words of Philip Rousseau, "the chief pastor of Caesarea."[11] In fact we have a number of sermons that can be dated with relative certainty to the time of his presbyterate, in particular a trilogy preached in response to a famine in Cappadocia where Basil takes it upon himself to make pastoral sense of the calamity.[12] Shortly after his election, Basil began work on what would be one of his most famous projects: the *Basileidos*. Called by Gregory a "new city" outside the city of Caesarea,[13] it was a complex of philanthropic institutions: a

[10]So Gregory of Nazianzus implies in his *Funeral Oration*. See Rousseau, 135.

[11]Rousseau, 133.

[12]See Paul Jonathan Fedwick, "A Chronology of the Life and Works of Basil of Caesarea," in *Basil of Caesarea: Christian, Humanist, Ascetic, vol. 1*, ed. Paul J. Fedwick (Toronto, ON: Pontifical Institute of Mediaeval Studies, 1981), 11. See also Rousseau, 136.

[13]Gregory of Nazianzus, *Ep.* 94. See Rousseau, 142 n. 33.

hospital, a hostel for poor travelers, and a "soup kitchen" where food was distributed to the hungry. Basil's tenure as pastor of Caesarea was also characterized by his concern for the ascetic communities under his jurisdiction. It was in constant dialogue with these that he produced what is known today as his monastic *Rule* or *Asketikon*. In one famous incident of his episcopate, the Arian Emperor Valens sent his highest ranking official, the Prefect Modestus, to pressure Basil into a theological compromise. In response to Basil's adamant refusal Modestus declared, "No one until now has spoken to me in such a manner and with such liberty of words." Basil answered in return, "Perhaps you have never met a bishop before."[14]

Basil's most pressing concern, which dominated his ecclesiastical career, was the chaotic state of the Church at large and the rampant run of heresies that had torn it apart from the inside out. Basil came to repudiate his former sympathy for the homoiousian position, and he became in the eyes of many the inheritor of Athanasius' mantle as leader of the Nicene coalition. Yet in those troubled times it was not always clear who was an ally and who an enemy in the fight over orthodoxy, and alliances shifted constantly. Concern for protecting the orthodoxy of his own flock and work for the unity of the Church at large under the banner of the council of Nicaea drove his episcopal ministry and caused him to forsake all else for this single-minded purpose, so that even his closest relationships suffered. He was at odds with his younger brother, Gregory of Nyssa, whose "simplicity" and "inexperience" in ecclesiastical maneuverings he blamed for a number of setbacks for the Nicene cause.[15] Also Gregory of Nazianzus came to resent Basil for pressuring him to become bishop of Sasima, a "one-horse town," which Basil had arranged to be elevated to episcopal status just for Gregory, so that he could count on his friend's vote at councils. Gregory remarks in his autobiography that Basil's presence, at times, was painful to him, and he felt it more as one would feel the presence of a domineering father than as that of

[14]As quoted in Quasten, 206. Cf. *Ethics* 6.1.
[15]See, for example, Basil's *Ep.* 58, *Ep.* 100 and *Ep.* 215.

a companion.[16] Basil reposed on 1 January 379, two years before the
vindication of Nicene orthodoxy at I Constantinople.

The Works

The centerpiece of this volume is Basil's *Ethics,* better known by its
Latin titles *Moralia* or *Regulae Morales.* This work is widely regarded
as Basil's most complete exposition of the Christian life,[17] and,
indeed, it stands well on its own as such. *On the Judgment of God*
and *On the Faith* are, however, included here in preface to the *Ethics*
because Basil himself disseminated the *Ethics* with these two prefaces attached. The prefaces, besides the fact that they are interesting
and worthwhile works themselves, help immensely to contextualize
the writing and intent of the *Ethics*, which might otherwise appear
to stand apart from any historical pressures.

In *On the Judgment of God* Basil lays out his reason for embark-
ing on the project of collecting the Scriptures and distilling them
into concise rules for the Christian life. We know from a reference in
On Baptism[18] that this work had already enjoyed a small, indepen-
dent circulation before Basil redacted it for the purpose of prefacing
the *Ethics,* yet it is clear that the two belong together. The *Ethics* grew
directly out of the concerns expressed in *On the Judgment of God,*
and Basil may have already begun drawing up a draft of the *Ethics*
when he first issued the earlier work.

Briefly put, the thesis of *On the Judgment of God* is that the theological turmoil of his day is a result of the great number of supposed
Christians, and especially Christian leaders, who elect to conduct
their lives not according to Scripture but according to their own
pleasure and reasoning, (effectively saying in their hearts, "There

[16]McGuckin, 89.

[17]See Paul Jonathan Fedwick, *The Church and the Charisma of Leadership in
Basil of Caesarea* (Toronto, ON: Pontifical Institute of Mediaeval Studies, 1979), 98;
also Rousseau, 232.

[18]*In baptisma* 2.5, where Basil calls it "an epistle concerning harmony."

is no God"). The pestilence ravaging the Church is fundamentally the rampant moral failure of disobedience to God's Word, which is manifesting itself in theological strife. The solution to the Church's problems is a return to Scripture as the norm governing Christian conduct. Basil discerns that the primary "reasoning" which has brought about such rampant disobedience is the assumption, following a "human tradition," that sins are rated on a kind of sliding scale. Christians then convince themselves that so long as they refrain from sins that are heinous (which they determine by their own reckoning), they can continue confidently in those they consider slight. Basil explodes this misconception, which is perhaps no less pervasive now than in his day, with a sustained appeal to Scripture. God, Basil discovers, judges all sins with the same terrible judgment, no matter how trivial they might appear to us. And so every sin, even the smallest, stands in need of repentance if the sinner is to stand on the Day of Judgment.

Human traditions of ethical reasoning rank deleterious behaviors as more or less bad, typically in proportion to their visible, harmful effects on society as a whole, and they are treated accordingly. We see this in our own society, not only in the obvious fact that different crimes are penalized with different severity, but also when media and popular culture vilify and dehumanize the pedophile, the terrorist, and the Neo-Nazi, while the philanderer, the wastrel, and the avaricious are given a pass. There is a certain "reasoning" lying behind this principle, rooted in the desire to sustain a functioning human society. But Basil points out that God does not abide by our reasoning, and his goals for humanity are not identical to the goals we have fashioned for ourselves. Those who would call themselves "Christian" need to attend to what God desires, and that is found in Scripture.

Here Basil lays down the foundation of a distinctive Christian ethics. All ethical systems begin with a set of assumed principles and proceed by way of rational argument to establish rules of behavior from those principles. Basil's is no different, but for him

the Christian "first principles" must be Scripture.[19] A cursory reading of *On the Judgment of God* might lead one to suspect that Basil's "fundamentalism" concerning Scripture leads him into anti-intellectualism, that there is no place for the "rational" in Basil's thinking. Does he not everywhere rail against trusting in one's own "reasonings"? However, it is clear by the logic he employs both here and especially in the *Ethics* itself that the "reasonings" Basil rejects are quite obviously not the use of reason generally (without which he would have a hard time making his case); rather they are any "reasons" (such as what we saw above) that a person might put forth for setting aside the teaching of Scripture. The fundamental philosophical insight behind Basil's stance is the nature of first principles. Since at least Aristotle, philosophers have understood that the use of reason, by which is meant the rules of logic and argument, is only possible once first principles have been established. And it is not possible for reason alone to establish these principles. They are necessarily un-provable assertions, and every system of thought must rest upon one set of them or another. The result, then as now, is that competing schools of thought develop, all operating according to their own agreed principles, which they have created for themselves. This is precisely the situation that Basil found so repugnant and the cause of such calamity in the Church: "Everyone [has] desert[ed] the teaching of our Lord Jesus Christ and adjudge[ed] on his own authority determinations and rules for himself and elect[ed] to rule over against the Lord rather than to be ruled by the Lord."[20] With this context in mind we are better able to appreciate Basil's identification

[19]There is a similar revolution occurring in the field of Christian ethics today, where many leading thinkers are struggling to discern just what it is that sets Christian ethics apart from secular ethics. See, for instance, the influential *Blackwell Companion to Christian Ethics* edited by Stanley Hauerwas and Samuel Wells (Oxford: Blackwell, 2004). The project of the editors is to ground Christian ethics in Christian worship, particularly the Eucharist (3). As laudable a goal as this seems, one cannot help but wonder whether the more obvious choice of Scripture was avoided because of the stigma associated with "fundamentalism" in the academy today. Basil's approach to the Scriptures surely has something to offer to this discussion.

[20]See p. 41 below.

in the *Ethics*[21] of the Christian's "struggle of faith" with trust in the authority and truth of Scripture. The Scriptures are the Christian's first principles of thought and action, and as such they can only be believed, not proven, since they are, in a sense, pre-rational; however, being inspired of God they are also infinitely more reliable than any others we might invent for ourselves. At the same time, there can be no purely rational grounds for doubting Scripture, since doubt is only possible if one assumes, by another act of faith, an alternate set of first principles from which to argue.

In Basil's second preface, *On the Faith*, we find a change of focus, which demonstrates sharply the uncertainty of alliances at the time. Basil's addressee(s)[22] have asked him for a written confession of faith. They are evidently theological conservatives, who had begun to suspect Basil of compromising the faith because of some polemical writings of his[23] in which he resorted to terms and phrases not found in the Scriptures. Basil fulfills their request, but only after a careful analysis of the nature of theological inquiry, according to which he justifies his departure from biblical language. The thesis of this work is that the words we use for talking about God are not up to the task. Even the words of Scripture, tailored as they are to our finite capacity of comprehension, afford only a hint of the truth, as though seen "darkly in a mirror." They are trustworthy insofar as they go, but when clever heretics raise new challenges to the faith, it is incumbent upon the Church's teachers to answer these in the spirit of the Scriptures when the letter alone is not sufficient.

On the Faith also appears to have had a life of its own before it was affixed to the *Ethics*. We have no report of a separate circulation, but a handful of manuscripts preserve the work apart from

[21] *Ethics* 80.22.

[22] We cannot be sure who the original recipients were, but Fedwick is probably right to suggest a group of ascetics who had looked on Eustathius favorably and were troubled by Basil's theological break with him. Paul J. Fedwick, "A Brief Analysis of Basil's Two Prefaces to the Moralia," in *Mémorial Dom Jean Gribomont (1920–1986)* (Rome: Institutum Patristicum "Augustinianum," 1988), 227.

[23] Perhaps his books *Against Eunomius*.

the *Ethics* and without the final paragraph, which Basil presumably added when he fused the three works together.[24] If this historical reconstruction is accurate, it is interesting that Basil does not alter the introduction to the work, where he addresses himself to the person or persons who had made the request for a written confession. Requests for a written confession were not uncommon in the early Church, especially from one bishop to another. It is possible that Basil used what he composed in *On the Faith* as a ready response to all such requests. In fact, the introduction is written in such a way as to be serviceable for sending, without alteration, to any bishop or head of a community, who would presumably "know well the mark of a faithful minister."[25] Perhaps the person(s) to whom he sent the *Ethics* had likewise asked a confession of him, but it may simply be that Basil could expect them to recognize the document for a stock letter of confession. It would be fair to say, then, that *On the Faith* is not a "natural" prologue to the *Ethics,* insofar as Basil did not compose the two in connection with each other. On the other hand, Basil recognizes how appropriate it is for an account of the Christian life to be prefaced by an account of the Christian faith, since he had already gone to great lengths in *On the Judgment of God* to demonstrate how inextricably tied the two are.

Indeed there is a consistent logic that runs through both prefaces which sets the stage for Basil's use of Scripture in the *Ethics.* In *On the Judgment of God* Basil emphasized the importance of looking to Scripture as the foundation upon which to build one's thinking. In *On the Faith*, he develops and nuances that assertion. The Scriptures are the firm foundation of the faith, and all of our theology must be rooted in them; however, they do not answer every question explicitly, and even what they do say directly is said using inadequate human language. Thus it requires the careful use of reason to faithfully apply the Scriptures to each question as it arises. In the realm of theology this problem is compounded by the ultimate ineffability

[24]Fedwick, "Chronology," 11 n. 59.
[25]See p. 69 below.

of the subject—God himself. But even in the realm of human behavior and interaction, the particular circumstances in which human beings might find themselves, and thus the possible ethical questions, are likewise infinite. It would be impossible for the Scriptures to contain direct answers to all of them. Thus for both realms of inquiry—theology and ethics—it is necessary to proceed from the straightforward assertions of Scripture with the use of reason toward resolutions that can properly be said to be in accordance with the spirit of Scripture if not, strictly speaking, found in the letter.

The explanation Basil gives in *On the Faith* for his divergence from the letter of Scripture in his polemical writings applies equally to his use of Scripture in the *Ethics*. He does not merely reproduce all the verses that contain explicit admonitions and prohibitions. He composes the rules in his own words, so that they speak directly to the concerns which he had observed in the Church of his day. In addition, a careful reading finds that the connection between the rules and the verses quoted is not always obvious. In numerous cases he insists on imitating Scriptural exemplars, so that all widows are to act as Anna and Dorcas,[26] all bishops as the apostles,[27] etc. The example of Christ is yet more complicated and in need of discernment. In some cases Basil understands his example to be for all Christians,[28] while in others it is specifically for those set over the Word.[29] In many other rules we see him expanding upon the letter of the Scriptures in other ways. For instance, in *Ethics* 45.1 Christ's command to "be like little children" is taken to mean "sharing equal honor." In 80.3, the rule is longer than the lone verse used to substantiate it. "I am the vine; you are the branches" is drawn out into a complicated metaphor.

Scripture is, for Basil, the very substance of the faith. He identifies the "mark of faith" as "unwavering conviction of the truth of the God-breathed words, unshaken by any reasoning," and the "mark of

[26]*Ethics* 74.
[27]E.g. *Ethics* 70.22.
[28]E.g. *Ethics* 34.1.
[29]E.g. *Ethics* 70.12.

a believer" is "with such conviction, to be of the disposition[30] that what is said is authoritative, and to undertake not to disregard or add anything."[31] He declares "That it is necessary not to waver over or doubt the things said by the Lord, but to be fully assured that every word of God is true and authoritative, even if nature might contradict, *for this is precisely the struggle of faith.*"[32] Faith is ultimately about one's trust in the words of God, since it is only by these words that we can come to know the Word of God, as St Paul says: "faith is from hearing, and hearing is through God's Word."[33]

Dating the Works

We know that Basil made a habit of revisiting his own works from time to time, making corrections and additions throughout his life. This is especially the case with the *Asketikon*, which is manifestly the product of many conversations and of reworking over many years.[34] There is evidence, both internal and external, for such a reworking also in the case of the *Ethics*. Apart from the minor revisions that might have been made over the course of the years after Basil first penned the document, there is reason to believe that rules 1–69 and 70–80 were composed separately from one another, or rather that 70–80 were added some time later. This complicates the dating of the work.

The first signal of this division is that 69 appears a fitting conclusion to what comes before it. Whereas every rule to that point is a specific injunction, 69 is a laundry list of commands and prohibitions in the Scriptures, as if to make sure that nothing is left out

---

[30]συνδιατίθεσθαι. See the excellent study of Basil's psychological use of this word and the difficulty of translating it in John Eudes Bamberger, "Μνήμη-Διάθεσις: The Psychic Dynamisms in the Ascetical Theology of Saint Basil," *Orientalia Christiana Periodica* 34 (1968): 233–251.

[31]*Ethics* 80.22.

[32]*Ethics* 8.1, emphasis added.

[33]Romans 10.17 as Basil quotes it in *Ethics* 80.22.

[34]See Anna M. Silvas, *The Asketikon of St Basil the Great* (Oxford: Oxford University Press, 2007), 130ff.

before the treatise ends. Secondly, one must account for a definite change both of tone and of subject matter between *Ethics* 1–69 and 70–80. Everything said before 70 is applied to all Christians indiscriminately, while rules 70–79 are each addressed to a particular stratum of society (clerics, married, soldiers, rulers, etc.) until a new conclusion is given to the work by returning to the universal and addressing the final rule to "the Christian." This represents an expansion of what seems to be the original intent of the work. Moreover, a tendency in the first part of the work for rules to be short and to the point is abandoned in the latter part. There the focus is on supplying a single rule to each group addressed, so that rule 70 on bishops, about whom he understandably has a lot to say, explodes almost into a treatise of its own. These differences of subject matter and rhetoric make sense if one supposes that the last eleven rules were composed after Basil had been away from the work for a time and was coming back to it with a different frame of mind. His concerns have changed, and he feels comfortable completing the work by a rhetorical strategy somewhat different from that by which he had begun.

There is also external evidence for dividing the work temporally. There are three manuscripts of the *Ethics* in which chapters 70–80 are absent.[35] It is possible that these manuscripts represent a circulation of the first 69 rules that continued alongside the fuller, later version in the same manner that we observe with the *Asketikon*. In the case of the latter work, older, less complete editions continued to circulate alongside the more complete even in Basil's own lifetime, and our manuscripts reflect these various redactions to the present day. However, a similar "parallel transmission" in the case of the *Ethics* is far from certain. The three manuscripts in question all come from Mt. Athos. All three may derive from the same late, corrupt manuscript.[36] Perhaps, as rules 70–79 have nothing to do with monks, an Athonite scribe who did not foresee his manuscript finding its way

[35] BBV III, 628.
[36] We know at least one of the three is a copy of another. See Fedwick, "Chronology," 14 n. 80.

out into the world conscientiously reserved the valuable parchment that would have been required to preserve the treatise whole.[37]

Another indicator from outside the *Ethics* is *Prologue* 2, one of several short introductions by later authors attached to the *Ascetical Works* in the manuscript tradition. Fedwick argues that this introduction indicates a division of the text into two by introducing them separately.[38] The section in question is poorly written and not at all straightforward:

> Then it is necessary to know all that is commanded us by the Scriptures and to be zealous for those things that aim at eternal life and the kingdom of heaven, and in like manner to set before oneself the things delegated to one's own degree or station. To accomplish this, in the form of an outline of a rule, the work aims to give to us from the Holy Scriptures more precisely and pointedly the character of a Christian, and, again, a similar characterization of the one set over the Word of the Lord's teachings; in which things a complete and utter purging reveals one's citizenship, and the worth of distinction in so doing, so that one will make a name for oneself, will shine forth.[39]

Some have taken these words to indicate that there was a manifest division in the manuscript that the author of the prologue had before him, which might indicate that the latter section had been added to an already extant edition of *Ethics* 1–69. However, all that can be said for sure is that the author has merely noticed the same phenomenon as contemporary scholars have—that there is an obvious breaking point between rules 69 and 70—and he considers the two sections to reflect two distinct purposes that Basil had in writing it: to set

[37]See Stephen Robinson Lloyd-Moffett, *Asceticism and the Common Life: Basil of Caesarea, Vedic India, and the Social Formation of Religion* (PhD Diss. University of California, 2005), 524.

[38]Fedwick, "Chronology," 14 n. 80.

[39]Edited in Jean Gribomont, *Histoire du Texte des Ascétiques de S. Basile* (Louvain: Publications Universitaires, 1953), 281–282.

out those things binding on all Christians, but also to include those things particular to their station in life, especially bishops. To push the evidence any further would seem to suggest that an ancient scribe could not have been as discerning of the work's contents as modern scholars.

Still, while the evidence for an early circulation of the *Ethics* without rules 70–80 is inconclusive, the internal evidence for a delay in their composition remains convincing. The hypothesis that an earlier composition of *Ethics* 1–69 went uncirculated accords well with what Basil says in his conclusion to *On the Faith*: Having written up the rules themselves, his first desire was to fill in a comprehensive list of citations for supporting passages from both the Old and the New Testaments, but given the restraints of time he ultimately contented himself with only a handful of possible New Testament passages. It is quite conceivable that rules 1–69 were drawn up at an earlier date, awaiting the day when Basil could devote the time necessary to completing the work along the lines he had first envisioned. When he finally did get around to finishing it, under the pressure of an outstanding promise, he felt it necessary to add the final eleven rules, but because of time constraints he compromised on the extent of the Scripture citations included.

Long the most popularly held date for the composition of the *Ethics* is around 360. It seems first to have been proposed by Dom Prudentius Marano in the *Vita* of Saint Basil that he composed for the third volume of Garnier's edition, which he completed in 1730 after Garnier's untimely death.[40] But this early date was stiffly challenged by Fedwick, who assigns a later date during Basil's episcopacy, and the most recent examination of the question, in the unpublished dissertation of Stephen Lloyd-Moffett,[41] largely bears out Fedwick's case.

---

[40]This date was accepted by Clarke, and it was most recently upheld by Rousseau (228–232), who repeats it without engaging the arguments of Fedwick.

[41]516–526.

The argument for the early date of 360 is based entirely on external evidence. In his sixth letter, addressed to Basil and firmly dated to around the end of 361, Gregory Nazianzus regrets that he is no longer living the life of retreat with Basil at Pontus, a life which they enjoyed together from 359 to the beginning of 361. One of his lines runs, "O for the contest and incitement of virtue which we secured by written rules and canons; O for the loving labour in the Divine Oracles, and the light we found in them by the guidance of the Holy Ghost."[42] The reference to "rules," which is the same word (ὅροι) used in the *Ethics*, and its proximity to "the Divine Oracles," is taken as a reference to an early draft of the *Ethics*. However, this is a very tenuous assumption. Fedwick demonstrates clearly that some of the concerns and seminal ideas of the *Ethics*, such as the equality of all sins and the distribution of charismata, do not surface in any of Basil's other datable writings until after the mid-360s when he is engaged in pastoral care as a presbyter. Thus, any document written in 360 with Gregory's help could only be considered, at best, an early ancestor of the *Ethics* in genre or form.[43]

Another piece of evidence offered for an early date is a line from *On the Judgment of God*, which is supposed to tie its composition to the rise of the Anomoeans associated with their success at the council in Antioch in 361.[44] The sentence in question reads,

> And, what is most horrible, its very leaders are in such disagreement with one another in judgment and opinion and act in such opposition to the commandments of our Lord Jesus Christ, mercilessly tearing apart the Church of God and unsparingly throwing his flock into confusion, that now if ever, with the outbreak of the Anomoeans, is fulfilled the Scripture: "From

[42]*Ep.* 6. The translation is from Charles Gordon Browne and James Edward Swallow, trans., *Nicene and Post-Nicene Fathers, Second Series*, Vol. 7, Philip Schaff and Henry Wace, eds. (Peabody, MA: Hendrickson, 2004), 448.

[43]Lloyd-Moffett (521–22) advances Basil's *Ep.* 2 as a possible candidate for the document Gregory describes, but this seems far-fetched.

[44]See Clarke, 15.

your own selves will arise men who speak perverse things to draw away disciples after them."[45]

Fedwick points out that the "now" (νῦν) in reference to the outbreak of the Anomoeans ought not to be taken to indicate that the Anomoean's prominence was a recent phenomenon at Basil's writing. Rather, it carries an historical meaning. The Anomoeans certainly contributed to the dreadful state of the Church, which *was* Basil's impetus for writing the *Ethics*, but this does not mean that it was composed in swift reaction to their ascendancy. On the contrary, the lines which follow would suggest just the opposite. Basil goes on to say:

> After seeing such things and wondering what the source of this evil was and what its cause, at first I dwelt in deep darkness, so to speak, and, as though on a balance, I inclined first one way, then another. A deceit at one time would draw me to itself, owing to the ancient habit of humanity. Then again it would repulse me on account of the truth I observed in the divine Scriptures. *After a long time of suffering so and investigating thoroughly the cause I was after*, I was reminded of what is recorded in the book of Judges . . .[46]

Clearly *On the Judgment of God* and the *Ethics* which followed it were the fruit of much reflection over time. Thus these works are better dated a considerable time after 361. Let us not forget that the Church remained in regrettable turmoil well after Basil's death in 379. Further, we must allow some time for *On the Judgment of God* to circulate independently before setting a *terminus post quem* for the *Ethics*.

Evidence of a later date is primarily internal to the text, and is most conclusive with respect to rules 70–80. These clearly reflect the

[45]See p. 39 below. Quoting Acts 20.30
[46]See pp. 39–41 below. Emphasis added.

era of Basil's episcopate, when his pastoral responsibilities require him to reflect on the proper behavior and activity of all of the various persons entrusted to him.[47] We have no writings of his prior to the episcopate where such persons are addressed or considered. Furthermore, it is unlikely that Basil would propose to instruct bishops on how to be a bishop if he were not already one himself. His own advice to "hearers" who are convinced that their bishop is either heretical or impious was not to correct or otherwise approach them in any way, as one would a brother,[48] but to "vehemently turn away" from them.[49]

Any attempt to assign a date to the *Ethics* has to account for the division we have observed between the original 69 rules and the 11 that were composed later. The dating of Fedwick seems the safest, though safety must come at the expense of precision. He gives ample consideration to the remove between the compositions of the two sets of rules. He gives the timeframe 365–372 for the first release of *On the Judgment of God*. He then dates the publication of *Ethics* 1–69 to 371–375, which he believes to have occurred before the writing of rules 70–80. According to Fedwick these were appended, along with the two reworked prefaces, in 376 or 377.

Fedwick's dating, however, is governed by his commitment to an earlier circulation of rules 1–69.[50] If we do not suppose there to have been an early circulation of the first 69 rules, then the possible dates of their composition widen considerably. No "real" time is necessary between *On the Judgment of God* and the first 69 rules, since it is possible that Basil had already begun work on them when that text was finished. We can assume that the *Ethics* was a work in progress for some time. We also no longer have a fixed end-point for rules 1–69, though we must allow a long enough lapse between the writing

[47]These are, in order: "Those set over the word" (bishops [and presbyters?]), deacons, hearers (laity), husbands and wives, widows, slaves and masters, children and parents, virgins, soldiers, rulers and subjects.

[48]See *Ethics* 52.

[49]*Ethics* 72.1–2.

[50]Fedwick, "Chronology," 14 n. 80.

of the first and second sections to account for the change in tone. Fedwick's dating of 376–377 for rules 70–80 is quite secure.[51] Therefore we might justly place the composition of rules 1–69 anywhere from 365–375, giving preference to a *terminus ad quem* earlier in the episcopate in order to give plenty of space for the manifest difference of mentality found in rules 70–80.

The Greek Text

The Greek text in this volume is taken from L. de Sinner's 1839 reprint of the Maurist edition executed by Dom Julien Garnier in 1722. De Sinner's printing is universally regarded as having best preserved Garnier's text. There is nothing more recent or of higher quality, yet despite its age and the relatively small number of manuscripts that Garnier consulted by today's standards,[52] over the years it has held up well to critical assessment.[53] However, Jean Gribomont demonstrated the great potential for an improved critical edition, identifying more than 150 manuscripts of the "Ascetic Works" (among which our texts are numbered) dating to before the year 1500.[54] Gribomont did much of the work of collating, and he classified the manuscripts into families, of which he identified five.[55] He also determined which manuscript families and even subfamilies retain the most conservative readings.[56] Fedwick has since confirmed Gribomont's

[51]Fedwick, "Chronology," 18 n. 96, where he allows for the possibility that the work had been sitting around for some time before Basil, in 376 or 377, included it in the *Outline of the Ascetic Life* (Basil's own edition of his collected Ascetic Works), which he compiled for publication at about this time.

[52]Garnier contented himself with mss and earlier editions accessible to him in Paris, and he did not even always collate all of these. See Stig Y. Rudberg, "Manuscripts and Editions of the Works of Basil of Caesarea," in Paul Jonathan Fedwick, ed., *Basil of Caesarea: Christian, Humanist, Ascetic. A Sixteen-Hundreth Anniversary Symposium* (Toronto: The Pontifical Institute of Mediaeval Studies, 1981), 58.

[53]So Clarke, 6, 19; Rudberg, 58; Gribomont, 329.

[54]Gribomont, 1.

[55]Ibid., 3–5.

[56]Ibid., 332.

judgments in the main. We await the motivated individual who will tackle the enormous task of completing the work begun by these scholars.

The process of preparing the Greek texts for this volume began with digital copies of the text of Migne's reprint. My publisher was able to supply the text of the *Ethics* while those of *On the Judgment of God* and *On the Faith* were graciously provided by the Thesaurus Linguae Graecae, a research center of the University of California, Irvine. These texts were reformatted and corrected against de Sinner. In the course of proofreading, I was able to correct a number of obvious misprints in de Sinner's edition and a few misattributions to the Scriptural quotes. These are noted in footnotes to the Greek text. I have also corrected obvious errors in punctuation, but these are not noted. In many other cases where the punctuation markings did not seem right but were not obviously misprinted, I have left them alone in the Greek text but have not felt obligated to reflect them in my translation. The same decision was made with respect to Garnier's conventions for capitalizing certain words and phrases, which he did not strictly follow himself in any case. I have adopted my own conventions of capitalization in the translation. I refer to the text throughout as "Garnier's" though I have not been able to consult the original 1722 edition. Thus I cannot say whether the errors I discovered are his or de Sinner's. I can only hope that I have corrected more errors than I have introduced.

In a few instances more substantial changes were made to Garnier's text, which are also noted in footnotes to the Greek text. These were made on the basis of four manuscripts, which I was able to consult myself, in cases where an oddity in the text of Garnier led me to suspect an error, the solution of which was not immediately obvious. The manuscripts consulted were BL Add MS 10069 (12th c.),[57]

---

[57]Readable at the British Library's website as of 17 October 2014: *http://www. bl.uk/manuscripts/FullDisplay.aspx?ref=Add_MS_10069*. This is MS i338 according to Fedwick's numbering. A complete description is in BBV III, 113. It is a damaged codex, the first extent folio of which begins in the middle of *Ethics* 12.3.

Vat. Gr. 413 (9th–10th c.),[58] Vat. Gr. 425 (12th c.),[59] and Vat. Gr. 428 (9th c.).[60] I have endeavored to make clear in each case my reasons for invoking the authority of these manuscripts.

The Translation

There are two earlier English translations of the works in this volume. W. K. Lowther Clarke's *The Ascetic Works of St Basil*, published in 1925, is an admirable achievement. It is the first English rendering of the ascetic corpus. It is clear and accurate on the whole, and it was a great help to me in the preparation of this new translation. However, Clarke's volume has been out of print for the better part of a century, its language is dated, and he often falls prey to his own, outdated assumptions about Basil's thought. These were based on the state of scholarship in his time, for much of which he was himself responsible; however, research into Basil's thinking has come a long way since 1925. M. Monica Wagner's 1950 translation of the *Ascetical Works* for the Fathers of the Church series did much to make these works more accessible to the average student; however, her translation is less to be relied upon than Clarke's. She adopted a freer style, which inevitably necessitates more error-prone judgments on the part of the translator. Her volume is likewise out of print.

Besides these considerations, it seems good finally to liberate the three works of Basil here from identification as strictly "monastic" works, which many suppose them to be when they are bound together with the *Asketikon*. Basil did not intend these works only for monks and nuns but for all who would call themselves "Christian." It is my belief that they remain a timely and necessary challenge to followers of Christ today, who are supposed to be recognizable from

---

[58]All of the Vatican MSS were accessed with helpful assistance from the Knights of Columbus Vatican Film Library, housed in Pius XII Memorial Library at Saint Louis University. Fedwick's MS i320; complete description in BBV III, 108.

[59]Fedwick's i254, described in BBV III, 81.

[60]Fedwick's i300, described in BBV III, 99–100.

their fruits[61] and from their love for one another.[62] For all these reasons, it seemed good to make a new, accurate, and contemporary translation of these works available in an affordable paperback edition for the use both of scholars and of laity seeking spiritual benefit.

My approach has been to err on the side of a literal or word-for-word translation. Many of the idioms of Greek actually come across well in English with only a little imagination on the part of the reader. When Basil speaks, for instance, of the great "disharmony with the commandments of the Lord and with one another" that he observed among the churches, though the expression "disharmony with the commandments of the Lord" is strange to our ears, it is not difficult to see that Basil is making an identification between the disharmony that exists among persons in the Church and the fact that their lives are not in harmony with the Scriptures. These two "disharmonies" are sides of the same coin. I hope that this approach has helped to minimize the number of my own error-prone judgments with respect to the meaning of the text. It will also make it easier, for those who are able, to read the English with an eye on the facing Greek. On the other hand, I have also made occasional use of what seemed to me a felicitous English idiom when I felt confident that nothing of the original sense was lost thereby.

For the blocks of New Testament Scripture quoted in the *Ethics*, I have used as a basis the Revised Standard Version, for which I acknowledge the generosity of the National Council of Churches, who hold copyright to that translation. The decision not to translate all of these Scriptures anew was an easy one. Unnecessary work was avoided, and readers are saved the distraction of entirely unfamiliar renderings of Scripture. Nevertheless, the RSV text for these Scriptures was emended in many places for a couple of important reasons.

The first, and by far the more frequent, reason changes were made to the text of the RSV is that Basil (or an early scribe) did

[61]Cf. Mt 7.16–20
[62]Cf. Jn 13.35

not always quote the Scriptures in accordance with modern critical editions of the New Testament, from which the RSV was translated. The manuscripts of the New Testament with which he was familiar generally follow what contemporary scholars call the "Byzantine" text type, which is no longer followed by the majority of biblical text critics. The vast majority of differences between Basil's text and most modern editions of the New Testament are without consequence to the larger meaning of the text, and often they do not at all affect the rendering of the text into English, e.g. a minor discrepancy in the order of words. However, in most cases I have found it appropriate to make changes to the English, however minor, in order to remain as faithful as possible to the text of the *Ethics* as Basil himself knew it.

The other reason changes were made to the text of the RSV, far less common than the first, was to make clearer the use to which Basil puts the verses he quotes. Often Basil composes his rules using the language of the Scriptures he quotes in support. In these cases, I have privileged my own translation of the rule and adjusted the RSV so that it is clear to the reader when this occurs. For example, a number of Basil's rules are concerned with "scandals." The RSV translates the Greek word σκάνδαλον variously as "hindrance," "offense," or "temptation," and its verb form σκανδαλίζω as "cause to sin," "cause to fall," or "give offense." In every case I have simply used the English cognates "scandal" and "scandalize" in my translation, so that when Basil brings his verses together, their relation to each other and to his rule is obvious to the reader. Words or phrases of the Scriptures in italics indicate where a divergence from the text of the RSV occurs. The presence of the facing Greek, against which all of my translation decisions may be checked, will hopefully atone for the fact that I have not thought it necessary to annotate these divergences. Interested readers may pick up and compare for themselves a modern critical edition with the Greek text here.

For Scriptures quoted in the course of Basil's prose—in the two prefaces and in rule 80—I have made my own translation. The flexibility afforded by this route was necessary to account for the ways

that Basil weaves Scripture into his own syntax and his train of thought. In a few cases, treating the Scriptures in these two ways in the volume has resulted in significantly different renderings of the same verse appearing in different places,[63] but this seems a small price to pay for the benefits already mentioned.

There is one particular word that Basil repeatedly uses to introduce the rules of the *Ethics*, to which I wish to alert the reader. The word is δεῖ, and it means "it is necessary." Something of Basil's elegance is lost when a three-letter word in Greek is translated by a three-word expression in English, and the reader may find the repetition of the phrase tiresome. Clarke compromised by using instead the shorter expression "One must." Yet this required him to alter the syntax of many rules, sometimes considerably. Much of the syntactical consistency, so characteristic of the work, was lost, and with it much of the text's emphatic nature. For Basil, these rules are not negotiable. He considered them definitive of the Christian life, and his repetitive use of the introductory phrase "That it is necessary . . ." helps to drive this point home.

Suggestions for Further Reading

Fedwick, Paul Jonathan. "A Brief Analysis of Basil's Two Prefaces to the Moralia" in *Mémorial Dom Jean Gribomont (1920–1986)*, 221–231. Rome: Institutum Patristicum "Augustinianum," 1988.

———, ed. *Basil of Caesarea: Christian, Humanist, Ascetic*, 2 vols. Toronto, ON: Pontifical Institute of Mediaeval Studies, 1981.

———. *The Church and the Charisma of Leadership in Basil of Caesarea*. Toronto, ON: Pontifical Institute of Mediaeval Studies, 1979.

Gribomont, Jean, O. S. B. *Histoire du Texte des Ascétiques de S. Basile*. Louvain: Publications Universitaires, 1953.

---

[63]E.g. Lk 12.47–48, which Basil quotes both in *On the Judgment of God* and following *Ethics* 9.5.

Hildebrand, Stephen M. *Basil of Caesarea*. Grand Rapids, MI: Baker Academic, 2014.

Monge, Ricco Gabriel. "Submission to One Head: Basil of Caesarea on Order and Authority in the Church." *St Vladimir's Theological Quarterly* 54, no. 2 (2010): 219–43.

Radde-Gallwitz, Andrew. *Basil of Caesarea: A Guide to His Life and Doctrine*. Eugene, OR: Cascade, 2012.

Rousseau, Philip. *Basil of Caesarea*. Berkeley: University of California Press, 1994.

Silvas, Anna M. *The Asketikon of St Basil the Great*. Oxford: Oxford University Press, 2007.

Wilken, Robert L. "The Spirit of Holiness: Basil of Caesarea and Early Christian Spirituality." *Worship* 42, no.2 (1968): 77–87.

ΠΕΡΙ ΚΡΙΜΑΤΟΣ ΘΕΟΥ

[298] Θεοῦ τοῦ ἀγαθοῦ χρηστότητι, καὶ φιλανθρωπίᾳ ἐν χάριτι τοῦ Κυρίου ἡμῶν Ἰησοῦ Χριστοῦ, κατ' ἐνέργειαν τοῦ ἁγίου Πνεύματος, τῆς μὲν κατὰ παράδοσιν τῶν ἔξωθεν πλάνης ῥυσθεὶς, ἄνωθεν δὲ καὶ ἐξ ἀρχῆς ὑπὸ Χριστιανοῖς γονεῦσιν ἀνατραφεὶς, παρ' αὐτοῖς μὲν ἀπὸ βρέφους καὶ τὰ ἱερὰ γράμματα ἔμαθον, ἄγοντά με πρὸς ἐπίγνωσιν τῆς ἀληθείας. Ὡς δὲ γέγονα ἀνὴρ, καὶ ἀποδημίαις πολλάκις χρώμενος, πράγμασί τε, ὡς εἰκὸς, ἐντυγχάνων πλείοσιν, ἐν μὲν ταῖς ἄλλαις τέχναις καὶ ἐπιστήμαις τοσαύτην πρὸς ἀλλήλους συμφωνίαν κατεμάνθανον τῶν ἀκριβῶς μετερχομένων ἑκάστην· ἐν μόνῃ δὲ τῇ Ἐκκλησίᾳ τοῦ Θεοῦ, ὑπὲρ ἧς Χριστὸς ἀπέθανε, καὶ τὸ Πνεῦμα τὸ ἅγιον ἐπ' αὐτὴν πλουσίως ἐξέχεε, πολλήν τινα καὶ ὑπερβάλλουσαν τήν τε πρὸς ἀλλήλους καὶ τὴν πρὸς τὰς θείας Γραφὰς διαφωνίαν τῶν πολλῶν ἐθεώρουν· καὶ τὸ φρικωδέστατον, αὐτοὺς τοὺς προεστῶτας αὐτῆς ἐν τοσαύτῃ[1] μὲν τῇ πρὸς ἀλλήλους διαφορᾷ γνώμης τε καὶ δόξης καθεστῶτας, τοσαύτῃ δὲ τῇ πρὸς τὰς ἐντολὰς τοῦ Κυρίου ἡμῶν Ἰησοῦ Χριστοῦ ἐναντιότητι χρωμένους, καὶ διασπῶντας μὲν ἀνηλεῶς τὴν Ἐκκλησίαν τοῦ Θεοῦ, ἐκταράσσοντας δὲ ἀφειδῶς τὸ ποίμνιον αὐτοῦ, ὡς καὶ ἐν αὐτοῖς πληροῦσθαι νῦν, εἴπερ ποτὲ, τῶν Ἀνομοίων ἐπιφυέντων, τὸ, ὅτι «Ἐξ ὑμῶν αὐτῶν ἀναστήσονται ἄνδρες λαλοῦντες διεστραμμένα, τοῦ ἀποσπᾶν τοὺς μαθητὰς ὀπίσω αὐτῶν.»

Ταῦτα καὶ τὰ τοιαῦτα ὁρῶν, καὶ πρὸς τούτοις ἐπαπορῶν, τίς καὶ πόθεν ἡ αἰτία τοῦ τοσούτου κακοῦ, τὰ μὲν πρῶτα, ὥσπερ ἐν βαθεῖ σκότῳ διῆγον, καὶ καθάπερ ἐπὶ ζυγοῦ, ποτὲ μὲν ὧδε, ποτὲ δὲ ἐκεῖσε ἔρρεπον· ἄλλου ἄλλως, ἢ πρὸς ἑαυτόν με ἕλκοντος,

---

[1]Corrected from τοσαύτῃ.

On the Judgment of God

The good God, in his kindness and love for humanity in the grace of our Lord Jesus Christ and through the operation of the Holy Spirit, preserved me from the delusion of pagan tradition, for I was raised by Christian parents from the very first. From the womb I learned from them the sacred writings, which brought me to a knowledge of the truth. Yet as I grew into manhood and began travelling widely and as, in the course of things, I engaged in more affairs, I observed among the devoted practitioners of the other arts and sciences such harmony, while in the Church of God alone, for which Christ died and upon which he richly poured out the Holy Spirit, I found so many in great and boundless disharmony, both with one another and with the divine Scriptures. And, what is most horrible, its very leaders are in such disagreement with one another in judgment and opinion and act in such opposition to the commandments of our Lord Jesus Christ, mercilessly tearing apart the Church of God and unsparingly throwing his flock into confusion, that now if ever, with the outbreak of the Anomoeans,[1] is fulfilled the Scripture: "From your own selves will arise men who speak perverse things to draw away disciples after them."[2]

After seeing such things and wondering what the source of this evil was and what its cause, at first I dwelt in deep darkness, so to speak, and, as though on a balance, I inclined first one way, then another. A deceit at one time would draw me to itself, owing to the ancient habit of humanity. Then again it would repulse me on

---

[1] The Anomoeans (literally: "Unlikers"), known also today as "radical Arians," are so called for teaching that the Son is "unlike" the Father in important ways.

[2] Acts 20.30

διὰ τὴν πολυχρόνιον τῶν ἀνθρώπων συνήθειαν, ἢ πάλιν ἄλλως ἀπωθουμένου διὰ τὴν ἐν [299] ταῖς θείαις Γραφαῖς ἐπιγινωσκομένην ἀλήθειαν. Ἐπιπολὺ δὲ τοῦτο πάσχων, καὶ τὴν αἰτίαν ἣν εἶπον πολυπραγμονῶν, εἰς μνήμην ἦλθον τῆς βίβλου τῶν Κριτῶν, ἱστορούσης μὲν, ὅτι ἕκαστος τὸ εὐθὲς ἐν ὀφθαλμοῖς αὐτοῦ ἐποίει, δηλούσης δὲ καὶ τὴν αἰτίαν ἐν τῷ εἰπεῖν· ὅτι «Ἐν ταῖς ἡμέραις ἐκείναις οὐκ ἦν βασιλεὺς ἐν Ἰσραήλ.» Τούτων τοίνυν ἐπιμνησθεὶς, ἐλογισάμην καὶ περὶ τῶν παρόντων ἐκεῖνο, ὅπερ εἰπεῖν μὲν φοβερὸν ἴσως καὶ παράδοξον, κατανοῆσαι δὲ ἀληθέστατον· ὅτι μή ποτε καὶ νῦν παρὰ τὴν τοῦ ἑνὸς καὶ μεγάλου τοῦ ἀληθινοῦ καὶ μόνου τῶν ὅλων βασιλέως καὶ Θεοῦ ἀθέτησιν, ἡ τοσαύτη διαφωνία καὶ μάχη τῶν ἐν τῇ Ἐκκλησίᾳ γίνεται, ἑκάστου τῆς μὲν τοῦ Κυρίου ἡμῶν Ἰησοῦ Χριστοῦ διδασκαλίας ἀφισταμένου, λογισμοὺς δέ τινας καὶ ὅρους ἰδίους ἐκδικοῦντος ἐξ αὐθεντίας, καὶ μᾶλλον ἄρχειν ἀπ᾽ ἐναντίας τοῦ Κυρίου, ἢ ἄρχεσθαι ὑπὸ τοῦ Κυρίου βουλομένου.

Τοῦτο δὴ λογισάμενος, καὶ πρὸς τὸ ὑπερβάλλον τῆς ἀσεβείας ἐπτοημένος, ἐπὶ πλεῖόν τε ἐρευνῶν, ἐπειθόμην οὐδὲν ἧττον, καὶ ἐκ τῶν ἐν τῷ βίῳ πραγμάτων ἀληθῆ εἶναι τὴν προειρημένην αἰτίαν. Ἑώρων γὰρ πᾶσαν μὲν πλήθους εὐταξίαν τε καὶ συμφωνίαν ἄχρι τότε κατορθουμένην, ἄχρις ἂν ἡ πρὸς ἕνα τινὰ τὸν ἄρχοντα σώζεται κοινὴ τῶν ἄλλων εὐπείθεια· πᾶσαν δὲ διαφωνίαν καὶ διάστασιν, ἔτι τε πολυαρχίαν, ἐξ ἀναρχίας ὁδοποιουμένην. Ἐγὼ δὲ εἶδόν ποτε² καὶ μελισσῶν πλῆθος νόμῳ φύσεως στρατηγούμενον, καὶ κατακολουθοῦν εὐτάκτως τῷ ἰδίῳ βασιλεῖ. Καὶ πολλὰ μὲν ἐγὼ τοιαῦτα εἶδον, πολλὰ δὲ ἤκουσα· ἴσασι δὲ καὶ πλείονα οἱ περὶ ταῦτα ἠσχολημένοι, ὡς καὶ ἐκ τούτων ἀληθὲς δείκνυσθαι τὸ λεγόμενον. Εἰ γὰρ τῶν πρὸς ἓν νεῦμα ἀποβλεπόντων, καὶ βασιλεῖ χρωμένων ἑνὶ, ἴδιον εὐταξία μετὰ συμφωνίας· ἄρα διαφωνία πᾶσα καὶ διάστασις σημεῖον ἀναρχίας. Κατὰ δὴ τὸν αὐτὸν λόγον, ἡ τοιαύτη πρός τε τὰς ἐντολὰς τοῦ Κυρίου καὶ πρὸς ἀλλήλους διαφωνία καὶ ἐν ἡμῖν εὑρισκομένη κατηγόρημα ἂν εἴη, ἢ ἀναχωρήσεως τοῦ ἀληθινοῦ βασιλέως, κατὰ τό· «Μόνον ὁ κατέχων ἄρτι, ἕως ἂν ἐκ μέσου γένηται·» ἢ ἀρνήσεως αὐτοῦ, κατὰ τό· «Εἶπεν ἄφρων ἐν τῇ καρδίᾳ

²Corrected from εἶδον ποτὲ.

account of the truth I observed in the divine Scriptures. After a long time of suffering so and investigating thoroughly the cause I was after, I was reminded of what is recorded in the book of Judges: that each did what was right in his own eyes, which it explains by saying, "In those days there was no king in Israel."[3] And thinking on this, I concluded that the same must be true of the present (which is perhaps dreadful and astonishing to say but most evident to perceive), that perhaps the great disharmony and strife now present among those in the Church has arisen likewise from rejecting the one, truly great and only king and God of all—from everyone deserting the teaching of our Lord Jesus Christ and adjudging on his own authority determinations and rules for himself and electing to rule over against the Lord rather than to be ruled by the Lord.

Having considered this, and distressed at the outpouring of impiety, I probed still further. And when I considered how it is with worldly affairs, I was no less persuaded that the aforementioned cause is correct. For I beheld all the good order and harmony of the multitude that is brought about when the common, willing obedience of all to a single ruler prevails, and likewise all the discord and division and even mob-rule that results from anarchy.[4] I even once saw a swarm of bees governed by the law of their nature, which were following their own king in good order. I have seen many examples like these and heard many more, and those who study such things know more than I, so that from these considerations my words are shown to be true. For if those who look to one command and are subject to one king are characterized by good order and harmony, then all discord and division is a sign of anarchy. By this logic, the appearance among us of such disharmony with the commandments of the Lord and with one another is a sign either that the true king has been deserted, according to what is written: "Only there is one now restraining, until he be removed,"[5] or that he has been denied,

[3]Judg 21.25
[4]That is, when people acknowledge no ruler but themselves.
[5]2 Thess 2.7

αὐτοῦ, οὐκ ἔστι Θεός.» Οὐ καθάπερ σημεῖόν τι ἢ ἔλεγχον [300] ἐπιφέρει τό· «Διεφθάρησαν, καὶ ἐβδελύχθησαν ἐν ἐπιτηδεύμασιν.»

Ἐνταῦθα μὲν οὖν ὥσπερ χαρακτῆρα τῆς τοιαύτης ἀσεβείας κατὰ τὸ λεληθὸς ἐμφωλευούσης τῇ ψυχῇ τὴν ἐπιφαινομένην κακίαν ὁ λόγος ἀπέδειξεν. Ὅ γε μὴν μακάριος ἀπόστολος Παῦλος σφοδρότερον ἐπιστρέφων εἰς φόβον τῶν τοῦ Θεοῦ κριμάτων τοὺς ἀπολωλεκότας τὴν καρδίαν, τοῦτο ἀντὶ τιμωρίας ὁρίζεται, καταδικάζεσθαι τοὺς τῆς ἀληθοῦς θεογνωσίας ἠμεληκότας. Τί γάρ φησι; «Καὶ καθὼς οὐκ ἐδοκίμασαν τὸν Θεὸν ἔχειν ἐν ἐπιγνώσει, παρέδωκεν αὐτοὺς ὁ Θεὸς εἰς ἀδόκιμον νοῦν, ποιεῖν τὰ μὴ καθήκοντα, πεπληρωμένους πάσης ἀδικίας, πονηρίας, πλεονεξίας, κακίας, μεστοὺς φθόνου,» καὶ τῶν ἑξῆς. Καὶ τοῦτο νενοηκέναι οἶμαι τὸν ἀπόστολον τὸ κρίμα, οὐκ ἀφ᾽ ἑαυτοῦ (Χριστὸν γὰρ εἶχεν ἐν ἑαυτῷ λαλοῦντα), ἀλλ᾽ ἐξ ἐκείνης αὐτοῦ τῆς φωνῆς ὁδηγηθέντα, ἐν ᾗ φησι διὰ τοῦτο ἐν παραβολαῖς λαλεῖν τοῖς ὄχλοις, ἵνα μὴ νοήσωσι τὰ θεῖα τοῦ εὐαγγελίου μυστήρια, ὅτι φθάσαντες αὐτοὶ τοὺς ὀφθαλμοὺς αὐτῶν ἐκάμμυσαν, καὶ τοῖς ὠσὶ βαρέως ἤκουσαν, καὶ ἐπαχύνθη ἡ ἀσύνετος αὐτῶν καρδία· ἵνα ἔχωσιν ἀντὶ τιμωρίας ὑπομένειν τὴν περὶ τὰ μείζονα ἀβλεψίαν, οἳ προφθάσαντες ἑκουσίως, τὸ ὄμμα τῆς ψυχῆς ἀποτυφλώσαντες, ἐσκοτίσθησαν· ὅπερ ὁ Δαβὶδ φοβούμενος παθεῖν, ἔλεγε· «Φώτισον τοὺς ὀφθαλμούς μου, μή ποτε ὑπνώσω εἰς θάνατον.» Ἐκ μὲν οὖν τούτων καὶ τοιούτων φανερὸν εἶναι ἐλογιζόμην, ὅτι καθόλου μὲν ἡ τῶν παθῶν κακία, διὰ τῆς περὶ Θεοῦ ἀγνωσίας, ἀδόκιμον γνῶσιν ἐντίθησιν· ἰδίως δὲ ἡ διαφωνία τῶν πολλῶν πρὸς ἀλλήλους, διὰ τὸ ἀναξίους ἡμᾶς ἑαυτοὺς κατασκευάσαι τῆς τοῦ Κυρίου ἐπιστασίας, ἐπισυμβαίνει.

Πρὸς δὲ τὴν ἐπίσκεψιν τοῦ τοιούτου βίου, εἴποτε δὴ καὶ ἐλθεῖν ἐβουλευσάμην, οὔτε μετρεῖν εἶχον τὸ μέγεθος τῆς τοιαύτης ἀναισθησίας, ἢ ἀλογίας, [301] ἢ ἀπονοίας, ἢ διὰ τὸ ὑπερβάλλον τῆς κακίας οὐκ ἔχω τί εἴπω. Εἰ γὰρ καὶ ἐν ἀλόγοις οὕτω κατορθουμένην εὑρίσκομεν τὴν ἐν ἀλλήλοις συμφωνίαν, διὰ

as: "The fool has said in his heart, 'There is no God'"[6]—to which it adds the following as a sure sign or confirmation: "They have become corrupt and loathsome in their pursuits."[7]

Here then the Word teaches that visible wickedness is a sign of this unseen impiety lurking in the soul. Indeed, the blessed apostle Paul, the more eagerly to convert those who have ruined their heart to fear God's judgments, sets this as their recompense: those who have neglected the true knowledge of God are condemned. For what does he say? "And even as they did not find it seemly to have God in their knowledge, God gave them over to an unseemly mind to do things unbecoming, filled with all unrighteousness, evil, covetousness, wickedness, full of malice,"[8] and what follows. And I do not think the Apostle perceived this judgment on his own (for he had Christ speaking in him), rather he was guided by Christ's explanation for speaking to the crowds in parables:[9] that they might not perceive the divine mysteries of the gospel because they had already closed their eyes and become hard of hearing, and their senseless heart had become hard—so that those who had first consented to be darkened might, in return, have to endure blindness to the greater things, since the eye of their soul was blinded. In fear of just this fate, David said, "Enlighten my eyes lest I sleep unto death."[10] Therefore, from these and similar considerations I concluded that, in general, it is clear that the wickedness of passions, due to ignorance of God, instills an unseemly "knowledge," and that, in particular, the mutual disharmony of so many arises because we render ourselves unfit for the Lord's care.

Now, if I should ever desire to study such a life, I would be incapable of measuring the enormity of such senselessness, such irrationality, such madness; nor do I know what to say in the face of such extreme wickedness. For if even among unreasoning creatures we find a proper, mutual harmony resulting from obedience to

[6]Ps 14.1 (LXX 13.1)
[7]Ibid.
[8]Rom 1.28–29
[9]Cf. Mt 13.13–15
[10]Ps 13.3 (LXX 12.4)

τὴν πρὸς τὸν καθηγούμενον εὐπείθειαν· τί ἂν εἴποιμεν ἡμεῖς ἐν
τοσαύτῃ μὲν τῇ πρὸς ἀλλήλους διαστάσει, τοσαύτῃ δὲ τῇ πρὸς τὰς
ἐντολὰς τοῦ Κυρίου ἐναντιότητι εὑρισκόμενοι; Ἢ οὐχὶ ταῦτα πάντα
ἡγούμεθα, νῦν μὲν εἰς διδασκαλίαν καὶ ἐντροπὴν ἡμετέραν ὑπὸ
τοῦ ἀγαθοῦ Θεοῦ προτεθεῖσθαι, ἐν δὲ τῇ μεγάλῃ καὶ φοβερᾷ τῆς
κρίσεως ἡμέρᾳ εἰς αἰσχύνην καὶ κατάκρισιν τῶν μὴ παιδευομένων
προσενεχθήσεσθαι ὑπ᾽ αὐτοῦ τοῦ καὶ εἰπόντος ἤδη, καὶ λέγοντος
ἀεὶ· ὅτι Ἔγνω βοῦς τὸν κτησάμενον, καὶ ὄνος τὴν φάτνην τοῦ
Κυρίου αὐτοῦ· Ἰσραὴλ δέ με οὐκ ἔγνω, καὶ ὁ λαός με οὐ συνῆκε·»
καὶ πολλὰ ἄλλα τοιαῦτα;

Ἐκεῖνο δὲ τὸ ὑπὸ τοῦ ἀποστόλου εἰρημένον, τό· «Εἴτε πάσχει
ἓν μέλος, συμπάσχει πάντα τὰ μέλη· εἴτε δοξάζεται ἓν μέλος,
συγχαίρει πάντα τὰ μέλη.» Καὶ τό· «Ἵνα μὴ ᾖ σχίσματα ἐν τῷ
σώματι, ἀλλὰ τὸ αὐτὸ ὑπὲρ ἀλλήλων μεριμνῶσι τὰ μέλη,» ὑπὸ μιᾶς
δηλονότι κινούμενα τῆς ἐνοικούσης ψυχῆς. Τίνος ἕνεκεν οὕτως
ᾠκονομήθη; Ἐγὼ μὲν οἶμαι, ἵνα σώζηται ἡ τοιαύτη ἀκολουθία τε καὶ
εὐταξία πολλῷ πλέον παρὰ τῇ Ἐκκλησίᾳ τοῦ Θεοῦ, πρὸς ἣν εἴρηται·
«Ὑμεῖς δέ ἐστε σῶμα Χριστοῦ, καὶ μέλη ἐκ μέρους·» κρατούσης
δηλονότι καὶ συναπτούσης ἕκαστον τῷ ἄλλῳ πρὸς ὁμόνοιαν τῆς
μιᾶς καὶ μόνης ἀληθῶς κεφαλῆς, ἥτις ἐστὶν ὁ Χριστός. Παρ᾽ οἷς δὲ
οὐχ ὁμόνοια κατορθοῦται, οὐχ ὁ σύνδεσμος τῆς εἰρήνης τηρεῖται,
οὐχ ἡ ἐν πνεύματι πραότης φυλάσσεται, ἀλλὰ καὶ διχοστασία καὶ
ἔρις καὶ ζῆλος εὑρίσκεται. Πολλῆς μὲν τόλμης ἂν εἴη μέλη Χριστοῦ
τοὺς τοιούτους ὀνομάζειν, ἢ ὑπ᾽ αὐτοῦ ἄρχεσθαι λέγειν· ἁπλῆς δὲ
διανοίας, μετὰ παρρησίας εἰπεῖν, ὅτι κρατεῖ ἐκεῖ καὶ βασιλεύει τὸ
τῆς σαρκὸς φρόνημα, κατὰ τὴν τοῦ ἀποστόλου φωνήν, λέγοντος
μὲν ὁριστικῶς, ὅτι «Ὧι παριστάνετε ἑαυτοὺς δούλους εἰς ὑπακοήν,
δοῦλοί ἐστε ᾧ ὑπακούετε·» διεξιόντος δὲ σαφῶς τοῦ τοιούτου
φρονήματος τὰ ἰδιώματα, ὡς ὅταν λέγῃ· «ὅπου γὰρ ἐν ὑμῖν ζῆλος
καὶ ἔρις, καὶ διχοστασίαι, οὐχὶ σαρκικοί ἐστε;» διδάσκοντος δὲ
ἅμα ἀποφαντικῶς τό τε χαλεπὸν αὐτῶν τῆς ἐκβάσεως, καὶ τὸ

their leader, what can we say, who are found in such strife with one another and in such opposition to the commandments of the Lord? Are these not all examples established by the good God? Now they serve for our instruction and warning, but in the great and fearful day of judgment they will be for the shame and condemnation of those who neglect the instruction of the one who said before and ever says: "The ox knows its owner and the ass its lord's manger, but Israel does not know me, and the people do not understand me,"[11] and many other similar things.

Now the Apostle says: "If one member suffers, all the members suffer together; if one member is glorified, all the members rejoice together,"[12] and, "So that there might not be schisms in the body but all the members might have the same care for one another,"[13] manifestly animated by a single indwelling soul. Why was it arranged so? I think in order to secure all the more the order and good organization of the Church of God, to which it is said: "You are the body of Christ and members individually"[14] with the one and only true head, Christ, who manifestly rules and joins together one to another in harmony. But among whom harmony is not maintained, nor the bond of peace kept, nor gentleness in spirit guarded, but rather dissension and strife and envy are found, it would take considerable nerve to call such as these members of Christ or to suggest that they are ruled by him; rather, lucid thinking declares boldly that the mind of the flesh rules and governs there, according to the word that the apostle spoke definitively: "To whom you present yourselves as slaves for obedience; you are slaves to whom you obey."[15] And he describes plainly the characteristics of such a mind when he says, for instance, "For wherever there is among you envy and strife and dissension, are you not carnal?"[16] At the same time he teaches clearly both the severity

[11] Is 1.3
[12] 1 Cor 12.26
[13] 1 Cor 12.25
[14] 1 Cor 12.27
[15] Rom 6.16
[16] 1 Cor 3.3

ἀκοινώνητον πρὸς θεοσέβειαν, δι' ὧν φησιν, ὅτι «Τὸ φρόνημα
τῆς σαρκὸς, ἔχθρα εἰς Θεόν· τῷ γὰρ νόμῳ [302] τοῦ Θεοῦ οὐχ
ὑποτάσσεται· οὐδὲ γὰρ δύναται·» διότι «Οὐδεὶς δύναται,» ὁ Κύριός
φησι, «δυσὶ κυρίοις δουλεύειν.»

Εἶτα αὐτοῦ τοῦ μονογενοῦς Υἱοῦ τοῦ Θεοῦ τοῦ Κυρίου καὶ
Θεοῦ ἡμῶν Ἰησοῦ Χριστοῦ βοῶντος, δι' οὗ τὰ πάντα ἐγένετο,
«Καταβέβηκα ἐκ τοῦ οὐρανοῦ, οὐχ ἵνα ποιῶ τὸ θέλημα τὸ ἐμὸν,
ἀλλὰ τὸ θέλημα τοῦ πέμψαντός με Πατρός·» καὶ ὅτι «Ἀπ' ἐμαυτοῦ
ποιῶ οὐδέν·» καὶ, «Ἐντολὴν ἔλαβον τί εἴπω, καὶ τί λαλήσω·» καὶ
τοῦ Πνεύματος τοῦ ἁγίου τοῦ διαιροῦντος μὲν τὰ μεγάλα καὶ
θαυμαστὰ χαρίσματα, ἐνεργοῦντος δὲ τὰ πάντα ἐν πᾶσι, λαλοῦντός
τε ἀφ' ἑαυτοῦ οὐδὲν, ἀλλ' ὅσα ἂν ἀκούσῃ παρὰ τοῦ Κυρίου, ταῦτα
λαλοῦντος· πῶς οὐ πολλῷ μᾶλλον ἀνάγκη πᾶσαν τὴν Ἐκκλησίαν
τοῦ Θεοῦ σπουδάζουσαν τηρεῖν τὴν ἑνότητα τοῦ πνεύματος ἐν
τῷ συνδέσμῳ τῆς εἰρήνης, πληροῦν ἐκεῖνο τὸ ἐν ταῖς Πράξεσιν
εἰρημένον, ὅτι «Τοῦ πλήθους τῶν πιστευσάντων ἦν ἡ καρδία καὶ
ἡ ψυχὴ μία·» οὐδενὸς μὲν, δηλονότι, τὸ ἴδιον βούλημα ἱστῶντος,
πάντων δὲ κοινῇ ζητούντων ἐν ἑνὶ τῷ ἁγίῳ Πνεύματι τὸ τοῦ ἑνὸς
Κυρίου Ἰησοῦ Χριστοῦ θέλημα, τοῦ εἰπόντος· «Καταβέβηκα ἐκ τοῦ
οὐρανοῦ, οὐχ ἵνα ποιῶ τὸ θέλημα τὸ ἐμὸν, ἀλλὰ τὸ θέλημα τοῦ
πέμψαντός με Πατρός·» πρὸς ὅν φησιν· «Οὐ περὶ τούτων δὲ ἐρωτῶ
μόνον, ἀλλὰ καὶ περὶ τῶν πιστευόντων διὰ τοῦ λόγου αὐτῶν εἰς ἐμὲ,
ἵνα πάντες ἓν ὦσιν;»

Ἐπὶ τούτοις, καὶ πλείοσι τοῖς σεσιωπημένοις, οὕτω σαφῶς καὶ
ἀναντιρρήτως ἀναγκαίαν μὲν εἶναι πληροφορηθεὶς τὴν παρὰ πάσης
ὁμοῦ τῆς τοῦ Θεοῦ Ἐκκλησίας, κατὰ τὸ θέλημα τοῦ Χριστοῦ ἐν
Πνεύματι ἁγίῳ, συμφωνίαν, ἐπικίνδυνον δὲ καὶ ὀλεθρίαν ἐν τῇ πρὸς
ἀλλήλους διαστάσει τὴν πρὸς Θεὸν ἀπείθειαν («Ὁ γὰρ ἀπειθῶν,»
φησὶ, «τῷ Υἱῷ, οὐκ ὄψεται τὴν ζωὴν, ἀλλ' ἡ ὀργὴ τοῦ Θεοῦ μενεῖ
ἐπ' αὐτόν»), ἐκεῖνο ἀκόλουθον ἡγησάμην ἐξετάσαι λοιπόν· ποῖα
μὲν ἄρα συγγνώμην τῶν ἁμαρτημάτων ἔχειν δύναται παρὰ τῷ Θεῷ,

of the consequence for such things and their incompatibility with godly piety when he says, "The mind of the flesh is hatred for God, for it does not submit to the law of God, for it is not able,"[17] because "No one is able," says the Lord, "to serve two masters."[18]

Therefore, since the same only-begotten Son of God through whom all things were made, our Lord and God Jesus Christ, cries out, "I am come down from heaven not to do my will but the will of the Father who sent me,"[19] and "I do nothing of myself,"[20] and "I received a commandment—what I should say and what I should speak,"[21] and the Holy Spirit, who distributes the great and wonderful charisms,[22] "working all in all,"[23] speaks nothing of himself but speaks whatever he should hear from the Lord,[24] how is it not all the more necessary for the whole Church of God to keep zealously the unity of the Spirit in the bond of peace? To fulfill what was spoken in the Acts: "The multitude of believers were of one heart and soul"[25]—no one, that is, erecting his own will, but all in common seeking in the one Holy Spirit the one will of the Lord Jesus Christ who said: "I am come down from heaven not to do my will but the will of the Father who sent me,"[26] and who says for this reason: "Not for these only do I ask, but also for those who believe in me through their word, that all may be one."[27]

From these verses and more which I have passed over in silence I was so thoroughly and incontrovertibly convinced that the harmony of the whole Church of God in accordance with the will of Christ in the Holy Spirit was necessary and that disobedience to God in mutual dissension was dangerous and deadly ("For whoever," it says, "is disobedient to the Son will not see life, but the wrath of God will remain on him"[28]), that I decided next to examine the following question: What kind of sins can be forgiven by God, and for what quantity and

[17]Rom 8.7
[18]Mt 6.24
[19]Jn 6.38
[20]Jn 8.28
[21]Jn 12.49
[22]Cf. 1 Cor 12.11

[23]1 Cor 12.6
[24]Cf. Jn 16.13
[25]Acts 4.32
[26]Jn 6.38
[27]Jn 17.20
[28]Jn 3.36

πόσα δέ τις καὶ πηλίκα ἁμαρτήσας, ὑπεύθυνος γίνεται τῷ κρίματι τῆς ἀπειθείας. Εὑρίσκω τοίνυν, ἀναλαβὼν τὰς θείας Γραφὰς, ἐν τῇ παλαιᾷ καὶ καινῇ Διαθήκῃ, οὔτε ἐν [303] τῷ πλήθει τῶν ἁμαρτανομένων, οὔτε ἐν τῷ μεγέθει τῶν ἁμαρτημάτων, ἐν μόνῃ δὲ τῇ παραβάσει οὑτινοσοῦν προστάγματος, σαφῶς κρινομένην τὴν πρὸς Θεὸν ἀπείθειαν, καὶ κοινὸν κατὰ πάσης παρακοῆς τοῦ Θεοῦ τὸ κρῖμα· ἐν μὲν τῇ Παλαιᾷ τὸ φοβερὸν ἐκεῖνο τοῦ Ἄχαρ ἀναγινώσκων τέλος, ἢ τὴν κατὰ τὸν ἐν σαββάτῳ ξύλα συλλέξαντα ἱστορίαν, ὧν ἑκάτερος οὐδὲν οὐδεπώποτε ἄλλως οὐκ εἰς Θεὸν ἡμαρτηκὼς, οὐκ ἄνθρωπον ἠδικηκὼς, οὐ μέγα, οὐ μικρὸν ὅλως εὑρίσκεται. Ἀλλ' ὁ μὲν, ἐπὶ μόνῃ καὶ πρώτῃ τῶν ξύλων συλλογῇ ἀπαραίτητον δίδωσι τὴν δίκην, οὐδὲ μετανοίας τόπον εὑρών· προστάγματι γὰρ τοῦ Θεοῦ παρὰ παντὸς τοῦ λαοῦ παραχρῆμα λιθοβολεῖται. Ὁ δὲ, ὅτι μόνον ὑφείλετό τι τῶν ἀναθεμάτων οὔπω εἰσενεχθέντων εἰς τὴν συναγωγὴν, οὐδὲ προσδεχθέντων ὑπὸ τῶν ἐπιτεταγμένων τὰ τοιαῦτα, αἴτιος ἀπωλείας, οὐκ αὐτῷ μόνον, ἀλλὰ καὶ γαμετῇ καὶ τέκνοις, πρὸς δὲ, καὶ αὐτῇ τῇ σκηνῇ σὺν πᾶσι τοῖς ἰδίοις ἐγένετο. Ἔμελλε δὲ ἤδη καὶ πάντα τὸν λαὸν, πυρὸς τρόπον, ἐπινέμεσθαι τῆς ἁμαρτίας τὸ κακὸν, καὶ ταῦτα, οὔτε εἰδότα τὸ γεγονὸς, οὐδὲ συνεγνωκότα τῷ ἁμαρτήσαντι, εἰ μὴ ταχέως ἐκ τῆς πτώσεως τῶν ἀναιρεθέντων ἀνδρῶν συνετρίβη μὲν ὁ λαὸς αἰσθόμενος τῆς ὀργῆς τοῦ Θεοῦ· ἔπεσε δὲ ἅμα τοῖς πρεσβυτέροις καταπασσάμενος χοῦν Ἰησοῦς ὁ τοῦ Ναυῆ· καὶ οὕτω διὰ κλήρου φωραθεὶς ὁ ἔνοχος τὴν εἰρημένην ἔδωκε δίκην.

Ἀλλ' ἴσως ἐρεῖ τις, ὑποπτεύεσθαι μὲν τούτους εἰκότως καὶ ἐπ' ἄλλοις ἁμαρτήμασιν, ἀφ' ὧν καὶ ἐν τούτοις ἑάλωσαν· μόνων δὲ τούτων, ὡς χαλεπωτέρων καὶ θανάτου ἀξίων, ἐπιμνησθῆναι τὴν ἁγίαν Γραφήν. Ἀλλ' εἰ καὶ λίαν εἴη ὁ τοιοῦτος τολμηρὸς προστιθέναι τι καὶ ὑφαιρεῖν, μὴ καὶ Μαρίας ἄρα τῆς ἀδελφῆς Μωϋσέως κατηγορήσει πλῆθος ἁμαρτημάτων, ἧς τὴν ἀρετὴν οὐδένα τῶν πιστῶν οἶμαι διαλανθάνειν; Αὕτη κατὰ Μωϋσέως ἐπειδὴ εἶπέ τι[3] μόνον ἐν καταγνώσεως μέρει, καὶ τοῦτο ἀληθὲς («Γυναῖκα» γὰρ,

---

[3] Corrected from εἶπε τί.

magnitude of sins does one become liable to the judgment against disobedience? Now I find when I take up the Holy Scripture, in both the Old and the New Testament, that disobedience to God is clearly adjudged neither from the multitude of sins nor their magnitude but from the mere overstepping of any ordinance whatsoever, and that the judgment of God against all disobedience is the same. For I read in the Old Testament of the fearful end of Achan[29] or the story of the man who gathered wood on the Sabbath,[30] neither of whom is found to have sinned against God at any other time or otherwise wronged another human being in any way great or small. Yet the one, for his first and only collection of wood, pays the inexorable penalty with no opportunity for repentance—for he was stoned on the spot by all the people at God's command—while the other, simply for pilfering some devoted items, which had never even entered the assembly nor been received by those responsible for such things, incurred not only his own destruction but even that of his wife and children in addition to his tent and all his possessions. And the evil of this sin would soon have spread like a wildfire to all the rest of the people (who were neither aware of what had happened, nor had they conspired with the sinner) were they not so swiftly struck by the calamity of those who perished, perceiving in it the wrath of God, and had Jesus the son of Nun not cast himself down with the elders, sprinkling himself with dust, and had the guilty party, who was discovered by drawing lots, not paid the aforementioned penalty.

But perhaps someone will say that it is reasonable to suspect these men of committing other sins as well, which also played into their condemnation, yet these only are recounted in Holy Scripture as being more grievous and worthy of death. And yet even if one should be so exceedingly bold as to add to and subtract from Scripture, will he also accuse Moses' sister Mary of a multitude of sins, whose virtue, I think, none of the faithful doubts? When she had merely said something against Moses in censure—and a truth at

[29]See Josh 7
[30]See Num 15.32–36

φησὶν, «Αἰθιόπισσαν ἔλαβεν ἑαυτῷ»), τοσαύτης ἐπειράθη τῆς ἀγανακτήσεως τοῦ Θεοῦ, ὡς μηδὲ αὐτοῦ Μωϋσέως ἱκετεύοντος συγχωρηθῆναι αὐτῇ τῆς ἁμαρτίας τὸ ἐπιτίμιον. Αὐτὸν τοίνυν ὅταν ἴδω Μωϋσέα, τὸν τοῦ Θεοῦ θεράποντα, τὸν μέγαν ἐκεῖνον, τὸν τοσαύτης μὲν καὶ τηλικαύτης ἀξιωθέντα τιμῆς παρὰ Θεοῦ, οὕτω δὲ πολλάκις ὑπ᾽ αὐτοῦ μαρτυρηθέντα, ὡς ἀκοῦσαι· «Οἶδά σε παρὰ [304] πάντας, καὶ εὕρηκας χάριν ἐνώπιόν μου·» τοῦτον ὅταν ἴδω ἐπὶ τοῦ ὕδατος τῆς ἀντιλογίας οὐδενὸς ἕνεκεν ἑτέρου, ἢ ἵνα μόνον εἴπῃ τῷ λαῷ γογγύζοντι διὰ ἀπορίαν ὕδατος, «Μὴ ἐκ ταύτης τῆς πέτρας ἐξάξομεν ὑμῖν ὕδωρ;» τούτου μόνου ἕνεκεν εὐθὺς ἀπειλὴν δεχόμενον, εἰς τὴν γῆν τῆς ἐπαγγελίας οὐκ εἰσελεύσεσθαι, ἥτις ἦν τότε τῶν πρὸς Ἰουδαίους ἐπαγγελιῶν τὸ κεφάλαιον· ὅταν ἴδω τοῦτον παρακαλοῦντα, καὶ μὴ συγχωρούμενον· ὅταν ἴδω μηδεμιᾶς συγγνώμης διὰ τὰ τοσαῦτα κατορθώματα ἐπὶ τῷ βραχεῖ ἐκείνῳ ῥήματι καταξιούμενον, ὄντως μὲν ὁρῶ «Θεοῦ ἀποτομίαν,» κατὰ τὸν ἀπόστολον, ὄντως δὲ ἐκεῖνο ἀληθὲς εἶναι πείθομαι, τό· «Εἰ ὁ δίκαιος μόλις σώζεται, ὁ ἀσεβὴς καὶ ἁμαρτωλὸς ποῦ φανεῖται;»

Καὶ τί ταῦτα λέγω; Ἐκείνης ὅταν ἀκούσω τῆς φοβερᾶς τοῦ Θεοῦ ἀποφάσεως, ἣν καὶ κατὰ τοῦ μίαν ἐντολὴν ἐπ᾽ ἀγνοίαι παραβεβηκότος ἀποφαίνεται, οὐκ ἔχω πῶς ἐπαξίως φοβηθῶ τῆς ὀργῆς τὸ μέγεθος. Γέγραπται γάρ· «Καὶ ψυχὴ ἐὰν ἁμάρτῃ, καὶ ποιήσῃ μίαν ἀπὸ πασῶν τῶν ἐντολῶν Κυρίου, ὧν οὐ δεῖ ποιεῖν, καὶ οὐκ ἔγνω, καὶ πλημμελήσῃ, καὶ λάβῃ τὴν ἁμαρτίαν, οἴσει κριὸν ἄμωμον ἐκ τῶν προβάτων, τιμῆς ἀργυρίου, εἰς πλημμέλειαν πρὸς τὸν ἱερέα. Καὶ ἐξιλάσεται περὶ αὐτοῦ ὁ ἱερεύς, περὶ τῆς ἀγνοίας αὐτοῦ, ἧς ἠγνόησε, καὶ αὐτὸς οὐκ ᾔδει, καὶ ἀφεθήσεται αὐτῷ. Ἐπλημμέλησε γὰρ πλημμέλειαν ἔναντι Κυρίου.» Εἰ δὲ ἐπὶ τῶν κατὰ ἄγνοιαν οὕτως ἀπαραίτητον τὸ κρίμα, καὶ ὑπὲρ τῆς καθάρσεως ἡ θυσία ἀναγκαία, ἣν καὶ ὁ δίκαιος Ἰὼβ μαρτυρεῖται προσφέρειν⁴ ὑπὲρ τῶν υἱῶν,

---

⁴Corrected from προσφέρεν.

that, for she said, "He has taken to himself an Ethiopian wife"[31]—she incited such vexation from God that not even the supplications of Moses himself could avert from her the penalty for the sin. And there is Moses himself, God's attendant, that great man, who was counted worthy of such great honor by God and is so often approved by him, as when he hears, "Of all people I know you, and you have found grace before me."[32] When I see him at the water of contention—for no reason but that he said to the people complaining for lack of water: "Shall we draw you water out of this rock?"[33] (immediately for this alone!)—assured that he would not enter the land of the promise (which at that time was the summation of all the promises to the Jews), when I see him supplicating and not exonerated, when I see that so many virtuous deeds stacked against that brief word can find no forbearance whatsoever, then do I truly see "the severity of God,"[34] as the apostle says, and I am utterly persuaded that the saying is true: "If the righteous is barely saved, where will the impious and the sinner appear?"[35]

Why do I say these things? When I hear that fearful oracle of God, which he declares against even the one who transgresses a commandment in ignorance, I have not the wherewithal to fear adequately this great wrath. For it is written: "And a soul, if it should sin and do any of the things which the Lord commanded not to be done, and it was not aware, and should it err and assume the sin, it shall bring an unblemished ram from the flock of the value of silver for a guilt offering to the priest, and the priest will make atonement for him concerning his ignorance of which he was unaware and did not know himself, and it will be forgiven for him. For he has committed an error before the Lord."[36] And if the judgment against things committed in ignorance is so inexorable, and the sacrifice for their

[31]Num 12.1
[32]Ex 33.12
[33]Num 20.10
[34]Rom 11.22
[35]1 Pet 4.18
[36]Lev 5.17–19

τί ἄν τις εἴποι περὶ τῶν ἐν γνώσει ἁμαρτανόντων, ἢ τῶν τούτοις
ἐφησυχαζόντων;
    Καὶ ἵνα μὴ δόξωμεν στοχασμοῖς αὐτὸ μόνον εἰκόσιν ἀναλογί-
ζεσθαι τὴν κατὰ τούτων ἀγανάκτησιν, αὐτῆς πάλιν ἀναγκαῖον
μνημονεῦσαι τῆς θεοπνεύστου Γραφῆς, ἀρκούσης ἐπὶ τοῦ παρόντος
καὶ διὰ μιᾶς ἱστορίας παραστῆσαι τὸ κρίμα τῶν τοιούτων. «Καὶ υἱοὶ,»
φησὶν, «Ἡλεὶ τοῦ ἱερέως, υἱοὶ λοιμοί.» Τούτοις δὲ τοιούτοις οὖσιν,
ὅτι μὴ ἐπεξῆλθε σφοδρότερον ὁ πατήρ, τοιαύτην ἐκίνησεν ὀργὴν τῇ
μακροθυμίᾳ τοῦ Θεοῦ, ὥστε ἐπαναστάντων τῶν ἀλλοφύλων, τοὺς
μὲν υἱοὺς αὐτοῦ ἐκείνοις ἀναιρεθῆναι κατὰ τὸν πόλεμον ἐν ἡμέρᾳ
μιᾷ, ἡττηθῆναι δὲ σύμπαντα τὸν λαὸν, καὶ τούτων πεσεῖν ἱκανοὺς,
γενέσθαι δὲ καὶ περὶ τὴν κιβωτὸν τῆς ἁγίας τοῦ Θεοῦ διαθήκης, ἃ
μήτε ἠκούσθη ποτὲ πρότερον, ὥστε, ἧς οὔτε Ἰσραηλίταις, οὔτε μὴν
αὐτοῖς ἱερεῦσιν ἅπασιν, οὐδὲ πάντοτε ἅπτεσθαι θεμιτὸν [305] ἦν,
οὐδὲ τόπος αὐτὴν ὁ τυχὼν ὑπεδέχετο, ταύτην ὑπὸ χειρῶν ἀσεβῶν
ἄλλοτε ἀλλαχόθεν μετακομίζεσθαι, καὶ ἀντὶ τῶν ἁγίων, εἰδώλων
ναοῖς ἐναποτίθεσθαι. Ἐφ᾽ οἷς πόσον τινὰ συνέβαινεν εἶναι, καὶ
κατ᾽ αὐτοῦ τοῦ ὀνόματος τοῦ Θεοῦ, γέλωτα καὶ χλεύην παρὰ
τοῖς ἀλλοφύλοις, στοχάζεσθαι πάρεστιν. Ἐπὶ τούτοις καὶ αὐτὸς
ὁ Ἡλεὶ τέλει χρησάμενος οἰκτροτάτῳ ἀναγέγραπται· δεξάμενος
ἀπειλὴν, τοῦ, καὶ τὸ σπέρμα αὐτοῦ ἀποκινηθήσεσθαι τοῦ ἱερατικοῦ
ἀξιώματος· ὅπερ καὶ γέγονε.
    Τοσαῦτα συμβέβηκε τῷ λαῷ. Τοιαῦτα πέπονθεν ὁ πατὴρ διὰ τὴν
τῶν υἱῶν παρανομίαν, ὃς καίπερ τοῦ μὲν ἰδίου βίου ἕνεκεν, οὐδὲν
ᾐτιάθη ποτέ. Καὶ αὐτοῖς δὲ ἐκείνοις οὐχ ὑπέμεινεν ἐφησυχάσαι,
ἀλλὰ πολλὰ μὲν παρῄνει, περὶ τοῦ μηκέτι τοῖς ὁμοίοις ἐπιμένειν·
«Μὴ, τέκνα,» λέγων, «μή· οὐκ ἀγαθαὶ αἱ ἀκοαὶ, ἃς ἐγὼ ἀκούω περὶ
ὑμῶν.» Σφοδρότερον δὲ κατασκευάζων τῆς ἁμαρτίας τὸ μέγεθος,
φοβερώτερον αὐτοῖς παρίστη τὸν κίνδυνον. «Ἐὰν γὰρ ἁμαρτάνων
ἁμάρτῃ ἄνθρωπος,» φησὶν, «εἰς ἄνθρωπον, προσεύξονται περὶ

cleansing necessary, which the righteous Job is found bringing on behalf of his sons,[37] what can be said for those who sin knowingly or those who observe the latter in silence?

And lest it appear that our reckoning of the anger against these last[38] rests only upon plausible speculation, it is necessary again to recall the same God-breathed Scripture, which is able to establish with a single story the judgment against them. "And the sons of Eli the priest," it says, "were plagues for sons."[39] And because their father was not sufficiently harsh with them, he stirred up such wrath in the longsuffering of God that when the foreigners rose up his sons were killed, and all the people together were defeated in a single day of combat, and a considerable number of them were slain. And the unthinkable happened to the ark of God's holy covenant: what neither the Israelites nor even all the priests were allowed to touch nor was just any place permitted to receive it, was carried off by impious hands and shuffled about from place to place, and, instead of holy places, it was housed in idols' temples. It is easy to imagine how much laughter and jesting issued at this among the foreigners at the expense of the very name of God. And in addition to these woes, it is recorded that Eli himself met with a most miserable end, for he was threatened that his seed would be removed from the dignity of the priesthood, and so it happened.[40]

Such was the fate of the people. Such did the father suffer for the lawlessness of his sons, though in his own life he was never accused of any wrongdoing. And it is not as though he remained silent at their misdeeds. On the contrary, he often exhorted them to persist in them no longer, saying, "No, my children, no! The reports that I hear about you are not good."[41] And to impress upon them the gravity of their sin, he presents the danger to them in more fearful terms: "For if in sinning a human should sin against another human," he says,

[37]See Job 1.5
[38]That is, those who observe sin committed and do nothing about it.
[39]1 Sam 2.12
[40]For the preceding narrative see 1 Sam 2–5.
[41]1 Sam 2.24

αὐτοῦ πρὸς Κύριον. Ἐὰν δὲ εἰς Θεὸν ἁμάρτῃ, τίς προσεύξεται περὶ αὐτοῦ;» ὅμως, ἐπειδήπερ, ὡς εἶπον, οὐχὶ τὸν πρέποντα ζῆλον κατ᾽ αὐτῶν ἐπεδείξατο, γέγονε τὰ εἰρημένα.

Τοιαῦτα μὲν οὖν πλεῖστα ὅσα κατὰ τὴν παλαιὰν Διαθήκην εὑρίσκω τὰ κατὰ πάσης παρακοῆς κρίματα· αὖθις δὲ ὅταν ἐπὶ τὴν Καινὴν ἔλθω, τοῦ Κυρίου ἡμῶν Ἰησοῦ Χριστοῦ οὐκ ἀπολύσαντος μὲν τῆς τιμωρίας, οὔτε τὰ κατὰ ἄγνοιαν, σφοδρότερον δὲ κατὰ τῶν ἐν γνώσει τὴν ἀπειλὴν ἐπιτείναντος, δι᾽ ὧν φησιν· «Ἐκεῖνος δὲ ὁ δοῦλος, ὁ γνοὺς τὸ θέλημα τοῦ κυρίου ἑαυτοῦ, καὶ μὴ ἑτοιμάσας ἑαυτὸν, μηδὲ ποιήσας πρὸς τὸ θέλημα αὐτοῦ, δαρήσεται πολλάς· ὁ δὲ μὴ γνοὺς, ποιήσας δὲ ἄξια πληγῶν, δαρήσεται ὀλίγας·» ὅταν εὕρω αὐτοῦ τοῦ μονογενοῦς Υἱοῦ τοῦ Θεοῦ τὰς τοιαύτας ἀποφάσεις, καὶ τῶν ἁγίων ἀποστόλων τὴν κατὰ τῶν ἁμαρτανόντων ἀγανάκτησιν· [306] τὰ τοιαῦτα καὶ τηλικαῦτα πάθη τῶν καὶ ἐν ὁτιοῦν ἡμαρτηκότων, οὐχ ἥττονα τῶν ἐκ τῆς Παλαιᾶς εἰρημένων, μᾶλλον δὲ καὶ πλείονα, καταμανθάνω τοῦ κρίματος τὴν σφοδρότητα. Ἐπεὶ καὶ «Ὧι παρέθεντο πολὺ, περισσότερον ἀπαιτήσουσιν αὐτόν.»

Ἰδοὺ τοίνυν καὶ ὁ μακάριος Παῦλος ὑποδεικνὺς ὁμοῦ τῆς τε κλήσεως τὸ ἀξίωμα, καὶ τὴν κατὰ παντὸς ἁμαρτήματος ἀγανάκτησιν, οἷά φησι· «Τὰ γὰρ ὅπλα τῆς στρατείας ἡμῶν οὐ σαρκικὰ, ἀλλὰ δυνατὰ τῷ Θεῷ πρὸς καθαίρεσιν ὀχυρωμάτων, λογισμοὺς καθαιροῦντες, καὶ πᾶν ὕψωμα ἐπαιρόμενον κατὰ τῆς γνώσεως τοῦ Θεοῦ, καὶ αἰχμαλωτίζοντες πᾶν νόημα εἰς τὴν ὑπακοὴν τοῦ Χριστοῦ·» οὐ μόνον δὲ, ἀλλὰ «Καὶ ἐν ἑτοίμῳ ἔχοντες ἐκδικῆσαι πᾶσαν παρακοήν.»

Ἔνθα καὶ ἐξετάσαντα τῶν εἰρημένων ἕκαστον ἐπιμελέστερον, ἔνεστι γνῶναι τὸ βούλημα τῆς θείας Γραφῆς ἀκριβέστερον, ὡς οὐκ ἀφῆκεν ἡμᾶς ἠπατημέναις τισὶ δόξαις πλάζεσθαι τὴν ἑκάστου ψυχὴν εἰς ἁμαρτίας ὄλισθον, οἰομένην τινὰ μὲν τῶν ἁμαρτημάτων ἐκδικεῖσθαι, τινὰ δὲ ἀφίεσθαι ἀνεκδίκητα. Ἀλλὰ τί φησι; «Λογισμοὺς καθαιροῦντες, καὶ πᾶν ὕψωμα ἐπαιρόμενον κατὰ τῆς γνώσεως

"they will pray to the Lord for him. But if he should sin against God, who will pray for him?"[42] Nevertheless, since, as I said, he was not fervent enough with them, all the aforementioned things occurred.

So I find in the Old Testament the greatest possible number of such judgments against all disobedience. And when I come, in turn, to the New, our Lord Jesus Christ by no means mitigates the penalty for things committed in ignorance, but he intensifies with greater strictness the threat against things done in awareness when he says, "That servant who knew his lord's will and neither prepared himself nor acted in accordance with his will, will be beaten with many blows; but the one who did not know and did things worthy of stripes will be flayed with few."[43] When I find such statements made by the only-begotten Son of God himself, and I behold the holy apostles' vexation against sinners; when I find described in terms no less harsh than in the Old Testament the great and numerous calamities that befall those who sin even in a single instance, I perceive the severity of the judgment. For he adds, "To whom they have provided much, they will demand of him even more in return."[44]

Observe therefore the blessed Paul also as he indicates at once both the dignity of our calling and the vexation against every sin, saying, "For the implements of our warfare are not fleshly, but they are able, through God, to demolish strongholds, demolishing calculations and every high thing erected against the knowledge of God and taking every thought captive to obedience to Christ,"[45] and not only this, but, "and being ready to requite all disobedience."[46] Here too, drawing out with extra care each of the words spoken, it is possible to know more precisely the intent of the divine Scripture, which has not abandoned us to perplexity in the face of certain deluded opinions, with every soul slipping into sin for supposing that only some sins are requited while others are left unrequited. But what does it say?

[42] 1 Sam 2.25
[43] Lk 12.47–48
[44] Lk 12.48
[45] 2 Cor 10.4–6
[46] 2 Cor 10.7

τοῦ Θεοῦ,» ὡς πᾶν ἁμάρτημα, διὰ τὴν ἐπὶ τῷ θείῳ προστάγματι καταφρόνησιν, «ὕψωμα ἐπαιρόμενον κατὰ τῆς γνώσεως τοῦ Θεοῦ» λέγεσθαι, ὅπερ καὶ ἐν τῇ βίβλῳ τῶν Ἀριθμῶν δηλοῦται τρανότερον. Ἐπειδὴ γὰρ τὰ ἀκούσια τῶν ἁμαρτημάτων ἀπαριθμησάμενος, καὶ τὰς ἐπ' αὐτοῖς θυσίας διαταξάμενος ὁ Θεὸς, ἔμελλεν ἤδη καὶ περὶ τῶν ἑκουσίων νομοθετεῖν τῷ λαῷ τὰ προσήκοντα, οὕτως ἄρχεται· «Καὶ ψυχὴ ἥτις ποιήσει ἐν χειρὶ ὑπερηφανίας» (χεῖρα ὑπερηφανίας καλῶν τὴν τόλμαν τῶν ἑκουσίως ἁμαρτανόντων, ὅπερ ὁ ἀπόστολος «ὕψωμα ἐπαιρόμενον κατὰ τῆς γνώσεως τοῦ Θεοῦ» ὀνομάζει), «Ψυχὴ» οὖν, φησὶν, «ἥτις ποιήσει ἐν χειρὶ ὑπερηφανίας, ἢ ἀπὸ τῶν αὐτοχθόνων, ἢ ἀπὸ τῶν προσηλύτων, τὸν Θεὸν οὗτος παροξυνεῖ, καὶ ἐξολοθρευθήσεται ἡ ψυχὴ ἐκείνη ἐκ μέσου τοῦ λαοῦ αὐτῆς. Ὅτι τὸ ῥῆμα Κυρίου ἐφαύλισε, καὶ τὰς ἐντολὰς αὐτοῦ διεσκέδασεν· ἐκτρίψει ἐκτριβήσεται ἡ ψυχὴ ἐκείνη· ἡ ἁμαρτία αὐτῆς ἐν αὐτῇ.» [307] Παρατηρητέον ἐνταῦθα ἐκεῖνο, ὅτι, ἐὰν μὴ ἐκτρίψει ἐκτριβῇ ἡ ψυχὴ ἐκείνη, ἡ ἁμαρτία αὐτῆς οὐκ ἐν αὐτῇ μόνον, ἀλλὰ καὶ ἐπὶ τοὺς μὴ ἐπιδειξαμένους τὸν ἀγαθὸν ζῆλον, καθὼς πολλαχοῦ γέγραπται, καὶ πολλάκις γέγονε. Καὶ ἵνα ἐκ τῶν ἡττόνων παιδευθῶμεν τὸν ἐπὶ τοῖς μείζοσι φόβον, τὴν κατὰ ἱερέως ἢ κριτοῦ παρακουόντων ἀγανάκτησιν οἵαν ποιεῖται ἐν τῷ Δευτερονομίῳ καταμάθωμεν. Λέγει οὖν· «Καὶ ἄνθρωπος, ὃς ἐὰν ποιήσῃ ἐν ὑπερηφανίᾳ τοῦ μὴ ὑπακοῦσαι τοῦ ἱερέως τοῦ παρεστηκότος λειτουργεῖν ἐπὶ τῷ ὀνόματι Κυρίου τοῦ Θεοῦ σου, ἢ τοῦ κριτοῦ, ὃς ἐὰν ᾖ ἐν ταῖς ἡμέραις ἐκείναις, καὶ ἀποθανεῖται ὁ ἄνθρωπος ἐκεῖνος, καὶ ἐξαρεῖς τὸν πονηρὸν ἐξ Ἰσραήλ. Καὶ πᾶς ὁ λαὸς ἀκούσας φοβηθήσεται, καὶ οὐκ ἀσεβήσουσιν ἔτι.» Πρὸς ἃ, πῶς ἄν τις ἀξιολόγως κινούμενος φρικωδέστερον καταπλαγείη, συνορᾷν ἀκόλουθον.

Εἶτά φησι·[5] «Καὶ αἰχμαλωτίζοντες πᾶν νόημα εἰς τὴν ὑπακοὴν τοῦ Χριστοῦ·» πᾶν νόημα· οὐχὶ τοῦτο, ἢ ἐκεῖνο. «Καὶ ἐν ἑτοίμῳ ἔχοντες ἐκδικῆσαι·» καὶ ἐνταῦθα πάλιν, οὐχὶ τήνδε, ἢ τινὰ, ἀλλὰ «Πᾶσαν παρακοήν.» Ἄρα γε ἠπάτησεν ἡμᾶς ἡ κακίστη

---

[5]Corrected from Εἶτα φησί.

"Demolishing calculations and every high thing erected against the knowledge of God." So every sin, because of its contempt for the ordinance of God, is called a "high thing exalted against the knowledge of God." This is shown even more clearly in the book of Numbers. For when God, who had already recounted the involuntary sins and ordained the sacrifices to be made for them, was ready also to establish the appropriate laws for the people concerning voluntary sins, he begins thus: "And whatever soul shall act high-handedly"—calling "high-handed" the boldness of those who sin voluntarily, which the Apostle calls a "high thing erected against the knowledge of God"— "Whatever soul," he says, therefore, "shall act high-handedly, whether native or proselyte, shall provoke God, and that soul will be utterly destroyed from the midst of its people, because it has shown contempt for the word of the Lord and has rejected his commandments. That soul shall be utterly wiped out; its sin is in it."[47] It is necessary to note here that unless that soul is "utterly wiped out" its sin is not in it alone, but it also rests upon those who did not demonstrate the proper zeal against it, as is often written and often happens. And that we might learn from less important things fear in the greater, let us examine in Deuteronomy what wrath is directed against those who disobey a priest or judge. So it says: "And a person who acts haughtily in defiance of the priest established to minister in the name of the Lord your God, or of the judge who should preside in those days, that person shall also die, and you shall remove the evil from Israel. And when they hear of it, all the people shall fear and no longer be impious."[48] How remarkably terrified a person would be—moved to trembling!—to witness the consequence of these things.

Then Paul says, "and taking every thought captive to obedience to Christ"—every thought, not this one or that one—"and being ready to requite" here again, not this or that thing, but "all disobedience."[49] It would appear that bad custom has deceived us,

[47]Num 15.30–31
[48]Deut 17.12–13
[49]2 Cor 10.5–6

συνήθεια· ἄρα κακῶν αἰτία ἡμῖν μεγάλων γέγονεν ἡ διεστραμμένη τῶν ἀνθρώπων παράδοσις, τὰ μὲν παραιτουμένη δῆθεν τῶν ἁμαρτημάτων, τὰ δὲ ἀδιαφόρως αἱρουμένη· καὶ κατὰ μέν τινων σφοδρῶς ἀγανακτεῖν προσποιουμένη, οἷον φόνου, καὶ μοιχείας, καὶ τῶν τοιούτων· τὰ δὲ οὐδὲ ψιλῆς γοῦν ἐπιτιμήσεως ἄξια κρίνουσα, οἷον ὀργὴν, ἢ λοιδορίαν, ἢ μέθην, ἢ πλεονεξίαν, καὶ ὅσα τοιαῦτα, καθ' ὧν ἁπάντων καὶ ἀλλαχοῦ ἔδωκε τὴν αὐτὴν ἀπόφασιν ὁ ἐν Χριστῷ λαλῶν Παῦλος, εἰπών· ὅτι «Οἱ τὰ τοιαῦτα πράσσοντες, ἄξιοι θανάτου εἰσίν.» Ὅπου δὲ πᾶν ὕψωμα ἐπαιρόμενον κατὰ τῆς γνώσεως τοῦ Θεοῦ καθαιρεῖται, καὶ πᾶν νόημα εἰς τὴν ὑπακοὴν τοῦ Χριστοῦ αἰχμαλωτίζεται, καὶ πᾶσα παρακοὴ ἐπίσης ἐκδικεῖται, ἐκεῖ οὐδὲν ἀκαθαίρετον, οὐδὲν ἀνεκδίκητον ἀφίεται, οὐδὲν τῆς τοῦ Χριστοῦ ὑπακοῆς ἐκτὸς ἀπολείπεται. Κοινὸν γὰρ καὶ μέγιστον ἀσέβημα κατὰ πάσης παρακοῆς ἔδειξεν ὁ ἀπόστολος Παῦλος, ἐκεῖνο εἰπών· «Ὃς ἐν νόμῳ καυχᾶσαι, διὰ τῆς παραβάσεως τοῦ νόμου τὸν Θεὸν ἀτιμάζεις.»

Ἀλλ' ἄρα μὴ ταῦτα λόγοι μόνον, καὶ οὐ πράγματα; Ἰδοὺ τοίνυν· ἐν Κορίνθῳ ὁ τὴν γυναῖκα τοῦ πατρὸς ἔχων, οὐδὲν ἕτερον ἐγκληθεὶς, εἰ [308] μὴ τοῦτο μόνον, οὐ μόνον αὐτὸς παραδίδοται τῷ σατανᾷ εἰς ὄλεθρον τῆς σαρκὸς, ἄχρις ἂν τοῖς ἀξίοις τῆς μετανοίας καρποῖς διορθώσηται τὸ πλημμέλημα, πᾶσαν δὲ ὁμοῦ τὴν ἐκκλησίαν, ἐπεὶ μὴ ἐπεξῆλθε τῷ ἁμαρτήματι, ἐκείνοις περιβάλλει τοῖς ἐγκλήμασιν· «Τί θέλετε; Ἐν ῥάβδῳ ἔλθω πρὸς ὑμᾶς;» Καὶ μετ' ὀλίγα, «Καὶ ὑμεῖς πεφυσιωμένοι ἐστὲ, καὶ οὐχὶ μᾶλλον ἐπενθήσατε, ἵνα ἐξαρθῇ ἐκ μέσου ὑμῶν ὁ τὸ ἔργον τοῦτο πράξας.» Τί δὲ ἄρα Ἀνανίας, ὁ ἐν ταῖς Πράξεσι; Τί ἄλλο κακὸν πεποιηκὼς εὑρίσκεται, ἢ ἐκεῖνο αὐτό; Ποῦ τοίνυν τοσαύτης ὀργῆς ἄξιον φαίνεται; Ἴδιον κτῆμα πωλήσας, ἤνεγκε τὰ χρήματα, καὶ ἔθηκε παρὰ τοὺς πόδας τῶν ἀποστόλων· νοσφισάμενος ἀπὸ τῆς τιμῆς, ἐπὶ τούτῳ, παρ' αὐτὴν τὴν ὥραν, ἅμα τῇ γυναικὶ θάνατον καταδικάζεται· οὐδὲ τοὺς περὶ τῆς μετανοίας

that perverted human tradition has caused us great evils. This tradition avoids some sins to be sure, but it indiscriminately embraces
others—affecting a violent irritation against some, such as murder,
adultery, and the like, while adjudging others unworthy even of censure, such as anger, an abusive tongue, drunkenness, arrogance, and
others like these. Yet elsewhere Paul, speaking in Christ, has assigned
to all of these the same sentence, saying, "Those who practice such
things are worthy of death."[50] Now, where every high thing erected
against the knowledge of God is demolished, and every thought
is taken captive to obedience to Christ, and every disobedience is
equally requited, there nothing is left undemolished, nothing goes
unrequited, nothing remains outside obedience to Christ. For the
apostle Paul indicated the common, great impiety of every disobedience when he said, "You who boast in the law, in transgressing the
law you dishonor God."[51]

But perhaps these are only words and not realities. Consider the
following: In Corinth, the man who had his father's wife, and was
accused of nothing else but this alone, was not only himself delivered
over to Satan for the destruction of his flesh until he should correct
the fault by worthy fruits of repentance, but he brings reproach likewise upon the whole Church, since it did not address the sin. "What
do you want? Shall I come for you with a rod?"[52] And a little further:
"And you are become puffed up and did not rather lament, so that the
doer of this deed might be ridded from among you."[53] And what of
Ananias in the Acts?[54] What other evil is he found to have committed
besides this one? How then does he become worthy of such wrath?
Having sold his own property, he brought the money and set it at the
feet of the apostles but kept some of the total back for himself. And for
this, at that very hour, he is consigned to death together with his wife.
Neither was given to hear the exhortation to repentance for their sin,

[50]Rom 1.32
[51]Rom 2.23
[52]Rom 2.23
[53]1 Cor 5.2
[54]See Acts 5.1–11

λόγους ἐπὶ τῷ ἁμαρτήματι μαθεῖν καταξιωθείς, οὐ τοῦ κατανυγῆναι
γοῦν ἐπὶ τούτῳ καιρὸν εὑρών, οὐ τοῦ μετανοῆσαι προθεσμίαν
λαβών.

Ὁ δὲ τοῦ τοιούτου καὶ τηλικούτου κρίματος ὑπηρέτης, ὁ
τῆς τοσαύτης τοῦ Θεοῦ ὀργῆς ἐπὶ τὸν ἡμαρτηκότα διάκονος, ὁ
μακάριος Πέτρος, ὁ πάντων μὲν τῶν μαθητῶν προκριθείς, μόνος
δὲ πλεῖον τῶν ἄλλων μαρτυρηθεὶς καὶ μακαρισθείς, ὁ τὰς κλεῖς
τῆς βασιλείας τῶν οὐρανῶν πιστευθείς, ὅταν ἀκούῃ παρὰ τοῦ
Κυρίου, «Ἐὰν μὴ νίψω σε, οὐκ ἔχεις μέρος μετ' ἐμοῦ,» ποίαν ἄρα
καὶ τὴν ὁπωσοῦν λιθίνην καρδίαν οὐ δυσωπήσει πρὸς φόβον καὶ
τρόμον τῶν τοῦ Θεοῦ κριμάτων; καὶ ταῦτα μὲν οὐδεμιᾶς ἁμαρτίας,
οὐδεμιᾶς δὲ καταφρονήσεως ἔμφασιν δούς, τιμῇ δὲ μᾶλλον τῇ περὶ
τὸν Δεσπότην ὑπερβαλλούσῃ χρησάμενος, καὶ τὴν προσήκουσαν
δούλῳ καὶ μαθητῇ εὐλάβειαν ἐπιδειξάμενος. Ἰδὼν γὰρ τὸν ἑαυτοῦ
καὶ πάντων Θεὸν καὶ Κύριον, καὶ βασιλέα, καὶ Δεσπότην, καὶ
διδάσκαλον, καὶ Σωτῆρα, καὶ ὁμοῦ τὰ πάντα, ἐν ὑπηρέτου σχήματι
διαζωσάμενον λέντιον, καὶ νίπτειν τοὺς πόδας αὐτοῦ βουλόμενον,
εὐθύς, ὥσπερ εἰς συναίσθησιν ἐλθὼν τῆς ἰδίας ἀναξιότητος, καὶ
τὸ ἀξίωμα τοῦ προσερχομένου καταπλαγείς, ἐξεβόησε· «Κύριε, σύ
μου νίπτεις τοὺς πόδας;» Καὶ πάλιν· «Οὐ μὴ νίψῃς τοὺς πόδας μου
εἰς τὸν αἰῶνα.» Ἐπὶ τούτῳ τὴν τοσαύτην εἰσδέχεται ἀπειλήν, ὡς εἰ
μὴ πάλιν εἰδὼς τὴν ἀλήθειαν τῶν ῥημάτων τοῦ Κυρίου, ἔφθασε
τῇ ὑπακοῇ διορθωσάμενος τὴν ἀντιλογίαν, οὐδὲν ἂν αὐτῷ τῶν
προλαβόντων, οὐ τῶν ἰδίων κατορθωμάτων, οὐ τῶν παρὰ τοῦ
Κυρίου μακαρισμῶν [309] τε καὶ δωρεῶν καὶ ἐπαγγελιῶν, οὐδὲ
αὐτὴ ἡ τοῦ Θεοῦ καὶ Πατρὸς τῆς τοιαύτης καὶ τοσαύτης εἰς τὸν
μονογενῆ Υἱὸν εὐδοκίας ἀποκάλυψις ἤρκεσε παραμυθήσασθαι τὴν
παροῦσαν ἀπείθειαν.

Ἀλλὰ ταῦτα μὲν ἐὰν θέλω καταλέγειν, ὅσα εὑρίσκω ἔκ τε
παλαιᾶς καὶ καινῆς Διαθήκης, ἐπιλείψει με τάχα διηγούμενον ὁ
χρόνος. Ἤδη δὲ καὶ ἐπ' αὐτὰς ὅταν ἔλθω τὰς τοῦ Κυρίου ἡμῶν
Ἰησοῦ Χριστοῦ ἐν τῷ εὐαγγελίῳ φωνάς, αὐτοῦ τοῦ μέλλοντος
κρίνειν ζῶντας καὶ νεκροὺς τὰ ῥήματα, ἃ πάσης μὲν ἱστορίας, πάσης
δὲ ἄλλης ἀποδείξεως παρὰ τοῖς πιστοῖς ἀξιοπιστότερα, πολλὴν

nor did they find time for the pricking of conscience, at least in this matter, nor were they afforded an opportunity to repent.

And the agent of so harsh and weighty a judgment, the server of God's great wrath to the one who had sinned, the blessed Peter—who was the most eminent of all the disciples, uniquely attested, and blessed more than the others, who was entrusted with the keys of the kingdom of the heavens—when he hears from the Lord, "If I do not wash you, you have no part with me,"[55] what heart, however stony, would not be reduced to fear and trembling at the judgments of God? And this was said to him though he gave no indication of any sin or contempt, but rather acquitted himself most honorably with the Master and demonstrated reverence befitting a servant and disciple. For when he beheld the God and Lord and King and Master and Teacher and Savior of himself and all in the guise of an attendant, girded with a towel and desiring to wash his feet, as one who has realized his own unworthiness and been struck by the worth of the one approaching, he immediately cried out: "Lord, do you wash my feet?"[56] And again: "You shall never wash my feet."[57] Yet at this he received so great a threat that unless he recognized the truth of the Lord's words and hastened to correct contention with obedience, nothing that had been attributed to him before—not his upright deeds, nor the blessings and gifts and promises of the Lord, nor even the very revelation of the exceeding good pleasure of the God and Father for the only-begotten Son[58]— would have sufficed to excuse his disobedience in that moment.

But should I wish to recount all that I find in the Old and New Testaments, time would soon fail me as I expounded it. Yet already when I but come to the voice of our Lord Jesus Christ in the Gospel, the words of the one coming to judge the living and the dead, which the faithful hold more trustworthy than all other accounts and

[55]Jn 13.8
[56]Jn 13.6
[57]Jn 13.8
[58]Basil is referring to the Transfiguration on Mount Tabor, which only Peter, James, and John of all the disciples were permitted to see. See Mt 17.1–8.

μὲν ἐν αὐτοῖς καταμανθάνω τῆς ἐν πᾶσι πρὸς Θεὸν εὐπειθείας, ἵνα οὕτως εἴπω, ἀνάγκην· οὐδεμίαν δὲ ὅλως, ἐπ᾽ οὐδενὶ προστάγματι, καταλειπομένην τοῖς μὴ μετανοοῦσι τῆς ἀπειθείας συγγνώμην, εἰ μή τι ἕτερόν ἐστι τολμῆσαι, καὶ μέχρις ἐννοίας λαβεῖν, πρὸς οὕτω γυμνὰς, σαφεῖς τε καὶ ἀπολύτους ἀποφάσεις· «Ὁ οὐρανὸς» γὰρ, φησὶ, «καὶ ἡ γῆ παρελεύσονται, οἱ δὲ λόγοι μου οὐ μὴ παρέλθωσιν.» Οὐκ ἔστιν ἐνταῦθα διαφορὰ, οὐκ ἔστι διαίρεσις, οὐδὲν οὐδαμοῦ ὅλως ὑπολέλειπται. Οὐκ εἶπεν· οὗτοι, ἢ ἐκεῖνοι, ἀλλ᾽, «Οἱ λόγοι μου·» πάντες ὁμοῦ δηλονότι, οὐ μὴ παρέλθωσι. Γέγραπται γάρ, «Πιστὸς Κύριος ἐν πᾶσι τοῖς λόγοις αὐτοῦ·» εἴτε ἀπαγορεύων ὁτιοῦν, εἴτε προστάσσων, εἴτε ἐπαγγελλόμενος, εἴτε ἀπειλῶν, καὶ εἴτε ἐπὶ τῇ πράξει τῶν ἀπηγορευμένων, εἴτε ἐπὶ τῇ ἐλλείψει τῶν ἐπιτεταγμένων. Ὅτι γὰρ ἐπίσης τῇ ἐνεργείᾳ τῶν κακῶν καὶ ἡ τῶν ἀγαθῶν ἔργων ἔλλειψις ἐκδικεῖται, ἤρκει μὲν καὶ πρὸς ἀπόδειξιν[6] καὶ πληροφορίαν τῇ γε μὴ παντελῇ ἀπιστίαν νοσούσῃ ψυχῇ τὸ προειρημένον ἐπὶ τῷ Πέτρῳ κρίμα· ὃς οὐκ ἀπηγορευμένον τι πράξας, οὐδὲ μὴν πρόσταγμά [310] τι τοιοῦτον ἐλλείψας, ὃ ῥαιθυμίαν ἢ καταφρόνησιν κατηγορεῖ τοῦ ἐλλείποντος, ὑπηρεσίαν δὲ καὶ τιμὴν τὴν παρὰ τοῦ Δεσπότου μόνον ὑποδέξασθαι εὐλαβηθεὶς, τοιαύτην ἐδέξατο τὴν ἀπειλὴν, ἣν οὐκ ἔφυγεν ἄν, εἰ μὴ, καθὼς προείρηται, ἔφθασε τὴν ὀργὴν τῇ ταχύτητι καὶ σφοδρότητι τῆς διορθώσεως.

Πλὴν ἐπειδὴ ὁ ἀγαθὸς καὶ εὔσπλαγχνος Θεὸς μακροθυμῶν ἐφ᾽ ἡμῖν εὐδόκησε, καὶ πολλάκις ἡμῖν τὸ αὐτὸ καὶ διὰ πολλῶν ὑποδεῖξαι, ἵνα τῷ πλήθει καὶ τῇ συνεχείᾳ δυνηθῇ μόλις ποτὲ μοχλευθεῖσα καὶ καταντληθεῖσα ἡ ψυχὴ ἀποτρίψασθαι τὴν πολυχρόνιον τῆς παρανομίας συνήθειαν, ἐκείνων μόνων πρὸς τὸ παρὸν μνημονεῦσαι ἀναγκαῖον τῶν ἐν τῇ μεγάλῃ καὶ φοβερᾷ τῆς κρίσεως ἡμέρᾳ ἐξ ἀριστερῶν τοῦ Κυρίου ἡμῶν Ἰησοῦ Χριστοῦ ἱσταμένων· πρὸς οὓς ἔλεγεν ὁ πᾶσαν τὴν ἐξουσίαν τῆς κρίσεως λαβὼν παρὰ τοῦ Πατρὸς, ὁ ἐρχόμενος «φωτίσαι τὰ κρυπτὰ τοῦ σκότους, καὶ φανερῶσαι τὰς βουλὰς τῶν καρδιῶν·» «Πορεύεσθε ἀπ᾽ ἐμοῦ, οἱ κατηραμένοι, εἰς τὸ πῦρ τὸ αἰώνιον, τὸ ἡτοιμασμένον τῷ διαβόλῳ καὶ τοῖς ἀγγέλοις

---

[6]Corrected from ἀπόδειξειν.

deductions, I learn in them the great necessity, so to speak, of ready obedience to God in all things. For there is no pardon whatsoever, no matter the command in question, for those who fail to repent of their disobedience, unless it is possible to venture a different conclusion in the face of such bald, plain, and unconditional statements. "For," he says, "heaven and earth will pass away, but my words will by no means pass away."[59] Here is no division observed, no distinction; nothing of the whole is left out. He did not say, "these" or "those," but "my words," a clear indication that all in common will by no means pass away. For it is written, "The Lord is faithful in all his words," whether forbidding or commanding anything, whether promising or threatening, with respect to doing what is forbidden or neglecting what is commanded. The judgment in Peter's case is sufficient to demonstrate and convince a soul that has any faith at all that leaving good deeds undone is requited the same as doing evil. For he did nothing forbidden, nor did he neglect any command which would have made him liable to an accusation of laziness or contempt. Yet merely for recoiling out of reverence from receiving the service and honor of the Master, he received this threat. And he would not have escaped it, as I said, had he not pre-empted the wrath with the speed and fervency of his correction.

However, since the God who is good, compassionate, and long-suffering with us is well pleased to demonstrate the same thing to us many times and in many ways, so that through overprovision and repetition our soul, dislodged and awash, might be just able eventually to rid itself of the long-standing habit of transgression, for now it is necessary only to recall those placed at the left hand of our Lord Jesus Christ in the great and fearful day of judgment. He who received from the Father all authority to judge, who comes to "enlighten the hidden things of darkness and to reveal the desires of the hearts,"[60] says to these, "Depart from me, accursed, into the eternal fire which was prepared for the devil and his angels."[61] And

[59]Mt 24.35
[60]1 Cor 4.5
[61]Mt 25.41

αὐτοῦ.» Καὶ τὴν αἰτίαν ἐπήγαγεν· οὐχ ὅτι ἐφονεύσατε λέγων, ἢ ἐπορνεύσατε, ἢ ἐψεύσασθε, ἤ τινα ἠδικήσατε, ἢ ἄλλο τι τῶν ἀπηγορευμένων, κἂν τὸ βραχύτατον γοῦν, ἐπράξατε· ἀλλὰ τί; ὅτι τῶν ἀγαθῶν ἔργων ἠμελήσατε. «Ἐπείνασα» γὰρ, φησὶ, «καὶ οὐκ ἐδώκατέ μοι φαγεῖν· ἐδίψησα, καὶ οὐκ ἐποτίσατέ⁷ με· ξένος ἤμην, καὶ οὐ συνηγάγετέ με· γυμνὸς, καὶ οὐ περιεβάλετέ με· ἀσθενὴς καὶ ἐν φυλακῇ, καὶ οὐκ ἐπεσκέψασθέ με.»

Ταῦτα καὶ τὰ τοιαῦτα Θεοῦ τοῦ ἀγαθοῦ χάριτι, τοῦ θέλοντος μὲν πάντας ἀνθρώπους σωθῆναι, καὶ εἰς ἐπίγνωσιν ἀληθείας ἐλθεῖν, διδάσκοντος δὲ ἄνθρωπον γνῶσιν, καταμαθὼν ἐν ταῖς θεοπνεύστοις Γραφαῖς, καὶ γνωρίσας μὲν τὴν φρικωδεστάτην αἰτίαν τῆς τοιαύτης τῶν πολλῶν πρός τε ἀλλήλους καὶ πρὸς τὰς ἐντολὰς τοῦ Κυρίου ἡμῶν Ἰησοῦ Χριστοῦ διαφωνίας, παιδευθεὶς δὲ τὸ φοβερὸν ἐκεῖνο κρίμα τῆς τοσαύτης παρανομίας, διδαχθεὶς δὲ καὶ πᾶσαν παρακοὴν παντὸς κρίματος Θεοῦ ἐπίσης ἐκδικεῖσθαι· ἔτι δὲ καὶ τὸ φοβερὸν ἐκεῖνο κρίμα καταμαθὼν, τὸ ἐπὶ τοὺς μὴ ἁμαρτήσαντας μὲν, παραπολαύσαντας δὲ ὅμως τῆς ὀργῆς, διὰ τὸ μὴ τὸν ἀγαθὸν ζῆλον κατὰ τῶν ἡμαρτηκότων ἐπιδείξασθαι, καίτοι πολλάκις μηδὲ συνεγνωκότας τὸ ἁμάρτημα· ἀναγκαῖον ἐλογισάμην, εἰ καὶ ὀψὲ τοῦ καιροῦ, διὰ τὸ ἀναμένειν ἀεὶ τοὺς τὸν αὐτὸν ἀγῶνα τῆς θεοσεβείας ἀνειληφότας, καὶ μὴ θαρρεῖν [311] ἑαυτῷ μόνῳ, ἀλλ' οὐκ ἀκαίρως γε τάχα, νῦν γοῦν πρὸς ὑπόμνησιν τοῖς ἀγωνιζομένοις τὸν ἀγῶνα τῆς θεοσεβείας, ἀναλεξάμενος ἐκ τῶν θεοπνεύστων Γραφῶν τά τε ἀπαρέσκοντα τῷ Θεῷ, καὶ οἷς εὐαρεστεῖται παραθέσθαι, ὡς ἂν οἷός τε ὦ, κατ' εὐχὰς κοινάς· ἵνα καταξιωθῶμεν χάριτι τοῦ Κυρίου ἡμῶν Ἰησοῦ Χριστοῦ καὶ διδασκαλίᾳ τοῦ ἁγίου Πνεύματος, ἀποπηδήσαντες μὲν τῆς τε τῶν ἰδίων θελημάτων συνηθείας, καὶ τῆς τῶν ἀνθρωπίνων παραδόσεων παρατηρήσεως· στοιχήσαντες δὲ τῷ εὐαγγελίῳ τοῦ μακαρίου Θεοῦ Ἰησοῦ Χριστοῦ, τοῦ Κυρίου ἡμῶν·

---

⁷Corrected from ἀποτίσατέ.

he presented the cause, which was not "you murdered" or "you fornicated" or "you lied" or "you were unjust to someone" or "you did anything else forbidden, even the least." But what? "Because you neglected good works." For he says, "I was hungry, and you did not give me to eat. I was thirsty and you did not give me to drink. I was a stranger, and you did not befriend me; naked, and you did not clothe me; sick and in prison, and you did not visit me."[62]

Having learned in the God-breathed Scriptures these and other such things by the grace of the good God who desires all humans to be saved and come to the knowledge of truth and who teaches a person knowledge; and having identified that most awful cause of the disharmony among everyone with one another and with the commandment of our Lord Jesus Christ; and having further-more been instructed in the fearful decree against such lawlessness and taught also that every disobedience of every decree of God is punished equally; and having further learned of the fearful decree against those who have not sinned yet share in the wrath against it nevertheless for not manifesting proper zeal against those who have, though often they are not even cognizant of the sin—having learned all this, I considered it necessary, if also late in time (for I had no confidence in myself alone and ever awaited those engaged in the same contest of piety[63]), though perhaps not untimely, to lay out all the things that are either displeasing or pleasing to God which I have collected from the God-breathed Scriptures to the best of my ability, by our common prayers, so that those struggling in the contest of piety might have them to mind. Thus when through the grace of our Lord Jesus Christ and the teaching of the Holy Spirit we have turned from the habit of our own desires and from the observance of human traditions, have aligned ourselves to the gospel of the blessed God

[62]Mt 25.42–43

[63]This is an ambiguous phrase. Perhaps it means that Basil hoped another, more capable individual would speak out first against the rampant immorality he observed in the Church, or perhaps it means that Basil had originally intended to compile the *Ethics* with the help of others, as he had the Philokalia with his friend St Gregory the Theologian.

καὶ κατὰ τὸν καιρὸν τὸν παρόντα εὐαρέστως αὐτῷ ζήσαντες, διά τε σφοδροτέρας ἀναχωρήσεως τῶν κεκωλυμένων, καὶ σπουδαιοτέρας ἐπιμελείας τῶν ἐγκεκριμένων, ἐν τῷ μέλλοντι αἰῶνι τῆς ἀθανασίας, φυγεῖν μὲν τὴν ὀργὴν τὴν ἐπερχομένην ἐπὶ τοὺς υἱοὺς τῆς ἀπειθείας δυναίμεθα, ἄξιοι δὲ εὑρεθῆναι τῆς αἰωνίου ζωῆς, καὶ ἐπουρανίου βασιλείας τῆς ἐπηγγελμένης παρὰ τοῦ Κυρίου Ἰησοῦ Χριστοῦ πᾶσι «Τοῖς φυλάσσουσι τὴν διαθήκην αὐτοῦ, καὶ μεμνημένοις τῶν ἐντολῶν αὐτοῦ, τοῦ ποιῆσαι αὐτάς.»

Μεμνημένος δὲ τοῦ ἀποστόλου εἰπόντος· «Ἐν Χριστῷ Ἰησοῦ οὔτε περιτομή τι ἰσχύει, οὔτε ἀκροβυστία, ἀλλὰ πίστις δι' ἀγάπης ἐνεργουμένη·» ἀκόλουθον ὁμοῦ καὶ ἀναγκαῖον ἐλογισάμην, τὴν ὑγιαίνουσαν πίστιν καὶ εὐσεβῆ δόξαν περί τε Πατρὸς καὶ Υἱοῦ καὶ ἁγίου Πνεύματος παραθέσθαι πρότερον, καὶ οὕτως ἐπισυνάψαι τὰ ἠθικά.

of Jesus Christ our Lord, and have lived this present life in a manner well-pleasing to him by retreating more fervently from things prohibited and showing more zealous diligence in things approved, we might be vouchsafed in the coming age of immortality to escape the wrath which is coming quickly upon the sons of disobedience and be found worthy of eternal life and the heavenly kingdom promised by the Lord Jesus Christ to all "who keep his covenant and, having his commandments in remembrance, do them."[64]

But remembering what the Apostle said: "In Christ Jesus neither does circumcision accomplish anything, nor uncircumcision, but faith working through love,"[65] I determined it necessary and fitting first to set forth the sound faith and pious conception of Father and Son and Holy Spirit, and then to attach the *Ethics*.

[64]Ps 103.18 (LXX 102.18)
[65]Gal 5.6

ΠΕΡΙ ΠΙΣΤΕΩΣ

Θεοῦ τοῦ ἀγαθοῦ χάριτι τὸ ἐπίταγμα τῆς ὑμετέρας εὐλαβείας καταμαθὼν ἄξιον τῆς ἐν Χριστῷ πρὸς τὸν Θεὸν ἀγάπης, ἐν ᾧ τῆς εὐσεβοῦς πίστεως ἔγγραφον ἐπεζητήσατε παρ' ἡμῶν ὁμολογίαν, τὰ μὲν πρῶτα ἐπαισθανόμενος τῆς ἐμαυτοῦ ταπεινώσεως [312] καὶ ἀσθενείας, ὤκνουν πρὸς τὴν ἀπόκρισιν· ὡς δὲ ἐμνημόνευσα τοῦ ἀποστόλου εἰπόντος, «Ἀνεχόμενοι ἀλλήλων ἐν ἀγάπῃ·» καὶ πάλιν, «Καρδίᾳ γὰρ πιστεύεται εἰς δικαιοσύνην, στόματι δὲ ὁμολογεῖται εἰς σωτηρίαν·» οὐκ ἀκίνδυνον ἡγησάμην τὸ ἀντειπεῖν μὲν ὑμῖν, σιωπῆσαι δὲ τὴν σωτήριον ὁμολογίαν, πεποίθησιν ἔχων διὰ τοῦ Χριστοῦ πρὸς τὸν Θεόν, ὡς γέγραπται· «Οὐχ ὅτι ἱκανοί ἐσμεν ἀφ' ἑαυτῶν λογίσασθαί τι, ὡς ἐξ ἑαυτῶν· ἀλλ' ἡ ἱκανότης ἡμῶν ἐκ τοῦ Θεοῦ,» τοῦ τότε μὲν ἐκείνους, νῦν δὲ καὶ ἡμᾶς, καὶ τοῦτο δι' ὑμᾶς, «ἱκανώσαντος γενέσθαι διακόνους καινῆς Διαθήκης, οὐ γράμματος, ἀλλὰ πνεύματος.» Διακόνου δὲ πιστοῦ ἴδιον ἴστε πάντως καὶ αὐτοί, τὸ, ἅπερ ἂν εἰς τοὺς συνδούλους οἰκονομῆσαι παρὰ τοῦ ἀγαθοῦ Δεσπότου πιστευθῇ, ταῦτα διασῶσαι τούτοις ἀνοθεύτως, καὶ ἀκαπηλεύτως.

Ὥστε κἀγώ, ἅπερ ἔμαθον ἐκ τῆς θεοπνεύστου Γραφῆς, ταῦτα ὑμῖν παραθέσθαι κατὰ τὸ ἀρέσκον Θεῷ, πρὸς τὸ κοινῇ συμφέρον ὀφειλέτης εἰμί. Εἰ γὰρ αὐτὸς ὁ Κύριος, ἐν ᾧ εὐδόκησεν ὁ Πατὴρ, «Ἐν ᾧ εἰσι πάντες οἱ θησαυροὶ τῆς σοφίας καὶ τῆς γνώσεως ἀπόκρυφοι,» ὁ πᾶσαν μὲν τὴν ἐξουσίαν, πᾶσαν δὲ τὴν κρίσιν

On the Faith

When I learned by the grace of the good God of Your Reverence's injunction, which was worthy of your love for God in Christ, and in which you sought from us a written confession of the pious faith, I first shrank from answering as I considered my lowliness and feebleness. But then I remembered the saying of the Apostle: "Bear with one another in love,"[1] and again, "For it is with the heart that one believes unto righteousness, but with the mouth one confesses unto salvation,"[2] and I determined it no safe thing to refuse you and not make the saving confession. So I took confidence in God through Christ, as it is written: "Not that we are adequate as to reckon anything of ourselves as our own, but our adequacy is from God, who has made" them then[3] and us now, for your sake, "adequate to be ministers of the New Covenant—not of the letter, but of the spirit."[4] And the mark of a faithful minister you especially know well: to maintain without adulteration or chicanery, for the benefit of our fellow servants, whatever the good Master has entrusted to us for the purpose of managing his household.

Therefore I too am obliged to set before you, for the common good, if it pleases God, that which I have learned from the God-breathed Scripture. For if the same Lord in whom the Father was well pleased,[5] "in whom are hidden all the treasures of wisdom and knowledge,"[6] the one who, after receiving from the Father all

[1] Eph 4.2
[2] Rom 10.10
[3] That is, the apostles.
[4] 2 Cor 3.5–6
[5] Cf. Mt 3.17
[6] Col 2.3

λαβὼν παρὰ τοῦ Πατρὸς, «Ἐντολὴν ἔδωκέ μοι, φησὶ, τί εἴπω, καὶ τί λαλήσω·» καὶ πάλιν, «Ἃ οὖν ἐγὼ λαλῶ, καθὼς εἴρηκέ μοι ὁ Πατὴρ, οὕτω λαλῶ· καὶ τὸ Πνεῦμα τὸ ἅγιον ἀφ' ἑαυτοῦ οὐ λαλεῖ, ἀλλ' ὅσα ἂν ἀκούσῃ παρ' αὐτοῦ, ταῦτα λαλεῖ· πόσῳ μᾶλλον ἡμῖν εὐσεβές τε ὁμοῦ καὶ ἀσφαλὲς τοῦτο φρονεῖν καὶ ποιεῖν ἐν ὀνόματι τοῦ Κυρίου ἡμῶν Ἰησοῦ Χριστοῦ;

Ἕως μὲν οὖν ἀγωνίζεσθαι πρὸς τὰς ἐπανισταμένας κατὰ καιρὸν αἱρέσεις ἐχρῆν, ἑπόμενος τοῖς προειληφόσιν, ἀκόλουθον ἡγούμην τῇ διαφορᾷ τῆς ἐπισπειρομένης ὑπὸ τοῦ διαβόλου ἀσεβείας, ταῖς ἀντιθέτοις φωναῖς κωλύειν, ἢ καὶ ἀνατρέπειν τὰς ἐπαγομένας βλασφημίας, καὶ ἄλλοτε ἄλλαις, ὡς ἂν ἡ χρεία τῶν νοσούντων κατηνάγκασε, καὶ ταύταις πολλάκις ἀγράφοις μὲν, ὅμως δ' οὖν οὐκ ἀπεξενωμέναις τῆς κατὰ τὴν Γραφὴν εὐσεβοῦς διανοίας· τοῦ ἀποστόλου πολλάκις καὶ Ἑλληνικοῖς ῥήμασι χρήσασθαι μὴ παραιτησαμένου πρὸς τὸν ἴδιον σκοπόν. Νῦν δὲ πρὸς τὸν κοινὸν ἡμῶν τε καὶ [313] ὑμῶν σκοπὸν ἁρμόζον ἐλογισάμην ἐν ἁπλότητι τῆς ὑγιαινούσης πίστεως τὸ ἐπίταγμα τῆς ὑμετέρας ἐν Χριστῷ ἀγάπης πληρῶσαι, εἰπὼν ἃ ἐδιδάχθην παρὰ τῆς θεοπνεύστου Γραφῆς· φειδόμενος μὲν καὶ τῶν ὀνομάτων, καὶ ῥημάτων ἐκείνων, ἃ λέξεσι μὲν αὐταῖς οὐκ ἐμφέρεται τῇ θείᾳ Γραφῇ, διάνοιάν γε μὴν τὴν ἐκείνην ἐγκειμένην τῇ Γραφῇ διασώζει· ὅσα δὲ πρὸς τῷ ξένῳ τῆς λέξεως ἔτι καὶ τὸν νοῦν ξένον ἡμῖν ἐπεισάγει, καὶ ἃ οὐκ ἔστιν ὑπὸ τῶν ἁγίων κηρυσσόμενα εὑρεῖν, ταῦτα ὡς ξένα καὶ ἀλλότρια τῆς εὐσεβοῦς πίστεως παντάπασι παραιτούμενος.

Πίστις μὲν οὖν ἐστι συγκατάθεσις ἀδιάκριτος τῶν ἀκουσθέντων ἐν πληροφορίᾳ τῆς ἀληθείας τῶν κηρυχθέντων Θεοῦ χάριτι, ἥντινα ἐπεδείξατο μαρτυρηθεὶς Ἀβραὰμ, ὅτι «Οὐ διεκρίθη τῇ ἀπιστίᾳ, ἀλλ' ἐνεδυναμώθη τῇ πίστει, δοὺς δόξαν τῷ Θεῷ, καὶ

authority and all judgment,[7] said "He has given me a commandment, what I should say and what I should speak,"[8] and again, "Therefore what I speak, just as the Father has spoken to me, so I speak,"[9] and if the Holy Spirit speaks not from himself but says whatever things he hears from him,[10] how much more pious and secure is it for us to think and to do likewise in the name of our Lord Jesus Christ?

Therefore, though when I had to contend with heresies as they arose in their season I found it necessary, as others before me, to use language tailored against the variety of the impieties sown by the devil, so that I might obstruct, or rather, overthrow the blasphemies brought forward, and though the language I used from time to time, as the needs of the afflicted[11] required, was often unwritten[12] (though it was not therefore estranged from the pious meaning of the Scripture, like the Apostle, who often taught using pagan expressions to achieve his aim), for the present purpose I considered it appropriate to our common aim to fulfill the injunction of your love in Christ in the simplicity of the sound faith. I will speak what I have been taught from the God-breathed Scripture, refraining from those names and expressions not found in the words of the divine Scripture (though they preserve the meaning wrapped within), and avoiding altogether as foreign and estranged from the pious faith those things which, besides being foreign in expression, introduce further a foreign sense, which cannot be found to have been used by the saints.

Now faith is unwavering assent to what is heard, in full assurance of the truth of what is proclaimed by the grace of God. This was shown by what was testified of Abraham, that "he did not waver in unbelief, rather he was strengthened in faith, giving glory to God,

[7]Cf. Jn 5.22, 27; 17.2; Mt 28.18
[8]Jn 12.49
[9]Jn 12.50
[10]Cf. Jn 16.13
[11]That is, the heretics.
[12]It is not clear whether Basil means by this "not found in Scripture," as the immediate context would suggest, or if he includes also the writings of the saints before him, which would accord with what he says toward the end of the paragraph.

πληροφορηθεὶς ὅτι, ὃ ἐπήγγελται, δυνατός ἐστι καὶ ποιῆσαι.» Εἰ
δὲ «Πιστὸς μὲν ὁ Κύριος ἐν πᾶσι τοῖς λόγοις αὐτοῦ,» «Πισταὶ δὲ
πᾶσαι αἱ ἐντολαὶ αὐτοῦ, ἐστηριγμέναι εἰς τὸν αἰῶνα τοῦ αἰῶνος,
πεποιημέναι ἐν ἀληθείᾳ καὶ εὐθύτητι,» φανερὰ ἔκπτωσις πίστεως
καὶ ὑπερηφανίας κατηγορία, ἢ ἀθετεῖν τι τῶν γεγραμμένων, ἢ
ἐπεισάγειν τῶν μὴ γεγραμμένων, τοῦ Κυρίου ἡμῶν Ἰησοῦ Χριστοῦ
εἰπόντος· «Τὰ ἐμὰ πρόβατα τῆς ἐμῆς φωνῆς ἀκούει·» καὶ πρὸ
τούτου δὲ εἰρηκότος· «Ἀλλοτρίῳ δὲ οὐ μὴ ἀκολουθήσωσιν, ἀλλὰ
φεύξονται ἀπ᾽ αὐτοῦ· ὅτι οὐκ οἴδασι τῶν ἀλλοτρίων τὴν φωνήν·»
καὶ τοῦ Ἀποστόλου ἐν ὑποδείγματι ἀνθρωπίνῳ σφοδρότερον
ἀπαγορεύοντος τὸ προσθεῖναι ἢ ὑφελεῖν τι ἐν ταῖς θεοπνεύστοις
Γραφαῖς, δι᾽ ὧν φησιν· «ὅμως ἀνθρώπου κεκυρωμένην διαθήκην
οὐδεὶς ἀθετεῖ, ἢ ἐπιδιατάσσεται.»

Πᾶσαν μὲν οὖν ἀλλοτρίαν τῆς τοῦ Κυρίου διδασκαλίας φωνὴν
καὶ ἔννοιαν οὕτως ἡμεῖς πάντοτε καὶ νῦν ἀποφεύγειν ἐγνώκαμεν,
καὶ τοῦ σκοποῦ δὲ, ὡς προεῖπον, τοῦ νῦν ἡμῖν τε καὶ ὑμῖν προκει-
μένου, καταπολὺ διαφέροντος τῶν ὑποθέσεων ἐκείνων, ὑφ᾽ ὧν
ἄλλοτε ἄλλως ἐπὶ τὸ γράψαι τι ἢ εἰπεῖν προήχθημεν. Διότι τότε
μὲν αἱρέσεως ἔλεγχος καὶ ἀνατροπὴ τῆς τοῦ διαβόλου μεθοδείας
ἐσπουδάζετο, [314] νῦν δὲ τῆς ὑγιαινούσης πίστεως ὁμολογία τε
καὶ φανέρωσις ἁπλῆ πρόκειται. Οὐκοῦν οὔτε τοῦ λόγου χαρακτὴρ
ὁ αὐτὸς ἡμῖν καὶ νῦν ἁρμόζει. Ὡς γὰρ οὐκ ἂν λάβοι μετὰ χεῖρας
ἄνθρωπος σκεύη τὰ αὐτὰ πολεμῶν καὶ γεωργῶν (ἄλλα γὰρ σκεύη
τῶν ἐν ἀδείᾳ τὰ πρὸς τὸ ζῆν ἑαυτοῖς ἐκπονούντων, ἄλλαι δὲ
πανοπλίαι τῶν ἐν πολέμῳ παρατασσομένων), οὕτως οὐκ ἂν εἴποι
τὰ αὐτὰ ὁ παρακαλῶν ἐν τῇ ὑγιαινούσῃ διδασκαλίᾳ. καὶ ὁ τοὺς
ἀντιλέγοντας ἐλέγχων. Ἄλλο γὰρ εἶδος λόγου ἐλεγκτικοῦ, καὶ
ἄλλο εἶδος λόγου παρακλητικοῦ. Ἄλλη ἁπλότης τῶν ἐν εἰρήνῃ
τὴν εὐσέβειαν ὁμολογούντων, καὶ ἄλλοι ἱδρῶτες τῶν πρὸς «τὰς
ἀντιθέσεις τῆς ψευδωνύμου γνώσεως» ἱσταμένων. Ὥστε ἂν

and was fully assured that what he promised he is able also to do."[13] But if "the Lord is faithful in all his words"[14] and "all his command-ments are faithful, established unto ages of ages, made in truth and uprightness,"[15] it is a clear indictment of abandoning the faith and of arrogance either to supplant anything that is written or to introduce anything not written. For our Lord Jesus Christ said, "My sheep hear my voice,"[16] and before this he said likewise, "A stranger they will not follow but will flee from him, because they do not know the voice of strangers."[17] And the Apostle, using an example from human affairs, more emphatically forbids adding or subtracting anything in the God-breathed Scripture, which he has in mind when he says, "Though a covenant be confirmed by human agency, no one denies it or makes addition to it."[18]

Thus we have always determined and determine still to flee from every word and thought foreign to the teaching of the Lord, and the aim, as I have said, now lying before us both differs greatly from those occasions in which we were compelled from time to time to write or to speak, because then we were eager to refute heresy and undo the craft of the devil, whereas the task before us now is to con-fess and plainly lay out the sound faith. Therefore the same manner of speech is now assuredly not fitting. For, as a person would not take in hand the same equipment for war as for farming (for the equipment used by those who produce their living in security is entirely different from the array of armor and weapons used by those drawn up for war), so the one who exhorts in sound doctrine and the one who refutes those who speak against it do not say the same things. There is one form of discourse for refutation and another for exhortation. The simplicity of those who confess piety in peace is one thing; the struggles of those who stand against "the oppositions

[13]Rom 4.20–21
[14]Ps 145.13 (LXX 144.13)
[15]Ps 111.7–8 (LXX 110.7–8)
[16]Jn 10.27
[17]Jn 10.5
[18]Gal 3.15

τούτῳ τῷ τρόπῳ καὶ ἡμεῖς οἰκονομοῦντες τοὺς λόγους ἡμῶν ἐν κρίσει, πανταχοῦ τοῖς πρὸς τὴν φυλακὴν ἢ οἰκοδομὴν τῆς πίστεως ἀκολούθως χρησαίμεθα, ποτὲ μὲν τοῖς ἐν μεθοδείᾳ τοῦ διαβόλου καταλύειν πειρωμένοις αὐτὴν ἀγωνιστικώτερον ἀνθιστάμενοι, ποτὲ δὲ τοῖς οἰκοδομεῖσθαι βουλομένοις ἐν αὐτῇ ἁπλοϊκώτερον καὶ οἰκειότερον αὐτὴν ἐξηγούμενοι, καὶ οὐδὲν ἄλλο ποιοῦντες ἢ ἐκεῖνο τὸ παρὰ τοῦ Ἀποστόλου εἰρημένον· «Εἰδέναι πῶς δεῖ ὑμᾶς ἑνὶ ἑκάστῳ ἀποκριθῆναι.»

Πρὶν δὲ ἐλθεῖν ἐπ' αὐτὴν τὴν τῆς πίστεως ὁμολογίαν, κἀκεῖνο ἐπισημήνασθαι ἄξιον· ὅτι τὴν τοῦ Θεοῦ μεγαλειότητα καὶ δόξαν, καὶ λόγῳ ἀπερίληπτον οὖσαν, καὶ νῷ ἀκατάληπτον, ἑνὶ μὲν ῥήματι ἢ νοήματι οὔτε δηλωθῆναι, οὔτε νοηθῆναι οἷόν τε ἦν· διὰ πλειόνων δὲ τῶν ἐνστρεφομένων τῇ ἡμετέρᾳ χρήσει ἡ θεόπνευστος Γραφὴ μόλις τοῖς καθαροῖς τῇ καρδίᾳ, ὡς δι' ἐσόπτρου, ᾐνίξατο. Τὸ μὲν γὰρ πρόσωπον πρὸς πρόσωπον, καὶ ἡ τελεία ἐπίγνωσις ἐν τῷ μέλλοντι αἰῶνι τοῖς ἀξίοις ἀποδοθῆναι ἐπήγγελται· νῦν δὲ, κἂν Παῦλός τις ᾖ, κἂν Πέτρος, βλέπει μὲν ἀληθῶς ἃ βλέπει, καὶ οὐ πλανᾶται, οὐδὲ φαντάζεται, δι' ἐσόπτρου δὲ ὅμως βλέπει, καὶ ἐν αἰνίγματι, καὶ τὸ ἐκ μέρους νῦν εὐχαρίστως δεχόμενος, τὸ τέλειον εἰς τὸ μέλλον περιχαρῶς ἀπεκδέχεται. Ὅπερ πιστοῦται μὲν ὁ ἀπόστολος Παῦλος, τῷ τοιούτῳ τινὶ τρόπῳ κατασκευάζων τὸν λόγον, ὅτι ὥσπερ, ὅτε μὲν ἤμην νήπιος, ἄρτι τὰ στοιχεῖα τῆς ἀρχῆς τῶν λογίων τοῦ Θεοῦ ἐκμανθάνων, ὡς νήπιος ἐλάλουν, ὡς νήπιος ἐφρόνουν, ὡς νήπιος ἐλογιζόμην· ὅτε δὲ γέγονα ἀνὴρ, [315] καὶ εἰς μέτρον ἡλικίας τοῦ πληρώματος τοῦ Χριστοῦ ἐπείγομαι φθάσαι, τὰ τοῦ νηπίου κατήργηκα. Καὶ τοσαύτην ἔσχον ἐν τῇ τῶν θείων καταλήψει τὴν προκοπὴν καὶ βελτίωσιν, ὥστε τὴν μὲν ἐν τῇ Ἰουδαϊκῇ λατρείᾳ ἐπίγνωσιν νηπίας φρενὸς ἐοικέναι κινήμασιν, ἀνδρὶ δὲ ἤδη τὰ πάντα τελείῳ προσήκουσαν τὴν διὰ τοῦ Εὐαγγελίου γνῶσιν. Οὕτως ἐν συγκρίσει τῆς ἐν τῷ μέλλοντι αἰῶνι τοῖς ἀξίοις ἀποκαλυφθησομένης γνώσεως, καὶ τὸ δοκοῦν

of knowledge falsely so called"[19] are another. And so in this way, apportioning our words with discretion, we ought everywhere to employ them fittingly for defending or for building up the faith, at one time resisting more contentiously those who diabolically try to undo it and, at another, explaining it more simply and more properly to those who wish to be edified in it, all the while doing nothing else but what was said by the Apostle: "To know how you must answer each one."[20]

Now, before coming to the confession of faith itself, it is also proper to add this in preface: The majesty and glory of God, insofar as it is both uncircumscribable by words and incomprehensible by intellect, is not the sort of thing that can be articulated or understood by a single phrase or notion; rather, through a great many which have been adapted to our use,[21] the God-breathed Scripture scarcely manages to speak but darkly to the pure in heart as in a mirror. For seeing face to face and perfect knowledge are promises for the age to come for those worthy of receiving them; whereas now, even if someone should be a Paul or a Peter, though what he sees he sees truly, and he is not misled or deluded, still he sees only through a mirror and in a riddle, and he awaits in anticipation of great joy the future perfection of what now is gratefully received in part. Of this the Apostle Paul assures us in a discourse along the following lines: "When I was a child just beginning to learn the fundamentals of the words of God, I spoke as a child, I thought as a child, I reasoned as a child. But having become a man, I am hastening to attain to the measure of the stature of the fullness of Christ, and I have put away childish things. And I made such progress and improvement in the apprehension of divine things that the knowledge afforded by the religion of the Jews seems to me like the impressions of a child's mind, while the knowledge had through the Gospel befits a man who is in all respects mature."[22] So too, when compared to the knowledge that

[19]1 Tim 6.20
[20]Col 4.6
[21]That is, to our ability to comprehend.
[22]Cf. 1 Cor 13.11; Eph 4.13

νῦν ἐν τῇ γνώσει τέλειον βραχύ τι καὶ ἀμυδρότερον τοσοῦτον, ὡς πλέον ἀπολιμπάνεσθαι τῆς ἐν τῷ μέλλοντι αἰῶνι τρανότητος, ἢ ὅσον ἀπολιμπάνεται τοῦ πρόσωπον πρὸς πρόσωπον τὸ δι' ἐσόπτρου βλέπειν καὶ ἐν αἰνίγματι. Συνιστῶσι δὲ τοῦτο καὶ οἱ περὶ τὸν μακάριον Πέτρον καὶ Ἰωάννην μαθηταὶ τοῦ Κυρίου, τῇ κατὰ τὸν παρόντα βίον ἀεὶ πρὸς τὸ μεῖζον ἐπιδόσει καὶ προκοπῇ τὸ ὑπερβάλλον τῆς ἐν τῷ μέλλοντι τηρουμένης αἰῶνι γνώσεως οὐκ ἔλαττον καὶ αὐτοὶ πιστούμενοι. Οἵτινες, μετὰ τὸ ἄξιοι φανῆναι τῆς παρὰ τοῦ Κυρίου ἐκλογῆς, τῆς σὺν αὐτῷ διαγωγῆς, τῆς παρ' αὐτοῦ ἀποστολῆς, τῆς τῶν πνευματικῶν χαρισμάτων διανομῆς, μετὰ τὸ ἀκοῦσαι· «Ὑμῖν δέδοται γνῶναι τὰ μυστήρια τῆς βασιλείας τῶν οὐρανῶν,» μετὰ τὴν τοιαύτην γνῶσιν, μετὰ τὴν ἀποκάλυψιν τῶν τοῖς λοιποῖς ἀπορρήτων, ὅμως ὕστερόν ποτε, περὶ αὐτὸ λοιπὸν τοῦ Κυρίου τὸ πάθος, ἀκούουσιν· «Ἔτι πολλὰ ἔχω λέγειν ὑμῖν, ἀλλ' οὐ δύνασθε βαστάζειν ἄρτι.»

Ἐκ τούτων καὶ τῶν τοιούτων μανθάνομεν, ὅτι τοσοῦτον μὲν οἶδεν ἡ θεόπνευστος Γραφὴ τῆς ἐπιγνώσεως τὸ ἀπέραντον, τοσοῦτον δὲ τῆς ἀνθρωπίνης φύσεως τὸ τῶν θείων μυστηρίων ἐν τῷ παρόντι ἀνέφικτον, ἀεὶ μὲν κατὰ προκοπὴν ἑκάστῳ προστιθεμένου [316] τοῦ πλείονος, ἀεὶ δὲ τοῦ πρὸς ἀξίαν ἀπολιμπανομένου ἁπάντων, ἄχρις ἂν ἔλθῃ τὸ τέλειον, ὅτε τὸ ἐκ μέρους καταργηθήσεται· οὐκοῦν οὔτε ἑνὸς ὀνόματος ἀρκοῦντος πάσας ὁμοῦ δηλῶσαι τὰς τοῦ Θεοῦ δόξας, οὔτε ἑκάστου ἐξ ὁλοκλήρου ἀκινδύνως παραλαμβανομένου. Ἄν τε γὰρ εἴπῃ τις, Θεὸς, οὐκ ἐδήλωσε τὸ, Πατὴρ· τῷ δὲ, Πατὴρ, λείπει τὸ, κτίστης. Τούτοις δὲ πάλιν χρεία ἀγαθότητος, σοφίας, δυνάμεως, καὶ τῶν λοιπῶν τῶν φερομένων ἐν τῇ ἁγίᾳ Γραφῇ. Πάλιν δὲ τὸ, Πατὴρ, ὁλόκληρον κατὰ τὴν ἡμετέραν χρῆσιν, ἐὰν ἐκλάβωμεν ἐπὶ Θεοῦ, ἀσεβοῦμεν· πάθος γὰρ καὶ ἀπόρροιαν, καὶ ἄγνοιαν, καὶ ἀσθένειαν, καὶ ὅσα τοιαῦτα ἐπιφημίζει. Ὁμοίως δὲ καὶ τὸ, κτίστης. Ἐφ' ἡμῶν γὰρ χρεία χρόνου, ὕλης, σκευῶν, βοηθείας· ὧν ἁπάντων καθαρεύειν δεῖ τὴν εὐσεβῆ περὶ Θεοῦ δόξαν, ὡς

will be revealed to the worthy in the age to come, even that which now seems perfect in knowledge will seem like something so shallow and vague as to be more greatly surpassed by the clarity in the age to come than seeing "face to face" surpasses "through a mirror and in a riddle." And the disciples of the Lord around the blessed Peter and John also confirm this. In their constant progress and advancement in this life toward greater things, they too confirm no less the surpassing knowledge reserved for the age to come. For, after appearing worthy of the Lord's call, of passing their days with him, of being sent out by him, of the distribution of spiritual charisms, after hearing: "To you it is given to know the mysteries of the kingdom of the heavens,"[23] after such knowledge, after the revelation of things hidden from everyone else, still at the end, when the Lord was going to his passion, they heard: "Still many things have I to tell you, but you are unable to bear them just now."[24]

From these and similar passages we learn that the God-breathed Scripture knows how great is the infinitude of knowledge and how unattainable the mysteries of God by human nature in the present life. Ever is more added to each as he progresses, yet ever does he fall short of being worthy of all things, until perfection comes when what is in part will be cast aside. Neither, therefore, is one name sufficient alone to articulate all the glories of God, nor is each name accepted in its full extent without danger. For, if someone says "God," this does not connote the notion "Father," and by "Father" is left out the notion "Creator." In these, moreover, is wanting Goodness, Wisdom, Power, and the rest of the things conveyed in the holy Scripture. Likewise, if we apply the term "Father" to God in its full extent according to our usage, we are impious. For this connotes passion and emanation and ignorance and weakness and other such things. Similarly the term "Creator"; for with us this implies time, matter, instruments, help—from all of which the pious conception of God must be purged insofar as this is humanly possible.

[23] Mt 13.11
[24] Jn 16.12

δυνατὸν ἀνθρώπῳ. Τοῦ γὰρ πρὸς ἀξίαν, ὡς ἔφην, κἂν εἰ πᾶσαι μὲν διάνοιαι πρὸς τὴν ἔρευναν συναφθεῖεν, πᾶσαι δὲ γλῶσσαι πρὸς τὴν ἐπαγγελίαν συνδράμοιεν, οὐδέποτε ἄν τις ἐφίκοιτο. Ταύτην δὲ ἡμῖν τὴν ἔννοιαν σαφῶς παρίστησι καὶ ὁ σοφώτατος Σολομὼν λέγων· «Εἶπα· Σοφισθήσομαι· καὶ αὕτη ἐμακρύνθη ἀπ' ἐμοῦ μακρὰν, ὑπὲρ ὃ ἦν·» οὐ τῷ φεύγειν, ἀλλὰ τῷ ἐκείνοις μάλιστα φανεροῦσθαι αὐτῆς τὸ ἀκατάληπτον, οἷς Θεοῦ χάριτι περισσοτέρως προσγέγονεν ἡ γνῶσις. Ἡ μὲν οὖν θεόπνευστος Γραφὴ πλείοσιν ὀνόμασιν ἀναγκαίως χρῆται καὶ ῥήμασιν εἰς μερικήν τινα, καὶ ταύτην αἰνιγματώδη, τῆς θείας δόξης παράστασιν.

Ἡμῖν δὲ πάντα μὲν τὰ πανταχοῦ ὑπὸ τῆς θεοπνεύστου Γραφῆς περί τε Πατρὸς καὶ Υἱοῦ καὶ ἁγίου Πνεύματος εἰρημένα τὸ παρὸν ἀναλέγειν οὔτε δύναμις, οὔτε σχολὴ, διὰ τὸ κατεπείγειν ὑμᾶς· ὀλίγα δὲ ἐκ πάντων παραθέμενοι, ἀρκεῖν ἡγούμεθα καὶ ταῦτα τῇ ὑμετέρᾳ συνειδήσει, πρός τε τὴν τοῦ ἡμετέρου ἐκ τῶν Γραφῶν φρονήματος φανέρωσιν, καὶ τὴν ὑμῶν αὐτῶν καὶ τῶν βουλομένων ἐφ' ἡμῖν πληροφορίαν. Ὡς γὰρ τὰ πολλὰ μίαν ἡμῖν τὴν εὐσεβῆ ἔννοιαν ἐξαγγέλλει, οὕτω καὶ ἐκ τῶν ὀλίγων ὁ εὐγνώμων, οἶμαι, τὸ ἐν πᾶσιν εὐσεβὲς ἐπιγινώσκει.

[317] Πιστεύομεν τοίνυν καὶ ὁμολογοῦμεν ἕνα μόνον ἀληθινὸν καὶ ἀγαθὸν Θεόν, καὶ Πατέρα παντοκράτορα, ἐξ οὗ τὰ πάντα· τὸν Θεὸν καὶ Πατέρα τοῦ Κυρίου ἡμῶν καὶ Θεοῦ Ἰησοῦ Χριστοῦ.

Καὶ ἕνα τὸν μονογενῆ αὐτοῦ Υἱὸν Κύριον καὶ Θεὸν ἡμῶν Ἰησοῦν Χριστὸν, μόνον ἀληθινὸν, δι' οὗ τὰ πάντα ἐγένετο, τά

For as I said, even if all minds were united in the inquiry and all tongues gathered together for the profession, never could one hit upon it worthily. The most wise Solomon also sets this idea clearly before us when he says, "I said, 'I will be wise,' and it was removed far from me beyond where it was"[25]—not because it fled, but it manifests its incomprehensibility the more to those who, by the grace of God, have accrued knowledge more abundantly. Therefore the God-breathed Scripture makes use of many names and expressions by necessity for a certain partial demonstration—and this in a riddle—of the divine glory.

Now, we have at present neither the ability nor the leisure to recite everything that is said throughout the God-breathed Scripture concerning Father and Son and Holy Spirit, on account of your urgency; but, having cited a few of the many,[26] we suppose that these will suffice your conscience for showing that our thinking derives from the Scriptures and assuring both you and those making demands of us. For, as many words affirm for us one pious conception, so even from these few words the charitable reader, I think, will recognize the piety of all our conceptions.

Therefore, we believe and confess: One,[27] alone true[28] and good,[29] God and Father almighty,[30] from whom are all things,[31] the God and Father of our Lord[32] and God Jesus Christ.

And One, his only-begotten Son,[33] our Lord and God Jesus Christ, alone true, through whom all things came into being,[34] both

---

[25]Eccl 7.23

[26]The following confession is a pastiche of Scripture. I have tried to identify at least one Scriptural passage on which each element is based, but I did not attempt a comprehensive list of Basil's sources.

[27]Eph 4.6
[28]Cf. Jn 17.3
[29]Cf. Mt 19.17
[30]Cf. 2 Cor 6.18
[31]Cf. 1 Cor 8.6
[32]Eph 1.3
[33]Jn 3.16
[34]Jn 1.3

τε ὁρατὰ καὶ τὰ ἀόρατα· καὶ ἐν ᾧ τὰ πάντα συνέστηκεν· ὃς ἐν ἀρχῇ ἦν πρὸς τὸν Θεὸν, καὶ Θεὸς ἦν· καὶ μετὰ ταῦτα, κατὰ τὴν Γραφὴν, ἐπὶ τῆς γῆς ὤφθη, καὶ τοῖς ἀνθρώποις συνανεστράφη· ὃς ἐν μορφῇ Θεοῦ ὑπάρχων, οὐχ ἁρπαγμὸν ἡγήσατο τὸ εἶναι ἴσα Θεῷ, ἀλλ᾽ ἑαυτὸν ἐκένωσε, καὶ διὰ τῆς ἐκ Παρθένου γεννήσεως μορφὴν δούλου λαβὼν, καὶ σχήματι εὑρεθεὶς ὡς ἄνθρωπος, πάντα τὰ εἰς αὐτὸν καὶ περὶ αὐτοῦ γεγραμμένα ἐπλήρωσε κατὰ τὴν ἐντολὴν τοῦ Πατρὸς, γενόμενος ὑπήκοος μέχρι θανάτου, θανάτου δὲ σταυροῦ· καὶ τῇ τρίτῃ ἡμέρᾳ ἐγερθεὶς ἐκ νεκρῶν, κατὰ τὰς Γραφὰς, ὤφθη τοῖς ἁγίοις αὐτοῦ μαθηταῖς, καὶ τοῖς λοιποῖς, ὡς γέγραπται· ἀνέβη τε εἰς οὐρανοὺς καὶ κάθηται ἐν δεξιᾷ τοῦ Πατρός· ὅθεν ἔρχεται ἐπὶ συντελείᾳ τοῦ αἰῶνος τούτου ἀναστῆσαι πάντας, καὶ ἀποδοῦναι ἑκάστῳ κατὰ τὴν πρᾶξιν αὐτοῦ· ὅτε οἱ μὲν δίκαιοι προσληφθήσονται εἰς ζωὴν αἰώνιον καὶ βασιλείαν οὐρανῶν, οἱ δὲ ἁμαρτωλοὶ κατακριθήσονται εἰς κόλασιν αἰώνιον, ὅπου ὁ σκώληξ αὐτῶν οὐ τελευτᾷ, καὶ τὸ πῦρ οὐ σβέννυται.

Καὶ ἓν μόνον Πνεῦμα ἅγιον, τὸ Παράκλητον, ἐν ᾧ ἐσφραγίσθημεν εἰς ἡμέραν ἀπολυτρώσεως· τὸ Πνεῦμα τῆς ἀληθείας, τὸ Πνεῦμα τῆς υἱοθεσίας, ἐν ᾧ κράζομεν· Ἀββᾶ, ὁ Πατήρ· τὸ διαιροῦν καὶ ἐνεργοῦν τὰ παρὰ τοῦ Θεοῦ χαρίσματα ἑκάστῳ πρὸς τὸ συμφέρον, καθὼς βούλεται· τὸ διδάσκον καὶ ὑπομιμνῆσκον πάντα, ὅσα ἂν ἀκούῃ παρὰ τοῦ Υἱοῦ· τὸ ἀγαθὸν, τὸ ὁδηγοῦν εἰς πᾶσαν τὴν ἀλήθειαν, καὶ στηρίζον πάντας τοὺς πιστεύοντας πρός τε γνῶσιν ἀσφαλῆ, καὶ ὁμολογίαν ἀκριβῆ, καὶ λατρείαν εὐσεβῆ, καὶ

visible and invisible,[35] and in whom all things cohere;[36] who was in the beginning with God and was God[37] and, afterwards, according to the Scripture, appeared on earth and dwelt among humans;[38] who, being in the form of God, did not consider being equal to God a thing to be grasped but emptied himself, and, taking the form of a servant through birth from a virgin[39] and having been found in frame as a human, he fulfilled in himself all the things that had been written about him,[40] according to the command of the Father,[41] becoming obedient unto death—a death on a cross[42]—and, having risen from the dead on the third day according to the Scriptures, he appeared to his holy disciples and the rest,[43] as it is written; who ascended into heaven and sits at the right hand of the Father,[44] from whence he comes at the end of this age[45] to raise all and to render to each according to their work,[46] when the righteous will be taken up into life eternal and the kingdom of the heavens while the sinners will be condemned to eternal punishment,[47] where their worm does not die and the fire is not quenched.[48]

And One only Holy Spirit, the Comforter,[49] in whom we have been sealed unto the day of redemption[50]; the Spirit of truth,[51] the Spirit of adoption, in whom we cry, "Abba, Father";[52] who divides and works the charisms that originate in God for the benefit of each just as he desires;[53] who teaches and brings to remembrance all things,[54] as many as he hears from the Son;[55] who is good;[56] who leads unto all truth[57] and establishes all those who believe with sure knowledge

[35]Cf. Col 1.16
[36]Col 1.17
[37]Cf. Jn 1.1–2
[38]Bar 3.38; Cf. Jn 1.10, 14
[39]Cf. Mt 1.23
[40]Cf. Lk 24.44–47
[41]Cf. Jn 6.38
[42]Phil 2.6–8
[43]Cf. 1 Cor 15.4–8
[44]Cf. Mk 16.19
[45]Cf. Mt 24.3
[46]Cf. Jn 5.27–29

[47]Cf. Mt 13.41–43; 25.46
[48]Cf. Mk 9.48
[49]Jn 14.26
[50]Cf. Eph 4.30
[51]Jn 14.17
[52]Rom 8.15
[53]Cf. 1 Cor 12.4–11
[54]Cf. Jn 14.26
[55]Cf. Jn 16.13–15
[56]Cf. Lk 11.13; Neh 9.20
[57]Cf. Jn 16.13

προσκύνησιν πνευματικὴν καὶ ἀληθῆ Θεοῦ Πατρὸς, [318] καὶ τοῦ μονογενοῦς Υἱοῦ αὐτοῦ τοῦ Κυρίου καὶ Θεοῦ ἡμῶν Ἰησοῦ Χριστοῦ, καὶ ἑαυτοῦ· ἑκάστου ὀνόματος τὴν τοῦ ὀνομαζομένου ἰδιότητα σαφῶς ἡμῖν διευκρινοῦντος, καὶ περὶ ἑκάστου τῶν ὀνομαζομένων πάντως τινῶν ἐξαιρέτων ἰδιωμάτων εὐσεβῶς θεωρουμένων, τοῦ μὲν Πατρὸς ἐν τῷ ἰδιώματι τοῦ Πατρὸς, τοῦ δὲ Υἱοῦ ἐν τῷ ἰδιώματι τοῦ Υἱοῦ, τοῦ δὲ ἁγίου Πνεύματος ἐν τῷ οἰκείῳ ἰδιώματι· μήτε τοῦ ἁγίου Πνεύματος ἀφ᾽ ἑαυτοῦ λαλοῦντος, μήτε τοῦ Υἱοῦ ἀφ᾽ ἑαυτοῦ τι ποιοῦντος· καὶ τοῦ μὲν Πατρὸς πέμποντος τὸν Υἱὸν, τοῦ δὲ Υἱοῦ πέμποντος τὸ ἅγιον Πνεῦμα.

Οὕτως φρονοῦμεν, καὶ οὕτως βαπτίζομεν εἰς Τριάδα ὁμοούσιον, κατὰ τὴν ἐντολὴν αὐτοῦ τοῦ Κυρίου ἡμῶν Ἰησοῦ Χριστοῦ εἰπόντος· «Πορευθέντες μαθητεύσατε πάντα τὰ ἔθνη, βαπτίζοντες αὐτοὺς εἰς τὸ ὄνομα τοῦ Πατρὸς καὶ τοῦ Υἱοῦ καὶ τοῦ ἁγίου Πνεύματος, διδάσκοντες αὐτοὺς τηρεῖν πάντα ὅσα ἐνετειλάμην ὑμῖν.» Ἅπερ τηροῦντες μὲν, τὴν εἰς αὐτὸν ἀγάπην ἐπιδεικνύμεθα, καὶ ἐν αὐτῇ μένειν καταξιούμεθα, καθὼς γέγραπται· μὴ τηροῦντες δὲ, ἐναντίως ἔχοντες ἐλεγχόμεθα. «Ὁ μὴ ἀγαπῶν με,» γάρ φησιν ὁ Κύριος, «τοὺς λόγους μου οὐ τηρεῖ·» καὶ πάλιν· «Ὁ ἔχων τὰς ἐντολάς μου, καὶ τηρῶν αὐτὰς, ἐκεῖνός ἐστιν ὁ ἀγαπῶν με.»

Θαυμάζω δὲ περισσοτέρως, ὅτι, αὐτοῦ τοῦ Κυρίου ἡμῶν Ἰησοῦ Χριστοῦ λέγοντος· «Μὴ χαίρετε, ὅτι τὰ δαιμόνια ὑμῖν ὑποτάσσεται· χαίρετε δὲ, ὅτι τὰ ὀνόματα ὑμῶν γέγραπται ἐν τοῖς οὐρανοῖς·» καὶ πάλιν· «Ἐν τούτῳ γνώσονται πάντες, ὅτι ἐμοὶ μαθηταί ἐστε, ἐὰν ἀγάπην ἔχητε μετ᾽ ἀλλήλων·» ὅθεν ὁ Ἀπόστολος, ἐν πᾶσι τὸ τῆς ἀγάπης ἀναγκαῖον δεικνὺς, διαμαρτύρεται λέγων· «Ἐὰν ταῖς γλώσσαις τῶν ἀνθρώπων λαλῶ καὶ τῶν ἀγγέλων, ἀγάπην δὲ μὴ ἔχω, γέγονα χαλκὸς ἠχῶν, ἢ κύμβαλον ἀλαλάζον· κἂν ἔχω προφητείαν, καὶ εἰδῶ τὰ μυστήρια πάντα, καὶ πᾶσαν τὴν γνῶσιν, καὶ ἐὰν ἔχω πᾶσαν τὴν πίστιν, ὥστε ὄρη μεθιστάνειν, ἀγάπην δὲ μὴ ἔχω,

and an accurate confession and pious religion and spiritual and true worship[58] of God the Father and of his only-begotten Son our Lord and God Jesus Christ and of himself. Each name correctly and clearly distinguishes for us the distinctive characteristic of the one named and all the particular characteristics that follow from these which we piously contemplate—the Father in the characteristics of father, the Son in the characteristics of son, and the Holy Spirit in the characteristics belonging to him. The Holy Spirit does not speak from himself[59] nor does the Son do anything from himself,[60] but the Father sends the Son, and the Son sends the Holy Spirit.[61]

Thus do we think, and thus do we baptize into the Trinity, one in essence, according to the commandment of our same Lord Jesus Christ, who said, "Go and make disciples of all nations, baptizing them in the name of the Father and of the Son and of the Holy Spirit, teaching them to keep everything which I have commanded you."[62] By keeping his commandments we demonstrate our love for him, and we are found worthy of living in him, just as it is written, and by not keeping them we prove ourselves his enemies. For "the one who does not love me," says the Lord, "does not keep my words."[63] And again: "The one who holds my commandments and keeps them—this is the one who loves me."[64]

I marvel greatly that when our Lord Jesus Christ himself says, "Do not rejoice because the demons submit to you, rather rejoice because your names are written in heaven,"[65] and again, "By this everyone will know that you are my disciples: if you have love for one another,"[66] and when the Apostle likewise, showing the necessity of love in all things, testifies: "If I should speak with the tongues of men and of angels, yet I have not love, I am become a sounding brass or a clanging cymbal, and if I should have prophetic utterance and know every mystery and all knowledge, and if I should have all

---

[58]Cf. Jn 4.24
[59]Cf. Jn 16.13
[60]Cf. Jn 5.19
[61]Cf. Jn 20.21–22; 15.26
[62]Mt 28.19–20
[63]Jn 14.24
[64]Jn 14.21
[65]Lk 10.20
[66]Jn 13.35

οὐθέν εἰμι·» καὶ μετ' ὀλίγα· «Εἴτε δὲ προφητεῖαι καταργηθήσονται, εἴτε γλῶσσαι παύσονται, εἴτε γνῶσις καταργηθήσεται,» καὶ τὰ ἑξῆς, οἷς ἐπιφέρει· «Νυνὶ δὲ μένει πίστις, ἐλπὶς, ἀγάπη, τὰ τρία ταῦτα· μείζων δὲ τούτων ἡ ἀγάπη·» τούτων [319] καὶ τῶν τοιούτων οὕτως ὑπό τε τοῦ Κυρίου καὶ τοῦ Ἀποστόλου διωρισμένων, θαυμάζων φημὶ, πῶς περὶ μὲν τὰ καταργούμενα καὶ παυόμενα τοσαύτην ἔχουσιν οἱ ἄνθρωποι σπουδὴν καὶ πτόησιν, περὶ δὲ τὰ μένοντα, καὶ μάλιστα τὴν μείζω πάντων ἀγάπην, τὴν χαρακτηρίζουσαν τὸν Χριστιανὸν, οὐ μόνον αὐτοὶ φροντίδα οὐδεμίαν ποιοῦνται, ἀλλὰ καὶ τοῖς ἐσπουδακόσιν ἐναντιοῦνται, καὶ μαχόμενοι πληροῦσι τὸ εἰρημένον· «Οὔτε αὐτοὶ εἰσέρχονται, καὶ τοὺς εἰσερχομένους κωλύουσιν εἰσελθεῖν.» Διόπερ παρακαλῶ καὶ δέομαι, παυσαμένους τῆς περιέργου ζητήσεως καὶ ἀπρεποῦς λογομαχίας, ἀρκεῖσθαι τοῖς ὑπὸ τῶν ἁγίων καὶ αὐτοῦ τοῦ Κυρίου εἰρημένοις, ἄξια δὲ τῆς ἐπουρανίου κλήσεως φρονεῖν· καὶ ἀξίως τοῦ Εὐαγγελίου τοῦ Χριστοῦ πολιτεύεσθαι, ἐπ' ἐλπίδι τῆς αἰωνίου ζωῆς, καὶ ἐπουρανίου βασιλείας, τῆς ἡτοιμασμένης πᾶσι τοῖς φυλάσσουσι τὰς ἐντολὰς τοῦ Θεοῦ καὶ Πατρὸς, τὰς κατὰ τὸ Εὐαγγέλιον τοῦ μακαρίου Θεοῦ Ἰησοῦ Χριστοῦ τοῦ Κυρίου ἡμῶν, ἐν Πνεύματι ἁγίῳ καὶ ἀληθείᾳ.

Ταῦτα ὑπομνησθέντες παρὰ τῆς ὑμετέρας εὐλαβείας ὑπαγορεῦσαι ἐν τοῖς τελευταίοις, καὶ τὸ ἑαυτῶν φρόνημα φανερὸν ποιῆσαι ὑμῖν τε καὶ δι' ὑμῶν τοῖς ἐν Χριστῷ ἀδελφοῖς, εἰς πληροφορίαν ὑμῶν τε καὶ αὐτῶν ἐν ὀνόματι τοῦ Κυρίου ἡμῶν Ἰησοῦ Χριστοῦ, ἀναγκαῖον καὶ ἡμῖν ἐπιβάλλον ἡγησάμεθα πρὸς τὸ μηδαμῶς περιφέρεσθαί τινων τὸν νοῦν ἐν τῇ διαφορᾷ τῶν ἄλλοτε μὲν ἄλλως παρ' ἡμῶν ἐκτεθέντων, ἀεὶ δὲ πρὸς τὴν ἐπεισαγομένην παρὰ τῶν ἀντιδιατιθεμένων τῇ ἀληθείᾳ ὑπόθεσιν ἀναγκαζομένων ἡμῶν ἐνίστασθαι, μήτε μὴν διασαλεύεσθαί τινας ἐν τῇ ἐναντιότητι τῶν ἐν ἡμῖν τὰ ἀλλότρια ἐπιφημίζειν θελόντων, ἢ καὶ τὰ ἴδια πάθη πολλάκις ἐπὶ τὸ συναρπάσαι τοὺς ἁπλουστέρους τοῦ ἡμετέρου φρονήματος

faith, so to move mountains, yet I have not love, I am nothing,"[67] and a little further: "Where there are prophecies they will be abolished, where there are tongues they will cease, where there is knowledge it will be abolished,"[68] and the rest, to which he adds, "But now remain faith, hope, love—these three—and the greatest of these is love,"[69] when these things and others like them have thus been ordained by the Lord and the Apostle, I marvel I say, that people are so earnest and obsessive about things passing away and ceasing, but to things which abide and especially to the greatest of all things, love, the distinctive mark of the Christian, they not only give absolutely no thought, but they even oppose those who hasten to pursue them! In fighting so, they fulfill what is spoken: "They themselves do not enter, and they hinder from entering those who would."[70] Therefore I exhort and I beg you: put an end to fastidious examination and unseemly polemic, and be satisfied with the words of the saints and of the Lord himself, and have a mind worthy of the heavenly calling. Conduct your affairs in a manner worthy of the Gospel of Christ in the hope of eternal life and of the heavenly kingdom prepared for all who keep the commandments of the God and Father, which are according to the Gospel of the blessed God Jesus Christ our Lord in the Holy Spirit and truth.

In conclusion, when we were called upon by Your Reverence to enumerate these things and to make our mind known to you and, through you, to the brethren in Christ, so that all might be fully assured in the name of our Lord Jesus Christ, we determined that it was necessary and proper for us, so that the mind of certain people should be in no way disturbed by the disparity of our expositions at different times (always compelled, as we were, to resist the novel position of those opposed to the truth), and that no one be confused by the contrariety of those who wish to allege foreign things to us or

[67] 1 Cor 13.1–2
[68] 1 Cor 13.8
[69] 1 Cor 13.13
[70] Lk 11.52

καταψευδομένων· οὓς καὶ ὑμῖν φυλάξασθαι, ὡς ἀλλοτρίους τῆς εὐαγγελικῆς καὶ ἀποστολικῆς πίστεώς τε καὶ ἀγάπης, ἀναγκαῖον· μεμνῆσθαι δὲ τοῦ Ἀποστόλου εἰπόντος· «Ἀλλὰ καὶ ἐὰν ἡμεῖς, ἢ ἄγγελος ἐξ οὐρανοῦ εὐαγγελίζηται ὑμῖν παρ' ὃ εὐηγγελισάμεθα ὑμῖν, ἀνάθεμα ἔστω·» ἵνα τηροῦντες κἀκεῖνο τό, «Προσέχετε ἀπὸ τῶν ψευδοπροφητῶν·» καὶ τό, «Στέλλεσθαι ὑμᾶς ἀπὸ παντὸς [320] ἀδελφοῦ ἀτάκτως περιπατοῦντος, καὶ μὴ κατὰ τὴν παράδοσιν, ἣν παρέλαβον παρ' ἡμῶν,» στοιχῶμεν τῷ κανόνι τῶν ἁγίων, ὡς «Ἐποικοδομηθέντες ἐπὶ τῷ θεμελίῳ τῶν ἀποστόλων καὶ προφητῶν, ὄντος ἀκρογωνιαίου αὐτοῦ τοῦ Κυρίου ἡμῶν Ἰησοῦ Χριστοῦ, ἐν ᾧ πᾶσα οἰκοδομὴ συναρμολογουμένη αὔξει εἰς ναὸν ἅγιον ἐν Κυρίῳ.» Ὁ δὲ Θεὸς τῆς εἰρήνης ἁγιάσαι ὑμᾶς ὁλοτελεῖς, καὶ ὁλόκληρον ὑμῶν τὸ πνεῦμα, καὶ ἡ ψυχή, καὶ τὸ σῶμα ἀμέμπτως ἐν τῇ παρουσίᾳ τοῦ Κυρίου ἡμῶν Ἰησοῦ Χριστοῦ τηρηθείη. «Πιστὸς ὁ Θεὸς ὁ καλῶν ὑμᾶς, ὃς καὶ ποιήσει,» ἐὰν τὰς ἐντολὰς αὐτοῦ τηρήσωμεν, χάριτι τοῦ Χριστοῦ ἐν Πνεύματι ἁγίῳ.

Τὰ περὶ τῆς ὑγιαινούσης πίστεως ἐν τοῖς πρὸ τούτων αὐτάρκως εἰρῆσθαι πρὸς τὸ παρὸν λογιζόμενοι, ἐντεῦθεν τὴν περὶ τῶν ἠθικῶν ἐπαγγελίαν ἐν ὀνόματι τοῦ Κυρίου ἡμῶν Ἰησοῦ Χριστοῦ πληρῶσαι σπουδάσωμεν. Ὅσα τοίνυν εὑρίσκομεν κατὰ τὴν Καινὴν τέως Διαθήκην σποράδην ἀπηγορευμένα ἢ ἐγκεκριμένα, ταῦτα, κατὰ τὸ δυνατὸν ἡμῖν, εἰς ὅρους κεφαλαιώδεις πρὸς τὸ εὔληπτον τοῖς βουλομένοις ἐσπουδάσαμεν συναγαγεῖν· παραθέντες ἑκάστῳ ὅρῳ καὶ τὸν ἀριθμὸν τῶν ἐμπεριειλημμένων αὐτῷ γραφικῶν κεφαλαίων,

even falsely ascribe their own afflictions to our way of thinking, as they often do in order to snatch away the simpler-minded. Against these you must be on your guard, for they are foreign to the Gospel and to apostolic faith and to love; and remember what the Apostle said: "But even if I or an angel from heaven should preach to you a gospel different from what we have preached, let him be anathema,"[71] so that, keeping the commands to "beware false prophets"[72] and to "withdraw yourself from every brother who walks out of step and not according to the tradition which they received from us,"[73] we might be aligned to the canon of the saints, as "having been built upon the foundation of the apostles and prophets, our Lord Jesus Christ himself being the chief cornerstone, in whom every block fitted together increases into a holy temple in the Lord."[74] The God of peace sanctify you entirely, and may your entire spirit and soul and body be kept blameless in the coming of our Lord Jesus Christ. "The God who calls you is faithful, who will also make good"[75] if we keep his commandments by the grace of Christ in the Holy Spirit.

What we have said above concerning the sound faith seems sufficient for the present. We should now hasten to fulfill in the name of our Lord Jesus Christ our promise of the *Ethics*. And so, as many things as we find forbidden or approved scattered throughout the New Testament we have eagerly gathered, as we were able, into concise rules for the easy digestion of the willing. We provided each rule also with the number of the scriptural passages[76] summarized

[71]Gal 1.8
[72]Mt 7.15
[73]2 Thess 3.6
[74]Eph 2.20
[75]1 Thess 5.23
[76]Basil employed a now defunct method of citing the Scriptures, by which books were divided into numbered chapters (κεφάλαια: rendered above as "passages") somewhat shorter than those with which we are familiar. There was no further division comparable to our verses. I have followed Garnier's edition in omitting the archaic chapter numbers and printing only the names of the books of Scripture to introduce each selection and providing complete references according to the now standard chapter and verse numbers following each selection.

εἴτε ἐκ τοῦ Εὐαγγελίου, εἴτε ἐκ τοῦ Ἀποστόλου, ἢ τῶν Πράξεων· ἵνα ὁ ἀναγνοὺς τὸν ὅρον, καὶ ἰδὼν παρακείμενον αὐτῷ τὸν πρῶτον, εἰ τύχοι, ἢ τὸν δεύτερον ἀριθμὸν, εἶτα ἀναλαβὼν αὐτὴν τὴν Γραφὴν, καὶ ἀναζητήσας τὸ κεφάλαιον τοῦ προειρημένου ἀριθμοῦ, οὕτως εὕρῃ τὴν μαρτυρίαν πρὸς ἣν ὁ ὅρος πεποίηται. Ἐβουλόμην μὲν οὖν τὰ πρῶτα καὶ ἐκ τῆς Παλαιᾶς Διαθήκης τὰ πρὸς ἕκαστον τῶν ἐν τῇ Καινῇ συμφώνως εἰρημένα παραθεῖναι τοῖς ὅροις· ἐπειδὴ δὲ κατήπειγεν ἡ χρεία, τῶν ἐν Χριστῷ ἀδελφῶν νῦν μάλιστα σπουδαιότερον [321] ἀπαιτησάντων ἡμᾶς τὰ πάλαι ἐπηγγελμένα, ἐμνημόνευσα τοῦ εἰπόντος· «Δίδου σοφῷ ἀφορμὴν, καὶ σοφώτερος ἔσται.» Ὥστε ἔξεστι τῷ βουλομένῳ ἀφορμὴν αὐτάρκη ἐκ τῶν παρακειμένων εἰληφότι ἀναλαβεῖν τὴν Παλαιὰν Διαθήκην, καὶ γνωρίσαι ἀφ' ἑαυτοῦ τὴν ἐν πάσαις ταῖς θεοπνεύστοις Γραφαῖς συμφωνίαν, ἄλλως τε καὶ μιᾶς φωνῆς ἀρκούσης τοῖς πιστοῖς καὶ πεπληροφορημένοις τὴν ἀλήθειαν τῶν τοῦ Κυρίου ῥημάτων. Διὸ καὶ τὰ ἐν τῇ Καινῇ Διαθήκῃ οὐ πάντα, ὀλίγα δὲ ἐκ πάντων παραθέσθαι αὔταρκες ἐλογισάμην.

in it, whether from the Gospel or the Apostle or the Acts, so that the reader, seeing beside the rule the first number or, where present, the second, might take up the Scripture itself, look up the passage of the given number, and find the testimony with which the rule was fashioned. Now, at first I desired to supply the rules also with those passages from the Old Testament that agree with each of those in the New. However, since the need was pressing, with the brethren in Christ now the more eagerly demanding from us our long-standing promises, I remembered the proverb: "Give means to one wise and he will be wiser."[77] So it is possible for one who is willing to seize from among the things which surround him the sufficient means—to take up the Old Testament and to learn for himself the harmony of all the God-breathed Scriptures. I considered also that a single utterance is sufficient for those who are faithful and fully convinced of the truth of the Lord's words. Therefore I determined it likewise sufficient to furnish not every possible passage in the New Testament, but a few of the many.

[77]Prov 9.9

[322] ΕΙΣΙΝ ΔΕ ΟΙ ΟΡΟΙ ΩΣ ΕΝ ΚΕΦΑΛΑΙΩι ΕΙΠΕΙΝ ΠΕΡΙ ΤΩΝΔΕ[1]

[1]The "table of contents" that follows is titled only "INDEX MORALIUM" by Garnier with no Greek equivalent. I have supplied the Greek heading on which Vat. Gr. 413 and Vat. Gr. 428 agree. Vat. Gr. 425 differs only superficially.

90

The Rules, in Brief,
Concern the Following:

1. On repentance, what the time for repentance is, its characteristics and its fruits.

2. On being pure of every opposing thing and spotless with respect to the zeal of those wishing to be well-pleasing to God.

3. On love for God, and how it is manifest.

4. What honors God and what dishonors him.

5. On love for one another and its characteristics.

6. On the need to speak openly in the confession of God and his Christ.

7. That the confession of the Lord does not avail unto salvation for those transgressing his commandments.

8. On faith in and certainty of the words of the Lord.

9. On knowledge or ignorance of our responsibilities.

10. What results from sin and from the commandment of God.

11. On the judgments of God and the fear of them.

12. On circumvention and contention as opposed to obedience and observance of the will of God.

ιγ΄. Περὶ τῆς ἐν παντὶ καιρῷ ἑτοιμότητος καὶ ἀνυπερθέτου σπουδῆς τῶν πρὸς εὐαρέστησιν Θεοῦ σπουδαζομένων.

ιδ΄. Περὶ τῆς ἑκάστου τῶν κατὰ μέρος κατορθουμένων εὐκαιρίας.

ιε΄. Ὅτι μὴ δεῖ τοῖς ἄλλων κατορθώμασιν ἐπελπίζοντα, τῶν καθ᾽ ἑαυτὸν ἀμελεῖν.

ις΄. Περὶ τῶν οἰομένων ὠφελεῖσθαί τι ἐκ τοῦ συζῆν τοῖς καλοῖς καὶ εὐαρέστοις, καὶ ἑαυτοὺς μὴ κατορθούντων. [323]

ιζ΄. Πῶς δεῖ πρὸς τὸν παρόντα καιρὸν διατίθεσθαι.

ιη΄. Περὶ τρόπου καὶ διαθέσεως τῶν περὶ τὴν ἐντολὴν τοῦ Θεοῦ ἐσπουδακότων.

ιθ΄. Περὶ ἐμποδίζοντος καὶ ἐμποδιζομένου εἰς τὴν ἐντολὴν τοῦ Θεοῦ.

κ΄. Περὶ βαπτίσματος, καὶ τίς ὁ λόγος καὶ ἡ δύναμις τοῦ βαπτίσματος.

κα΄. Περὶ κοινωνίας τοῦ σώματος, καὶ τοῦ αἵματος τοῦ Χριστοῦ, καὶ τίς ὁ ταύτης λόγος.

κβ΄. Πῶς ἀπαλλοτριοῦταί τις Θεοῦ, καὶ διὰ τίνων οἰκειοῦται Θεῷ.

κγ΄. Περὶ τῶν ἡττωμένων καὶ εἰς ἃ μισοῦσιν ἁμαρτήματα.

κδ΄. Περὶ ψεύδους καὶ ἀληθείας.

κε΄. Περὶ ἀργολογίας, καὶ περὶ τῆς τῶν σπουδαίων λόγων οἰκονομίας.

κς΄. Περὶ τοῦ δεῖν κεχρῆσθαι πρῶτον μὲν ταῖς ἀπὸ τῶν Γραφῶν μαρτυρίαις εἰς σύστασιν τῶν παρ᾽ ἡμῶν γινομένων ἢ λεγομένων, ἔπειτα δὲ καὶ τοῖς ἐν τῇ συνηθείᾳ γνωριζομένοις.

13. On constant readiness and consummate zeal for pursuing the good pleasure of God.

14. On the proper time for each particular righteous act.

15. That it is necessary not to neglect one's own duty, hoping in the good works of others.

16. On those supposing that they benefit somehow from living among those who are good and well-pleasing without acting aright themselves.

17. How it is necessary to make arrangements for the time at hand.

18. On the manner and disposition of those zealous for the commandment of God.

19. On hindering and being hindered with respect to the commandment of God.

20. On baptism, and what the reason for and the power of baptism is.

21. On communion with the body and the blood of Christ, and what the reason for this is.

22. How one is estranged from God and by what means one relates to God.

23. On those ensnared even by the sins they hate.

24. On falsehood and truth.

25. On idle speech and on the regulation of hasty words.

26. On the necessity to make use first of the testimonies of the Scriptures for grounding our deeds or words, and then of what is known from experience.

κζ΄. Περὶ τῆς πρὸς Θεὸν καὶ πρὸς τοὺς ἁγίους κατὰ δύναμιν ἐξομοιώσεως.

κη΄. Περὶ τοῦ διακριτικὸν εἶναι περὶ τῶν ἀγαθῶν ἀνδρῶν, καὶ τῶν ἐναντίων.

κθ΄. Περὶ τοῦ, ποίῳ τρόπῳ τὸ ἐπάγγελμα ἑαυτῶν πιστούμεθα.

λ΄. Περὶ τιμῆς ἀναθημάτων Θεοῦ.

λα΄. Περὶ χρήσεως τῶν τοῖς ἁγίοις ἀφωρισμένων.

λβ΄. Περὶ χρεῶν καὶ ἀποδόσεων.

λγ΄. Περὶ σκανδαλιζόντων καὶ σκανδαλιζομένων.

λδ΄. Περὶ τοῦ δεῖν ἕκαστον ἐν τῷ ἰδίῳ μέτρῳ τύπον τῶν καλῶν προκεῖσθαι τοῖς ἄλλοις.

λε΄. Περὶ τῶν τὰ καλὰ φαυλιζόντων.

λς΄. Περὶ τῆς εἰς τοὺς ἁγίους τιμῆς καὶ διαθέσεως.

λζ΄. Περὶ τῶν ὀλίγα κατὰ δύναμιν προθυμουμένων.

λη΄. Ὅπως χρὴ δεξιοῦσθαι. [324]

λθ΄. Περὶ τῆς ἐν τοῖς σκανδάλοις στερρότητος.

μ΄. Περὶ ἑτεροδιδασκαλούντων.

μα΄. Περὶ ἐκκοπῆς τῶν σκανδαλιζόντων, καὶ φειδοῦς τῶν ἀσθενεστέρων.

μβ΄. Περὶ τοῦ τὸν Κύριον ἐπὶ τῷ πληρῶσαι τὸν νόμον ἐληλυθέναι.

μγ΄. Περὶ διαφορᾶς ἐντολῶν τοῦ νόμου καὶ τοῦ εὐαγγελίου.

μδ΄. Ὅτι ἐλαφρὸν τὸ τοῦ Κυρίου φορτίον, βαρεῖα δὲ ἡ ἁμαρτία.

με΄. Περὶ ἰσοτιμίας καὶ ταπεινοφροσύνης.

μς΄. Περὶ σπουδῆς κατορθωμάτων μειζόνων ἢ ἐλαττόνων.

μζ΄. Περὶ πλούτου καὶ πτωχείας, καὶ τῶν τούτοις παρεπομένων.

48. On beneficence for the brethren and work for this purpose.

49. On going to law and avenging oneself or even another.

50. On peace and peacemaking.

51. Of what sort the one who would correct his neighbor ought to be.

52. On grief over sinners and how it is necessary to meet with them, and when to turn away from them and when to receive them.

53. What the judgment is for those who hold grudges against any they believe to have wronged them.

54. On judging and on vacillating.

55. On regard for and acknowledgment of the graces of God, and on giving thanks for them.

56. On prayer, and when and what and how and for what things it is necessary to pray.

57. On being puffed up because of our virtues.

58. On acquiring charisms from God and on their distribution.

59. On human honor and glory.

60. On the diversity of God's charisms and the harmony between those superior in them and those inferior.

61. On the meagerness (by human reckoning) of those who receive the grace of God.

62. On temptations, and when it is necessary to withdraw and when to stand firm, and how to meet the opposition.

63. On cowardice and courage in crises.

64. On joy in sufferings on account of Christ.

ξε'. Ὅπως δεῖ καὶ ἐν αὐτῷ τῷ τέλει προσεύχεσθαι.

ξϛ'. Περὶ τῶν ἐγκαταλιμπανόντων τοὺς ὑπὲρ εὐσεβείας ἀγωνιζομένους, καὶ περὶ τῶν τούτοις συναγωνιζομένων.

ξζ'. Περὶ τῶν ἐπὶ τοῖς ἀποθνήσκουσι λυπουμένων.

ξη'. Περὶ διαφορᾶς τοῦ παρόντος αἰῶνος καὶ τοῦ μέλλοντος.

ξθ'. Περὶ τῶν ὁμοῦ καὶ κατὰ συνάφειαν ἀπαγορευομένων ὑπὸ τῆς Γραφῆς, ἢ ἐγκρινομένων.

ο'. Περὶ τῶν τὸ κήρυγμα τοῦ εὐαγγελίου ἐγχειριζομένων, καὶ πότε, καὶ τίνας, καὶ τί διδάσκειν, καὶ πῶς ἑαυτοὺς προκατορθοῦν τοὺς τοιούτους χρή· καὶ ὅπως ἐν τῷ κηρύγματι παρρησιάζεσθαι, καὶ πῶς ἐπιμελεῖσθαι τῶν πεπιστευμένων, καὶ ποίᾳ διαθέσει, καὶ περὶ ποῖα τῶν σπουδασμάτων προηγουμένως καταγίνεσθαι· καὶ ὅπως καθαρεύειν ἀπὸ τῶν ὡς ἐπὶ τὸ πλεῖστον παρεπομένων ἐλαττωμάτων, καὶ ἐπὶ ποῖον ἄγειν μέτρον τοὺς διδασκομένους, καὶ πῶς ἐνάγειν τοὺς ἀντιδιατιθεμένους, καὶ τίνα τρόπον εἴκειν τοὺς διὰ φόβον παραιτουμένους, καὶ πῶς ἀναχωρεῖν τῶν δι' ἀγνωμοσύνην μὴ καταδεχομένων· καὶ πῶς τινας χειροτονεῖν, ἢ ἀποβάλλειν τοὺς κεχειροτονημένους· καὶ ὅτι χρὴ τῶν προεστώτων ἕκαστον ὑπεύθυνον ἑαυτὸν ἡγεῖσθαι, καὶ τοῖς πεπιστευμένοις αὐτῷ εἰς τὴν περὶ ὧν ποιεῖ καὶ λέγει πληροφορίαν.

οα'. Περὶ τῶν κατὰ συνάφειαν ἐπὶ τοῖς προεστῶσι διατεταγμένων.
[326]

οβ'. Ὅπως δεῖ τοὺς διδασκομένους διακρίνειν τοὺς πνευματικοὺς τῶν διδασκάλων ἀπὸ τῶν μὴ τοιούτων, καὶ ὅπως πρὸς αὐτοὺς διατίθεσθαι, ἢ τὰ παρ' αὐτῶν δέχεσθαι.

65. In what manner it is necessary to pray even at the very end.

66. On the deserters of those struggling on behalf of piety and on those struggling alongside them.

67. On those who grieve for the dead.

68. On the difference between the present age and that to come.

69. On things prohibited together and conjointly by the Scriptures, and things approved.

70. On those entrusted with the preaching of the Gospel, and when and to whom and what they are to teach, and how it is necessary for them to first practice as much; also how to be frank in preaching, and how to care for those entrusted to them, and with what disposition, and with what kinds of pursuits they ought to be principally concerned; and that they should be free, as much as possible, of abiding defects, and to what measure they should lead those they teach and how they are to bring in resistors, and the way to yield to those who, because of fear, beg them off, and how to withdraw from those who, because of ignorance, do not receive them; and how they ought to ordain certain individuals or cast out those already ordained; and that it is necessary for each of those set over [the word][1] to consider himself accountable even to those entrusted to him, who stand surety for what he does and says.

71. On those things laid down conjointly for those set over [the word].

72. The manner in which it is necessary for those taught to discern the spirits of teachers and those who are not, and how to be disposed toward them or to receive what issues forth from them.

---

[1]In the *Ethics* itself Basil always adds this direct object (e.g. 70.37, which is here condensed), though in his other works "ὁ προεστώς" is often used alone to speak of a bishop or the head of an ascetic community.

ογ΄. Περὶ τῶν ἐν γάμῳ.

οδ΄. Περὶ χηρῶν.

οε΄. Περὶ δούλων καὶ δεσποτῶν.

ος΄. Περὶ τέκνων καὶ γονέων.

οζ΄. Περὶ παρθένων.

οη΄. Περὶ στρατευομένων.

οθ΄. Περὶ ἀρχόντων καὶ ὑπηκόων.

π΄. Ποταποὺς εἶναι βούλεται καθόλου ὁ λόγος τοὺς Χριστιανούς, καὶ ποταποὺς τοὺς προεστῶτας.

73. On those who are married.

74. On widows.

75. On slaves and masters.

76. On children and parents.

77. On virgins.

78. On soldiers.

79. On rulers and subjects.

80. Of what sort the Word desires Christians to be in general, and of what sort those set over [the word].

[327] ΑΡΧΗ ΤΩΝ ΗΘΙΚΩΝ.

ΟΡΟΣ Α΄.

[1.1] Ὅτι δεῖ τοὺς πιστεύοντας τῷ Κυρίῳ μετανοῆσαι πρῶτον, κατὰ τὸ κήρυγμα Ἰωάννου, καὶ αὐτοῦ τοῦ Κυρίου ἡμῶν Ἰησοῦ Χριστοῦ· χεῖρον γὰρ τῶν πρὸ τοῦ Εὐαγγελίου κατακριθέντων οἱ νῦν μὴ μετανοοῦντες κατακρίνονται.

Κεφάλαιον α΄.

ΜΑΤΘΑΙΟΣ. Ἀπὸ τότε ἤρξατο ὁ Ἰησοῦς κηρύσσειν, καὶ λέγειν, μετανοεῖτε· ἤγγικε γὰρ ἡ βασιλεία τῶν οὐρανῶν ... Τότε ἤρξατο ὀνειδίζειν τὰς πόλεις, ἐν ᾧς ἐγένοντο αἱ πλεῖσται δυνάμεις αὐτοῦ, ὅτι οὐ μετενόησαν. Οὐαί σοι Χωραζὶν, οὐαί σοι Βηθσαϊδά· ὅτι εἰ ἐν Τύρῳ καὶ Σιδῶνι ἐγένοντο αἱ δυνάμεις αἱ γενόμεναι ἐν ὑμῖν, πάλαι ἂν ἐν σάκκῳ καὶ σποδῷ καθήμεναι μετενόησαν. Πλὴν Τύρῳ καὶ Σιδῶνι ἀνεκτότερον ἔσται ἐν ἡμέρᾳ κρίσεως, ἢ ὑμῖν· καὶ τὰ ἑξῆς.

[1.2] Ὅτι τῆς μετανοίας καὶ τῆς ἀφέσεως τῶν ἁμαρτιῶν ὁ παρών ἐστι καιρός· ἐν δὲ τῷ μέλλοντι αἰῶνι ἡ δικαία κρίσις τῆς ἀνταποδόσεως.

Κεφάλ. β΄.

ΜΑΤΘΑΙΟΣ.[1] Ἵνα δὲ εἰδῆτε, ὅτι ἐξουσίαν ἔχει ὁ Υἱὸς τοῦ ἀνθρώπου ἐπὶ τῆς γῆς ἁμαρτίας ἀφιέναι, [328] λέγει.

ΜΑΤΘΑΙΟΣ. Ἀμὴν λέγω ὑμῖν, ὅσα ἂν δήσητε ἐπὶ τῆς γῆς, ἔσται δεδεμένα ἐν τῷ οὐρανῷ· καὶ ὅσα ἂν λύσητε ἐπὶ τῆς γῆς, ἔσται λελυμένα ἐν τῷ οὐρανῷ. Πάλιν ἀμὴν λέγω ὑμῖν, ὅτι ἐὰν δύο

---

[1]Garnier cites Mark 2:10 here, but Vat. Gr. 413, 425, and 428 all have Matthew, and the text of the line in question is closer to the UBS wording of Matthew 9:6 than it is to that of Mark 2:10.

The Beginning of the Ethics

1.1 That it is necessary for those believing in the Lord first to repent, according to the preaching of John and of our Lord Jesus Christ himself; for those now who do not repent are more severely judged than those condemned prior to the Gospel.

MATTHEW: From that time Jesus began to preach, saying, "Repent, for the kingdom of heaven is at hand" (4.17).

MATTHEW: Then he began to upbraid the cities where most of his mighty works had been done, because they did not repent, "Woe to you, Chorazin! Woe to you, Bethsaida! For if the mighty works done in you had been done in Tyre and Sidon, they would have repented long ago, *sitting* in sackcloth and ashes. *It* shall be more tolerable on the day of judgment for Tyre and Sidon than for you" (11.20–22); *and what follows.*

1.2 That now is the time for repentance and for the forgiveness of sins, but in the coming age is the righteous judgment of retribution.

MATTHEW: "But that you may know that the Son of Man has authority on earth to forgive sins," he said (9.6), "Truly I say to you, whatever you bind on earth shall be bound in heaven, and whatever you loose on earth shall be loosed in heaven. Again, *truly* I say to

ὑμῶν συμφωνήσωσιν ἐπὶ τῆς γῆς περὶ παντὸς πράγματος, οὗ ἐὰν αἰτήσωνται, γενήσεται αὐτοῖς παρὰ τοῦ Πατρός μου τοῦ ἐν οὐρανοῖς.

ΙΩΑΝΝΗΣ. Ὅτι ἔρχεται ὥρα, ἐν ᾗ πάντες οἱ ἐν τοῖς μνημείοις ἀκούσονται τῆς φωνῆς αὐτοῦ, καὶ ἐκπορεύσονται, οἱ τὰ ἀγαθὰ ποιήσαντες, εἰς ἀνάστασιν ζωῆς· οἱ δὲ τὰ φαῦλα πράξαντες, εἰς ἀνάστασιν κρίσεως.

ΠΡΟΣ ΡΩΜ. Ἢ τοῦ πλούτου τῆς χρηστότητος αὐτοῦ, καὶ τῆς ἀνοχῆς, καὶ τῆς μακροθυμίας καταφρονεῖς; ἀγνοῶν, ὅτι τὸ χρηστὸν τοῦ Θεοῦ εἰς μετάνοιάν σε ἄγει. Κατὰ δὲ τὴν σκληρότητά σου, καὶ ἀμετανόητον καρδίαν, θησαυρίζεις ἑαυτῷ ὀργὴν ἐν ἡμέρᾳ ὀργῆς, καὶ ἀποκαλύψεως, καὶ δικαιοκρισίας τοῦ Θεοῦ, ὃς ἀποδώσει ἑκάστῳ κατὰ τὰ ἔργα αὐτοῦ.

ΠΡΑΞΕΙΣ. Τοὺς μὲν οὖν χρόνους τῆς ἀγνοίας ὑπεριδὼν ὁ Θεὸς, τὰ νῦν παραγγέλλει τοῖς ἀνθρώποις πᾶσι πανταχοῦ μετανοεῖν· καθότι ἔστησεν ἡμέραν, ἐν ᾗ μέλλει κρίνειν τὴν οἰκουμένην.

[1.3]   Ὅτι δεῖ τοὺς μετανοοῦντας κλαίειν πικρῶς, καὶ τὰ λοιπὰ, ὅσα ἴδια τῆς μετανοίας, ἐκ καρδίας ἐπιδείκνυσθαι.
Κεφάλ. γ′.
ΜΑΤΘΑΙΟΣ. Καὶ ἐμνήσθη ὁ Πέτρος τοῦ ῥήματος Ἰησοῦ εἰρηκότος αὐτῷ, ὅτι πρὶν ἢ ἀλέκτορα φωνῆσαι, τρὶς ἀπαρνήσῃ με. Καὶ ἐξελθὼν ἔξω, ἔκλαυσε πικρῶς.

ΠΡΟΣ ΚΟΡ. β′. Ἀλλ᾽ ὁ παρακαλῶν τοὺς ταπεινοὺς, παρεκάλεσεν ἡμᾶς ἐν τῇ παρουσίᾳ Τίτου. Οὐ μόνον δὲ ἐν τῇ παρουσίᾳ αὐτοῦ, ἀλλὰ καὶ ἐν τῇ παρακλήσει ᾗ παρεκλήθη ὑφ᾽ ὑμῖν, ἀναγγέλλων ἡμῖν τὴν ὑμῶν ἐπιπόθησιν, τὸν ὑμῶν ὀδυρμὸν, τὸν ὑμῶν ζῆλον ὑπὲρ ἐμοῦ. Καὶ μετ᾽ ὀλίγα, Ἰδοὺ γὰρ αὐτὸ τοῦτο τὸ κατὰ Θεὸν λυπηθῆναι ὑμᾶς, πόσην κατειργάσατο ἐν ὑμῖν σπουδήν· ἀλλὰ ἀπολογίαν, ἀλλὰ ἀγανάκτησιν, ἀλλὰ φόβον, ἀλλὰ ἐπιπόθησιν, ἀλλὰ ζῆλον, ἀλλὰ ἐκδίκησιν· ἐν παντὶ συνεστήσατε ἑαυτοὺς ἁγνοὺς εἶναι ἐν τῷ πράγματι.

ΠΡΑΞΕΙΣ. Πολλοί τε τῶν πεπιστευκότων ἤρχοντο, ἐξομολογούμενοι καὶ ἀναγγέλλοντες τὰς πράξεις αὐτῶν. Ἱκανοί τε τῶν

you, if two of you agree on earth about anything they ask, it will be done for them by my Father in heaven" (18.18–19).

JOHN: For the hour is coming when all who are in the tombs will hear his voice and come forth: those who have done good to the resurrection of life, and those who have done evil to the resurrection of judgment (5.28–29).

ROMANS: Or do you presume upon the riches of his kindness and forbearance and *patience, knowing* that God's kindness is meant to lead you to repentance? But by your hard and impenitent heart you are storing up wrath for yourself on the *day of wrath and revelation and God's righteous judgment*. For he will render to every man according to his works (2.4–6).

ACTS: The times of ignorance God overlooked, but now he *exhorts* all men everywhere to repent, because he has fixed a day on which he will judge the world (17.30–31).

1.3   That it is necessary for those who repent to weep bitterly, and to exhibit from the heart all else that is proper to repentance.

MATTHEW: And Peter remembered *the words of Jesus spoken to him*, "Before the cock crows, you will deny me three times." And he went out and wept bitterly (26.75).

2 CORINTHIANS: But *he* who comforts the downcast comforted us by the coming of Titus, and not only by his coming but also by the comfort with which he was comforted *by* you, as he told us of your longing, your mourning, your zeal for me (7.6–7). *And a little further*: For see what earnestness this godly grief *of yours* has produced in you, what eagerness to clear yourselves, what indignation, what alarm, what longing, what zeal, what punishment! At every point you have proved yourselves guiltless in the matter (7.11).

ACTS: Many also of those who were now believers came, confessing and divulging their practices. And a number of those who

τὰ περίεργα πραξάντων συγκομίσαντες τὰς βίβλους κατέκαιον ἐνώπιον αὐτῶν. [329]

[1.4] Ὅτι τοῖς μετανοοῦσιν οὐκ ἀρκεῖ πρὸς σωτηρίαν ἡ ἀναχώρησις μόνη τῶν ἁμαρτημάτων, χρεία δὲ αὐτοῖς καὶ καρπῶν ἀξίων τῆς μετανοίας.

Κεφάλ. δ'.

ΜΑΤΘΑΙΟΣ. Ἰδὼν δὲ πολλοὺς τῶν Φαρισαίων καὶ Σαδδουκαίων ἐρχομένους ἐπὶ τὸ βάπτισμα αὐτοῦ, εἶπεν αὐτοῖς· γεννήματα ἐχιδνῶν, τίς ὑπέδειξεν ὑμῖν φυγεῖν ἀπὸ τῆς μελλούσης ὀργῆς; Ποιήσατε οὖν καρποὺς ἀξίους τῆς μετανοίας, καὶ μὴ δόξητε λέγειν ἐν ἑαυτοῖς, πατέρα ἔχομεν τὸν Ἀβραάμ. Λέγω γὰρ ὑμῖν, ὅτι δύναται ὁ Θεὸς ἐκ τῶν λίθων τούτων ἐγεῖραι τέκνα τῷ Ἀβραάμ. Ἤδη δὲ καὶ ἡ ἀξίνη πρὸς τὴν ῥίζαν τῶν δένδρων κεῖται. Πᾶν οὖν δένδρον, μὴ ποιοῦν καρπὸν καλὸν, ἐκκόπτεται, καὶ εἰς πῦρ βάλλεται.

[1.5] Ὅτι μετὰ τὴν ἐντεῦθεν ἀπαλλαγὴν οὐκ ἔστι καιρὸς κατορθωμάτων, τοῦ Θεοῦ τὸν παρόντα καιρὸν ἐπιμετρήσαντος ἐν μακροθυμίᾳ εἰς ἐργασίαν τῶν πρὸς τὴν αὐτοῦ εὐαρέστησιν.

Κεφάλ. ε'.

ΜΑΤΘΑΙΟΣ. Τότε ὁμοιωθήσεται ἡ βασιλεία τῶν οὐρανῶν δέκα παρθένοις, αἵτινες, λαβοῦσαι τὰς λαμπάδας αὐτῶν, ἐξῆλθον εἰς ἀπάντησιν τοῦ νυμφίου. Πέντε δὲ ἦσαν ἐξ αὐτῶν φρόνιμοι, καὶ πέντε μωραί· αἵτινες μωραὶ, λαβοῦσαι τὰς λαμπάδας αὐτῶν, οὐκ ἔλαβον μεθ' ἑαυτῶν ἔλαιον· αἱ δὲ φρόνιμοι ἔλαβον ἔλαιον ἐν τοῖς ἀγγείοις αὐτῶν μετὰ τῶν λαμπάδων αὐτῶν. Χρονίζοντος δὲ τοῦ νυμφίου, ἐνύσταξαν πᾶσαι καὶ ἐκάθευδον. Μέσης δὲ νυκτὸς κραυγὴ γέγονεν· ἰδοὺ ὁ νυμφίος ἔρχεται, ἐξέρχεσθε εἰς ἀπάντησιν αὐτοῦ. Τότε ἠγέρθησαν πᾶσαι αἱ παρθένοι ἐκεῖναι, καὶ ἐκόσμησαν τὰς λαμπάδας αὐτῶν· αἱ δὲ μωραὶ ταῖς φρονίμοις εἶπον· δότε ἡμῖν ἐκ τοῦ ἐλαίου ὑμῶν, ὅτι αἱ λαμπάδες ἡμῶν σβέννυνται. Ἀπεκρίθησαν² δὲ αἱ φρόνιμοι, λέγουσαι· μή ποτε οὐκ ἀρκέση ἡμῖν καὶ ὑμῖν· πορεύεσθε δὲ μᾶλλον πρὸς τοὺς πωλοῦντας, καὶ ἀγοράσατε ἑαυταῖς. Ἀπερχομένων

---

²Corrected from Ἀπερκίθησαν.

practiced magic arts *gathered* their books together and burned them in *their presence* (19.18–19).

1.4 That for those who repent, retreat from sins alone is not sufficient for salvation, but it is necessary also for them to bear fruits worthy of repentance.

MATTHEW: But when he saw many of the Pharisees and Sadducees coming for baptism, he said to them, "You brood of vipers! Who warned you to flee from the wrath to come? Bear *fruits worthy of* repentance, and do not presume to say to yourselves, 'We have Abraham as our father'; for I tell you, God is able from these stones to raise up children to Abraham. *But* even now the axe is laid to the root of the trees; every tree therefore that does not bear good fruit is cut down and thrown into the fire" (3.7–10).

1.5 That after the release from this life is not a time for good works, inasmuch as God has patiently measured out the present time for doing what pleases Him.

MATTHEW: Then the kingdom of heaven shall be compared to ten maidens who took their lamps and went to meet the bridegroom. *Five of them were wise, and five were foolish.* Whichever were foolish, *when they* took their lamps, took no oil with them; but the wise took *their* flasks of oil with their lamps. As the bridegroom was delayed, they all slumbered and slept. But at midnight there was a cry, "Behold, the bridegroom *is coming*! Come out to meet him." Then all those maidens rose and trimmed their lamps. And the foolish said to the wise, "Give us some of your oil, for our lamps are going out." But the wise replied, "Perhaps there will not be enough for us and for you; *but* go rather to the dealers and buy for yourselves." And while they went to buy, the bridegroom came, and those who were ready went in with him to the marriage feast; and the door was shut. Afterward

δὲ αὐτῶν ἀγοράσαι, ἦλθεν ὁ νυμφίος, καὶ αἱ ἕτοιμοι εἰσῆλθον μετ᾿ αὐτοῦ εἰς τοὺς γάμους, καὶ ἐκλείσθη ἡ θύρα. Ὕστερον δὲ ἔρχονται καὶ αἱ λοιπαὶ παρθένοι, λέγουσαι· Κύριε, Κύριε, ἄνοιξον ἡμῖν. Ὁ δὲ ἀποκριθεὶς, εἶπεν· ἀμὴν [330] λέγω ὑμῖν, οὐκ οἶδα ὑμᾶς.

ΛΟΥΚΑΣ. Ἀγωνίσασθε εἰσελθεῖν διὰ τῆς στενῆς πύλης, ὅτι πολλοὶ, λέγω ὑμῖν, ζητήσουσιν εἰσελθεῖν, καὶ οὐκ ἰσχύσουσιν. Ἀφ᾿ οὗ ἂν ἐγερθῇ ὁ οἰκοδεσπότης, καὶ ἀποκλείσῃ τὴν θύραν, καὶ ἄρξησθε ἔξω ἑστάναι, καὶ κρούειν τὴν θύραν, λέγοντες, Κύριε, Κύριε, ἄνοιξον ἡμῖν· καὶ ἀποκριθεὶς ἐρεῖ ὑμῖν, οὐκ οἶδα ὑμᾶς πόθεν ἐστέ.

ΠΡΟΣ ΚΟΡ. β´. Ἰδοὺ νῦν καιρὸς εὐπρόσδεκτος, ἰδοὺ νῦν ἡμέρα σωτηρίας· μηδεμίαν ἐν μηδενὶ διδόντες προσκοπὴν,[3] ἵνα μὴ μωμηθῇ ἡ διακονία, ἀλλ᾿ ἐν παντὶ συνιστῶντες ἑαυτοὺς, ὡς Θεοῦ διάκονοι. ΠΡΟΣ ΓΑΛ. Ἄρα οὖν ὡς καιρὸν ἔχομεν, ἐργαζώμεθα τὸ ἀγαθὸν πρὸς πάντας.

ΟΡΟΣ Β´.

[2.1]   Ὅτι ἀδύνατον δουλεῦσαι Θεῷ τὸν καὶ τοῖς ἀλλοτρίοις τῆς θεοσεβείας ἐπιμιγνύμενον πράγμασιν.

Κεφάλαιον α´.

ΜΑΤΘΑΙΟΣ. Οὐδεὶς δύναται δυσὶ κυρίοις δουλεύειν· ἢ γὰρ τὸν ἕνα μισήσει, καὶ τὸν ἕτερον ἀγαπήσει· ἢ ἑνὸς ἀνθέξεται, καὶ τοῦ ἑτέρου καταφρονήσει. Οὐ δύνασθε Θεῷ δουλεύειν καὶ μαμωνᾷ. ΠΡΟΣ ΚΟΡ. β´. Μὴ γίνεσθε ἑτεροζυγοῦντες ἀπίστοις. Τίς γὰρ μετοχὴ δικαιοσύνῃ καὶ ἀνομίᾳ; ἢ τίς κοινωνία φωτὶ πρὸς σκότος; τίς δὲ συμφώνησις Χριστῷ πρὸς Βελίαλ; ἢ τίς μερὶς πιστῷ μετὰ ἀπίστου; τίς δὲ συγκατάθεσις ναῷ Θεοῦ μετὰ εἰδώλων;

[2.2]   Ὅτι τὸν ὑπακούσαντα τῷ εὐαγγελίῳ δεῖ πρῶτον καθαρισθῆναι ἀπὸ παντὸς μολυσμοῦ σαρκὸς καὶ πνεύματος, ἵνα οὕτως εὐπρόσδεκτος τῷ Θεῷ γένηται ἐν τοῖς τῆς ἁγιωσύνης κατορθώμασιν.

Κεφάλ. β´.

ΜΑΤΘΑΙΟΣ. Οὐαὶ ὑμῖν, γραμματεῖς καὶ Φαρισαῖοι ὑποκριταὶ, ὅτι καθαρίζετε τὸ ἔξωθεν τοῦ ποτηρίου καὶ τῆς παροψίδος, ἔσωθεν δὲ

---

[3] Corrected from προκοπήν.

the other maidens came also, saying, "Lord, lord, open to us." But he replied, "Truly, I say to you, I do not know you" (25.1–12).

LUKE: Strive to enter by the narrow *gate*; for many, I tell you, will seek to enter and will not be able. When once the householder has risen up and shut the door, you will begin to stand outside and to knock at the door, saying, "Lord, *lord*, open to us." He will answer you, "I do not know where you come from" (13.24–25).

2 CORINTHIANS: Behold, now is the acceptable time; behold, now is the day of salvation. We put no obstacle in anyone's way, so that no fault may be found with our ministry, but as servants of God we commend ourselves in every way (6.2–4).

GALATIANS: So then, as we have opportunity, let us do good to all (6.10).

2.1   That the one who associates with those opposed to godly piety is powerless to serve God.

MATTHEW: No one can serve two masters; for either he will hate the one and love the other, or he will be devoted to the one and despise the other. You cannot serve God and mammon (6.24).

2 CORINTHIANS: Do not be mismated with unbelievers. For what partnership have righteousness and iniquity? Or what fellowship has light with darkness? What accord has Christ with Belial? Or what has a believer in common with an unbeliever? What agreement has the temple of God with idols (6.14–16)?

2.2   That for the one who has hearkened to the Gospel it is necessary first to be cleansed from all defilement of flesh and spirit, so that he might thus become acceptable to God in the good works of holiness.

MATTHEW: Woe to you, scribes and Pharisees, hypocrites! For you cleanse the outside of the cup and of the plate, but inside they

γέμουσιν ἐξ ἁρπαγῆς καὶ ἀκρασίας. Φαρισαῖε τυφλέ, καθάρισον πρῶτον τὸ ἐντὸς τοῦ ποτηρίου καὶ τῆς παροψίδος, ἵνα γένηται καὶ τὸ ἐκτὸς αὐτῶν καθαρόν. ΠΡΟΣ ΚΟΡ. β'. Ταύτας οὖν ἔχοντες τὰς ἐπαγγελίας, [331] ἀγαπητοί, καθαρίσωμεν ἑαυτοὺς ἀπὸ παντὸς μολυσμοῦ σαρκὸς καὶ πνεύματος, ἐπιτελοῦντες ἁγιωσύνην ἐν φόβῳ Θεοῦ.

[2.3] Ὅτι ἀδύνατον μαθητὴν τοῦ Κυρίου γενέσθαι τὸν προσπαθῶς ἔχοντα πρός τι τῶν παρόντων, ἢ ἀνεχόμενόν τινος τῶν καὶ ἐπ᾽ ὀλίγον ἀφελκόντων ἐντολῆς Θεοῦ.
Κεφάλ. γ'.
ΜΑΤΘΑΙΟΣ. Ὁ φιλῶν πατέρα ἢ μητέρα ὑπὲρ ἐμὲ, οὐκ ἔστι μου ἄξιος. Καὶ ὁ φιλῶν υἱὸν ἢ θυγατέρα ὑπὲρ ἐμὲ, οὐκ ἔστι μου ἄξιος. Καὶ ὃς οὐ λαμβάνει τὸν σταυρὸν αὐτοῦ, καὶ ἀκολουθεῖ ὀπίσω μου, οὐκ ἔστι μου ἄξιος.
ΜΑΤΘΑΙΟΣ. Εἴ τις θέλει ὀπίσω μου ἐλθεῖν, ἀπαρνησάσθω ἑαυτὸν, καὶ ἀράτω τὸν σταυρὸν αὐτοῦ, καὶ ἀκολουθείτω μοι. Ὃς γὰρ ἂν θέλῃ τὴν ψυχὴν αὐτοῦ σῶσαι, ἀπολέσει αὐτήν.
ΟΡΟΣ Γ'.
[3.1] Ὅτι πρώτη καὶ μεγάλη ἐντολὴ ἐν τῷ νόμῳ ὑπὸ τοῦ Κυρίου ἐμαρτυρήθη, ἀγαπᾶν τὸν Θεὸν ἐξ ὅλης τῆς καρδίας· καὶ δευτέρα, ἀγαπᾶν τὸν πλησίον ὡς ἑαυτόν.
Κεφάλ. α'.
ΜΑΤΘΑΙΟΣ. Ὁ δὲ Ἰησοῦς ἔφη αὐτῷ· «ἀγαπήσεις Κύριον τὸν Θεόν σου ἐξ ὅλης τῆς καρδίας σου, καὶ ἐξ ὅλης τῆς ψυχῆς σου, καὶ ἐξ ὅλης τῆς ἰσχύος σου, καὶ ἐξ ὅλης τῆς διανοίας σου.» Αὕτη ἐστὶν ἡ πρώτη καὶ μεγάλη ἐντολή· δευτέρα δὲ ὁμοία, αὕτη· «ἀγαπήσεις τὸν πλησίον σου ὡς ἑαυτόν.»

[3.2] Ὅτι ἔλεγχος τοῦ μὴ ἀγαπᾶν τὸν Θεὸν, καὶ τὸν Χριστὸν αὐτοῦ, τὸ, τὰς ἐντολὰς αὐτοῦ μὴ τηρεῖν· [332] ἀπόδειξις δὲ τοῦ ἀγαπᾶν, ἡ τήρησις τῶν ἐντολῶν τοῦ Χριστοῦ, ἐν ὑπομονῇ τῶν αὐτοῦ παθημάτων μέχρι θανάτου.

are full of extortion and rapacity. You blind Pharisee! First cleanse the inside of the cup and of the plate, that the outside also may be clean (23.25–26).

2 CORINTHIANS: Since we have these promises, beloved, let us cleanse ourselves from every defilement of body and spirit, and make holiness perfect in the fear of God (7.1).

2.3   That the one who is disposed toward any of the things of this life or who tolerates anything that separates him from God's commandment in the slightest is incapable of becoming a disciple of the Lord.

MATTHEW: He who loves father or mother more than me is not worthy of me; and he who loves son or daughter more than me is not worthy of me; and he who does not take his cross and follow me is not worthy of me (10.37–38).

MATTHEW: If anyone would come after me, let him deny himself and take up his cross and follow me. For whoever would save his life will lose it (16.24–25).

3.1   That the first and great commandment in the law was witnessed to by the Lord: to love God from the whole heart; and the second: to love one's neighbor as oneself.

MATTHEW: And *Jesus* said to him, " 'You shall love the Lord your God *from* all your heart, and *from* all your soul, *and from all your strength*, and *from* all your mind.'[1] This is the *first and great* commandment. And a second is like it, 'You shall love your neighbor as yourself' "[2] (22.37–39).

3.2   That the proof of not loving God and his Christ is not keeping his commandments, whereas the evidence of love is keeping the commandments of Christ in endurance of his sufferings even unto death.

[1]Deut 6.5.
[2]Lev 19.18.

Κεφάλ. β΄.

ΙΩΑΝΝΗΣ. Ὁ ἔχων τὰς ἐντολάς μου, καὶ τηρῶν αὐτὰς, ἐκεῖνός ἐστιν ὁ ἀγαπῶν με. Ὁ μὴ ἀγαπῶν με, τοὺς λόγους μου οὐ τηρεῖ. Ἐὰν τὰς ἐντολάς μου τηρήσητε, μενεῖτε ἐν τῇ ἀγάπῃ μου, καθὼς ἐγὼ τὰς ἐντολὰς τοῦ Πατρός μου τετήρηκα, καὶ μένω αὐτοῦ ἐν τῇ ἀγάπῃ.

ΠΡΟΣ ΡΩΜ. Τίς ἡμᾶς χωρίσει ἀπὸ τῆς ἀγάπης τοῦ Χριστοῦ; θλίψις; ἢ στενοχωρία; ἢ διωγμός; ἢ λιμός; ἢ γυμνότης; ἢ κίνδυνος; ἢ μάχαιρα; Καθὼς γέγραπται, «ὅτι ἕνεκα σοῦ θανατούμεθα πᾶσαν ἡμέραν· ἐλογίσθημεν ὡς πρόβατα σφαγῆς.» Ἀλλ᾽ ἐν τούτοις πᾶσιν ὑπερνικῶμεν διὰ τοῦ ἀγαπήσαντος ἡμᾶς, καὶ τὰ ἑξῆς.

ΟΡΟΣ Δ΄.

[4.1] Ὅτι τιμᾷ καὶ δοξάζει τὸν Θεὸν ὁ τὸ θέλημα αὐτοῦ ἐργαζόμενος· ἀτιμάζει δὲ, ὁ παραβαίνων αὐτοῦ τὸν νόμον.

Κεφάλ. α΄.

ΙΩΑΝΝΗΣ. Ἐγώ σε ἐδόξασα ἐπὶ τῆς γῆς· τὸ ἔργον ἐτελείωσα, ὃ δέδωκάς μοι ἵνα ποιήσω.

ΜΑΤΘΑΙΟΣ. Οὕτως λαμψάτω τὸ φῶς ὑμῶν ἔμπροσθεν τῶν ἀνθρώπων, ὅπως ἴδωσιν ὑμῶν τὰ καλὰ ἔργα, καὶ δοξάσωσι τὸν Πατέρα ὑμῶν τὸν ἐν τοῖς οὐρανοῖς.

ΠΡΟΣ ΦΙΛΙΠ. Ἵνα ἦτε εἰλικρινεῖς καὶ ἀπρόσκοποι εἰς ἡμέραν Χριστοῦ, πεπληρωμένοι καρπῶν δικαιοσύνης τῶν διὰ Ἰησοῦ Χριστοῦ, εἰς δόξαν καὶ ἔπαινον Θεοῦ.

ΠΡΟΣ ΡΩΜ. Ὃς ἐν νόμῳ καυχᾶσαι, διὰ τῆς παραβάσεως τοῦ νόμου τὸν Θεὸν ἀτιμάζεις. [333]

ΟΡΟΣ Ε΄.

[5.1] Ὅτι δεῖ, παντὸς μίσους πρὸς πάντας καθαρεύοντα, καὶ τοὺς ἐχθροὺς ἀγαπᾷν· ὑπὲρ δὲ τῶν φίλων τὴν ψυχὴν τιθέναι, ὅταν χρεία καλῇ, τοιαύτην ἔχοντα ἀγάπην, οἵαν ἔσχε πρὸς ἡμᾶς ὁ Θεὸς, καὶ ὁ Χριστὸς αὐτοῦ.

Κεφάλ. α΄.

ΜΑΤΘΑΙΟΣ. Ἠκούσατε, ὅτι ἐρρέθη τοῖς ἀρχαίοις· Ἀγαπήσεις τὸν πλησίον σου, καὶ μισήσεις τὸν ἐχθρόν σου. Ἐγὼ δὲ λέγω ὑμῖν·

JOHN: He who has my commandments and keeps them, he it is who loves me (14.21). He who does not love me does not keep my words (14.24). If you keep my commandments, you will abide in my love, just as I have kept my Father's commandments and abide in his love (15.10).

ROMANS: Who shall separate us from the love of Christ? Shall tribulation, or distress, or persecution, or famine, or nakedness, or peril, or sword? As it is written, "For thy sake we are being killed all the day long; we are regarded as sheep to be slaughtered."[3] No, in all these things we are more than conquerors through him who loved us (8.35–37); *and what follows.*

4.1   That the one who does his will honors and glorifies God and the one who transgresses his law dishonors him.

JOHN: I glorified thee on earth; *I accomplished* the work which thou gavest me to do (17.4).

MATTHEW: Let your light so shine before men, that they may see your good works and give glory to your Father who is in heaven (5.16).

PHILIPPIANS: So that you may be pure and blameless for the day of Christ, filled with the fruits of righteousness which come through Jesus Christ, to the glory and praise of God (1.10–11).

ROMANS: You who boast in the law, do you dishonor God by breaking the law (2.23)?

5.1   That it is necessary, being cleansed of all hatred toward everyone, to love even one's enemies and to lay down one's life on behalf of one's friends whenever the need calls, having such love as God and his Christ had for us.

MATTHEW: You have heard that it was said *in times of old*, "You shall love your neighbor and hate your enemy." But I say to you,

---

[3]Ps 44.22 (LXX 43.23)

Ἀγαπᾶτε τοὺς ἐχθροὺς ὑμῶν. Καὶ μετ᾽ ὀλίγα· Ἔσεσθε οὖν ὑμεῖς
τέλειοι, ὥσπερ ὁ Πατὴρ ὑμῶν ὁ οὐράνιος τέλειός ἐστιν.

ΙΩΑΝΝΗΣ. Οὕτως γὰρ ἠγάπησεν ὁ Θεὸς τὸν κόσμον, ὥστε τὸν
Υἱὸν αὐτοῦ τὸν μονογενῆ ἔδωκεν. Αὕτη ἐστὶν ἡ ἐντολὴ ἡ ἐμὴ, ἵνα
ἀγαπᾶτε ἀλλήλους, καθὼς ἐγὼ ἠγάπησα ὑμᾶς. Μείζονα ταύτης
ἀγάπην οὐδεὶς ἔχει, ἵνα τις τὴν ψυχὴν αὐτοῦ θῇ ὑπὲρ τῶν φίλων
αὐτοῦ.

ΛΟΥΚΑΣ. Καὶ ἔσεσθε υἱοὶ τοῦ Ὑψίστου, ὅτι αὐτὸς χρηστός ἐστιν
ἐπὶ τοὺς ἀχαρίστους καὶ πονηρούς. Γίνεσθε οὖν οἰκτίρμονες, καθὼς
καὶ ὁ Πατὴρ ὑμῶν οἰκτίρμων ἐστί.

ΠΡΟΣ ΡΩΜ. Συνίστησι δὲ τὴν ἑαυτοῦ ἀγάπην ὁ Θεὸς εἰς ἡμᾶς, ὅτι,
ἔτι ἁμαρτωλῶν ἡμῶν ὄντων, Χριστὸς ὑπὲρ ἡμῶν ἀπέθανεν.

ΠΡΟΣ ΕΦΕΣ. Γίνεσθε οὖν μιμηταὶ τοῦ Θεοῦ ὡς τέκνα ἀγαπητὰ,
καὶ περιπατεῖτε ἐν ἀγάπῃ, καθὼς καὶ ὁ Χριστὸς ἠγάπησεν ἡμᾶς, καὶ
παρέδωκεν ἑαυτὸν ὑπὲρ ἡμῶν προσφορὰν καὶ θυσίαν τῷ Θεῷ.

[5.2]   Ὅτι ἀπόδειξις τῶν τοῦ Χριστοῦ μαθητῶν ἡ ἐν αὐτῷ πρὸς
ἀλλήλους ἀγάπη.
                                    Κεφάλ. β΄.
ΙΩΑΝΝΗΣ. Ἐν τούτῳ γνώσονται πάντες, ὅτι ἐμοὶ μαθηταί ἐστε,
ἐὰν ἀγάπην ἔχητε ἐν ἀλλήλοις.

[5.3]   Ὅτι ἔλεγχος τοῦ μὴ ἔχειν τὴν Χριστοῦ ἀγάπην πρὸς τὸν
πλησίον τὸ ποιῆσαί τι τῶν βλαπτόντων ἢ λυπούντων αὐτὸν εἰς
ἐκκοπὴν τῆς πίστεως, κἂν συγκεχωρημένον ὑπὸ τῆς Γραφῆς τῷ ἰδίῳ
λόγῳ τὸ γινόμενον ᾖ. [334]
                                    Κεφάλ. γ΄.
ΠΡΟΣ ΡΩΜ. Εἰ γὰρ διὰ βρῶμα ὁ ἀδελφός σου λυπεῖται, οὐκέτι
κατὰ ἀγάπην περιπατεῖς. Μὴ τῷ βρώματί σου ἐκεῖνον ἀπόλλυε, ὑπὲρ
οὗ ὁ Χριστὸς ἀπέθανεν.

[5.4]   Ὅτι δεῖ τὸν Χριστιανὸν καὶ τὸν λυπούμενον κατ᾽ αὐτοῦ παντὶ
τρόπῳ τό γε ἐπ᾽ αὐτῷ θεραπεύειν.

"Love your enemies" (5.43–44). *And a little further*: You therefore must be perfect, *even* as your heavenly Father is perfect (5.48).

JOHN: For God so loved the world that he gave his only Son (3.16).

JOHN: This is my commandment: that you love one another as I have loved you. Greater love has no man than this: that a man lay down his life for his friends (15.12–13).

LUKE: And you will be sons of the Most High; for he is kind to the ungrateful and the evil. *Therefore* be merciful, even as your Father is merciful (6.35–36).

ROMANS: But God shows his love for us in that while we were yet sinners Christ died for us (5.8).

EPHESIANS: Therefore be imitators of God, as beloved children. And walk in love as Christ loved us and gave himself up for us, *an offering* and sacrifice to God (5.1–2).

5.2 That a mark of Christ's disciples is their love in Him for each other.

JOHN: By this all men will know that you are my disciples: if you have love for one another (13.35).

5.3 That the proof of not having the love of Christ for one's neighbor is doing anything that harms or grieves his faith, even if the act itself is allowed by the letter of the Scriptures.

ROMANS: If your brother is being injured by what you eat, you are no longer walking in love. Do not let what you eat cause the ruin of one for whom Christ died (14.15).

5.4 That it is necessary for the Christian to care by all means even for the one who hates him.

Κεφάλ. δ΄.

ΜΑΤΘΑΙΟΣ. Ἐὰν οὖν προσφέρῃς τὸ δῶρόν σου ἐπὶ τὸ θυσια-
στήριον, κἀκεῖ μνησθῇς, ὅτι ὁ ἀδελφός σου ἔχει τι κατὰ σοῦ, ἄφες
ἐκεῖ τὸ δῶρόν σου ἔμπροσθεν τοῦ θυσιαστηρίου, καὶ ὕπαγε πρῶτον,
διαλλάγηθι τῷ ἀδελφῷ σου, καὶ τότε ἐλθὼν πρόσφερε τὸ δῶρόν
σου.

ΠΡΟΣ ΚΟΡ. α΄. Λοιδορούμενοι εὐλογοῦμεν, διωκόμενοι ἀνεχό-
μεθα, βλασφημούμενοι παρακαλοῦμεν.

[5.5]   Ὅτι τὴν κατὰ Χριστὸν ἀγάπην ὁ ἔχων ἔστιν ὅτε καὶ λυπεῖ
πρὸς τὸ συμφέρον τὸν ἀγαπώμενον.
Κεφάλ. ε΄.

ΙΩΑΝΝΗΣ. Νῦν δὲ ὑπάγω πρὸς τὸν πέμψαντά με, καὶ οὐδεὶς ἐξ
ὑμῶν ἐρωτᾷ με, ποῦ ὑπάγεις; ἀλλ᾽ ὅτι ταῦτα λελάληκα ὑμῖν, ἡ λύπη
πεπλήρωκεν ὑμῶν τὴν καρδίαν. Ἀλλ᾽ ἐγὼ τὴν ἀλήθειαν λέγω ὑμῖν·
συμφέρει ὑμῖν, ἵνα ἐγὼ ἀπέλθω. Ἐὰν γὰρ μὴ ἀπέλθω, ὁ Παράκλητος
οὐκ ἐλεύσεται πρὸς ὑμᾶς.

ΠΡΟΣ ΚΟΡ. β΄. Ὥστε με μᾶλλον χαρῆναι, ὅτι, εἰ καὶ ἐλύπησα ὑμᾶς
ἐν τῇ ἐπιστολῇ, οὐ μεταμέλομαι, εἰ καὶ μετεμελόμην. Βλέπω γὰρ, ὅτι
ἡ ἐπιστολὴ ἐκείνη, εἰ καὶ πρὸς ὥραν, ἐλύπησεν ὑμᾶς. Νῦν χαίρω, οὐχ
ὅτι ἐλυπήθητε, ἀλλ᾽ ὅτι ἐλυπήθητε εἰς μετάνοιαν. Ἐλυπήθητε γὰρ
κατὰ Θεόν, ἵνα ἐν μηδενὶ ζημιωθῆτε ἐξ ἡμῶν. [335]

ΟΡΟΣ ς΄.
[6.1]   Ὅτι δεῖ ἀφόβως καὶ ἀνεπαισχύντως παρρησιάζεσθαι ἐν τῇ
ὁμολογίᾳ τοῦ Κυρίου ἡμῶν Ἰησοῦ Χριστοῦ καὶ τῶν λόγων αὐτοῦ.
Κεφάλ. α΄.

ΜΑΤΘΑΙΟΣ. Ὃ λέγω ὑμῖν ἐν τῇ σκοτίᾳ, εἴπατε ἐν τῷ φωτί· καὶ ὃ
εἰς τὸ οὖς ἠκούσατε, κηρύξατε ἐπὶ τῶν δωμάτων. Καὶ μὴ φοβεῖσθε
ἀπὸ τῶν ἀποκτεινόντων τὸ σῶμα, τὴν δὲ ψυχὴν μὴ δυναμένων
ἀποκτεῖναι· φοβήθητε δὲ μᾶλλον τὸν δυνάμενον καὶ ψυχὴν καὶ
σῶμα ἀπολέσαι ἐν γεέννῃ. Πᾶς οὖν, ὅστις ὁμολογήσει ἐν ἐμοὶ
ἔμπροσθεν τῶν ἀνθρώπων, ὁμολογήσω κἀγὼ ἐν αὐτῷ ἔμπροσθεν
τοῦ Πατρός μου τοῦ ἐν οὐρανοῖς.

MATTHEW: So if you are offering your gift at the altar, and there remember that your brother has something against you, leave your gift there before the altar and go; first be reconciled to your brother, and then come and offer your gift (5.23–24).

1 CORINTHIANS: When reviled, we bless; when persecuted, we endure; when slandered, we try to conciliate (4.12–13).

5.5 That the one who loves as Christ does will even grieve for their benefit those whom he loves.

JOHN: But now I am going to him who sent me; yet none of you asks me, "Where are you going?" But because I have said these things to you, sorrow has filled your hearts. Nevertheless I tell you the truth: it is to your advantage that I go away, for if I do not go away, the Counselor will not come to you (16.5–7).

2 CORINTHIANS: So that I rejoiced still more, for even if I made you sorry with my letter, I do not regret it (though I did regret it), for I see that that letter grieved you, though only for a while. As it is, I rejoice, not because you were grieved, but because you were grieved into repenting; for you felt a godly grief, so that you suffered no loss through us (7.7–9).

6.1 That it is necessary to speak openly, without fear or shame, in the confession of our Lord Jesus Christ and of his words.

MATTHEW: What I tell you in the dark, utter in the light; and what you *have heard* whispered, proclaim upon the housetops. And do not fear those who kill the body but cannot kill the soul; rather fear him who can destroy both soul and body in hell (10.27–28). So everyone who acknowledges me before men, I also will acknowledge before my Father who is in heaven (10.32).

ΛΟΥΚΑΣ. Ὃς γὰρ ἂν ἐπαισχυνθῇ με καὶ τοὺς ἐμοὺς λόγους, τοῦτον ὁ Υἱὸς τοῦ ἀνθρώπου ἐπαισχυνθήσεται, ὅταν ἔλθῃ ἐν τῇ δόξῃ αὐτοῦ, καὶ τοῦ Πατρὸς, καὶ τῶν ἁγίων ἀγγέλων.

ΠΡΟΣ ΤΙΜ. β΄. Μὴ οὖν ἐπαισχυνθῇς τὸ μαρτύριον τοῦ Κυρίου ἡμῶν, μηδὲ ἐμὲ τὸν δέσμιον αὐτοῦ, ἀλλὰ συγκακοπάθησον τῷ εὐαγγελίῳ, ὡς καλὸς στρατιώτης Ἰησοῦ Χριστοῦ.

ΟΡΟΣ Ζ΄.

[7.1]   Ὅτι, κἂν δοκῇ τις ὁμολογεῖν τὸν Κύριον, καὶ ἀκούῃ τῶν λόγων αὐτοῦ, ἀπειθῇ δὲ ταῖς ἐντολαῖς αὐτοῦ, κατακέκριται, κἂν ἐν χαρίσμασι πνευματικοῖς διά τινα οἰκονομίαν γενέσθαι συγχωρηθῇ.

Κεφάλ. α΄.

ΜΑΤΘΑΙΟΣ. Οὐ πᾶς ὁ λέγων μοι, Κύριε, Κύριε, εἰσελεύσεται εἰς τὴν βασιλείαν τῶν οὐρανῶν, ἀλλ᾽ ὁ ποιῶν τὸ θέλημα τοῦ Πατρός μου τοῦ ἐν οὐρανοῖς. Πολλοὶ ἐροῦσί μοι ἐν ἐκείνῃ τῇ ἡμέραι, Κύριε, Κύριε, οὐ τῷ σῷ ὀνόματι προεφητεύσαμεν; καὶ τῷ σῷ ὀνόματι δαιμόνια ἐξεβάλομεν; καὶ τῷ σῷ ὀνόματι δυνάμεις πολλὰς ἐποιήσαμεν; Καὶ τότε [336] ὁμολογήσω αὐτοῖς, ὅτι οὐδέποτε ἔγνων ὑμᾶς. Ἀποχωρεῖτε ἀπ᾽ ἐμοῦ οἱ ἐργαζόμενοι τὴν ἀνομίαν, καὶ τὰ ἑξῆς.

ΛΟΥΚΑΣ. Τί δέ με καλεῖτε, Κύριε, Κύριε, καὶ οὐ ποιεῖτε ἃ λέγω; καὶ τὰ ἑξῆς.

ΠΡΟΣ ΤΙΤ. Θεὸν ὁμολογοῦσιν εἰδέναι, τοῖς δὲ ἔργοις ἀρνοῦνται· βδελυκτοὶ ὄντες, καὶ ἀπειθεῖς, καὶ πρὸς πᾶν ἔργον ἀγαθὸν ἀδόκιμοι.

ΟΡΟΣ Η΄.

[8.1]   Ὅτι οὐ δεῖ διακρίνεσθαι καὶ διστάζειν ἐπὶ τοῖς ὑπὸ τοῦ Κυρίου λεγομένοις, ἀλλὰ πεπληροφορῆσθαι πᾶν ῥῆμα Θεοῦ ἀληθὲς εἶναι καὶ δυνατόν, κἂν ἡ φύσις μάχηται. Ἐνταῦθα γὰρ καὶ ὁ ἀγὼν τῆς πίστεως.

Κεφάλ. α΄.

ΜΑΤΘΑΙΟΣ. Τετάρτῃ δὲ φυλακῇ τῆς νυκτὸς ἔρχεται ὁ Ἰησοῦς πρὸς αὐτοὺς περιπατῶν ἐπὶ τῆς θαλάσσης· καὶ ἰδόντες αὐτὸν οἱ μαθηταὶ ἐπὶ τὴν θάλασσαν περιπατοῦντα, ἐταράχθησαν, λέγοντες· φάντασμά ἐστι, καὶ ἀπὸ τοῦ φόβου ἔκραξαν. Εὐθέως δὲ ἐλάλησεν αὐτοῖς ὁ Ἰησοῦς λέγων· θαρσεῖτε. Ἐγώ εἰμι, μὴ φοβεῖσθε. Ἀποκριθεὶς

LUKE: For whoever is ashamed of me and of my words, of him will the Son of man be ashamed when he comes in his glory and the glory of the Father and of the holy angels (9.26).

2 TIMOTHY: Do not be ashamed then of testifying to our Lord, nor of me his prisoner, but share in suffering for the gospel (1.8) as a good soldier of Jesus Christ (2.3).

7.1 That even if someone may seem to confess the Lord and hear his words, but he disobeys his commandments, he is condemned, even if he is allowed to receive spiritual gifts through some dispensation.

MATTHEW: Not everyone who says to me, "Lord, Lord," shall enter the kingdom of heaven, but he who does the will of my Father who is in heaven. On that day many will say to me, "Lord, Lord, did we not prophesy in your name, and cast out demons in your name, and do many mighty works in your name?" And then will I declare to them, "I never knew you; depart from me, you evildoers" (7.21–23), *and what follows.*

LUKE: Why do you call me "Lord, Lord," and not do what I tell you? (6.46), *and what follows.*

TITUS: They profess to know God, but they deny him by their deeds; they are detestable, disobedient, unfit for any good deed (1.16).

8.1 That it is necessary not to waver over or doubt the things said by the Lord, but to be fully assured that every word of God is true and authoritative, even if nature might contradict, for this is precisely the struggle of faith.

MATTHEW: And in the fourth watch of the night *Jesus* came to them, walking on the sea. *And* when the disciples saw him walking on the sea, they were terrified, saying, "It is a ghost!" And they cried out for fear. But immediately *Jesus* spoke to them, saying, "Take heart; it is I. Have no fear." And Peter answered him, "Lord, if it is

δὲ αὐτῷ ὁ Πέτρος εἶπε· Κύριε, εἰ σὺ εἶ, κέλευσόν με πρὸς σὲ ἐλθεῖν ἐπὶ τὰ ὕδατα. Ὁ δὲ εἶπεν, ἐλθέ. Καὶ καταβὰς ἀπὸ τοῦ πλοίου ὁ Πέτρος, περιεπάτησεν ἐπὶ τὰ ὕδατα, ἐλθεῖν πρὸς τὸν Ἰησοῦν. Βλέπων δὲ τὸν ἄνεμον ἰσχυρὸν, ἐφοβήθη· καὶ ἀρξάμενος καταποντίζεσθαι, ἔκραξε λέγων· Κύριε, σῶσόν με. Εὐθέως δὲ ὁ Ἰησοῦς ἐκτείνας τὴν χεῖρα, ἐπελάβετο αὐτοῦ, καὶ λέγει αὐτῷ, ὀλιγόπιστε, εἰς τί ἐδίστασας; ΙΩΑΝΝΗΣ. Ἐμάχοντο οὖν πρὸς ἀλλήλους οἱ Ἰουδαῖοι, λέγοντες· πῶς δύναται οὗτος ἡμῖν τὴν σάρκα δοῦναι φαγεῖν; Εἶπεν οὖν αὐτοῖς· ἀμὴν ἀμὴν λέγω ὑμῖν, ἐὰν μὴ φάγητε τὴν σάρκα τοῦ Υἱοῦ τοῦ ἀνθρώπου, καὶ πίητε αὐτοῦ τὸ αἷμα, οὐκ ἔχετε ζωὴν ἐν ἑαυτοῖς. ΛΟΥΚΑΣ. Εἶπε δὲ αὐτῷ ὁ ἄγγελος· μὴ φοβοῦ, Ζαχαρία, διότι εἰσηκούσθη ἡ δέησίς σου· καὶ ἡ γυνή σου Ἐλισάβετ γεννήσει υἱόν σοι. Καὶ μετ᾽ ὀλίγα· Καὶ εἶπε Ζαχαρίας πρὸς τὸν ἄγγελον· κατὰ τί γνώσομαι τοῦτο; Ἐγὼ γάρ εἰμι πρεσβύτης, καὶ ἡ γυνή μου προβεβηκυῖα ἐν ταῖς ἡμέραις αὐτῆς. [337] Καὶ ἀποκριθεὶς ὁ ἄγγελος εἶπεν αὐτῷ· ἐγώ εἰμι Γαβριὴλ, ὁ παρεστηκὼς ἐνώπιον τοῦ Θεοῦ, καὶ ἀπεστάλην λαλῆσαι πρὸς σὲ, καὶ εὐαγγελίσασθαί σοι ταῦτα. Καὶ ἰδοὺ ἔσῃ σιωπῶν, καὶ μὴ δυνάμενος λαλῆσαι ἄχρι ἧς ἡμέρας γένηται ταῦτα, ἀνθ᾽ ὧν οὐκ ἐπίστευσας τοῖς λόγοις μου, οἵτινες πληρωθήσονται εἰς τὸν καιρὸν αὐτῶν. ΠΡΟΣ ΡΩΜ. Καὶ μὴ ἀσθενήσας τῇ πίστει, οὐ κατενόησε τὸ ἑαυτοῦ σῶμα ἤδη νενεκρωμένον, ἑκατονταέτης που ὑπάρχων, καὶ τὴν νέκρωσιν τῆς μήτρας Σάρρας. Εἰς δὲ τὴν ἐπαγγελίαν τοῦ Θεοῦ οὐ διεκρίθη τῇ ἀπιστίᾳ, ἀλλ᾽ ἐνεδυναμώθη τῇ πίστει· δοὺς δόξαν τῷ Θεῷ, καὶ πληροφορηθεὶς, ὅτι ὃ ἐπήγγελται, δυνατός ἐστι καὶ ποιῆσαι. Διὸ καὶ «ἐλογίσθη αὐτῷ εἰς δικαιοσύνην.»

[8.2]   Ὅτι ὁ ἐπὶ τοῖς ἐλάττοσι μὴ πιστεύων τῷ Κυρίῳ δῆλός ἐστι πολὺ πρότερον ἐπὶ τοῖς μείζοσιν ἀπιστῶν.

Κεφάλ. β'.

ΙΩΑΝΝΗΣ. Εἰ τὰ ἐπίγεια εἶπον ὑμῖν, καὶ οὐ πιστεύετε, πῶς, ἐὰν εἴπω ὑμῖν τὰ ἐπουράνια, πιστεύσετε;

you, bid me come to you on the water." He said, "Come." So Peter got out of the boat and walked on the water *to go* to Jesus; but when he saw the *mighty* wind he was afraid, and, beginning to sink, he cried out, "Lord, save me." Jesus immediately reached out his hand and caught him, saying to him, "O you of little faith, why did you doubt?" (14.25–31).

JOHN: The Jews then disputed among themselves saying, "How can this man give us his flesh to eat?" So *he* said to them, "Truly, truly, I say to you, unless you eat the flesh of the Son of man and drink his blood, you have no life in you" (6.52–53).

LUKE: But the angel said to him, "Do not be afraid, Zechariah, for your prayer is heard, and your wife Elizabeth will bear you a son" (1.13). *And a little further:* And Zechariah said to the angel, "How shall I know this? For I am an old man, and my wife is advanced in years." And the angel answered him, "I am Gabriel, who stand in the presence of God, and I was sent to speak to you and to bring you this good news. And behold, you will be silent and unable to speak until the day that these things come to pass, because you did not believe my words, which will be fulfilled in their time" (1.18–20).

ROMANS: *Not weakening in faith, he did not consider* his own body, which was as good as dead because he was about a hundred years old, or when he considered the barrenness of Sarah's womb. No distrust made him waver concerning the promise of God, but he grew strong in his faith as he gave glory to God, fully convinced that God was able to do what he had promised. That is why "*it* was reckoned to him as righteousness"[4] (4.19–22).

8.2 That the one who does not trust the Lord in the lesser things is manifestly much more faithless in the greater things.

JOHN: If I have told you earthly things and you do not believe, how can you believe if I tell you heavenly things (3.12)?

---

[4] Gen 15.6

ΛΟΥΚΑΣ. Ὁ πιστὸς ἐν ἐλαχίστῳ καὶ ἐν πολλῷ πιστός ἐστι· καὶ ὁ ἐν ἐλαχίστῳ ἄδικος, καὶ ἐν πολλῷ ἄδικός ἐστιν.

[8.3] Ὅτι οὐ χρὴ λογισμοῖς ἰδίοις στηρίζεσθαι ἐπὶ ἀθετήσει τῶν ὑπὸ τοῦ Κυρίου λεγομένων· ἀξιοπιστότερα δὲ εἰδέναι τῆς ἰδίας πληροφορίας τὰ τοῦ Κυρίου ῥήματα.

Κεφάλ. γ'.

ΜΑΤΘΑΙΟΣ. Τότε λέγει αὐτοῖς ὁ Ἰησοῦς· πάντες ὑμεῖς σκανδαλισθήσεσθε ἐν ἐμοὶ ἐν τῇ νυκτὶ ταύτῃ. Ἀποκριθεὶς δὲ ὁ Πέτρος, εἶπεν αὐτῷ· καὶ εἰ πάντες σκανδαλισθήσονται ἐν σοὶ, ἐγὼ δὲ οὐδέποτε σκανδαλισθήσομαι. Ἔφη αὐτῷ ὁ Ἰησοῦς· ἀμὴν λέγω σοι, ἐν ταύτῃ τῇ νυκτὶ, πρὶν ἀλέκτορα φωνῆσαι, τρὶς ἀπαρνήσῃ με.

ΜΑΤΘΑΙΟΣ. Ὀψίας δὲ γενομένης, ἀνέκειτο μετὰ τῶν δώδεκα μαθητῶν· καὶ ἐσθιόντων αὐτῶν, λέγει αὐτοῖς· λέγω ὑμῖν, ὅτι εἷς ἐξ ὑμῶν παραδώσει με. Καὶ λυπούμενοι σφόδρα, ἤρξαντο λέγειν αὐτῷ ἕκαστος αὐτῶν· μή τι ἐγώ εἰμι, Κύριε; [338]

ΠΡΑΞΕΙΣ. Καὶ ἐγένετο φωνὴ πρὸς αὐτόν· ἀναστὰς, Πέτρε, θῦσον, καὶ φάγε. Ὁ δὲ Πέτρος εἶπε· Μηδαμῶς, Κύριε, ὅτι οὐδέποτε ἔφαγον πᾶν κοινὸν ἢ ἀκάθαρτον. Καὶ φωνὴ πάλιν ἐκ δευτέρου πρὸς αὐτόν· ἃ ὁ Θεὸς ἐκαθάρισε, σὺ μὴ κοίνου.

ΠΡΟΣ ΚΟΡ. β'. Λογισμοὺς καθαιροῦντες, καὶ πᾶν ὕψωμα ἐπαιρόμενον κατὰ τῆς γνώσεως τοῦ Θεοῦ, καὶ αἰχμαλωτίζοντες πᾶν νόημα εἰς τὴν ὑπακοὴν τοῦ Χριστοῦ.

ΟΡΟΣ Θ'.

[9.1] Ὅτι οὐ δεῖ ἀμελεῖν τῆς τῶν ἐπιβαλλόντων γνώσεως· μετὰ προσοχῆς δὲ τῶν τοῦ Κυρίου λόγων ἀκούοντα συνιέναι, καὶ ποιεῖν τὸ θέλημα αὐτοῦ.

Κεφάλ. α'

ΜΑΤΘΑΙΟΣ. Ἀποκριθεὶς δὲ ὁ Πέτρος εἶπεν αὐτῷ· φράσον ἡμῖν τὴν παραβολὴν ταύτην. Ὁ δὲ Ἰησοῦς εἶπεν· Ἀκμὴν καὶ ὑμεῖς ἀσύνετοί ἐστε; Οὔπω νοεῖτε, ὅτι πᾶν τὸ εἰσπορευόμενον εἰς τὸ στόμα εἰς τὴν κοιλίαν χωρεῖ, καὶ εἰς ἀφεδρῶνα ἐκβάλλεται; τὰ δὲ ἐκπορευόμενα ἐκ τοῦ στόματος, ἐκ τῆς καρδίας ἐξέρχεται, καὶ κοινοῖ τὸν ἄνθρωπον;

LUKE: He who is faithful in a very little is faithful also in much; and he who is *unrighteous* in a very little is *unrighteous* also in much (16.10).

8.3 That it is necessary not to be fixed on one's own reasonings to the rejection of what is said by the Lord, but to understand that the words of the Lord are worthier of belief than one's own convictions.

MATTHEW: Then Jesus said to them, "You will all fall away because of me this night" (26.31). Peter declared to him, "Though they all fall away because of you, I will never fall away." Jesus said to him, "Truly, I say to you *that* this very night, before the cock crows, you will deny me three times" (26.33–34).

MATTHEW: When it was evening, he sat at table with the twelve disciples; and as they were eating, he said *to them*, "*I say* to you, one of you will betray me." And they were very sorrowful, and *each of them began to say to him*, "Is it I, Lord?" (26.20–22).

ACTS: And there came a voice to him, "Rise, Peter; kill and eat." But Peter said, "No, Lord; for I have never eaten anything that is common or unclean." And the voice came to him again a second time, "What God has cleansed, you must not call common" (10.13–15).

2 CORINTHIANS: We destroy arguments and every proud obstacle to the knowledge of God, and take every thought captive to obey Christ (10.5).

9.1 That it is necessary not to be neglectful of knowing one's responsibilities but, listening attentively to the words of the Lord, also to do his will.

MATTHEW: But Peter said to him, "Explain the parable to us." And *Jesus* said, "Are you also still without understanding? Do you not *yet* see that whatever goes into the mouth passes into the stomach, and so passes on? But what comes out of the mouth proceeds from the heart, and *defiles* a man?" (15.15–18).

ΜΑΤΘΑΙΟΣ. Παντὸς ἀκούοντος τὸν λόγον τῆς βασιλείας, καὶ μὴ συνιέντος, ἔρχεται ὁ πονηρὸς, καὶ ἁρπάζει τὸ ἐσπαρμένον ἐν τῇ καρδίᾳ αὐτοῦ. Οὗτός ἐστιν ὁ παρὰ τὴν ὁδὸν σπαρείς. Καὶ μετ᾽ ὀλίγον· Ὁ δὲ ἐπὶ τὴν γῆν τὴν καλὴν σπαρεὶς, οὗτός ἐστιν ὁ τὸν λόγον ἀκούων καὶ συνιὼν, ὃς δὴ καρποφορεῖ, καὶ ποιεῖ ὁ μὲν ἑκατὸν, ὁ δὲ ἑξήκοντα, ὁ δὲ τριάκοντα.

ΜΑΡΚΟΣ. Καὶ προσκαλεσάμενος πάντα τὸν ὄχλον, εἶπεν αὐτοῖς· Ἀκούετέ μου, καὶ συνίετε.

ΠΡΟΣ ΕΦΕΣ. Βλέπετε οὖν πῶς ἀκριβῶς περιπατεῖτε· μὴ ὡς ἄσοφοι, ἀλλ᾽ ὡς σοφοί· ἐξαγοραζόμενοι τὸν καιρὸν, ὅτι αἱ ἡμέραι πονηραί εἰσι. Διὰ τοῦτο μὴ γίνεσθε ἄφρονες, ἀλλὰ συνιέντες τί τὸ θέλημα τοῦ Θεοῦ. [339]

[9.2]   Ὅτι περὶ τῶν μὴ ἐπιβαλλόντων οὐ δεῖ πολυπραγμονεῖν.
Κεφάλ. β′.

ΙΩΑΝΝΗΣ. Καὶ μετὰ τὸ ψωμίον, τότε εἰσῆλθεν εἰς ἐκεῖνον ὁ Σατανᾶς. Λέγει αὐτῷ ὁ Ἰησοῦς· ὃ ποιεῖς, ποίησον τάχιον. Τοῦτο δὲ οὐδεὶς ἔγνω τῶν ἀνακειμένων, πρὸς τί εἶπεν αὐτῷ.

ΠΡΑΞΕΙΣ. Οἱ μὲν οὖν συνελθόντες ἐπηρώτων αὐτὸν λέγοντες· Κύριε, εἰ ἐν τῷ χρόνῳ τούτῳ ἀποκαθιστάνεις τὴν βασιλείαν τῷ Ἰσραήλ; Εἶπε δὲ πρὸς αὐτούς· οὐχ ὑμῶν ἐστι γνῶναι χρόνους ἢ καιροὺς, οὓς ὁ Πατὴρ ἔθετο ἐν τῇ ἰδίᾳ ἐξουσίᾳ.

[9.3]   Ὅτι ἴδιον τῶν ἐχόντων σπουδὴν τῆς πρὸς Θεὸν εὐαρεστή-σεως, τὸ, καὶ ἐπερωτᾶν περὶ ὧν δεῖ.
Κεφάλ. γ′.

ΜΑΤΘΑΙΟΣ. Καὶ προσῆλθον αὐτῷ οἱ μαθηταὶ αὐτοῦ λέγοντες· φράσον ἡμῖν τὴν παραβολὴν τῶν ζιζανίων τοῦ ἀγροῦ.

ΜΑΤΘΑΙΟΣ. Καὶ ἰδοὺ, εἷς προσελθὼν, εἶπεν αὐτῷ· διδάσκαλε ἀγαθὲ, τί ἀγαθὸν ποιήσω, ἵνα ἔχω ζωὴν αἰώνιον;

ΛΟΥΚΑΣ. Ἔλεγεν οὖν τοῖς ἐκπορευομένοις ὄχλοις βαπτισθῆναι ὑπ᾽ αὐτοῦ· γεννήματα ἐχιδνῶν, τίς ὑπέδειξεν ὑμῖν φυγεῖν ἀπὸ τῆς

MATTHEW: When anyone hears the word of the kingdom and does not understand it, the evil one comes and snatches away what is sown in his heart; this is what was sown along the path (13.19). *And a little further:* As for what was sown on good soil, this is he who hears the word and understands it; he indeed bears fruit, and yields, in one case a hundredfold, in another sixty, and in another thirty (13.23).

MARK: And he called *all* the people to *him* and said to them, "*Hear me and understand*" (7.14).

EPHESIANS: Look carefully then how you walk, not as unwise men but as wise, making the most of the time, because the days are evil. Therefore do not be foolish, but understand what the will of the Lord is (5.15–17).

9.2 That it is necessary not to meddle in what is not one's responsibility.

JOHN: Then after the morsel, Satan entered into him. Jesus said to him, "What you are going to do, do quickly." Now no one at the table knew why he said this to him (13.27–28).

ACTS: So when they had come together, they asked him, "Lord, will you at this time restore the kingdom to Israel?" He said to them, "It is not for you to know times or seasons which the Father has fixed by his own authority" (1.6–7).

9.3 That it is fitting for those who are zealous for the good pleasure of God even to ask what they should do.

MATTHEW: And his disciples came to him, saying, "Explain to us the parable of the weeds of the field" (13.36).

MATTHEW: And behold, one came up to him, saying, "*Good* teacher, what good deed must I do, to have eternal life?" (19.16).

LUKE: He said therefore to the multitudes that came out to be baptized by him, "You brood of vipers! Who warned you to flee from the wrath to come?" (3.7). *And a little further:* And the multitudes

μελλούσης ὀργῆς; Καὶ μετ᾽ ὀλίγα· Καὶ ἐπηρώτων αὐτὸν οἱ ὄχλοι λέγοντες, τί ποιήσομεν; Ὁμοίως τελῶναι, ὁμοίως στρατευόμενοι. ΠΡΑΞΕΙΣ. Ἀκούσαντες δὲ κατενύγησαν τὴν καρδίαν, εἶπόν τε πρὸς τὸν Πέτρον, καὶ τοὺς λοιποὺς ἀποστόλους· τί ποιήσομεν, ἄνδρες ἀδελφοί;

[9.4] Ὅτι δεῖ ἐπερωτωμένῳ φροντίζειν ἀξιολόγως ἀποκρίνεσθαι.
Κεφάλ. δ΄.
ΛΟΥΚΑΣ. Καὶ ἰδοὺ, νομικός τις ἀνέστη ἐκπειράζων αὐτὸν, καὶ λέγων· διδάσκαλε, τί ποιήσας, ζωὴν αἰώνιον κληρονομήσω; Εἶπε δὲ πρὸς αὐτόν· ἐν τῷ νόμῳ τί γέγραπται; πῶς ἀναγινώσκεις; Ὁ [340] δὲ ἀποκριθεὶς εἶπεν· «ἀγαπήσεις Κύριον τὸν Θεόν σου ἐξ ὅλης τῆς καρδίας σου, καὶ ἐξ ὅλης τῆς ψυχῆς σου, καὶ ἐξ ὅλης τῆς διανοίας σου, καὶ τὸν πλησίον σου ὡς ἑαυτόν.» Εἶπε δὲ πρὸς αὐτόν· ὀρθῶς ἀπεκρίθης. Τοῦτο ποίει, καὶ ζήσῃ.
ΠΡΟΣ ΚΟΛΟΣΣ. Ὁ λόγος ὑμῶν πάντοτε ἐν χάριτι, ἅλατι ἠρτυμένος, εἰδέναι πῶς δεῖ ὑμᾶς ἑνὶ ἑκάστῳ ἀποκρίνεσθαι.

[9.5] Ὅτι χεῖρον μὲν τὸ κρῖμα τῶν συνιέντων, καὶ μὴ ποιούντων· οὔτε δὲ τὸ κατὰ ἄγνοιαν ἁμαρτάνειν ἀκίνδυνον.
Κεφάλ. ε΄.
ΛΟΥΚΑΣ. Ἐκεῖνος δὲ ὁ δοῦλος, ὁ γνοὺς τὸ θέλημα τοῦ κυρίου αὐτοῦ, καὶ μὴ ἑτοιμάσας, μηδὲ ποιήσας πρὸς τὸ θέλημα αὐτοῦ, δαρήσεται πολλάς. Ὁ δὲ μὴ γνοὺς, ποιήσας δὲ ἄξια πληγῶν, δαρήσεται ὀλίγας.
ΟΡΟΣ Ι΄.

[10.1] Ὅτι τέλος ἁμαρτίας θάνατος.
Κεφάλ. α΄.
ΙΩΑΝΝΗΣ. Ὁ δὲ ἀπειθῶν τῷ Υἱῷ οὐκ ὄψεται τὴν ζωὴν, ἀλλ᾽ ἡ ὀργὴ τοῦ Θεοῦ μενεῖ ἐπ᾽ αὐτόν.
ΠΡΟΣ ΡΩΜ. Ὅτε γὰρ δοῦλοι ἦτε τῆς ἁμαρτίας, ἐλεύθεροι ἦτε τῇ δικαιοσύνῃ. Τίνα οὖν καρπὸν εἴχετε τότε, ἐφ᾽ οἷς νῦν ἐπαισχύνεσθε;

asked him, "What then shall we do?" (3.10), *tax collectors and soldiers alike.*[5]

ACTS: Now when they heard this they were cut to the heart, and said to Peter and the rest of the apostles, "Brethren, what shall we do?" (2.37).

9.4 That it is necessary for the one who is asked a question to answer carefully with fitting words.

LUKE: And behold, a lawyer stood up to put him to the test, saying, "Teacher, what shall I do to inherit eternal life?" He said to him, "What is written in the law? How do you read?" And he answered, "You shall love the Lord your God with all your heart, and with all your *soul, and* with all your mind; and your neighbor as yourself."[6] And he said to him, "You have answered right; do this, and you will live" (10.25–28).

COLOSSIANS: Let your speech always be gracious, seasoned with salt, so that you may know how you ought to answer every one (4.6).

9.5 That though the judgment of those who fail to do as they have pledged is worse, neither is it without danger to sin from ignorance.

LUKE: And that servant who knew his master's will, but did not make ready *nor* act according to his will, shall receive a severe beating. But he who did not know, and did what deserved a beating, shall receive a light beating (12.47–48).

10.1 That the result of sin is death.

JOHN: He who does not obey the Son shall not see life, but the wrath of God rests upon him (3.36).

ROMANS: When you were slaves of sin, you were free in regard to righteousness. But then what return did you get from the things

[5]Cf. Lk 3.12–14.
[6]Cf. Deut 6.5; Lev 19.18

Τὸ μὲν γὰρ τέλος ἐκείνων θάνατος. Καὶ μετ' ὀλίγα· Τὰ γὰρ ὀψώνια τῆς ἁμαρτίας θάνατος. ... Τὸ δὲ κέντρον τοῦ θανάτου ἡ ἁμαρτία.

[10.2]   Ὅτι τέλος ἐντολῆς Θεοῦ ζωὴ αἰώνιος.
Κεφάλ. β'.

ΙΩΑΝΝΗΣ. Ἀμὴν ἀμὴν λέγω ὑμῖν, ἐάν τις τὸν λόγον τὸν ἐμὸν τηρήσῃ, θάνατον οὐ μὴ θεωρήσῃ εἰς τὸν αἰῶνα.

ΙΩΑΝΝΗΣ. Ἀλλ' ὁ πέμψας με Πατήρ, αὐτός μοι ἐντολὴν ἔδωκε, τί εἴπω, καὶ τί λαλήσω, καὶ οἶδα, ὅτι ἡ ἐντολὴ αὐτοῦ ζωὴ αἰώνιός ἐστι.

ΠΡΟΣ ΡΩΜ. Νυνὶ δὲ ἐλευθερωθέντες ἀπὸ τῆς ἁμαρτίας, δουλω-θέντες δὲ τῷ Θεῷ, ἔχετε τὸν καρπὸν ὑμῶν εἰς ἁγιασμόν, τὸ δὲ τέλος ζωὴν αἰώνιον. [341]

ΟΡΟΣ ΙΑ'.

[11.1]   Ὅτι οὐ δεῖ καταφρονεῖν κριμάτων Θεοῦ, ἀλλὰ φοβεῖσθαι, κἂν μὴ παραυτίκα τὴν ἀνταπόδοσιν ἔχῃ.
Κεφάλ. α'.

ΜΑΤΘΑΙΟΣ. Φοβήθητε δὲ μᾶλλον τὸν δυνάμενον καὶ ψυχὴν καὶ σῶμα ἀπολέσαι ἐν γεέννῃ.

ΛΟΥΚΑΣ. Ἐὰν δὲ εἴπῃ ὁ δοῦλος ἐκεῖνος ἐν τῇ καρδίᾳ αὐτοῦ· χρονίζει ὁ κύριός μου ἔρχεσθαι· καὶ ἄρξηται τύπτειν τοὺς παῖδας καὶ τὰς παιδίσκας, ἐσθίειν τε καὶ πίνειν, καὶ μεθύσκεσθαι· ἥξει ὁ κύριος τοῦ δούλου ἐκείνου ἐν ἡμέρᾳ ᾗ οὐ προσδοκᾷ, καὶ ἐν ὥρᾳ ᾗ οὐ γινώσκει, καὶ διχοτομήσει αὐτόν, καὶ τὸ μέρος αὐτοῦ μετὰ τῶν ἀπίστων θήσει.

ΙΩΑΝΝΗΣ. Ἴδε, ὑγιὴς γέγονας· μηκέτι ἁμάρτανε, ἵνα μὴ χεῖρόν τί σοι γένηται.

ΠΡΟΣ ΕΦΕΣ. Μηδεὶς ὑμᾶς ἀπατάτω κενοῖς λόγοις· διὰ ταῦτα γὰρ ἔρχεται ἡ ὀργὴ τοῦ Θεοῦ ἐπὶ τοὺς υἱοὺς τῆς ἀπειθείας.

[11.2]   Ὅτι ὁ ἐπὶ τοῖς πρώτοις ἁμαρτήμασι παιδευθείς, καὶ τῆς ἀφέσεως καταξιωθείς, ἐὰν πάλιν ἁμάρτῃ, χεῖρον τοῦ προτέρου κατασκευάζει ἑαυτῷ τὸ κρῖμα τῆς ὀργῆς.

of which you are now ashamed? The *result* of those things is death (6.20–21). *And a little further:* For the wages of sin is death (6.23).

1 CORINTHIANS: The sting of death is sin (15.56).

10.2 That the result of God's commandment is life eternal.

JOHN: Truly, truly, I say to you, if any one keeps my word, he will never see death (8.51).

JOHN: The Father who sent me has himself given me commandment what to say and what to speak. And I know that his commandment is eternal life (12.49–50).

ROMANS: But now that you have been set free from sin and have become slaves of God, the return you get is sanctification and its end, eternal life (6.22).

11.1 That it is necessary not to regard God's judgments lightly, but to fear them, even if retribution is not immediate.

MATTHEW: Rather fear him who can destroy both soul and body in hell (10.28).

LUKE: But if that servant says to himself, "My master is delayed in coming," and begins to beat the menservants and the maidservants, and to eat and drink and get drunk, the master of that servant will come on a day when he does not expect him and at an hour he does not know, and will punish him, and put him with the unfaithful (12.45–46).

JOHN: See, you are well. Sin no more, that nothing worse befall you (5.14).

EPHESIANS: Let no one deceive you with empty words, for it is because of these things that the wrath of God comes upon the sons of disobedience (5.6).

11.2 That the one instructed with regard to his former sins and counted worthy of forgiveness, if he should sin again, brings upon himself the judgment of wrath more so than before his repentance.

Κεφάλ. β'.

ΙΩΑΝΝΗΣ. Ἴδε, ὑγιὴς γέγονας, μηκέτι ἁμάρτανε, ἵνα μὴ χεῖρον τί σοι γένηται.

[11.3] Ὅτι, κρίματι ὀργῆς Θεοῦ τινων ὑποπεσόντων, τοὺς λοιποὺς φοβουμένους παιδεύεσθαι δεῖ.

Κεφάλ. γ'.

ΛΟΥΚΑΣ. Παρῆσαν δέ τινες ἐν αὐτῷ τῷ καιρῷ, ἀπαγγέλλοντες αὐτῷ περὶ τῶν Γαλιλαίων, ὧν τὸ αἷμα Πιλᾶτος ἔμιξε μετὰ τῶν θυσιῶν αὐτῶν. Καὶ ἀποκριθεὶς ὁ Ἰησοῦς εἶπεν αὐτοῖς· δοκεῖτε ὅτι οἱ [342] Γαλιλαῖοι οὗτοι ἁμαρτωλοὶ παρὰ πάντας τοὺς Γαλιλαίους ἐγένοντο, ὅτι τοιαῦτα πεπόνθασιν; Οὐχί, λέγω ὑμῖν· ἀλλ' ἐὰν μὴ μετανοῆτε, πάντες ὡσαύτως ἀπολεῖσθε· Ἢ ἐκεῖνοι οἱ δέκα καὶ ὀκτώ, ἐφ' οὓς ἔπεσεν ὁ πύργος ἐν τῷ Σιλωὰμ, καὶ ἀπέκτεινεν⁴ αὐτούς, δοκεῖτε ὅτι οὗτοι ὀφειλέται ἐγένοντο παρὰ πάντας τοὺς ἀνθρώπους τοὺς κατοικοῦντας ἐν Ἱερουσαλήμ; Οὐχί, λέγω ὑμῖν· ἀλλ' ἐὰν μὴ μετανοῆτε, πάντες ὡσαύτως ἀπολεῖσθε.

ΠΡΑΞΕΙΣ. Ἀκούων δὲ Ἀνανίας τοὺς λόγους τούτους, πεσὼν ἐξέψυξε. Καὶ ἐγένετο φόβος μέγας ἐπὶ πάντας τοὺς ἀκούοντας ταῦτα.

ΠΡΟΣ ΚΟΡ. α'. Μηδὲ γογγύζετε, καθάπερ τινὲς αὐτῶν ἐγόγγυσαν, καὶ ἀπώλοντο ὑπὸ τοῦ ὀλοθρευτοῦ. Ταῦτα δὲ τύποι συνέβαινον ἐκείνοις· ἐγράφη δὲ πρὸς νουθεσίαν ἡμῶν, εἰς οὓς τὰ τέλη τῶν αἰώνων κατήντησεν.

[11.4] Ὅτι καὶ αὐτοῖς τοῖς τῆς κακίας ἔργοις πρὸς τιμωρίαν πολλάκις παραδίδοταί τις, διὰ προϋπάρχουσαν ἀσέβειαν.

Κεφάλ. δ'.

ΠΡΟΣ ΡΩΜ. Καὶ καθὼς οὐκ ἐδοκίμασαν τὸν Θεὸν ἔχειν ἐν ἐπιγνώσει, παρέδωκεν αὐτοὺς ὁ Θεὸς εἰς ἀδόκιμον νοῦν, ποιεῖν τὰ μὴ καθήκοντα.

ΠΡΟΣ ΘΕΣΣ. β'. Ἀνθ' ὧν τὴν ἀγάπην τῆς ἀληθείας οὐκ ἐδέξαντο, εἰς τὸ σωθῆναι αὐτούς, διὰ τοῦτο πέμπει αὐτοῖς ὁ Θεὸς ἐνέργειαν πλάνης, εἰς τὸ πιστεῦσαι αὐτοὺς τῷ ψεύδει.

⁴Corrected from ἀπέκτεινειν.

JOHN: See, you are well. Sin no more, that nothing worse befall you (5.14).

11.3   That when someone falls under the judgment of God's wrath, it is necessary for the rest to correct themselves out of fear.

LUKE: There were some present at that very time who told him of the Galileans whose blood Pilate had mingled with their sacrifices. And *Jesus* answered them, "Do you think that these Galileans were worse sinners than all the other Galileans, because they suffered thus? I tell you, No; but unless you repent you will all likewise perish. Or those eighteen upon whom the tower in Siloam fell and killed them, do you think that *these* were worse offenders than all the others who dwelt in Jerusalem? I tell you, No; but unless you repent you will all likewise perish" (13.1–5).

ACTS: When Ananias heard these words, he fell down and died. And great fear came upon all who heard of *these things* (5.5).

1 CORINTHIANS: Nor grumble, as some of them did and were destroyed by the Destroyer.[7] Now these *types happened to them*, but they were written down for our instruction, upon whom the end of the ages has come (10.10–11).

11.4   That a person, because of previous impiety, is often delivered for punishment even to the very works of evil.

ROMANS: And since they did not see fit to acknowledge God, God gave them up to a base mind and to improper conduct (1.28).

2 THESSALONIANS: Because they refused to love the truth and so be saved, therefore God sends upon them a strong delusion, to make them believe what is false (2.10–11).

[7]Cf. Num 16

[11.5] Ὅτι οὐχὶ πλῆθος ἁμαρτωλῶν δυσωπεῖ τὸν Θεόν, ἀλλ᾽ ὁ εὐαρεστῶν αὐτῷ, κἂν ἀνὴρ τυγχάνῃ, κἂν γυνή.

Κεφάλ. εʹ.

ΛΟΥΚΑΣ. Ἐπ᾽ ἀληθείας λέγω ὑμῖν, ὅτι πολλαὶ χῆραι ἦσαν ἐν ταῖς ἡμέραις Ἠλίου ἐν τῷ Ἰσραὴλ, ὅτε ἐκλείσθη ὁ οὐρανὸς ἐπὶ ἔτη τρία καὶ μῆνας ἕξ, ὡς ἐγένετο λιμὸς μέγας ἐπὶ πᾶσαν τὴν γῆν, καὶ πρὸς οὐδεμίαν αὐτῶν ἐπέμφθη Ἠλίας, εἰ μὴ εἰς Σάραφθα τῆς Σιδῶνος πρὸς γυναῖκα χήραν.

ΠΡΟΣ ΚΟΡ. αʹ. Οὐ θέλω γὰρ ὑμᾶς ἀγνοεῖν, ἀδελφοί, ὅτι οἱ πατέρες ἡμῶν πάντες ὑπὸ τὴν νεφέλην ἦσαν, καὶ πάντες διὰ τῆς θαλάσσης διῆλθον, καὶ πάντες εἰς τὸν Μωσῆν ἐβαπτίσθησαν ἐν τῇ νεφέλῃ καὶ ἐν [343] τῇ θαλάσσῃ, καὶ πάντες τὸ αὐτὸ βρῶμα πνευματικὸν ἔφαγον, καὶ πάντες τὸ αὐτὸ πόμα πνευματικὸν ἔπιον· ἔπινον γὰρ ἐκ πνευματικῆς ἀκολουθούσης πέτρας· ἡ δὲ πέτρα ἦν ὁ Χριστός. Ἀλλ᾽ οὐκ ἐν τοῖς πλείοσιν αὐτῶν εὐδόκησεν ὁ Θεός· κατεστρώθησαν γὰρ ἐν τῇ ἐρήμῳ.

ΟΡΟΣ ΙΒʹ.

[12.1] Ὅτι πᾶσα ἀντιλογία, κἂν ἐκ φιλικῆς καὶ εὐλαβοῦς διαθέσεως γένηται, ἀπαλλοτριοῖ τοῦ Κυρίου τὸν ἀντιλέγοντα· πᾶν δὲ ῥῆμα Κυρίου μετὰ πάσης πληροφορίας καταδέχεσθαι δεῖ.

Κεφάλ. αʹ.

ΙΩΑΝΝΗΣ. Καὶ ἤρξατο νίπτειν τοὺς πόδας τῶν μαθητῶν, καὶ ἐκμάσσειν τῷ λεντίῳ, ᾧ ἦν διεζωσμένος. Ἔρχεται οὖν πρὸς Σίμωνα Πέτρον, καὶ λέγει αὐτῷ ἐκεῖνος· Κύριε, σύ μου νίπτεις τοὺς πόδας; Ἀπεκρίθη Ἰησοῦς, καὶ εἶπεν αὐτῷ· ὃ ἐγὼ ποιῶ, σὺ οὐκ οἶδας ἄρτι, γνώσῃ δὲ μετὰ ταῦτα. Λέγει αὐτῷ Πέτρος· οὐ μὴ νίψεις τοὺς πόδας μου εἰς τὸν αἰῶνα. Ἀπεκρίθη αὐτῷ ὁ Ἰησοῦς· ἐὰν μὴ νίψω σε, οὐκ ἔχεις μέρος μετ᾽ ἐμοῦ.

[12.2] Ὅτι οὐ δεῖ παραδόσεσιν ἀνθρώπων ἀκολουθεῖν ἐπ᾽ ἀθετήσει ἐντολῆς Θεοῦ.

Κεφάλ. βʹ.

ΜΑΡΚΟΣ. Ἔπειτα ἐπερωτῶσιν αὐτὸν οἱ Φαρισαῖοι καὶ οἱ γραμματεῖς· διὰ τί οἱ μαθηταί σου οὐ περιπατοῦσι κατὰ τὴν παράδοσιν

11.5   That a host of sinners will by no means entreat God's favor, but one who pleases him will, whether a man or a woman.

LUKE: *In* truth, I tell you, there were many widows in Israel in the days of Elijah, when the heaven was shut up three years and six months, when there came a great famine over all the land; and Elijah was sent to none of them but only to Zarephath of the *Sidonians*, to a woman who was a widow[8] (4.25–26).

1 CORINTHIANS: I want you to know, brethren, that *your* fathers were all under the cloud,[9] and all passed through the sea,[10] and all were baptized into Moses in the cloud and in the sea, and all ate the same supernatural food[11] and all drank the same supernatural drink. For they drank from the supernatural Rock which followed them,[12] and the Rock was Christ. Nevertheless with most of them God was not pleased; for they were overthrown in the wilderness (10.1–5).

12.1   That all contention, even if it comes from a loving and reverent disposition, alienates one from the Lord, and that it is necessary for every word of the Lord to be accepted with all certainty.

JOHN: Then he poured water into a basin, and began to wash the disciples' feet, and to wipe them with the towel with which he was girded. He came to Simon Peter; and Peter said to him, "Lord, do you wash my feet?" Jesus answered him, "What I am doing you do not know now, but afterward you will understand." Peter said to him, "You shall never wash my feet." Jesus answered him, "If I do not wash you, you have no part in me" (13.5–8).

12.2   That it is necessary not to follow human traditions unto circumvention of the commandment of God.

MARK: *Then* the Pharisees and the scribes asked him, "Why do your disciples not live according to the tradition of the elders, but

[8]See 1 Kg (LXX 3 Kingdoms) 17.8–24
[9]See Ex 13.21; Ps 105.39 (LXX 104.39)
[10]See Ex 14.22
[11]See Ex 16.4
[12]See Ex 17.6; Num 20.11

τῶν πρεσβυτέρων, ἀλλὰ ἀνίπτοις χερσὶν ἐσθίουσι τὸν ἄρτον; Ὁ
δὲ ἀποκριθεὶς εἶπεν αὐτοῖς· ὅτι καλῶς προεφήτευσεν Ἡσαΐας περὶ
ὑμῶν τῶν ὑποκριτῶν, ὡς γέγραπται· «Οὗτος ὁ λαὸς τοῖς χείλεσί με
τιμᾷ, ἡ δὲ καρδία αὐτῶν πόρρω ἀπέχει ἀπ' ἐμοῦ. Μάτην δὲ σέβονταί
με, διδάσκοντες διδασκαλίας, ἐντάλματα ἀνθρώπων.» Ἀφέντες γὰρ
τὴν ἐντολὴν τοῦ Θεοῦ, κρατεῖτε τὴν παράδοσιν τῶν ἀνθρώπων· καὶ
τὰ ἑξῆς. [344]

[12.3]   Ὅτι δεῖ πάντα ἀπαραλείπτως φυλάττειν, τὰ διὰ τοῦ
εὐαγγελίου καὶ τῶν ἀποστόλων ὑπὸ τοῦ Κυρίου παραδεδομένα.
                              Κεφάλ. γ'.
   ΜΑΤΘΑΙΟΣ. Πορευθέντες, μαθητεύσατε πάντα τὰ ἔθνη, βαπτίζοντες αὐτοὺς εἰς τὸ ὄνομα τοῦ Πατρὸς καὶ τοῦ Υἱοῦ καὶ τοῦ ἁγίου
Πνεύματος· διδάσκοντες αὐτοὺς τηρεῖν πάντα, ὅσα ἐνετειλάμην
ὑμῖν.
   ΛΟΥΚΑΣ. Ἦσαν δὲ δίκαιοι ἀμφότεροι ἐνώπιον τοῦ Θεοῦ,
πορευόμενοι ἐν πάσαις ταῖς ἐντολαῖς καὶ δικαιώμασι τοῦ Κυρίου
ἄμεμπτοι.
   ΛΟΥΚΑΣ. Ὁ ἀκούων ὑμῶν ἐμοῦ ἀκούει· ὁ δὲ ἀθετῶν ὑμᾶς ἐμὲ
ἀθετεῖ.
   ΠΡΟΣ ΘΕΣΣ. β'. Ἄρα οὖν, ἀδελφοί, στήκετε, καὶ κρατεῖτε τὰς
παραδόσεις, ἃς ἐδιδάχθητε εἴτε διὰ λόγου, εἴτε δι' ἐπιστολῆς, ὡς δι'
ἡμῶν.

[12.4]   Ὅτι οὐ δεῖ θέλημα ἴδιον παρὰ τὸ θέλημα τοῦ Κυρίου
ἐγκρίνειν· ἀλλ' ἐν παντὶ πράγματι ζητεῖν καὶ ποιεῖν τὸ θέλημα τοῦ
Θεοῦ.
                              Κεφάλ. δ'.
   ΙΩΑΝΝΗΣ. Ὅτι οὐ ζητῶ τὸ θέλημα τὸ ἐμόν, ἀλλὰ τὸ θέλημα τοῦ
πέμψαντός με Πατρός.
   ΛΟΥΚΑΣ. Καὶ θεὶς τὰ γόνατα, προσηύξατο λέγων· Πάτερ, εἰ
βούλει, παρένεγκε τὸ ποτήριον τοῦτο. Πλὴν μὴ τὸ θέλημα τὸ ἐμόν,
ἀλλὰ τὸ σὸν γενέσθω.

eat with hands *unwashed*?" And he *answered* them, "Well did Isaiah prophesy of you hypocrites, as it is written, 'This people honors me with their lips, but their heart is far from me; in vain do they worship me, teaching as doctrines the precepts of men.'[13] *For* you leave the commandment of God, and hold fast to the tradition of men" (7.5–8), *and what follows.*

12.3 That it is necessary to observe all in its entirety that has been delivered by the Lord through the Gospel and the apostles.

MATTHEW: Go therefore and make disciples of all nations, baptizing them in the name of the Father and of the Son and of the Holy Spirit, teaching them to observe all that I have commanded you (28.19–20).

LUKE: And they were both righteous *in the face of* God, walking in all the commandments and ordinances of the Lord blameless (1.6).

LUKE: He who hears you hears me, and he who rejects you rejects me, and he who rejects me rejects him who sent me (10.16).

2 THESSALONIANS: So then, brethren, stand firm and hold to the traditions which you were taught, *either by word of mouth or by letter, as by us* (2.15).

12.4 That it is necessary not to consider one's own will before the Lord's, but, in all things, to seek and to do the will of God.

JOHN: Because I seek not my own will but the will of *the Father* who sent me (5.30).

LUKE: And he withdrew from them about a stone's throw, and knelt down and prayed, "Father, if thou art willing, remove this *cup*; nevertheless not my will, but thine, be done" (22.41–42).

---

[13] Is 29.13

ΠΡΟΣ ΕΦΕΣ. Ἐν οἷς καὶ ἡμεῖς πάντες ἀνεστράφημέν ποτε ἐν ταῖς ἐπιθυμίαις τῆς σαρκὸς ἡμῶν, ποιοῦντες τὸ θέλημα τῆς σαρκὸς καὶ τῶν διανοιῶν ἡμῶν· καὶ ἦμεν τέκνα φύσει ὀργῆς, ὡς καὶ οἱ λοιποί. ΟΡΟΣ ΙΓʹ.

[13.1] Ὅτι δεῖ νήφειν ἀεὶ, καὶ ἕτοιμον εἶναι ἐν τῇ σπουδῇ τῶν κατορθωμάτων τοῦ Θεοῦ, γνωρίζοντα τῆς ἀναβολῆς τὸ ἐπικίνδυνον. Κεφάλ. αʹ.

ΛΟΥΚΑΣ. Ἔστωσαν ὑμῶν αἱ ὀσφύες περιεζωσμέναι, καὶ οἱ λύχνοι καιόμενοι· καὶ ὑμεῖς ὅμοιοι [345] ἀνθρώποις προσδεχομένοις τὸν κύριον ἑαυτῶν, πότε ἀναλύσει ἐκ τῶν γάμων· ἵνα ἐλθόντος, καὶ κρούσαντος, εὐθέως ἀνοίξωσιν αὐτῷ. Μακάριοι οἱ δοῦλοι ἐκεῖνοι, οὓς ἐλθὼν ὁ κύριος εὑρήσει γρηγοροῦντας. Ἀμὴν λέγω ὑμῖν, ὅτι περιζώσεται, καὶ ἀνακλινεῖ αὐτοὺς, καὶ παρελθὼν διακονήσει αὐτοῖς. Καὶ ἐὰν ἔλθῃ ἐν τῇ δευτέρᾳ φυλακῇ, καὶ ἐν τῇ τρίτῃ φυλακῇ ἔλθῃ, καὶ εὕρῃ οὕτω, μακάριοί εἰσιν οἱ δοῦλοι ἐκεῖνοι. Τοῦτο δὲ γινώσκετε, ὅτι εἰ ᾔδει ὁ οἰκοδεσπότης ποίᾳ ὥρᾳ ὁ κλέπτης ἔρχεται, ἐγρηγόρησεν ἄν, καὶ οὐκ⁵ ἂν ἀφῆκε διορυγῆναι τὴν οἰκίαν αὐτοῦ. Καὶ ὑμεῖς οὖν γίνεσθε ἕτοιμοι, ὅτι ᾗ ὥρᾳ οὐ δοκεῖτε ὁ Υἱὸς τοῦ ἀνθρώπου ἔρχεται, καὶ τὰ ἑξῆς.

ΠΡΟΣ ΘΕΣΣ. αʹ. Περὶ δὲ τῶν χρόνων καὶ τῶν καιρῶν, ἀδελφοὶ, οὐ χρείαν ἔχετε γράφεσθαι ὑμῖν· αὐτοὶ γὰρ ἀκριβῶς οἴδατε, ὅτι ἡ ἡμέρα Κυρίου ὡς κλέπτης ἐν νυκτὶ, οὕτως ἔρχεται. Καὶ μετ' ὀλίγα· Ἄρα οὖν μὴ καθεύδωμεν ὡς καὶ οἱ λοιποί, ἀλλὰ γρηγορῶμεν, καὶ νήφωμεν.

[13.2] Ὅτι δεῖ πάντα καιρὸν εὔθετον ἡγεῖσθαι εἰς τὴν σπουδὴν τῶν ἀρεσκόντων Θεῷ. Κεφάλ. βʹ.

ΙΩΑΝΝΗΣ. Ἐμὲ δεῖ ἐργάζεσθαι τὰ ἔργα τοῦ πέμψαντός με, ἕως ἡμέρα ἐστίν.

ΠΡΟΣ ΦΙΛΙΠ. Ὥστε, ἀγαπητοί μου, καθὼς πάντοτε ὑπηκούσατε, μὴ ὡς ἐν τῇ παρουσίᾳ μου μόνον, ἀλλὰ νῦν πολλῷ μᾶλλον ἐν τῇ ἀπουσίᾳ μου, μετὰ φόβου καὶ τρόμου τὴν ἑαυτῶν σωτηρίαν κατεργάζεσθε.

⁵Corrected from αὐκ.

EPHESIANS: Among these we all once lived in the passions of our flesh, following the *desire* of our body and mind, and so we were by nature children of wrath like the rest (2.3).

13.1   That it is necessary to be always vigilant and ready in zeal for the good works of God, ever mindful of the danger of delay.

LUKE: Let your loins be girded and your lamps burning, and be like men who are waiting for their master to come home from the marriage feast, so that they may open to him at once when he comes and knocks. Blessed are those servants whom the master finds awake when he comes; truly, I say to you, he will gird himself and have them sit at table, and he will come and serve them. If he comes in the second watch, *and in the third watch he comes*, and finds them so, blessed are those servants! But know this, that if the householder had known at what hour the thief was coming, he would not have left his house to be broken into. *Therefore* you also must be ready; for the Son of man is coming at an unexpected hour (12.35–40), *and what follows*.

1 THESSALONIANS: But as to the times and the seasons, brethren, you have no need to have anything written to you. For you yourselves know well that the day of the Lord will come like a thief in the night (5.1–2). *And a little further*: So then let us not sleep, *even* as others do, but let us keep awake and be sober (5.6).

13.2   That it is necessary to consider every moment appropriate for zeal in those things which please God.

JOHN: *I* must work the works of him who sent me, while it is day; night comes, when no one can work (9.4).

PHILIPPIANS: Therefore, my beloved, as you have always obeyed, so now, not only as in my presence but much more in my absence, work out your own salvation with fear and trembling (2.12).

ΟΡΟΣ ΙΔ΄.

[14.1] Ὅτι οὐ δεῖ τὰ ἀνοίκεια μιγνύναι, ἀλλ᾽ ἑκάστου τῶν γινομένων ἢ λεγομένων τὸν ἴδιον καιρὸν γνωρίζειν.

Κεφάλ. α΄.

ΜΑΤΘΑΙΟΣ. Τότε προσέρχονται αὐτῷ οἱ μαθηταὶ Ἰωάννου,
λέγοντες· διὰ τί ἡμεῖς καὶ οἱ Φαρισαῖοι [346] νηστεύομεν πολλὰ,
οἱ δὲ μαθηταί σου οὐ νηστεύουσι; Καὶ εἶπεν αὐτοῖς ὁ Ἰησοῦς· μὴ
δύνανται οἱ υἱοὶ τοῦ νυμφῶνος πενθεῖν, ἐφ᾽ ὅσον μετ᾽ αὐτῶν ἐστιν ὁ
νυμφίος; Ἐλεύσονται δὲ ἡμέραι, ὅταν ἀπαρθῇ ἀπ᾽ αὐτῶν ὁ νυμφίος,
καὶ τότε νηστεύσουσιν ἐν ἐκείναις ταῖς ἡμέραις· καὶ τὰ ἑξῆς.

ΠΡΟΣ ΓΑΛ. Ἄρα, ἀδελφοὶ, οὐκ ἐσμὲν παιδίσκης τέκνα, ἀλλὰ τῆς
ἐλευθέρας· τῇ ἐλευθερίᾳ οὖν, ᾗ Χριστὸς ἡμᾶς ἠλευθέρωσε, στήκετε,
καὶ μὴ πάλιν ζυγῷ δουλείας ἐνέχεσθε.

ΟΡΟΣ ΙΕ΄.

[15.1] Ὅτι οὐ δεῖ τοῖς ἄλλων κατορθώμασιν ἐλπίζοντα, τῶν καθ᾽
ἑαυτὸν ἀμελεῖν.

Κεφάλ. α΄.

ΜΑΤΘΑΙΟΣ. Ποιήσατε οὖν καρποὺς ἀξίους τῆς μετανοίας, καὶ μὴ
δόξητε λέγειν ἐν ἑαυτοῖς· πατέρα ἔχομεν τὸν Ἀβραάμ.

ΟΡΟΣ Ις΄.

[16.1] Ὅτι οὐδὲν ὠφελοῦνται οἱ συζῶντες τοῖς ἀρέσκουσι τῷ Θεῷ,
καὶ τὸ ἑαυτῶν φρόνημα μὴ κατορθοῦντες, κἂν κατὰ τὸ φαινόμενον
σώζωσι τὴν πρὸς αὐτοὺς ὁμοιότητα.

Κεφάλ. α΄.

ΜΑΤΘΑΙΟΣ. Τότε ὁμοιωθήσεται ἡ βασιλεία τῶν οὐρανῶν δέκα
παρθένοις, αἵτινες λαβοῦσαι τὰς λαμπάδας αὐτῶν, ἐξῆλθον εἰς
ἀπάντησιν τοῦ νυμφίου. Πέντε δὲ ἐξ αὐτῶν ἦσαν φρόνιμοι, καὶ αἱ
πέντε μωραί. Αἵτινες μωραὶ, λαβοῦσαι τὰς λαμπάδας αὐτῶν, οὐκ
ἔλαβον μεθ᾽ ἑαυτῶν ἔλαιον· αἱ δὲ φρόνιμοι ἔλαβον ἐν τοῖς ἀγγείοις
αὐτῶν μετὰ τῶν λαμπάδων αὐτῶν. Οἷς ἐπιφέρει μετ᾽ ὀλίγα περὶ τῶν
μωρῶν·Ὕστερον δὲ ἔρχονται αἱ λοιπαὶ παρθένοι λέγουσαι· Κύριε,
Κύριε, ἄνοιξον ἡμῖν. Ὁ δὲ ἀποκριθεὶς [347] εἶπε· Λέγω ὑμῖν, οὐκ
οἶδα ὑμᾶς.

14.1   That it is necessary not to mingle incongruous things, but to know the proper time for every deed and word.

MATTHEW: Then the disciples of John came to him, saying, "Why do we and the Pharisees fast, but your disciples do not fast?" And Jesus said to them, "Can the wedding guests mourn as long as the bridegroom is with them? The days will come, when the bridegroom is taken away from them, and then they will fast *in those days*" (9.14–15), *and what follows.*

GALATIANS: So, brethren, we are not children of the slave but of the free woman. *Therefore stand in the freedom for which Christ has set us free*, and do not submit again to a yoke of slavery (4.31–5.1).

15.1   That it is necessary not to neglect one's own duty, hoping in the good works of others.

MATTHEW: Bear *fruits that befit* repentance, and do not presume to say to yourselves, "We have Abraham as our father" (3.8–9).

16.1   That they who live among those who please God but do not correct their way of thinking benefit in no way, even if in appearance they maintain a similar way of life.

MATTHEW: Then the kingdom of heaven shall be compared to ten maidens who took their lamps and went to meet the bridegroom. *Five of them were wise, and five were foolish. When* the foolish took their lamps, they took no oil with them; but the wise took *some in their flasks* with their lamps (25.1–4). *To which it adds a little further, concerning the foolish*: Afterward the other maidens *came*, saying, "Lord, lord, open to us." But he replied, "*I say* to you, I do not know you" (25.11–12).

ΛΟΥΚΑΣ. Λέγω ὑμῖν· ταύτῃ τῇ νυκτὶ δύο ἔσονται ἐπὶ κλίνης μιᾶς· εἷς παραληφθήσεται, καὶ ὁ ἕτερος ἀφεθήσεται. Δύο ἀλήθουσαι ἐπὶ τὸ αὐτό· μία παραληφθήσεται, καὶ ἡ ἑτέρα ἀφεθήσεται. Καὶ ἀποκριθέντες λέγουσιν αὐτῷ· ποῦ, Κύριε; Ὁ δὲ εἶπεν αὐτοῖς· ὅπου τὸ πτῶμα, ἐκεῖ συναχθήσονται καὶ οἱ ἀετοί.

ΟΡΟΣ ΙΖ΄.

[17.1] Ὅτι δεῖ, τὸν ἐνεστῶτα καιρὸν ἀπὸ τῶν δεδηλωμένων ἡμῖν παρὰ τῆς Γραφῆς ἰδιωμάτων γνωρίζοντας, ὁποῖός ἐστιν, ἐστοχασμένως τούτου τὰ καθ᾽ ἑαυτοὺς διατιθέναι.

Κεφάλ. α΄.

ΜΑΤΘΑΙΟΣ. Ἀπὸ δὲ τῆς συκῆς μάθετε τὴν παραβολήν. Ὅταν ἤδη ὁ κλάδος αὐτῆς γένηται ἁπαλὸς, καὶ τὰ φύλλα ἐκφύῃ, γινώσκετε, ὅτι ἐγγὺς τὸ θέρος. Οὕτω καὶ ὑμεῖς, ὅταν ἴδητε ταῦτα πάντα, γινώσκετε, ὅτι ἐγγύς ἐστιν ἐπὶ θύραις.

ΛΟΥΚΑΣ. Ὅταν ἴδητε τὴν νεφέλην ἀνατέλλουσαν ἀπὸ δυσμῶν, εὐθέως λέγετε, ὅτι ὄμβρος ἔρχεται· καὶ γίνεται οὕτως. Καὶ ὅταν νότον πνέοντα, λέγετε, ὅτι καύσων ἔσται· καὶ γίνεται. Ὑποκριταὶ, τὸ πρόσωπον τῆς γῆς καὶ τοῦ οὐρανοῦ οἴδατε δοκιμάζειν, τὸν δὲ καιρὸν τοῦτον πῶς οὐ δοκιμάζετε;

ΠΡΟΣ ΚΟΡ. α΄. Ὁ καιρὸς συνεσταλμένος ἐστὶν τὸ λοιπὸν, ἵνα καὶ οἱ ἔχοντες γυναῖκας ὡς μὴ ἔχοντες ὦσι· καὶ οἱ κλαίοντες, ὡς μὴ κλαίοντες· καὶ οἱ χαίροντες, ὡς μὴ χαίροντες· καὶ οἱ ἀγοράζοντες, ὡς μὴ κατέχοντες· καὶ οἱ χρώμενοι τῷ κόσμῳ, ὡς μὴ καταχρώμενοι· παράγει γὰρ τὸ σχῆμα τοῦ κόσμου τούτου. [348]

ΟΡΟΣ ΙΗ΄.

[18.1] Ὅτι δεῖ τὰς ἐντολὰς τοῦ Θεοῦ οὕτω ποιεῖν, ὡς ὁ Κύριος προσέταξεν. Ὁ γὰρ περὶ τὸν τρόπον τῆς ἐργασίας διαπταίων, κἂν δόξῃ ποιεῖν τὴν ἐντολὴν, ἀδόκιμός ἐστι παρὰ τῷ Θεῷ.

LUKE: I tell you, in that night there will be two in one bed; one will be taken and the other left. There will be two women grinding together; one will be taken and the other left" (17.34–35). And they said to him, "Where, Lord?" He said to them, "Where the *corpse* is, there the eagles will be gathered together" (17.37).

17.1 That it is necessary to arrange our affairs in accordance with the time at hand, which we recognize from the signs set forth for us in Scripture.

MATTHEW: From the fig tree learn its lesson: as soon as its branch becomes tender and puts forth its leaves, you know that summer is near. So also, when you see all these things, you know that he is near, at the very gates (24.32–33).

LUKE: When you see *the* cloud rising *from* the west, you say at once, "A shower is coming"; and so it happens. And when you see the south wind blowing, you say, "There will be scorching heat"; and it happens. You hypocrites! You know how to interpret the appearance of earth and sky; but why do you not *interpret* the present time (12.54–56)?

1 CORINTHIANS: The appointed time has grown very short; from now on, let those who have wives live as though they had none, and those who mourn as though they were not mourning, and those who rejoice as though they were not rejoicing, and those who buy as though they had no goods, and those who deal with the world as though they had no dealings with it. For the form of this world is passing away (7.29–31).

18.1 That it is necessary to carry out the commandments of God just as the Lord ordained, for the one who errs in the manner of the work, though he seems to fulfill the commandment, is unseemly to the Lord.

Κεφάλ. α'.

ΛΟΥΚΑΣ. Ἔλεγε δὲ καὶ τῷ κεκληκότι αὐτόν· ὅταν ποιῇς ἄριστον ἢ δεῖπνον, μὴ φώνει τοὺς φίλους σου, μηδὲ τοὺς ἀδελφούς σου, μηδὲ τοὺς συγγενεῖς σου, μηδὲ γείτονας πλουσίους, μήποτε καὶ αὐτοί σε ἀντικαλέσωσι, καὶ γένηταί σοι ἀνταπόδομα. Ἀλλ᾽ ὅταν ποιῇς δοχὴν, κάλει πτωχοὺς, ἀναπήρους, χωλοὺς, τυφλοὺς, καὶ μακάριος ἔσῃ, ὅτι οὐκ ἔχουσιν ἀνταποδοῦναί σοι· ἀνταποδοθήσεται γάρ σοι ἐν τῇ ἀναστάσει τῶν δικαίων.

[18.2] Ὅτι οὐ δεῖ τὴν τοῦ Θεοῦ ἐντολὴν διὰ τὴν πρὸς ἀνθρώπους ἀρέσκειαν, ἢ δι᾽ ἄλλο τι πάθος, ποιεῖν, ἀλλ᾽ ἐν παντὶ σκοπὸν ἔχειν, τῷ Θεῷ ἀρέσαι, καὶ Θεὸν δοξάσαι.

Κεφάλ. β'.

ΜΑΤΘΑΙΟΣ. Προσέχετε τὴν ἐλεημοσύνην ὑμῶν μὴ ποιεῖν ἔμπρο-σθεν τῶν ἀνθρώπων, πρὸς τὸ θεαθῆναι αὐτοῖς· εἰ δὲ μήγε, μισθὸν οὐκ ἔχετε παρὰ τῷ Πατρὶ ὑμῶν τῷ ἐν τοῖς οὐρανοῖς. Ὅταν οὖν ποιῇς ἐλεημοσύνην, μὴ σαλπίσῃς ἔμπροσθεν τῶν ἀνθρώπων, ὥσπερ οἱ ὑποκριταὶ ποιοῦσιν ἐν ταῖς συναγωγαῖς καὶ ἐν ταῖς ῥύμαις, ὅπως δοξασθῶσιν ὑπὸ τῶν ἀνθρώπων. Ἀμὴν λέγω ὑμῖν, ἀπέχουσι τὸν μισθὸν αὐτῶν, καὶ τὰ ἑξῆς.

ΠΡΟΣ ΚΟΡ. α'. Εἴτε οὖν ἐσθίετε, εἴτε πίνετε, εἴτε τι ποιεῖτε, πάντα εἰς δόξαν Θεοῦ ποιεῖτε.

ΠΡΟΣ ΘΕΣΣ. α'. Ἀλλὰ καθὼς δεδοκιμάσμεθα ὑπὸ τοῦ Θεοῦ, πιστευθῆναι τὸ εὐαγγέλιον, οὕτω λαλοῦμεν, οὐχ ὡς ἀνθρώποις ἀρέσκοντες, ἀλλὰ τῷ Θεῷ τῷ δοκιμάζοντι τὰς καρδίας ἡμῶν. Οὔτε γάρ ποτε ἐν λόγῳ κολακείας ἐγενήθημεν, [349] καθὼς οἴδατε· οὔτε προφάσει πλεονεξίας, Θεὸς μάρτυς· οὔτε ζητοῦντες ἐξ ἀνθρώπων δόξαν, οὔτε ἀφ᾽ ὑμῶν, οὔτε ἀπ᾽ ἄλλων.

[18.3] Ὅτι δεῖ τὰς ἐντολὰς τοῦ Κυρίου μετὰ συνειδήσεως καὶ διαθέσεως ἀγαθῆς πρός τε Θεὸν καὶ ἀνθρώπους ποιεῖν. Ὁ γὰρ μὴ οὕτω ποιῶν κατακέκριται.

LUKE: He said also to the man who had invited him, "When you give a dinner or a banquet, do not invite your friends or your brothers or your kinsmen or rich neighbors, lest they also invite you in return, and you be repaid. But when you give a feast, invite the poor, the maimed, the lame, the blind, and you will be blessed, because they cannot repay you. You will be repaid at the resurrection of the just" (14.12–14).

18.2   That it is necessary not to fulfill the commandment of God out of a desire for human approval or any other passion, but in all things to have as one's aim to please God and to glorify God.

MATTHEW: Beware of practicing your *charity* before men in order to be seen by them; for then you will have no reward from your Father who is in heaven. Thus, when you give alms, sound no trumpet before *others*, as the hypocrites do in the synagogues and in the streets, that they may be praised by men. Truly, I say to you, they have received their reward (6.1–2), *and what follows.*

1 CORINTHIANS: So, whether you eat or drink, or whatever you do, do all to the glory of God (10.31).

1 THESSALONIANS: But just as we have been approved by God to be entrusted with the gospel, so we speak, not to please men, but to please God who tests our hearts. *For we engaged neither in flattering speech, as you know, nor in a pretext for our gain*, as God is witness; nor did we seek glory from men, whether from you or from others (2.4–6).

18.3   That it is necessary to fulfill the commandments of the Lord conscientiously and with a good disposition toward both God and human beings, for the one who does not do so is condemned.

Κεφάλ. γ'.

ΜΑΤΘΑΙΟΣ. Οὐαὶ ὑμῖν, γραμματεῖς, καὶ Φαρισαῖοι ὑποκριταὶ, ὅτι καθαρίζετε τὸ ἔξωθεν τοῦ ποτηρίου καὶ τῆς παροψίδος, ἔσωθεν δὲ γέμουσιν ἐξ ἁρπαγῆς καὶ ἀκρασίας. Φαρισαῖε τυφλὲ, καθάρισον πρῶτον τὸ ἐντὸς τοῦ ποτηρίου καὶ τῆς παροψίδος, ἵνα γένηται καὶ τὸ ἐκτὸς αὐτοῦ καθαρόν. ΠΡΟΣ ΡΩΜ. Ὁ μεταδιδοὺς ἐν ἁπλότητι. ΠΡΟΣ ΦΙΛΙΠ. Πάντα ποιεῖτε χωρὶς γογγυσμῶν καὶ διαλογισμῶν. ΠΡΟΣ ΤΙΜ. α'. Τὸ δὲ τέλος τῆς παραγγελίας ἐστὶν ἀγάπη ἐκ καθαρᾶς καρδίας καὶ συνειδήσεως ἀγαθῆς ... Ἔχων πίστιν, καὶ ἀγαθὴν συνείδησιν, ἥντινες ἀπωσάμενοι, περὶ τὴν πίστιν ἐναυάγησαν.

[18.4]   Ὅτι ἀπὸ τῆς περὶ τὰ ἐλάττονα εὐγνωμοσύνης ἡ ἐπὶ τοῖς μείζοσι τῆς ἀνταποδόσεως⁶ κρίσις δικαιοῦται.

Κεφάλ. δ'.

ΜΑΤΘΑΙΟΣ. Εὖ, δοῦλε ἀγαθὲ καὶ πιστὲ, ἐπὶ ὀλίγα ἧς πιστός, ἐπὶ πολλῶν σε καταστήσω· εἴσελθε εἰς τὴν χαρὰν τοῦ κυρίου σου. Καὶ μετ' ὀλίγα· Τῷ γὰρ ἔχοντι παντὶ δοθήσεται, καὶ περισσευθήσεται· ἀπὸ δὲ τοῦ μὴ ἔχοντος, καὶ ὃ ἔχει, ἀρθήσεται ἀπ' αὐτοῦ. ΛΟΥΚΑΣ. Εἰ οὖν ἐν τῷ ἀδίκῳ μαμμωνᾷ⁷ πιστοὶ οὐκ ἐγένεσθε, τὸ ἀληθινὸν τίς ὑμῖν πιστεύσει; Καὶ εἰ ἐν τῷ ἀλλοτρίῳ πιστοὶ οὐκ ἐγένεσθε, τὸ ὑμέτερον τίς ὑμῖν δώσει;

[18.5]   Ὅτι δεῖ τὰς ἐντολὰς τοῦ Κυρίου μετὰ ἐπιθυμίας ἀκορέστου ποιεῖν, ἀεὶ πρὸς τὸ πλέον ἐπειγόμενον.

Κεφάλ. ε'.

ΜΑΤΘΑΙΟΣ. Μακάριοι οἱ πεινῶντες καὶ διψῶντες τὴν δικαιοσύνην. ΠΡΟΣ ΦΙΛΙΠ. Ἐγὼ, [350] ἀδελφοὶ, ἐμαυτὸν οὔπω λογίζομαι κατειληφέναι. Ἕν δὲ, τῶν μὲν ὄπισθεν ἐπιλανθανόμενος, τοῖς δὲ ἔμπροσθεν ἐπεκτεινόμενος, κατὰ σκοπὸν διώκω ἐπὶ τὸ βραβεῖον τῆς ἄνω κλήσεως ἐν Χριστῷ Ἰησοῦ.

---

⁶Corrected from ἀνταποδοώσεως.
⁷Corrected from μαμωνᾷ.

MATTHEW: Woe to you, scribes and Pharisees, hypocrites! For you cleanse the outside of the cup and of the plate, but inside they are full of extortion and rapacity. You blind Pharisee! First cleanse the inside of the cup and of the plate, that the outside also may be clean (23.25–26).

ROMANS: He who contributes, in liberality (12.8).

PHILIPPIANS: Do all things without grumbling or questioning (2.14).

1 TIMOTHY: Whereas the aim of our charge is love that issues from a pure heart and a good conscience (1.5), *having* faith and a good conscience, *which certain persons have rejected, making* shipwreck of their faith (1.19).

18.4 That based on prudence in little things is the decision made to grant greater things in return.

MATTHEW: Well done, good and faithful servant; you have been faithful over a little, I will set you over much; enter into the joy of your master (25.23). *And a little further*: For to everyone who has will more be given, and he will have abundance; but from him who has not, even what he has will be taken away (25.29).

LUKE: If then you have not been faithful in the unrighteous mammon, who will entrust to you the true riches? And if you have not been faithful in that which is another's, who will give you that which is your own (16.11–12)?

18.5 That it is necessary to fulfill the commandments of the Lord with an insatiable desire, ever pressing on to more.

MATTHEW: Blessed are those who hunger and thirst for righteousness (5.6).

PHILIPPIANS: Brethren, I do not consider that I have made it my own; but one thing I do, forgetting what lies behind and straining forward to what lies ahead, I press on toward the goal for the prize of the upward call of God in Christ Jesus (3.13–14).

[18.6] Ὅτι δεῖ τὰς ἐντολὰς τοῦ Θεοῦ οὕτω ποιεῖν, ὥστε, ὅσον ἐπὶ τῷ ποιοῦντι, φωτίζεσθαι τοὺς πάντας, καὶ τὸν Θεὸν δοξάζεσθαι.

Κεφάλ. ς'.

ΜΑΤΘΑΙΟΣ. Ὑμεῖς ἐστε τὸ φῶς τοῦ κόσμου. Οὐ δύναται πόλις κρυβῆναι ἐπάνω ὄρους κειμένη· οὐδὲ καίουσι λύχνον, καὶ τιθέασιν ὑπὸ τὸν μόδιον, ἀλλ' ἐπὶ τὴν λυχνίαν, καὶ λάμπει πᾶσι τοῖς ἐν τῇ οἰκίᾳ. Οὕτω λαμψάτω τὸ φῶς ὑμῶν ἔμπροσθεν τῶν ἀνθρώπων, ὅπως ἴδωσι τὰ καλὰ ἔργα ὑμῶν, καὶ δοξάσωσι τὸν⁸ Πατέρα ὑμῶν τὸν ἐν τοῖς οὐρανοῖς.

ΛΟΥΚΑΣ. Οὐδεὶς δὲ, λύχνον ἅψας, κρύπτει αὐτὸν σκεύει, ἢ ὑποκάτω κλίνης τίθησιν, ἀλλ' ἐπὶ λυχνίας ἐπιτίθησιν, ἵνα οἱ εἰσπορευόμενοι βλέπωσι τὸ φῶς.

ΠΡΟΣ ΦΙΛΙΠ. Ἵνα ἦτε εἰλικρινεῖς, καὶ ἀπρόσκοποι εἰς ἡμέραν Χριστοῦ, πεπληρωμένοι καρπῶν δικαιοσύνης, διὰ Ἰησοῦ Χριστοῦ, εἰς δόξαν καὶ ἔπαινον Θεοῦ.

ΟΡΟΣ ΙΘ'

[19.1] Ὅτι οὐ δεῖ ἐμποδίζειν τῷ ποιοῦντι θέλημα Θεοῦ, εἴτε κατ' ἐντολὴν Θεοῦ, εἴτε κατὰ λόγον ἀκολουθοῦντα τῇ ἐντολῇ· οὔτε μὴν ποιοῦντα ἀνέχεσθαι τῶν κωλυόντων, κἂν γνήσιοι ὦσιν, ἀλλ' ἐπιμένειν τῇ κρίσει.

Κεφάλ. α'.

ΜΑΤΘΑΙΟΣ. Τότε παραγίνεται ὁ Ἰησοῦς ἀπὸ τῆς Γαλιλαίας ἐπὶ τὸν Ἰορδάνην πρὸς τὸν Ἰωάννην, τοῦ βαπτισθῆναι ὑπ' αὐτοῦ. Ὁ δὲ Ἰωάννης διεκώλυεν αὐτὸν, λέγων· ἐγὼ χρείαν ἔχω ὑπὸ σοῦ βαπτισθῆναι, καὶ σὺ ἔρχῃ πρός με; Ἀποκριθεὶς δὲ ὁ Ἰησοῦς εἶπε πρὸς αὐτόν· ἄφες ἄρτι· οὕτω γὰρ πρέπον ἡμῖν ἐστι πληρῶσαι πᾶσαν δικαιοσύνην, καὶ τὰ ἑξῆς.

ΜΑΤΘΑΙΟΣ. Ἀπὸ τότε ἤρξατο ὁ [350] Ἰησοῦς δεικνύειν τοῖς μαθηταῖς αὐτοῦ, Ὅτι δεῖ αὐτὸν ἀπελθεῖν εἰς Ἱεροσόλυμα, καὶ πολλὰ παθεῖν ὑπὸ τῶν πρεσβυτέρων, καὶ ἀρχιερέων, καὶ γραμματέων· καὶ ἀποκτανθῆναι, καὶ τῇ τρίτῃ ἡμέρᾳ ἐγερθῆναι. Καὶ προσλαβόμενος αὐτὸν ὁ Πέτρος, ἤρξατο ἐπιτιμᾶν αὐτῷ λέγων· ἵλεώς σοι, Κύριε· οὐ μὴ ἔσται σοι τοῦτο. Ὁ δὲ, στραφεὶς, εἶπε τῷ Πέτρῳ· ὕπαγε ὀπίσω

⁸Corrected from τὴν.

18.6   That it is necessary to fulfill the commandments of God in such a way that, as much as possible, all are enlightened and God is glorified.

MATTHEW: You are the light of the world. A city set on a hill cannot be hid. Nor do *they* light a lamp and put it under a bushel, but on a stand, and it gives light to all in the house. Let your light so shine before men, that they may see your good works and give glory to your Father who is in heaven (5.14–16).

LUKE: No one after lighting a lamp *hides* it with a vessel, or puts it under a bed, but puts it on a stand, that those who enter may see the light (8.16).

PHILIPPIANS: So that you may be pure and blameless for the day of Christ, filled with the fruits of righteousness *through* Jesus Christ, to the glory and praise of God (1.10–11).

19.1   That it is necessary not to hinder the one doing God's will, whether he obeys because of the command or on account of his own reasoning; nor for the doer to be held back in any way by those who would hinder him, even if they are close relations, but to persevere in his resolve.

MATTHEW: Then Jesus came from Galilee to the Jordan to John, to be baptized by him. John would have prevented him, saying, "I need to be baptized by you, and do you come to me?" But Jesus answered him, "Let it be so now; for thus it is fitting for us to fulfill all righteousness" (3.13–15), *and what follows.*

MATTHEW: From that time Jesus began to show his disciples that he must go to Jerusalem and suffer many things from the elders and chief priests and scribes, and be killed, and on the third day be raised. And Peter took him and began to rebuke him, saying, "God forbid, Lord! This shall never happen to you." But he turned and said

μου, σατανᾶ· σκάνδαλόν μου εἶ, ὅτι οὐ φρονεῖς τὰ τοῦ Θεοῦ, ἀλλὰ τὰ τῶν ἀνθρώπων.

ΜΑΡΚΟΣ. Καὶ προσέφερον αὐτῷ παιδία, ἵνα αὐτῶν ἅψηται. Οἱ δὲ μαθηταὶ ἐπετίμων τοῖς προσφέρουσιν. Ἰδὼν δὲ ὁ Ἰησοῦς, ἠγανάκτησε, καὶ εἶπεν αὐτοῖς· ἄφετε τὰ παιδία ἔρχεσθαι πρός με, καὶ μὴ κωλύετε αὐτά· τῶν γὰρ τοιούτων ἐστὶν ἡ βασιλεία τῶν οὐρανῶν.

ΠΡΑΞΕΙΣ. Ἐπιμενόντων δὲ ἡμέρας πλείους, κατῆλθέ τις ἀπὸ τῆς Ἰουδαίας προφήτης ὀνόματι Ἄγαβος. Καὶ ἐλθὼν πρὸς ἡμᾶς, καὶ ἄρας τὴν ζώνην Παύλου, καὶ δήσας ἑαυτοῦ τοὺς πόδας καὶ τὰς χεῖρας, εἶπε· τάδε λέγει τὸ Πνεῦμα τὸ ἅγιον· τὸν ἄνδρα, οὗ ἐστιν ἡ ζώνη αὕτη, οὕτω δήσουσιν ἐν Ἱερουσαλὴμ οἱ Ἰουδαῖοι, καὶ παραδώσουσιν εἰς χεῖρας ἐθνῶν. Ὡς δὲ ἠκούσαμεν ταῦτα, παρεκαλοῦμεν ἡμεῖς τε καὶ οἱ ἐντόπιοι, τοῦ μὴ ἀναβαίνειν εἰς Ἱερουσαλήμ. Ἀπεκρίθη δὲ ὁ Παῦλος· τί ποιεῖτε κλαίοντες, καὶ συνθρύπτοντές μου τὴν καρδίαν; Ἐγὼ γὰρ οὐ μόνον δεθῆναι, ἀλλὰ καὶ ἀποθανεῖν ἑτοίμως ἔχω ὑπὲρ τοῦ ὀνόματος τοῦ Κυρίου Ἰησοῦ. Μὴ πειθομένου δὲ αὐτοῦ, ἡσυχάσαμεν εἰπόντες· τὸ θέλημα τοῦ Κυρίου γενέσθω.

ΠΡΟΣ ΘΕΣΣ. α΄. Τῶν καὶ τὸν Κύριον ἀποκτεινάντων Ἰησοῦν, καὶ τοὺς ἰδίους προφήτας, καὶ ἡμᾶς ἐκδιωξάντων, καὶ Θεῷ μὴ ἀρεσκόντων, καὶ πᾶσιν ἀνθρώποις ἐναντίων, κωλυόντων ἡμᾶς τοῖς ἔθνεσι λαλῆσαι, ἵνα σωθῶσιν, εἰς τὸ ἀναπληρῶσαι αὐτῶν τὰς ἁμαρτίας πάντοτε· ἔφθασε δὲ ἐπ᾽ αὐτοὺς ἡ ὀργὴ εἰς τέλος.

[19.2] Ὅτι τὸν ποιοῦντα ἐντολὴν Θεοῦ μὴ ἐκ διαθέσεως ὑγιοῦς, κατά γε μὴν τὸ φαινόμενον σώζοντα τὴν ἀκρίβειαν τῆς τοῦ Κυρίου διδασκαλίας, κωλύειν μὲν οὐ χρὴ διὰ τὸ ὅσον ἐπὶ τῷ πράγματι μηδένα βλάπτεσθαι, ἐνίοτε δὲ καὶ ὠφελεῖσθαί τινας ἐξ αὐτοῦ· παραινεῖν δὲ αὐτῷ ἀξίαν τοῦ κατορθώματος ἔχειν τὴν διάνοιαν.

Κεφάλ. β΄.

ΜΑΤΘΑΙΟΣ. Ὅταν οὖν ποιῇς ἐλεημοσύνην, [352] μὴ σαλπίσῃς ἔμπροσθέν σου, ὥσπερ οἱ ὑποκριταὶ ποιοῦσιν ἐν ταῖς συναγωγαῖς, καὶ ἐν ταῖς ῥύμαις, ὅπως δοξασθῶσιν ὑπὸ τῶν ἀνθρώπων. Ἀμὴν λέγω ὑμῖν, ἀπέχουσι τὸν μισθὸν αὐτῶν. Σοῦ δὲ ποιοῦντος ἐλεημοσύνην, μὴ γνώτω ἡ ἀριστερά σου τί ποιεῖ ἡ δεξιά σου· ὅπως ᾖ σου ἡ ἐλεημοσύνη

to Peter, "Get behind me, Satan! You are a *scandal* to me; for you are not on the side of God, but of men" (16.21–23).

MARK: And they were bringing children to him that he might touch them; and the disciples rebuked *those who brought* them. But when Jesus saw it he was indignant and said to them, "Let the children come to me, *and* do not hinder them; for to such belongs the kingdom of *heaven*" (10.13–14).

ACTS: While we were staying for some days, a prophet named Agabus came down from Judea. And coming to us he took Paul's girdle and bound his own feet and hands and said, "Thus says the Holy Spirit, 'So shall the Jews at Jerusalem bind the man who owns this girdle and deliver him into the hands of the Gentiles.'" When we heard this, we and the people there begged him not to go up to Jerusalem. *Paul* answered, "What are you doing, weeping and breaking my heart? For I am ready not only to be imprisoned but even to die at Jerusalem for the name of the Lord Jesus." And when he would not be persuaded, we ceased and said, "The will of the Lord be done" (21.10–14).

1 THESSALONIANS: *They* killed both the Lord Jesus and *his* prophets, and drove us out, and displease God and oppose all men by hindering us from speaking to the Gentiles that they may be saved—so as always to fill up the measure of their sins. But *wrath* has come upon them at last (2.15–16).

19.2 That the one who fulfills the command of God from an unwholesome disposition, yet to all appearances preserves the strictness of the Lord's teaching, must not be hindered since no one is harmed by him and at times some are even benefited; but exhort him to make his mind worthy of his virtuous deeds.

MATTHEW: Thus when you give alms sound no trumpet before you as the hypocrites do in the synagogues and in the streets that they may be praised by men. Truly I say to you, they have received their reward. But when you give alms do not let your left hand know what your right hand is doing, so that your alms may be in

ἐν τῷ κρυπτῷ· καὶ ὁ Πατήρ σου, ὁ βλέπων ἐν τῷ κρυπτῷ, ἀποδώσει σοι αὐτὸς ἐν τῷ φανερῷ. Καὶ περὶ προσευχῆς ὁμοίως.

ΜΑΡΚΟΣ. Ἀπεκρίθη δὲ αὐτῷ ὁ Ἰωάννης λέγων, διδάσκαλε, εἴδομέν τινα ἐν τῷ ὀνόματί σου ἐκβάλλοντα δαιμόνια, ὃς οὐκ ἀκολουθεῖ μεθ᾽ ἡμῶν, καὶ ἐκωλύσαμεν, ὅτι οὐκ ἀκολουθεῖ ἡμῖν. Ὁ δὲ Ἰησοῦς εἶπε· μὴ κωλύετε αὐτόν· οὐδεὶς γάρ ἐστιν, ὃς ποιήσει δύναμιν ἐπὶ τῷ ὀνόματί μου, καὶ δυνήσεται ταχὺ κακολογῆσαί με. Ὃς γὰρ οὐκ ἔστι καθ᾽ ἡμῶν, ὑπὲρ ἡμῶν ἐστιν.

ΠΡΟΣ ΦΙΛΙΠ. Τινὲς μὲν καὶ διὰ φθόνον καὶ ἔριν, τινὲς δὲ καὶ δι᾽ εὐδοκίαν τὸν Χριστὸν κηρύσσουσιν. Οἱ μὲν ἐξ ἀγάπης, εἰδότες, ὅτι εἰς ἀπολογίαν τοῦ εὐαγγελίου κεῖμαι· οἱ δὲ ἐξ ἐριθείας Χριστὸν καταγγέλλουσιν, οὐχ ἁγνῶς, οἰόμενοι θλίψιν ἐπιφέρειν τοῖς δεσμοῖς μου; Τί γάρ; Πλὴν παντὶ τρόπῳ, εἴτε προφάσει, εἴτε ἀληθείᾳ, Χριστὸς καταγγέλλεται, καὶ ἐν τούτῳ χαίρω, ἀλλὰ καὶ χαρήσομαι.

ΟΡΟΣ Κ´.

[20.1]　Ὅτι δεῖ τοὺς πιστεύοντας τῷ Κυρίῳ βαπτίζεσθαι εἰς τὸ ὄνομα τοῦ Πατρὸς, καὶ τοῦ Υἱοῦ, καὶ τοῦ ἁγίου Πνεύματος.

Κεφάλ. α´.

ΜΑΤΘΑΙΟΣ. Πορευθέντες, μαθητεύσατε πάντα τὰ ἔθνη, βαπτίζοντες αὐτοὺς εἰς τὸ ὄνομα τοῦ Πατρὸς, καὶ τοῦ Υἱοῦ, καὶ τοῦ ἁγίου Πνεύματος.

ΙΩΑΝΝΗΣ. Ἀμὴν ἀμὴν λέγω σοι, ἐὰν μή τις γεννηθῇ ἄνωθεν, οὐ δύναται ἰδεῖν τὴν βασιλείαν τοῦ Θεοῦ. Καὶ πάλιν· Ἀμὴν ἀμὴν λέγω σοι· ἐὰν μή τις γεννηθῇ ἐξ ὕδατος καὶ Πνεύματος, οὐ δύναται εἰσελθεῖν εἰς τὴν βασιλείαν τοῦ Θεοῦ. [353]

[20.2]　Τίς ὁ λόγος ἢ ἡ δύναμις τοῦ βαπτίσματος; Τὸ ἀλλοιωθῆναι τὸν βαπτιζόμενον κατά τε νοῦν, καὶ λόγον, καὶ πρᾶξιν, καὶ γενέσθαι ἐκεῖνο κατὰ τὴν δοθεῖσαν δύναμιν, ὅπερ ἐστὶ τὸ ἐξ οὗ ἐγεννήθη.

Κεφάλ. β´.

ΙΩΑΝΝΗΣ. Τὸ γεγεννημένον ἐκ τῆς σαρκὸς, σάρξ ἐστι, καὶ τὸ γεγεννημένον ἐκ τοῦ πνεύματος, πνεῦμά ἐστι. Μὴ θαυμάσῃς, ὅτι εἶπόν σοι· δεῖ ὑμᾶς γεννηθῆναι ἄνωθεν. Τὸ πνεῦμα ὅπου θέλει πνεῖ,

secret, and your Father who sees in secret will reward you *openly* (6.2–4).

MARK: John *answered* him, "Teacher, we saw a man casting out demons in your name *who was not following with us,* and we forbade him because he was not following us." But Jesus said, "Do not forbid him, for no one who does a mighty work in my name will be able soon after to speak evil of me. For he that is not against us is for us" (9.38–40).

PHILIPPIANS: Some indeed preach Christ from envy and rivalry, but others from good will. The latter do it out of love, knowing that I am put here for the defense of the gospel; the former proclaim Christ out of partisanship, not sincerely but thinking to afflict me in my imprisonment. What then? *Only* in every way, whether in pretense or in truth, Christ is proclaimed; and in that I rejoice, yes, and I shall rejoice (1.15–18).

20.1 That it is necessary for those who believe in the Lord to be baptized in the name of the Father and of the Son and of the Holy Spirit.

MATTHEW: Go therefore and make disciples of all nations, baptizing them in the name of the Father and of the Son and of the Holy Spirit (28.19).

JOHN: Truly, truly I say to you, unless one is born anew, he cannot see the kingdom of God (3.3). *And again*: Truly, truly I say to you, unless one is born of water and the Spirit, he cannot enter the kingdom of God (3.5).

20.2 What is the reason for or the power of Baptism? The one baptized is changed according to mind and reason and activity and becomes, by the power given, that very thing from which he was born.

JOHN: That which is born of the flesh is flesh, and that which is born of the Spirit is spirit. Do not marvel that I said to you, "You must be born anew." The wind blows where it wills, and you hear the

καὶ τῆς φωνῆς αὐτοῦ ἀκούεις· ἀλλ' οὐκ οἶδας πόθεν ἔρχεται, καὶ ποῦ ὑπάγει. Οὕτως ἐστὶ πᾶς ὁ γεγεννημένος ἐκ τοῦ πνεύματος.

ΠΡΟΣ ΡΩΜ. Τὸ νεκρωθῆναι μὲν τῇ ἁμαρτίᾳ, ζῆσαι δὲ τῷ Θεῷ ἐν Χριστῷ Ἰησοῦ. Ὅσοι ἐβαπτίσθημεν εἰς Χριστὸν Ἰησοῦν, εἰς τὸν θάνατον αὐτοῦ ἐβαπτίσθημεν. Συνετάφημεν οὖν αὐτῷ διὰ τοῦ βαπτίσματος εἰς τὸν θάνατον· ἵνα ὥσπερ ἠγέρθη Χριστὸς ἐκ νεκρῶν διὰ τῆς δόξης τοῦ Πατρὸς, οὕτω καὶ ἡμεῖς ἐν καινότητι ζωῆς περιπατήσωμεν. Εἰ γὰρ σύμφυτοι γεγόναμεν τῷ ὁμοιώματι τοῦ θανάτου αὐτοῦ, ἀλλὰ καὶ τῆς ἀναστάσεως ἐσόμεθα· τοῦτο γινώσκοντες, ὅτι ὁ παλαιὸς ἡμῶν ἄνθρωπος συνεσταυρώθη, ἵνα καταργηθῇ τὸ σῶμα τῆς ἁμαρτίας, τοῦ μηκέτι δουλεύειν ἡμᾶς τῇ ἁμαρτίᾳ. Ὁ γὰρ ἀποθανὼν δεδικαίωται ἀπὸ τῆς ἁμαρτίας.

ΠΡΟΣ ΚΟΛ. Ἐν ᾧ καὶ περιετμήθητε περιτομῇ ἀχειροποιήτῳ, ἐν τῇ ἀπεκδύσει τοῦ σώματος τῶν ἁμαρτιῶν τῆς σαρκὸς, ἐν τῇ περιτομῇ τοῦ Χριστοῦ, συνταφέντες αὐτῷ ἐν τῷ βαπτίσματι, ἐν ᾧ καὶ συνηγέρθητε διὰ τῆς πίστεως τῆς ἐνεργείας τοῦ Θεοῦ, τοῦ ἐγείροντος αὐτὸν ἐκ νεκρῶν.

ΠΡΟΣ ΓΑΛ. Ὅσοι γὰρ εἰς Χριστὸν ἐβαπτίσθητε, Χριστὸν ἐνεδύσασθε. Οὐκ ἔνι Ἰουδαῖος, οὐδὲ Ἕλλην· οὐκ [354] ἔνι δοῦλος, οὐδὲ ἐλεύθερος· οὐκ ἔνι ἄρσεν καὶ θῆλυ· πάντες γὰρ ὑμεῖς ἕν ἐστε ἐν Χριστῷ Ἰησοῦ.

ΠΡΟΣ ΚΟΛ. Ἀπεκδυσάμενοι τὸν παλαιὸν ἄνθρωπον σὺν ταῖς πράξεσιν αὐτοῦ, καὶ ἐνδυσάμενοι τὸν νέον τὸν ἀνακαινούμενον εἰς ἐπίγνωσιν κατ' εἰκόνα τοῦ κτίσαντος αὐτόν· ὅπου οὐκ ἔνι Ἕλλην καὶ Ἰουδαῖος, περιτομὴ καὶ ἀκροβυστία, βάρβαρος, Σκύθης, δοῦλος, ἐλεύθερος, ἀλλὰ τὰ πάντα, καὶ ἐν πᾶσι Χριστός.

ΟΡΟΣ ΚΑ΄.

[21.1]   Ὅτι ἀναγκαία καὶ πρὸς αὐτὴν τὴν αἰώνιον ζωὴν ἡ μετάληψις τοῦ σώματος καὶ αἵματος τοῦ Χριστοῦ.

Κεφάλ. α΄.

ΙΩΑΝΝΗΣ. Ἀμὴν ἀμὴν λέγω ὑμῖν· ἐὰν μὴ φάγητε τὴν σάρκα τοῦ Υἱοῦ τοῦ ἀνθρώπου, καὶ πίητε αὐτοῦ τὸ ἆμα, οὐκ ἔχετε ζωὴν ἐν ἑαυτοῖς. Ὁ τρώγων μου τὴν σάρκα καὶ πίνων μου τὸ ἆμα, ἔχει ζωὴν αἰώνιον, καὶ τὰ ἑξῆς.

sound of it, but you do not know whence it comes or whither it goes; so it is with everyone who is born of the Spirit (3.6–8).

ROMANS: *To have died to sin, but to live to God in Christ Jesus* (6.11). Do you not know that all of us who have been baptized into Christ Jesus were baptized into his death? We were buried, therefore, with him by baptism into death, so that as Christ was raised from the dead by the glory of the Father, we too might walk in newness of life. For if we have been united with him in a death like his, we shall certainly be united with him in a resurrection like his. We know that our old humanity was crucified with him so that the *body of sin* might be destroyed, and we might no longer be enslaved to sin. For he who has died is freed from sin (6.3–7).

COLOSSIANS: In him also you were circumcised with a circumcision made without hands, by putting off the body *of the sins* of the flesh in the circumcision of Christ, and you were buried with him in baptism, in which you were also raised with him through faith in the working of God, who raised him from the dead (2.11–12).

GALATIANS: For as many of you as were baptized into Christ have put on Christ. There is neither Jew nor Greek, there is neither slave nor free, there is neither male nor female; for you are all one in Christ Jesus (3.27–28).

COLOSSIANS: Seeing that you have put off the old *humanity* with its practices and have put on the new *humanity*, which is being renewed in knowledge after the image of its creator. Here there cannot be Greek and Jew, circumcised and uncircumcised, barbarian, Scythian, slave, *free*, but Christ is all and in all (3.9–11).

21.1   That necessary also for eternal life is partaking of the body and blood of Christ.

JOHN: Truly, truly I say to you, unless you eat the flesh of the Son of man and drink his blood, you have no life in you; he who eats my flesh and drinks my blood has eternal life (6.53–54), *and what follows.*

[21.2] Ὅτι οὐδὲν ὠφελεῖται ὁ ἄνευ τῆς κατανοήσεως τοῦ λόγου, καθ᾿ ὃν δίδοται ἡ μετάληψις τοῦ σώματος καὶ τοῦ αἵματος τοῦ Χριστοῦ, προσερχόμενος τῇ κοινωνίᾳ· ὁ δὲ ἀναξίως μεταλαμβάνων, κατακέκριται.

Κεφάλ. β΄.

ΙΩΑΝΝΗΣ. Ἀμὴν ἀμὴν λέγω ὑμῖν, ἐὰν μὴ φάγητε τὴν σάρκα τοῦ Υἱοῦ τοῦ ἀνθρώπου, καὶ πίητε αὐτοῦ τὸ αἷμα, οὐκ ἔχετε ζωὴν ἐν ἑαυτοῖς. Καὶ μετ᾿ ὀλίγα· Εἰδὼς δὲ ὁ Ἰησοῦς ἐν ἑαυτῷ, ὅτι γογγύζουσι περὶ τούτου οἱ μαθηταὶ αὐτοῦ, εἶπεν αὐτοῖς· τοῦτο ὑμᾶς σκανδαλίζει; Ἐὰν οὖν θεωρῆτε τὸν Υἱὸν τοῦ ἀνθρώπου ἀναβαίνοντα ὅπου ἦν τὸ πρότερον; Ἡ σὰρξ οὐκ ὠφελεῖ οὐδέν, τὸ πνεῦμά ἐστι τὸ ζωοποιοῦν. Τὰ ῥήματα ἃ ἐγὼ λελάληκα ὑμῖν, πνεῦμά ἐστι, καὶ ζωή ἐστι.

ΠΡΟΣ ΚΟΡ. α΄. Ὥστε ὃς ἂν ἐσθίῃ τὸν ἄρτον τοῦτον, ἢ πίνῃ τὸ ποτήριον τοῦτο τοῦ Κυρίου ἀναξίως, ἔνοχος ἔσται τοῦ σώματος [355] καὶ τοῦ αἵματος τοῦ Κυρίου. Δοκιμαζέτω δὲ ἄνθρωπος ἑαυτόν, καὶ οὕτως ἐκ τοῦ ἄρτου ἐσθιέτω, καὶ ἐκ τοῦ ποτηρίου πινέτω. Ὁ γὰρ ἐσθίων καὶ πίνων ἀναξίως, κρῖμα ἑαυτῷ ἐσθίει καὶ πίνει, μὴ διακρίνων τὸ σῶμα τοῦ Κυρίου.

[21.3] Ποίῳ λόγῳ δεῖ ἐσθίειν τὸ σῶμα, καὶ πίνειν τὸ ἅμα τοῦ Κυρίου, εἰς ἀνάμνησιν τῆς τοῦ Κυρίου μέχρι θανάτου ὑπακοῆς, ἵνα οἱ ζῶντες μηκέτι ἑαυτοῖς ζῶσιν, ἀλλὰ τῷ ὑπὲρ αὐτῶν ἀποθανόντι καὶ ἐγερθέντι.

Κεφάλ. γ΄.

ΛΟΥΚΑΣ. Καὶ λαβὼν ἄρτον, εὐχαριστήσας ἔκλασε, καὶ ἔδωκεν αὐτοῖς λέγων· τοῦτό ἐστι τὸ σῶμά μου, τὸ ὑπὲρ ὑμῶν διδόμενον· τοῦτο ποιεῖτε εἰς τὴν ἐμὴν ἀνάμνησιν. Ὡσαύτως καὶ τὸ ποτήριον, μετὰ τὸ δειπνῆσαι, λέγων· τοῦτο τὸ ποτήριον ἡ καινὴ διαθήκη ἐστὶν ἐν τῷ αἵματί μου, τῷ ὑπὲρ ὑμῶν ἐκχυνομένῳ.

ΠΡΟΣ ΚΟΡ. α΄. Ὅτι ὁ Κύριος Ἰησοῦς ἐν τῇ νυκτί, ᾗ παρεδίδοτο, ἔλαβεν ἄρτον, καὶ εὐχαριστήσας, ἔκλασε, καὶ εἶπε· λάβετε, φάγετε· τοῦτό μου ἐστὶ τὸ σῶμα, τὸ ὑπὲρ ὑμῶν κλώμενον· τοῦτο ποιεῖτε εἰς τὴν ἐμὴν ἀνάμνησιν. Ὡσαύτως καὶ τὸ ποτήριον, μετὰ τὸ δειπνῆσαι, λέγων· Τοῦτο τὸ ποτήριον ἡ καινὴ διαθήκη ἐστὶν ἐν τῷ ἐμῷ αἵματι.

21.2 That the one who comes to communion without consideration for the reason why the participation of the flesh and blood of Christ is given is in no way benefited, rather the one receiving unworthily is condemned.

JOHN: Truly, truly I say to you, unless you eat the flesh of the Son of man and drink his blood, you have no life in you (6.53). *And a little further:* But Jesus, knowing in himself that his disciples murmured at it, said to them, "*Does this scandalize you?* Then what if you were to see the Son of man ascending where he was before? *The flesh is of no avail; it is the spirit that gives life.* The words that I have spoken to you are spirit and life" (6.61–63).

1 CORINTHIANS: Whoever, therefore, eats *this* bread or drinks *this* cup of the Lord in an unworthy manner will be guilty of profaning the body and blood of the Lord. Let a man examine himself and so eat of the bread and drink of the cup. For anyone who eats and drinks *unworthily*, without discerning the body *of the Lord*, eats and drinks judgment upon himself (11.27–29).

21.3 With what understanding is it necessary to eat the body and to drink the blood of the Lord? Unto remembrance of the Lord's obedience until death: so that the living no longer live for themselves but for the one who died and was raised on their behalf.

LUKE: And he took bread, and when he had given thanks he broke it and gave it to them, saying, "This is my body which is given for you. Do this in remembrance of me." And likewise the cup, after supper, saying, "*This cup is the new covenant in my blood, which is poured out for you*" (22.19–20).

1 CORINTHIANS: That the Lord Jesus, on the night when he was betrayed, took bread, and when he had given thanks he broke it and said, "*Take, eat.* This is my body which is *broken* for you. Do this in remembrance of me." In the same way also the cup, after supper, saying, "This cup is the new covenant in my blood. Do this, as often

Τοῦτο ποιεῖτε, ὁσάκις ἂν πίνητε, εἰς τὴν ἐμὴν ἀνάμνησιν. Ὁσάκις γὰρ ἂν ἐσθίητε τὸν ἄρτον τοῦτον, καὶ τὸ ποτήριον τοῦτο πίνητε, τὸν θάνατον τοῦ Κυρίου καταγγέλλετε ἄχρις οὗ ἂν ἔλθῃ.

ΠΡΟΣ ΚΟΡ. β'. Ἡ γὰρ ἀγάπη τοῦ Χριστοῦ συνέχει ἡμᾶς, κρίναντας τοῦτο, ὅτι, εἰ εἷς ὑπὲρ πάντων ἀπέθανεν, ἄρα οἱ πάντες ἀπέθανον· καὶ ὑπὲρ πάντων ἀπέθανεν, ἵνα οἱ ζῶντες μηκέτι ἑαυτοῖς ζῶσιν, ἀλλὰ τῷ ὑπὲρ αὐτῶν ἀποθανόντι, καὶ ἐγερθέντι, εἰς τὸ γενέσθαι τοὺς πολλοὺς ἓν σῶμα ἐν Χριστῷ.

ΠΡΟΣ ΚΟΡ. α'. Ὁ ἄρτος ὃν κλῶμεν οὐχὶ κοινωνία τοῦ σώματος τοῦ Χριστοῦ ἐστιν; ὅτι εἷς ἄρτος, ἓν σῶμα οἱ πολλοί ἐσμεν. Οἱ γὰρ πάντες ἐκ τοῦ ἑνὸς ἄρτου μετέχομεν. [356]

[21.4] Ὅτι δεῖ τὸν μεταλαμβάνοντα τῶν ἁγίων ὑμνεῖν τὸν Κύριον.

Κεφάλ. δ'.

ΜΑΤΘΑΙΟΣ. Ἐσθιόντων δὲ αὐτῶν, λαβὼν ὁ Ἰησοῦς τὸν ἄρτον, καὶ εὐχαριστήσας ἔκλασε, καὶ ἐδίδου τοῖς μαθηταῖς, καὶ τὰ ἑξῆς. Οἷς ἐπιφέρει· Καὶ ὑμνήσαντες, ἐξῆλθον εἰς τὸ ὄρος τῶν ἐλαιῶν.

ΟΡΟΣ ΚΒ'.

[22.1] Ὅτι ἡ ἐργασία τῆς ἁμαρτίας ἀπαλλοτριοῖ τοῦ Κυρίου, καὶ προσοικειοῖ τῷ διαβόλῳ.

Κεφάλ. α'.

ΙΩΑΝΝΗΣ. Ἀμὴν ἀμὴν λέγω ὑμῖν, ὅτι πᾶς ὁ ποιῶν τὴν ἁμαρτίαν, δοῦλός ἐστι τῆς ἁμαρτίας. Ὑμεῖς ἐκ τοῦ Πατρὸς τοῦ διαβόλου ἐστὲ, καὶ τὰς ἐπιθυμίας τοῦ Πατρὸς ὑμῶν θέλετε ποιεῖν.

ΠΡΟΣ ΡΩΜ. Ὅτε γὰρ δοῦλοι ἦτε τῆς ἁμαρτίας, ἐλεύθεροι ἦτε τῇ δικαιοσύνῃ.

[22.2] Ὅτι ἡ πρὸς τὸν Κύριον οἰκειότης οὐκ ἐν τῇ κατὰ σάρκα συγγενείᾳ γνωρίζεται, ἀλλ' ἐν τῇ σπουδῇ τῶν θελημάτων τοῦ Θεοῦ κατορθοῦται.

Κεφάλ. β'.

ΙΩΑΝΝΗΣ. Ὁ ὢν ἐκ τοῦ Θεοῦ, τὰ ῥήματα τοῦ Θεοῦ ἀκούει.

ΛΟΥΚΑΣ. Καὶ ἀπηγγέλη αὐτῷ, λεγόντων· ἡ μήτηρ σου καὶ οἱ ἀδελφοί σου ἑστήκασιν ἔξω, ἰδεῖν σε θέλοντες. Ὁ δὲ ἀποκριθεὶς

as you drink it, in remembrance of me." For as often as you eat this bread and drink *this* cup, you proclaim the Lord's death until he comes (11.23–26).

2 CORINTHIANS: For the love of Christ controls us, because we are convinced that one has died for all; therefore all have died. And he died for all, that those who live might live no longer for themselves but for him who for their sake died and was raised, in order for many to become one body in Christ (5.14–15).

1 CORINTHIANS: The bread which we break, is it not a participation in the body of Christ? Because there is one bread we who are many are one body, for we all partake of the one bread (10.16–17).

21.4 That it is necessary for the one who receives the holy things to praise the Lord.

MATTHEW: Now as they were eating, Jesus took *the* bread, and *gave thanks*, and broke it, and gave it to the disciples (26.26), *and what follows; to which it adds*: And when they had sung a hymn, they went out to the Mount of Olives (26.30).

22.1 That committing sins estranges one from the Lord and unites one with the devil.

JOHN: Truly, truly I say to you, everyone who commits sin is a slave to sin (8.34). You are of your father the devil, and your will is to do your father's desires (8.44).

ROMANS: When you were slaves of sin, you were free in regard to righteousness (6.20).

22.2 That relation to the Lord is not known in kinship according to the flesh, but in zeal for the will of God is it established.

JOHN: He who is of God hears the words of God (8.47).

LUKE: And he was told, "Your mother and your brothers are standing outside desiring to see you." But he said to them, "My

εἶπεν αὐτοῖς· μήτηρ μου καὶ ἀδελφοί μου οὗτοί εἰσιν οἱ τὸν λόγον τοῦ Θεοῦ ἀκούοντες καὶ ποιοῦντες.

ΙΩΑΝΝΗΣ. Ὑμεῖς φίλοι μου ἐστέ, ἐὰν ποιῆτε ὅσα ἐγὼ ἐντέλλομαι ὑμῖν.

ΠΡΟΣ ΡΩΜ. Ὅσοι γὰρ Πνεύματι Θεοῦ ἄγονται, οὗτοι υἱοὶ Θεοῦ εἰσιν. [357]

ΟΡΟΣ ΚΓ΄.

[23.1]   Ὅτι ὁ ἄκων ἑλκόμενος ὑπὸ ἁμαρτίας ὀφείλει γνωρίζειν ἑαυτὸν ὑφ' ἑτέρας προενυπαρχούσης κρατούμενον ἁμαρτίας, ᾗ ἑκὼν δουλεύων, ἄγεται λοιπὸν ὑπ' αὐτῇ καὶ ἐφ' ἃ μὴ θέλει.

Κεφάλ. α΄.

ΠΡΟΣ ΡΩΜ. Οἴδαμεν δὲ ὅτι ὁ νόμος πνευματικός ἐστιν, ἐγὼ δὲ σαρκικός εἰμι, πεπραμένος ὑπὸ τὴν ἁμαρτίαν. Ὃ γὰρ κατεργάζομαι, οὐ γινώσκω. Οὐ γὰρ ὃ θέλω, τοῦτο πράσσω· ἀλλ' ὃ μισῶ, τοῦτο ποιῶ. Εἰ δὲ ὃ οὐ θέλω, τοῦτο ποιῶ, σύμφημι τῷ νόμῳ, ὅτι καλός. Νυνὶ δὲ οὐκέτι ἐγὼ κατεργάζομαι αὐτὸ, ἀλλ' ἡ οἰκοῦσα ἐν ἐμοὶ ἁμαρτία. Οἶδα δὲ ὅτι οὐκ οἰκεῖ ἐν ἐμοὶ, τουτέστιν, ἐν τῇ σαρκί μου, ἀγαθόν· τὸ γὰρ θέλειν παράκειταί μοι, τὸ δὲ κατεργάζεσθαι τὸ καλὸν, οὐχ εὑρίσκω. Οὐ γὰρ ὃ θέλω, ποιῶ ἀγαθὸν, ἀλλ' ὃ οὐ θέλω κακὸν, τοῦτο πράσσω. Εἰ δὲ ὃ οὐ θέλω ἐγὼ, τοῦτο ποιῶ, οὐκέτι ἐγὼ κατεργάζομαι αὐτὸ, ἀλλ' ἡ οἰκοῦσα ἐν ἐμοὶ ἁμαρτία.

ΟΡΟΣ ΚΔ΄.

[24.1]   Ὅτι οὐ δεῖ ψεύδεσθαι, ἀλλ' ἀληθεύειν ἐν παντί.

Κεφάλ. α΄.

ΜΑΤΘΑΙΟΣ. Ἔστω δὲ ὁ λόγος ὑμῶν, ναὶ, ναί· οὔ, οὔ· τὸ δὲ περισσὸν τούτων ἐκ τοῦ πονηροῦ ἐστιν.

ΠΡΟΣ ΕΦΕΣ. Ἀποθέμενοι τὸ ψεῦδος, λαλεῖτε ἀλήθειαν ἕκαστος μετὰ τοῦ πλησίον αὐτοῦ.

ΠΡΟΣ ΚΟΛ. Μὴ ψεύδεσθε εἰς ἀλλήλους.

ΟΡΟΣ ΚΕ΄.

[25.1]   Ὅτι οὐ δεῖ ζητήσεις ἀνωφελεῖς ἢ ἐμφιλονείκους ποιεῖσθαι.

Κεφάλ. α΄.

ΠΡΟΣ ΤΙΜ. β΄. Ταῦτα ὑπομίμνησκε διαμαρτυρόμενος [358] ἐνώπιον τοῦ Κυρίου· μὴ λογομαχεῖν εἰς οὐδὲν χρήσιμον, ἐπὶ καταστροφῇ

mother and my brothers are those who hear the word of God and do it" (8.20–21).

JOHN: You are my friends if you do *all that* I command you (15.14).

ROMANS: For all who are led by the Spirit of God are sons of God (8.14).

23.1   That the one drawn into sin unwillingly ought to know that he is mastered by another sin already, which he serves willingly, and by the power of which he is led to the rest even against his will.

ROMANS: We know that the law is spiritual, but I am carnal, sold under sin. I do not understand my own actions. For I do not do what I want, but I do the very thing I hate. Now if I do what I do not want, I agree that the law is good. So then it is no longer I that do it but sin which dwells within me. For I know that nothing good dwells within me, that is, in my flesh. I can will what is right, but I cannot do it. For I do not do the good I want, but the evil I do not want is what I do. Now if I do what I do not want, it is no longer I that do it but sin, which dwells within me (7.14–20).

24.1   That it is necessary not to lie but always to speak the truth.

MATTHEW: Let what you say be simply "Yes" or "No"; anything more than this comes from evil (5.37).

EPHESIANS: *Putting* away falsehood, let everyone speak the truth with his neighbor (4.25).

COLOSSIANS: Do not lie to one another (3.9).

25.1   That it is necessary not to make useless or contentious inquiries.

2 TIMOTHY: Remind them of this and charge them before the Lord to avoid disputing about words, which does no good, but only

τῶν ἀκουόντων. Τὰς δὲ μωρὰς καὶ ἀπαιδεύτους ζητήσεις παραιτοῦ, εἰδὼς, ὅτι γεννῶσι μάχας.

[25.2] Ὅτι οὐ δεῖ φθέγγεσθαι λόγον ἀργὸν, ἐξ οὗ οὐδὲν ὄφελος. Τὸ γὰρ μὴ πρὸς οἰκοδομὴν τῆς πίστεως λαλεῖν, ἢ καὶ ποιεῖν αὐτὸ τὸ ἀγαθὸν, λυπεῖν ἐστι τὸ Πνεῦμα τὸ ἅγιον τοῦ Θεοῦ.
Κεφάλ. β′.
ΜΑΤΘΑΙΟΣ. Λέγω δὲ ὑμῖν, ὅτι πᾶν ῥῆμα ἀργὸν ὃ ἐὰν λαλήσωσιν οἱ ἄνθρωποι, ἀποδώσουσι περὶ αὐτοῦ λόγον ἐν ἡμέρᾳ κρίσεως.
ΠΡΟΣ ΕΦΕΣ. Πᾶς λόγος σαπρὸς ἐκ τοῦ στόματος ὑμῶν μὴ ἐκπορευέσθω· ἀλλ᾽ εἴ τις ἀγαθὸς πρὸς οἰκοδομὴν τῆς πίστεως, ἵνα δῷ χάριν τοῖς ἀκούουσι, καὶ μὴ λυπῆτε τὸ Πνεῦμα τὸ ἅγιον τοῦ Θεοῦ, ἐν ᾧ ἐσφραγίσθητε εἰς ἡμέραν ἀπολυτρώσεως.
ΟΡΟΣ Κς′.
[26.1] Ὅτι δεῖ πᾶν ῥῆμα ἢ πρᾶγμα πιστοῦσθαι τῇ μαρτυρίᾳ τῆς θεοπνεύστου Γραφῆς εἰς πληροφορίαν μὲν τῶν ἀγαθῶν, ἐντροπὴν δὲ τῶν πονηρῶν.
Κεφάλ. α′.
ΜΑΤΘΑΙΟΣ. Καὶ προσελθὼν αὐτῷ ὁ πειράζων εἶπεν· εἰ Υἱὸς εἶ τοῦ Θεοῦ, εἰπὲ, ἵνα οἱ λίθοι οὗτοι ἄρτοι γένωνται. Ὁ δὲ ἀποκριθεὶς εἶπε· γέγραπται, «Οὐκ ἐπ᾽ ἄρτῳ μόνῳ ζήσεται ἄνθρωπος, ἀλλ᾽ ἐπὶ παντὶ ῥήματι ἐκπορευομένῳ διὰ στόματος Θεοῦ.»
ΠΡΑΞΕΙΣ. Καὶ ἐπλήσθησαν ἅπαντες Πνεύματος ἁγίου, καὶ ἤρξαντο λαλεῖν ἑτέραις γλώσσαις, καθὼς τὸ Πνεῦμα ἐδίδου αὐτοῖς ἀποφθέγγεσθαι. Ἐξίσταντο δὲ πάντες, καὶ διηπόρουν, ἄλλος πρὸς ἄλλον λέγοντες· τί ἂν θέλοι εἶναι τοῦτο; Ἕτεροι δὲ χλευάζοντες ἔλεγον, ὅτι γλεύκους μεμεστωμένοι εἰσίν. Σταθεὶς δὲ ὁ Πέτρος σὺν τοῖς ἕνδεκα, ἐπῆρε τὴν φωνὴν αὐτοῦ, καὶ ἀπεφθέγξατο αὐτοῖς· ἄνδρες Ἰουδαῖοι, καὶ οἱ κατοικοῦντες Ἱερουσαλὴμ ἅπαντες, τοῦτο ὑμῖν γνωστὸν ἔστω, καὶ ἐνωτίσασθε τὰ ῥήματά μου. Οὐ γὰρ, ὡς ὑμεῖς ὑπολαμβάνετε, οὗτοι [359] μεθύουσιν· ἔστι γὰρ ὥρα τρίτη τῆς ἡμέρας, ἀλλὰ τοῦτό ἐστι τὸ εἰρημένον διὰ τοῦ προφήτου Ἰωήλ· «Καὶ ἔσται ἐν ταῖς ἐσχάταις ἡμέραις, λέγει ὁ Θεός, ἐκχεῶ ἀπὸ τοῦ Πνεύματός μου ἐπὶ πᾶσαν σάρκα, καὶ προφητεύσουσι·» καὶ τὰ

ruins the hearers (2.14). Have nothing to do with stupid, senseless controversies; you know that they breed quarrels (2.23).

25.2 That it is necessary not to utter an idle word from which there can be no benefit; for speaking things mean and unedifying of faith, let alone doing such, is to grieve the Holy Spirit of God.

MATTHEW: I tell you, on the day of judgment men will render account for every careless word they utter (12.36).

EPHESIANS: Let no evil talk come out of your mouths, but only such as is good for *the edification of faith*, that it may impart grace to those who hear. And do not grieve the Holy Spirit of God, in whom you were sealed for the day of redemption (4.29–30).

26.1 That it is necessary to confirm every word or matter with the testimony of the God-breathed Scripture, so that the good is established and the evil reproached.

MATTHEW: And the tempter *came to him and said*, "If you are the Son of God, command these stones to become loaves of bread." But he answered, "It is written, 'Man shall not live by bread alone, but by every word that proceeds from the mouth of God' "[14] (4.3–4).

ACTS: And they were all filled with the Holy Spirit and began to speak in other tongues as the Spirit gave them utterance (2.4). And all were amazed and perplexed, saying to one another, "What *might* this mean?" But others, mocking, said, "They are filled with new wine." But Peter, standing with the eleven, lifted up his voice and addressed them, "Men of Judea and all who dwell in Jerusalem, let this be known to you, and give ear to my words. For these men are not drunk as you suppose, since it is only the third hour of the day; but this is what was spoken by the prophet Joel: 'And in the last days it shall be, God declares, that I will pour out my Spirit upon all flesh, and they shall prophesy' "[15] (2.12–17), *and what follows*.

[14]Deut 8.3
[15]Joel 2.28

ἑξῆς.

[26.2] Ὅτι δεῖ καὶ τοῖς ἐν τῇ φύσει καὶ τῇ συνηθείᾳ τοῦ βίου γνωριζομένοις κεχρῆσθαι εἰς βεβαίωσιν τῶν γινομένων ἢ λεγομένων.
Κεφάλ. β'.
ΜΑΤΘΑΙΟΣ. Προσέχετε δὲ ἀπὸ τῶν ψευδοπροφητῶν, οἵτινες
ἔρχονται πρὸς ὑμᾶς ἐν ἐνδύμασι προβάτων, ἔσωθεν δέ εἰσι λύκοι
ἅρπαγες. Ἀπὸ τῶν καρπῶν αὐτῶν ἐπιγνώσεσθε αὐτούς. Μήτι
συλλέγουσιν ἀπὸ ἀκανθῶν σταφυλὴν, ἢ ἀπὸ τριβόλων σῦκα; Οὕτω
πᾶν δένδρον ἀγαθὸν καρποὺς καλοὺς ποιεῖ· τὸ δὲ σαπρὸν δένδρον
καρποὺς πονηροὺς ποιεῖ· καὶ τὰ ἑξῆς.
ΛΟΥΚΑΣ. Καὶ ἐγόγγυζον οἱ γραμματεῖς αὐτῶν, καὶ οἱ Φαρισαῖοι,
πρὸς τοὺς μαθητὰς αὐτοῦ λέγοντες· διὰ τί μετὰ τελωνῶν καὶ
ἁμαρτωλῶν ἐσθίετε καὶ πίνετε; Καὶ ἀποκριθεὶς ὁ Ἰησοῦς εἶπεν
αὐτοῖς· οὐ χρείαν ἔχουσιν οἱ ὑγιαίνοντες ἰατροῦ, ἀλλ᾽ οἱ κακῶς
ἔχοντες.
ΠΡΟΣ ΤΙΜ. β'. Οὐδεὶς στρατευόμενος ἐμπλέκεται ταῖς τοῦ βίου
πραγματείαις, ἵνα τῷ στρατολογήσαντι ἀρέσῃ. Ἐὰν δὲ καὶ ἀθλῇ τις,
οὐ στεφανοῦται, ἐὰν μὴ νομίμως ἀθλήσῃ.
ΟΡΟΣ ΚΖ'.
[27.1] Ὅτι οὐ δεῖ τοῖς ἀλλοτρίοις τῆς τοῦ Κυρίου διδασκαλίας
ἐξομοιοῦσθαι· μιμεῖσθαι δὲ τὸν Θεὸν καὶ τοὺς ἁγίους αὐτοῦ κατὰ
τὴν δοθεῖσαν ἡμῖν παρ᾽ αὐτοῦ δύναμιν.
Κεφάλ. α'.
ΜΑΤΘΑΙΟΣ. Οἴδατε, ὅτι οἱ ἄρχοντες τῶν ἐθνῶν [360] κατακυρι-
εύουσιν αὐτῶν, καὶ οἱ μεγάλοι κατεξουσιάζουσιν αὐτῶν. Οὐχ οὕτως
ἔσται ἐν ὑμῖν· ἀλλ᾽ ὃς ἐὰν θέλῃ ἐν ὑμῖν γενέσθαι πρῶτος, ἔσται
ὑμῶν διάκονος· καὶ ὃς ἐὰν θέλῃ ἐν ὑμῖν πρῶτος εἶναι, ἔσται ὑμῶν
δοῦλος· ὥσπερ ὁ Υἱὸς τοῦ ἀνθρώπου οὐκ ἦλθε διακονηθῆναι, ἀλλὰ
διακονῆσαι, καὶ δοῦναι τὴν ψυχὴν αὐτοῦ λύτρον ἀντὶ πολλῶν.
ΠΡΟΣ ΡΩΜ. Μὴ σχηματίζεσθε τῷ αἰῶνι τούτῳ, ἀλλὰ μεταμορ-
φοῦσθε τῇ ἀνακαινώσει τοῦ νοὸς ὑμῶν, εἰς τὸ δοκιμάζειν ὑμᾶς τί τὸ
θέλημα τοῦ Θεοῦ.
ΠΡΟΣ ΚΟΡ. α'. Μιμηταί μου γίνεσθε, καθὼς κἀγὼ Χριστοῦ.

26.2   That it is necessary also to use things known in nature and life experience for establishing matters or words.

MATTHEW: Beware of false prophets, who come to you in sheep's clothing but inwardly are ravenous wolves. You will know them by their fruits. Are grapes gathered from thorns or figs from thistles? So every sound tree bears good fruit, but the bad tree bears evil fruit (7.15–17), *and what follows.*

LUKE: And *their scribes and Pharisees* murmured against his disciples, saying, "Why do you eat and drink with tax collectors and sinners?" And Jesus answered them, "Those who are well have no need of a physician, but those who are sick" (5.30–31).

2 TIMOTHY: No soldier on service gets entangled in civilian pursuits, since his aim is to satisfy the one who enlisted him. An athlete is not crowned unless he competes according to the rules (2.4–5).

27.1   That it is necessary not to be like those estranged from the teaching of the Lord, but to mimic God and his saints as he has empowered us.

MATTHEW: You know that the rulers of the Gentiles lord it over them, and their great men exercise authority over them. It shall not be so among you; but whoever would be *first* among you must be your servant, and whoever would be first among you must be your slave, even as the Son of man came not to be served but to serve and to give his life as a ransom for many" (20.25–28).

ROMANS: Do not be conformed to this world, but be transformed by the renewal of your mind that you may prove what is the will of God (12.2).

1 CORINTHIANS: Be imitators of me as I am of Christ (11.1).

ΟΡΟΣ ΚΗ΄.

[28.1] Ὅτι οὐ δεῖ ἁπλῶς, οὐδὲ ἀνεξετάστως ὑπὸ τῶν ὑποκρινο-μένων τὴν ἀλήθειαν συναρπάζεσθαι· ἀπὸ δὲ τοῦ δεδομένου ἡμῖν παρὰ τῆς Γραφῆς χαρακτῆρος γνωρίζειν ἕκαστον.

Κεφάλ. α΄.

ΜΑΤΘΑΙΟΣ. Προσέχετε δὲ ἀπὸ τῶν ψευδοπροφητῶν, οἵτινες ἔρχονται πρὸς ὑμᾶς ἐν ἐνδύμασι προβάτων, ἔσωθεν δέ εἰσι λύκοι ἅρπαγες. Ἀπὸ τῶν καρπῶν αὐτῶν ἐπιγνώσεσθε αὐτούς.

ΙΩΑΝΝ. Ἐν τούτῳ γνώσονται πάντες, ὅτι ἐμοὶ μαθηταί ἐστε, ἐὰν ἀγάπην ἔχητε ἐν ἀλλήλοις.

ΠΡΟΣ ΚΟΡ. α΄. Διὸ γνωρίζω ὑμῖν, ὅτι οὐδεὶς ἐν Πνεύματι Θεοῦ λαλῶν, λέγει ἀνάθεμα Ἰησοῦν.

ΟΡΟΣ ΚΘ΄.

[29.1] Ὅτι δεῖ ἕκαστον διὰ τῶν οἰκείων ἔργων πιστοῦσθαι τὸ ἑαυτοῦ ἐπάγγελμα.

Κεφάλ. α΄.

ΙΩΑΝΝΗΣ. Αὐτὰ τὰ ἔργα, ἃ ἐγὼ ποιῶ, μαρτυρεῖ περὶ ἐμοῦ, ὅτι ὁ Πατήρ με ἀπέστειλεν. Εἰ οὐ ποιῶ τὰ ἔργα τοῦ Πατρός μου, μὴ πιστεύετέ μοι· εἰ δὲ ποιῶ, κἂν ἐμοὶ μὴ πιστεύητε, τοῖς ἔργοις [361] μου πιστεύσατε· ἵνα γνῶτε καὶ πιστεύσητε, ὅτι ἐν ἐμοὶ ὁ Πατὴρ, κἀγὼ ἐν αὐτῷ.

ΠΡΟΣ ΚΟΡ. β΄. Μηδεμίαν ἐν μηδενὶ διδόντες προσκοπὴν, ἵνα μὴ μωμηθῇ ἡ διακονία. Ἀλλ' ἐν παντὶ συνιστῶντες ἑαυτοὺς ὡς Θεοῦ διάκονοι, ἐν ὑπομονῇ πολλῇ, ἐν θλίψεσι· καὶ τὰ ἑξῆς.

ΟΡΟΣ Λ΄.

[30.1] Ὅτι οὐ δεῖ τὰ ἅγια τῇ ἐπιμιξίᾳ τῶν πρὸς τὴν κοινὴν χρείαν καθυβρίζειν.

Κεφάλ. α΄.

ΜΑΤΘΑΙΟΣ. Καὶ εἰσῆλθεν ὁ Ἰησοῦς εἰς τὸ ἱερὸν τοῦ Θεοῦ, καὶ ἐξέβαλε πάντας τοὺς πωλοῦντας καὶ ἀγοράζοντας ἐν τῷ ἱερῷ, καὶ τὰς τραπέζας τῶν κολλυβιστῶν κατέστρεψε, καὶ τὰς καθέδρας τῶν πωλούντων τὰς περιστεράς· καὶ λέγει αὐτοῖς· γέγραπται· «Ὁ οἶκός μου οἶκος προσευχῆς κληθήσεται·» ὑμεῖς δὲ ἐποιήσατε αὐτὸν «σπήλαιον ληστῶν.»

28.1   That it is necessary not to be carried away simply or gullibly by those playing at the truth, but to recognize each from the description given by Scripture.

MATTHEW: Beware of false prophets who come to you in sheep's clothing but inwardly are ravenous wolves. You will know them by their fruits (7.15–16).

JOHN: By this all men will know that you are my disciples, if you have love for one another (13.35).

1 CORINTHIANS: Therefore I want you to understand that no one speaking by the Spirit of God ever says, "Jesus be cursed!" (12.3).

29.1   That it is necessary for each to be confirmed in his confession by the appropriate works.

JOHN: These very works which I am doing bear me witness that the Father has sent me (5.36).

JOHN: If I am not doing the works of my Father then do not believe me, but if I do them, even though you do not believe me, believe *my* works, that you may know and *believe* that the Father is in me and I am in the Father (10.37–38).

2 CORINTHIANS: We put no obstacle in anyone's way, so that no fault may be found with our ministry, but as servants of God we commend ourselves in every way: through great endurance, in afflictions (6.3–4), *and what follows*.

30.1   That it is necessary not to disrespect the holy things by mingling them with things of common use.

MATTHEW: And Jesus entered the temple of God and drove out all who sold and bought in the temple, and he overturned the tables of the money-changers and the seats of those who sold pigeons. He said to them, "It is written, 'My house shall be called a house of prayer,'[16] but you *have made* it 'a den of robbers'"[17] (21.12–13).

[16] Is 56.7
[17] Jer 7.11

ΠΡΟΣ ΚΟΡ. α'. Μὴ γὰρ οἰκίας οὐκ ἔχετε εἰς τὸ ἐσθίειν καὶ πίνειν; ἢ τῆς Ἐκκλησίας τοῦ Θεοῦ καταφρονεῖτε, καὶ καταισχύνετε τοὺς μὴ ἔχοντας; Εἰ δέ τις πεινᾷ, ἐν οἴκῳ ἐσθιέτω, ἵνα μὴ εἰς κρίμα συνέρχησθε.

[30.2] Ὅτι τὸ ἐπονομαζόμενον τῷ Θεῷ μέχρι τότε ὡς ἅγιον τιμᾶν δεῖ, μέχρις ἂν τὸ τοῦ Θεοῦ θέλημα φυλάσσηται ἐπ' αὐτῷ.

Κεφάλ. β'.

ΜΑΤΘΑΙΟΣ. Ἱερουσαλὴμ, Ἱερουσαλὴμ, ἡ ἀποκτείνουσα τοὺς προφήτας, καὶ λιθοβολοῦσα τοὺς ἀπεσταλμένους πρὸς αὐτήν· ποσάκις ἠθέλησα ἐπισυναγαγεῖν τὰ τέκνα σου, ὃν τρόπον ὄρνις ἐπισυνάγει τὰ νοσσία ἑαυτῆς ὑπὸ τὰς πτέρυγας, καὶ οὐκ ἠθελήσατε; Ἰδοὺ, ἀφίεται ὑμῖν ὁ οἶκος ὑμῶν ἔρημος. [362]

ΟΡΟΣ ΛΑ'.

[31.1] Ὅτι οὐ δεῖ τὰ τοῖς ἀνακειμένοις τῷ Θεῷ ἀφωρισμένα εἰς ἑτέρους ἀναλίσκειν, εἰ μή τι ἂν ἐκ τοῦ περισσεύματος.

Κεφάλ. α'.

ΜΑΡΚΟΣ. Ἦν δὲ γυνὴ Ἑλληνὶς Συροφοίνισσα τῷ γένει, καὶ ἐπηρώτα αὐτὸν, ἵνα τὸ δαιμόνιον ἐκβάλῃ ἐκ τῆς θυγατρὸς αὐτῆς. Ὁ δὲ εἶπεν· ἄφες πρῶτον χορτασθῆναι τὰ τέκνα· οὐ γὰρ καλόν ἐστι λαβεῖν τὸν ἄρτον τῶν τέκνων, καὶ βαλεῖν τοῖς κυναρίοις. Ἡ δὲ ἀπεκρίθη καὶ εἶπεν αὐτῷ· ναί, Κύριε· καὶ τὰ κυνάρια ὑποκάτω τῆς τραπέζης ἐσθίει ἀπὸ τῶν ψιχίων τῶν παίδων. Καὶ εἶπεν αὐτῇ· διὰ τοῦτον τὸν λόγον ὕπαγε, ἐξελήλυθε τὸ δαιμόνιον ἐκ τῆς θυγατρός σου.

ΟΡΟΣ ΛΒ'.

[32.1] Ὅτι δεῖ τὰ ἐπιβάλλοντα ἑκάστῳ εὐγνωμόνως ἀποδιδόναι.

Κεφάλ. α'.

ΛΟΥΚΑΣ. Καὶ ἐπηρώτησαν αὐτὸν, λέγοντες· διδάσκαλε, οἴδαμεν ὅτι ὀρθῶς λέγεις καὶ διδάσκεις, καὶ οὐ λαμβάνεις πρόσωπον, ἀλλ' ἐπ' ἀληθείας τὴν ὁδὸν τοῦ Θεοῦ διδάσκεις· ἔξεστιν ἡμῖν Καίσαρι φόρον δοῦναι, ἢ οὔ; Κατανοήσας δὲ αὐτῶν τὴν πανουργίαν, εἶπε πρὸς αὐτούς· τί με πειράζετε; Δείξατέ μοι δηνάριον. Τίνος ἔχει εἰκόνα καὶ ἐπιγραφήν; Ἀποκριθέντες δὲ εἶπον, Καίσαρος. Ὁ δὲ εἶπεν αὐτοῖς· ἀπόδοτε οὖν τὰ Καίσαρος Καίσαρι, καὶ τὰ τοῦ Θεοῦ τῷ Θεῷ.

1 CORINTHIANS: What! Do you not have houses to eat and drink in? Or do you despise the church of God and humiliate those who have nothing (11.22)? If anyone is hungry, let him eat at home—lest you come together to be condemned (11.34).

30.2   That it is necessary to honor as holy what is dedicated to God so long as the will of God is preserved in it.

MATTHEW: O Jerusalem, Jerusalem, killing the prophets and stoning those who are sent to you! How often would I have gathered your children together as a hen gathers her brood under her wings, and you would not! Behold, your house is forsaken and desolate (23.37–38).

31.1   That it is necessary not to squander on others what has been reserved for those dedicated to God, unless there is something extra.

MARK: Now the woman was a Greek, a Syrophoenician by birth. And she begged him to cast the demon out of her daughter. And *he said*, "Let the children first be fed, for it is not right to take the children's bread and throw it to the dogs." But she answered him, "Yes, Lord; yet even the dogs under the table eat the children's crumbs." And he said to her, "For this saying you may go your way; the demon has left your daughter" (7.26–29).

32.1   That it is necessary to give to each what is due in fairness.

LUKE: They asked him, "Teacher, we know that you speak and teach rightly and show no partiality but truly teach the way of God. Is it lawful for us to give tribute to Caesar, or not?" But he perceived their craftiness and said to them, "*Why do you tempt me?* Show me a coin. Whose likeness and inscription has it?" They *answered*, "Caesar's." He said to them, "Then render to Caesar the things that are Caesar's and to God the things that are God's" (20.21–25).

ΠΡΟΣ ΡΩΜ. Ἀπόδοτε οὖν πᾶσι τὰς ὀφειλὰς, τῷ τὸν φόρον, τὸν φόρον· τῷ τὸ τέλος, τὸ τέλος· τῷ τὸν φόβον, τὸν φόβον· τῷ τὴν τιμὴν τὴν τιμήν. Μηδενὶ μηδὲν ὀφείλετε, εἰ μὴ τὸ ἀλλήλους ἀγαπᾷν. [363]

ΟΡΟΣ ΛΓ΄.

[33.1]   Ὅτι οὐ δεῖ σκανδαλίζειν.

Κεφάλ. α΄.

ΜΑΤΘΑΙΟΣ. Ὅς δ᾽ ἂν σκανδαλίσῃ ἕνα τῶν μικρῶν τούτων τῶν πιστευόντων εἰς ἐμὲ, συμφέρει αὐτῷ, ἵνα κρεμασθῇ μύλος ὀνικὸς περὶ τὸν τράχηλον αὐτοῦ, καὶ καταποντισθῇ ἐν τῷ πελάγει τῆς θαλάσσης. Καὶ πάλιν· Οὐαὶ τῷ ἀνθρώπῳ ἐκείνῳ, δι᾽ οὗ τὸ σκάνδαλον ἔρχεται.

ΠΡΟΣ ΡΩΜ. Ἀλλὰ τοῦτο κρίνατε μᾶλλον, τὸ μὴ τιθέναι πρόσκομμα τῷ ἀδελφῷ, ἢ σκάνδαλον.

[33.2]   Ὅτι πᾶν τὸ ἀντικείμενον τῷ τοῦ Κυρίου θελήματι σκάνδαλόν ἐστιν.

Κεφάλ. β΄.

ΜΑΤΘΑΙΟΣ. Ἀπὸ τότε ἤρξατο ὁ Ἰησοῦς δεικνύειν τοῖς μαθηταῖς αὐτοῦ, Ὅτι δεῖ αὐτὸν ἀπελθεῖν εἰς Ἰεροσόλυμα, καὶ πολλὰ παθεῖν ἀπὸ τῶν πρεσβυτέρων, καὶ ἀρχιερέων, καὶ γραμματέων, καὶ ἀποκτανθῆναι, καὶ τῇ τρίτῃ ἡμέρᾳ[9] ἀναστῆναι. Καὶ προσλαβόμενος αὐτὸν ὁ Πέτρος, ἤρξατο ἐπιτιμᾷν αὐτῷ, λέγων· Ἵλεώς σοι, Κύριε, οὐ μὴ ἔσται σοι τοῦτο. Ὁ δὲ, στραφεὶς, εἶπε τῷ Πέτρῳ· ὕπαγε ὀπίσω μου, σατανᾶ, σκάνδαλόν μου εἶ, ὅτι οὐ φρονεῖς τὰ τοῦ Θεοῦ, ἀλλὰ τὰ τῶν ἀνθρώπων.

[33.3]   Ὅτι δεῖ καὶ τὸ συγκεχωρημένον ὑπὸ τῆς Γραφῆς πρᾶγμα ἢ ῥῆμα παραιτεῖσθαι, ὅταν οἰκοδομῶνται ἄλλοι ἐκ τοῦ ὁμοίου εἰς ἁμαρτίαν· ἢ ἐκκόπτωνται τὴν περὶ τὰ καλὰ προθυμίαν.

Κεφάλ. γ΄.

ΠΡΟΣ ΚΟΡ. α΄. Περὶ τῆς βρώσεως οὖν τῶν εἰδωλοθύτων, οἴδαμεν, ὅτι οὐδὲν εἴδωλον ἐν κόσμῳ, καὶ ὅτι οὐδεὶς Θεὸς, εἰ μὴ εἷς. Καὶ γὰρ εἴπερ εἰσὶ λεγόμενοι θεοὶ, εἴτε ἐν οὐρανῷ, εἴτε ἐπὶ τῆς γῆς (ὥσπερ εἰσὶ

---

[9]Corrected from ἡμέρα.

ROMANS: *Therefore* pay all of them their dues, taxes to whom taxes are due, revenue to whom revenue is due, respect to whom respect is due, honor to whom honor is due. Owe no one anything except to love one another (13.7–8).

33.1   That it is necessary not to scandalize.

MATTHEW: *But whoever scandalizes one of these little ones*, it would be better for him to have a great millstone fastened round his neck and to be drowned in the depth of the sea (18.6). *And again*: Woe to the man by whom the *scandal* comes (18.7)!

ROMANS: But rather decide never to put a stumbling block or *scandal* in the way of a brother (14.13).

33.2   That everything opposed to the will of the Lord is a scandal.

MATTHEW: From that time Jesus began to show his disciples that he must go to Jerusalem and suffer many things from the elders and chief priests and scribes and be killed and on the third day be raised. And Peter took him and began to rebuke him, saying, "God forbid, Lord! This shall never happen to you." But he turned and said to Peter, "Get behind me, Satan! You are a *scandal* to me, for you are not on the side of God but of men" (16.21–23).

33.3   That it is necessary to be averted even from what is authorized by the Scriptures, whether deed or word, when others might be encouraged to sin thereby or might be driven from their zeal for the good.

1 CORINTHIANS: Hence, as to the eating of food offered to idols, we know that an idol has no real existence and that there is no God but one. For although there may be so-called gods in heaven or on earth—as indeed there are many gods and many lords—yet for us

θεοὶ πολλοὶ καὶ κύριοι πολλοὶ), ἀλλ' ἡμῖν εἷς Θεὸς, ὁ Πατήρ, ἐξ οὗ τὰ πάντα, καὶ ἡμεῖς [364] εἰς αὐτόν· καὶ εἷς Κύριος, Ἰησοῦς Χριστὸς, δι' οὗ τὰ πάντα, καὶ ἡμεῖς δι' αὐτοῦ· ἀλλ' οὐκ ἐν πᾶσιν ἡ γνῶσις. Τινὲς δὲ τῇ συνειδήσει ἕως ἄρτι τοῦ εἰδώλου ὡς εἰδωλόθυτον ἐσθίουσι, καὶ ἡ συνείδησις αὐτῶν ἀσθενὴς οὖσα μολύνεται. Βρῶμα δὲ ἡμᾶς οὐ παρίστησι τῷ Θεῷ. Οὔτε γὰρ ἐὰν φάγωμεν, περισσεύομεν· οὔτε ἐὰν μὴ φάγωμεν, ὑστερούμεθα. Βλέπετε δὲ μήπως ἡ ἐξουσία ὑμῶν αὕτη πρόσκομμα γένηται τοῖς ἀσθενοῦσιν. Ἐὰν γάρ τις ἴδῃ σὲ, τὸν ἔχοντα γνῶσιν, ἐν εἰδωλείῳ κατακείμενον, οὐχὶ ἡ συνείδησις αὐτοῦ ἀσθενοῦς ὄντος οἰκοδομηθήσεται εἰς τὸ τὰ εἰδωλόθυτα ἐσθίειν; καὶ ἀπόλλυται ὁ ἀσθενῶν ἐν τῇ σῇ γνώσει ἀδελφὸς, δι' ὃν Χριστὸς ἀπέθανεν; Οὕτω δὲ ἁμαρτάνοντες εἰς τοὺς ἀδελφοὺς, καὶ τύπτοντες αὐτῶν τὴν συνείδησιν ἀσθενοῦσαν, εἰς Χριστὸν ἁμαρτάνετε. Διόπερ εἰ βρῶμα σκανδαλίζει τὸν ἀδελφόν μου, οὐ μὴ φάγω κρέα εἰς τὸν αἰῶνα, ἵνα μὴ τὸν ἀδελφόν μου σκανδαλίσω. Μὴ οὐκ ἔχομεν ἐξουσίαν φαγεῖν καὶ πίνειν;[10] Μὴ οὐκ ἔχομεν ἐξουσίαν ἀδελφὴν γυναῖκα περιάγειν, ὡς καὶ οἱ λοιποὶ ἀπόστολοι, καὶ οἱ ἀδελφοὶ τοῦ Κυρίου, καὶ Κηφᾶς; Ἢ μόνος ἐγὼ καὶ Βαρνάβας οὐκ ἔχομεν ἐξουσίαν τοῦ μὴ ἐργάζεσθαι; Τίς στρατεύεται ἰδίοις ὀψωνίοις ποτέ; τίς φυτεύει ἀμπελῶνα, καὶ ἐκ τοῦ καρποῦ αὐτοῦ οὐκ ἐσθίει; Ἢ τίς ποιμαίνει ποίμνην, καὶ ἐκ τοῦ γάλακτος τῆς ποίμνης οὐκ ἐσθίει; καὶ τὰ ἑξῆς.

[33.4] Ὅτι, ὑπὲρ τοῦ μὴ σκανδαλίσαι τινὰ, ποιεῖν δεῖ καὶ ὃ μὴ ἐπάναγκες.

Κεφάλ. δ'.

ΜΑΤΘΑΙΟΣ. Ἐλθόντων δὲ αὐτῶν εἰς Καπερναοὺμ, προσῆλθον οἱ τὰ δίδραχμα λαμβάνοντες τῷ Πέτρῳ, καὶ εἶπον· ὁ διδάσκαλος ὑμῶν οὐ τελεῖ τὰ δίδραχμα; Λέγει, ναί. Καὶ ὅτε εἰσῆλθεν εἰς τὴν οἰκίαν, προέφθασεν αὐτὸν ὁ Ἰησοῦς λέγων· τί σοι δοκεῖ, Σίμων; Οἱ βασιλεῖς τῆς γῆς ἀπὸ τίνων λαμβάνουσι τέλη, ἢ κῆνσον; Ἀπὸ τῶν υἱῶν αὐτῶν, ἢ ἀπὸ τῶν ἀλλοτρίων; Λέγει αὐτῷ ὁ Πέτρος· ἀπὸ τῶν ἀλλοτρίων. Λέγει αὐτῷ ὁ Ἰησοῦς· ἄρα γε ἐλεύθεροί εἰσιν οἱ υἱοί. Ἵνα δὲ μὴ σκανδαλίσωμεν αὐτοὺς, [365] πορευθεὶς εἰς τὴν θάλασσαν,

---

[10]Corrected from ποιεῖν.

there is one God, the Father, from whom are all things and for whom we exist, and one Lord, Jesus Christ, through whom are all things and through whom we exist. However, not all possess this knowledge. But some, through being hitherto accustomed to idols, eat food as really offered to an idol; and their conscience, being weak, is defiled. Food *does* not commend us to God. *For* we are no worse off if we do not eat and no better off if we do. Only take care lest this liberty of yours somehow become a stumbling block to the weak. For if anyone sees you, a man of knowledge, at table in an idol's temple, might he not be encouraged, if his conscience is weak, to eat food offered to idols? And so by your knowledge this *weak brother is destroyed*, for whom Christ died. Thus, sinning against your brethren and wounding their conscience when it is weak, you sin against Christ. Therefore if food *scandalizes my brother*, I will never eat meat, lest I *scandalize my brother* (8.4–13). Do we not have the right to our food and drink? Do we not have the right to be accompanied by a wife as the other apostles and the brothers of the Lord and Cephas? Or is it only Barnabas and I who have no right to refrain from working for a living? Who serves as a soldier at his own expense? Who plants a vineyard without eating any of its fruit? Who tends a flock without getting some of the milk (9.4–7)? *and what follows*.

33.4   That in order not to scandalize anyone, it is necessary to do even things that are not mandated.

MATTHEW: When they came to Capernaum, the collectors of the half–shekel tax went up to Peter and said, "Does not your teacher pay the tax?" He said, "Yes." And when he came home, Jesus spoke to him first, saying, "What do you think, Simon? From whom do kings of the earth take toll or tribute? From their sons or from others?" *Peter said to him*, "From others." Jesus said to him, "Then the sons are free. However, not to *scandalize* them, go to the sea and cast a hook, and take the first fish that comes up, and when you open its

βάλε ἄγκιστρον, καὶ τὸν ἀναβάντα πρῶτον ἰχθὺν ἆρον· καὶ ἀνοίξας τὸ στόμα αὐτοῦ, εὑρήσεις στατῆρα· ἐκεῖνον λαβών, δὸς αὐτοῖς ἀντὶ ἐμοῦ καὶ σοῦ.

[33.5] Ὅτι ἐπὶ τοῖς τοῦ Κυρίου θελήμασι, κἂν σκανδαλίζωνταί τινες, ἀνένδοτον ἐπιδείκνυσθαι δεῖ τὴν παῤῥησίαν.

Κεφάλ. ε΄.

ΜΑΤΘΑΙΟΣ. Οὐ τὸ εἰσερχόμενον εἰς τὸ στόμα κοινοῖ τὸν ἄνθρωπον, ἀλλὰ τὸ ἐκπορευόμενον ἐκ τοῦ στόματος, τοῦτο κοινοῖ τὸν ἄνθρωπον. Τότε προσελθόντες οἱ μαθηταὶ αὐτοῦ, εἶπον αὐτῷ· οἶδας ὅτι οἱ Φαρισαῖοι ἀκούσαντες τὸν λόγον, ἐσκανδαλίσθησαν; Ὁ δὲ ἀποκριθεὶς εἶπε· πᾶσα φυτεία, ἣν οὐκ ἐφύτευσεν ὁ Πατήρ μου ὁ οὐράνιος, ἐκριζωθήσεται. Ἄφετε αὐτούς· τυφλοί εἰσιν, ὁδηγοὶ τυφλῶν. Τυφλὸς δὲ τυφλὸν ἐὰν ὁδηγῇ, ἀμφότεροι εἰς βόθυνον πεσοῦνται.

ΙΩΑΝΝΗΣ. Ἀμὴν ἀμὴν λέγω ὑμῖν· ἐὰν μὴ φάγητε τὴν σάρκα τοῦ Υἱοῦ τοῦ ἀνθρώπου, καὶ πίητε αὐτοῦ τὸ αἷμα, οὐκ ἔχετε ζωὴν ἐν ἑαυτοῖς. Καὶ μετ᾽ ὀλίγα· Ἐκ τούτου πολλοὶ τῶν μαθητῶν αὐτοῦ ἀπῆλθον εἰς τὰ ὀπίσω, καὶ οὐκέτι μετ᾽ αὐτοῦ περιεπάτουν. Εἶπεν οὖν ὁ Ἰησοῦς τοῖς δώδεκα· μὴ καὶ ὑμεῖς θέλετε ἀπελθεῖν;

ΠΡΟΣ ΚΟΡ. β΄. Ὅτι Χριστοῦ εὐωδία ἐσμὲν τῷ Θεῷ, ἐν τοῖς σωζομένοις, καὶ ἐν τοῖς ἀπολλυμένοις, οἷς μὲν ὀσμὴ θανάτου εἰς θάνατον, οἷς δὲ ὀσμὴ ζωῆς εἰς ζωήν. Καὶ πρὸς ταῦτα τίς ἱκανός;

ΟΡΟΣ ΛΔ΄.

[34.1] Ὅτι δεῖ τύπον τῶν καλῶν προκεῖσθαι τοῖς ἄλλοις, ἕκαστον ἐν τῷ ἰδίῳ μέτρῳ.

Κεφάλ. α΄.

ΜΑΤΘΑΙΟΣ. Μάθετε ἀπ᾽ ἐμοῦ, ὅτι πρᾶός εἰμι, καὶ ταπεινὸς τῇ καρδίᾳ.

ΠΡΟΣ ΚΟΡ. β΄. Οἶδα γὰρ τὴν προθυμίαν ὑμῶν, ἣν ὑπὲρ ὑμῶν καυχῶμαι Μακεδόσιν, ὅτι Ἀχαΐα μὲν παρεσκεύασται [366] ἀπὸ πέρυσι, καὶ ὁ ἐξ ὑμῶν ζῆλος ἠρέθισε τοὺς πλείονας.

ΠΡΟΣ ΘΕΣΣ. α΄. Καὶ ὑμεῖς μιμηταὶ ἡμῶν ἐγενήθητε[11] καὶ τοῦ Κυρίου,

---

[11]Corrected from ἐγεννήθητε.

mouth you will find a shekel; take that and give it to them for me and for yourself" (17.24–27).

33.5 That with respect to those things the Lord desires, even if someone might be scandalized, it is necessary to continue without yielding our freedom.

MATTHEW: "Not what goes into the mouth defiles a man, but what comes out of the mouth, this defiles a man." Then *his* disciples came and said to him, "Do you know that the Pharisees were *scandalized* when they heard this saying?" He answered, "Every plant which my heavenly Father has not planted will be rooted up. Let them alone; they are blind guides *of the blind*. And if a blind man leads a blind man, both will fall into a pit" (15.11–14).

JOHN: Truly, truly I say to you, unless you eat the flesh of the Son of man and drink his blood, you have no life in you (6.53). *And a little further*: After this many of his disciples drew back and no longer went about with him. Jesus said to the twelve, "Do you also wish to go away?" (6.66–67).

2 CORINTHIANS: For we are the aroma of Christ to God among those who are being saved and among those who are perishing, to one *a fragrance of death unto death*, to the other *a fragrance of life unto life*. Who is sufficient for these things (2.15–16)?

34.1 That it is necessary to set an example of good works for others, each in his own measure.

MATTHEW: Learn from me; for I am gentle and lowly in heart (11.29).

2 CORINTHIANS: For I know your readiness, of which I boast about you to the people of Macedonia saying that Achaia has been ready since last year, and your zeal has stirred up most of them (9.2).

1 THESSALONIANS: And you became imitators of us and of the Lord, for you received the word in much affliction with joy inspired

δεξάμενοι τὸν λόγον ἐν θλίψει πολλῇ μετὰ χαρᾶς Πνεύματος ἁγίου·
ὥστε γενέσθαι ὑμᾶς τύπους πᾶσι τοῖς πιστεύουσιν ἐν τῇ Μακεδονίᾳ
καὶ ἐν τῇ Ἀχαΐᾳ.

ΟΡΟΣ ΛΕ΄.

[35.1] Ὅτι οἱ τὸν καρπὸν τοῦ ἁγίου Πνεύματος ἔν τινι ὁρῶντες
πανταχοῦ τὸ ὁμαλὸν τῆς θεοσεβείας σώζοντα, καὶ μὴ τῷ ἁγίῳ
Πνεύματι ἀνατιθέντες, ἀλλὰ τῷ ἐναντίῳ ἐπιφημίζοντες, εἰς αὐτὸ τὸ
ἅγιον Πνεῦμα βλασφημοῦσιν.

Κεφάλ. α΄.

ΜΑΤΘΑΙΟΣ. Τότε προσηνέχθη αὐτῷ δαιμονιζόμενος τυφλὸς καὶ
κωφὸς, καὶ ἐθεράπευσεν αὐτόν, ὥστε τὸν κωφὸν καὶ τυφλὸν καὶ
λαλεῖν καὶ βλέπειν. Καὶ ἐξίσταντο πάντες οἱ ὄχλοι, καὶ ἔλεγον· μήτι
οὗτός ἐστιν ὁ υἱὸς Δαβίδ; Οἱ δὲ Φαρισαῖοι, ἀκούσαντες, εἶπον·
οὗτος οὐκ ἐκβάλλει τὰ δαιμόνια εἰ μὴ ἐν Βεελζεβοὺλ ἄρχοντι τῶν
δαιμονίων. Εἰδὼς δὲ ὁ Ἰησοῦς τὰς ἐνθυμήσεις αὐτῶν, εἶπεν αὐτοῖς·
εἰ δὲ ἐν Πνεύματι Θεοῦ ἐκβάλλω ἐγὼ τὰ δαιμόνια, ἄρα ἔφθασεν ἐφ'
ὑμᾶς ἡ βασιλεία τοῦ Θεοῦ. Οἷς ἑξῆς ἐπιφέρει· Διὰ τοῦτο λέγω ὑμῖν,
πᾶσα ἁμαρτία καὶ βλασφημία ἀφεθήσεται τοῖς ἀνθρώποις· ἡ δὲ τοῦ
Πνεύματος βλασφημία οὐκ ἀφεθήσεται τοῖς ἀνθρώποις. Καὶ ὃς ἐὰν
εἴπῃ λόγον κατὰ τοῦ Υἱοῦ τοῦ ἀνθρώπου, ἀφεθήσεται αὐτῷ· ὃς δ'
ἂν εἴπῃ κατὰ τοῦ Πνεύματος τοῦ ἁγίου, οὐκ ἀφεθήσεται αὐτῷ, οὔτε
ἐν τῷ νῦν αἰῶνι, οὔτε ἐν τῷ μέλλοντι.

ΟΡΟΣ Λς΄.

[36.1] Ὅτι τοὺς φυλάσσοντας τὸν τύπον τῆς τοῦ Κυρίου διδασκαλίας μετὰ πάσης σπουδῆς καὶ τιμῆς δέχεσθαι δεῖ εἰς δόξαν αὐτοῦ τοῦ
Κυρίου· ὁ δὲ μὴ ἀκούσας, μηδὲ δεξάμενος, κατακρίνεται.

Κεφάλ. α΄.

ΜΑΤΘΑΙΟΣ. Ὁ δεχόμενος ὑμᾶς, ἐμὲ δέχεται· [367] καὶ ὁ ἐμὲ
δεχόμενος δέχεται τὸν ἀποστείλαντά με. Καὶ ὃς ἐὰν μὴ δέξηται
ὑμᾶς, μηδὲ ἀκούσῃ τοὺς λόγους ὑμῶν, ἐξερχόμενοι τῆς οἰκίας
ἐκείνης, ἢ τῆς πόλεως, ἐκτινάξατε τὸν κονιορτὸν τῶν ποδῶν ὑμῶν.
Ἀμὴν λέγω ὑμῖν, ἀνεκτότερον ἔσται γῇ Σοδόμων, καὶ Γομόρρων ἐν
ἡμέρᾳ κρίσεως ἢ τῇ πόλει ἐκείνῃ.

by the Holy Spirit, so that you became *examples* to all the believers in Macedonia and in Achaia (1.6–7).

35.1 That those who behold the fruit of the Holy Spirit in someone constant in piety and do not ascribe it to the Holy Spirit but rather to the opposing spirit, blaspheme against the same Holy Spirit.

MATTHEW: Then a blind and dumb demoniac was brought to him, and he healed him, so that the dumb *and blind* man *both* spoke and saw. And all the people were amazed and said, "Can this be the Son of David?" But when the Pharisees heard it they said, "It is only by Beelzebul the prince of demons that this man casts out demons." Knowing their thoughts, *Jesus* said to them, "Every kingdom divided against itself is laid waste, and no city or house divided against itself will stand" (12.22–25). "But if it is by the Spirit of God that I cast out demons, then the kingdom of God has come upon you" (12.28). *To which it adds the following*: Therefore I tell you, every sin and blasphemy will be forgiven men, but the blasphemy against the Spirit will not be forgiven. And whoever says a word against the Son of man will be forgiven; but whoever speaks against the Holy Spirit will not be forgiven, either in *the present* age or in the age to come (12.31–32).

36.1 That it is necessary to receive those who keep the model of the Lord's teaching with all zeal and honor unto the glory of the same Lord, and that the one who neither hears nor receives them is condemned.

MATTHEW: He who receives you receives me, and he who receives me receives him who sent me (10.40). And if anyone will not receive you or listen to your words, shake off the dust from your feet as you leave that house or town. Truly, I say to you, it shall be more tolerable on the day of judgment for the land of Sodom and Gomorrah than for that town (10.14–15).

ΙΩΑΝΝΗΣ. Ὁ λαμβάνων, ἐάν τινα πέμψω, ἐμὲ λαμβάνει· ὁ δὲ ἐμὲ λαμβάνων, λαμβάνει τὸν ἀποστείλαντά με.

ΠΡΟΣ ΦΙΛ. Ἀναγκαῖον δὲ ἡγησάμην Ἐπαφρόδιτον τὸν ἀδελφὸν, καὶ συνεργὸν, καὶ συστρατιώτην μου, ὑμῶν δὲ ἀπόστολον, καὶ λειτουργὸν τῆς χρείας μου, πέμψαι πρὸς ὑμᾶς. Καὶ μετ' ὀλίγα· Προσδέχεσθε οὖν αὐτὸν ἐν Κυρίῳ μετὰ πάσης χαρᾶς, καὶ τοὺς τοιούτους ἐντίμους ἔχετε.

ΟΡΟΣ ΛΖ'.

[37.1] Ὅτι ἡ κατὰ δύναμιν κἂν ᾖ ἐν τοῖς ἐλαχίστοις, προθυμία εὐπρόσδεκτός ἐστι τῷ Θεῷ, κἂν παρὰ γυναικῶν ᾖ.

Κεφάλ. α'.

ΜΑΤΘΑΙΟΣ. Καὶ ὃς ἐὰν ποτίσῃ ἕνα τῶν μικρῶν τούτων ποτήριον ψυχροῦ μόνον εἰς ὄνομα μαθητοῦ, ἀμὴν λέγω ὑμῖν οὐ μὴ ἀπολέσῃ τὸν μισθὸν αὐτοῦ.

ΛΟΥΚΑΣ. Ἀναβλέψας δὲ εἶδε τοὺς βάλλοντας τὰ δῶρα αὐτῶν εἰς τὸ γαζοφυλάκιον πλουσίους. Εἶδε δέ τινα χήραν πενιχρὰν βάλλουσαν ἐκεῖ δύο λεπτὰ, καὶ εἶπεν· ἀληθῶς λέγω ὑμῖν, ὅτι ἡ χήρα αὕτη ἡ πτωχὴ πλεῖον πάντων ἔβαλεν. Ἅπαντες γὰρ οὗτοι ἐκ τοῦ περισσεύοντος αὐτοῖς ἔβαλον εἰς τὰ δῶρα τοῦ Θεοῦ· αὕτη δὲ ἐκ τοῦ ὑστερήματος αὐτῆς ἅπαντα τὸν βίον ὃν εἶχεν ἔβαλεν.

ΜΑΤΘΑΙΟΣ. Τοῦ δὲ Ἰησοῦ γενομένου ἐν Βεθανίᾳ ἐν οἰκίᾳ Σίμωνος τοῦ λεπροῦ, προσῆλθεν αὐτῷ γυνὴ ἀλάβαστρον μύρου ἔχουσα βαρυτίμου, καὶ κατέχεεν ἐπὶ τὴν κεφαλὴν αὐτοῦ ἀνακειμένου. Ἰδόντες δὲ οἱ μαθηταὶ αὐτοῦ, ἠγανάκτησαν, λέγοντες· εἰς τί ἡ ἀπώλεια αὕτη τοῦ μύρου; Ἠδύνατο γὰρ τοῦτο πραθῆναι πολλοῦ, καὶ δοθῆναι πτωχοῖς. Γνοὺς δὲ ὁ Ἰησοῦς, εἶπεν αὐτοῖς· τί κόπους παρέχετε τῇ γυναικί; Ἔργον γὰρ καλὸν εἰργάσατο [368] εἰς ἐμέ.

ΠΡΑΞΕΙΣ. Περὶ τῆς Λυδίας· Ὡς δὲ ἐβαπτίσθη, καὶ ὁ οἶκος αὐτῆς, παρεκάλεσε λέγουσα· εἰ κεκρίκατέ με πιστὴν τῷ Κυρίῳ εἶναι, εἰσελθόντες εἰς τὸν οἶκόν μου, μείνατε. Καὶ παρεβιάσατο ἡμᾶς.

ΟΡΟΣ ΛΗ'.

[38.1] Ὅτι δεῖ τὸν Χριστιανὸν καὶ τὴν εἰς τοὺς ἀδελφοὺς δεξίωσιν ἀθόρυβον καὶ λιτοτέραν ποιεῖσθαι.

JOHN: He who receives anyone whom I send receives me; and he who receives me receives him who sent me (13.20).

PHILIPPIANS: I have thought it necessary to send to you Epaphroditus, my brother and fellow worker and fellow soldier and your messenger and minister to my need (2.25). *And a little further*: So receive him in the Lord with all joy, and honor such men (2.29).

37.1 That zeal according to one's ability, even in the smallest things, is acceptable to God, even if it be from a woman.

MATTHEW: And whoever gives to one of these little ones even a cup of cold water because he is a disciple, truly, I say to you, he shall not lose his reward (10.42).

LUKE: He looked up and saw the rich putting their gifts into the treasury, and he saw a poor widow put in two copper coins. And he said, "Truly I tell you, this poor widow has put in more than all of them; for they all contributed *to God's gifts* out of their abundance, but she out of her poverty put in all the living that she had" (21.1–4).

MATTHEW: Now when Jesus was at Bethany in the house of Simon the leper, a woman came up to him with an alabaster flask of very expensive ointment, and she poured it on his head as he sat at table. But when the disciples saw it they were indignant, saying, "Why this waste *of the ointment*? For *it* might have been sold for a large sum and given to the poor." But Jesus, aware of this, said to them, "Why do you trouble the woman? For she has done a beautiful thing to me" (26.6–10).

ACTS: *Concerning Lydia*: And when she was baptized with her household, she besought us, saying, "If you have judged me to be faithful to the Lord, come to my house and stay." And she prevailed upon us (16.15).

38.1 That it is necessary for the Christian to show hospitality to the brethren without commotion and more simply.

Κεφάλ. α΄.

ΙΩΑΝΝΗΣ. Λέγει αὐτῷ εἷς τῶν μαθητῶν αὐτοῦ, Ἀνδρέας ὁ ἀδελφὸς Σίμωνος· ἔστι παιδάριον ἓν ὧδε, καὶ ἔχει πέντε ἄρτους κριθίνους καὶ δύο ὀψάρια· ἀλλὰ ταῦτα τί ἐστιν εἰς τοσούτους; Εἶπε δὲ ὁ Ἰησοῦς· ποιήσατε τοὺς ἀνθρώπους ἀναπεσεῖν. Ἦν δὲ χόρτος πολὺς ἐν τῷ τόπῳ. Ἀνέπεσον οὖν οἱ ἄνδρες τὸν ἀριθμὸν ὡσεὶ πεντακισχίλιοι. Ἔλαβε δὲ τοὺς ἄρτους ὁ Ἰησοῦς, καὶ εὐχαριστήσας, διέδωκε τοῖς ἀνακειμένοις. Ὁμοίως δὲ καὶ ἐκ τῶν ὀψαρίων ὅσον ἤθελον. ΛΟΥΚΑΣ. Γυνὴ δέ τις ὀνόματι Μάρθα ὑπεδέξατο αὐτὸν εἰς τὸν οἶκον αὐτῆς. Καὶ τῇδε ἦν ἀδελφὴ καλουμένη Μαρία, ἣ καὶ παρακαθίσασα παρὰ τοὺς πόδας τοῦ Ἰησοῦ, ἤκουε τὸν λόγον αὐτοῦ. Ἡ δὲ Μάρθα περιεσπᾶτο περὶ πολλὴν διακονίαν. Ἐπιστᾶσα δὲ εἶπε· Κύριε, οὐ μέλει σοι, ὅτι ἡ ἀδελφή μου μόνην με κατέλιπε διακονεῖν; Εἰπὲ οὖν αὐτῇ, ἵνα μοι συναντιλάβηται. Ἀποκριθεὶς δὲ εἶπεν αὐτῇ ὁ Ἰησοῦς· Μάρθα, Μάρθα, μεριμνᾷς καὶ τυρβάζῃ¹² περὶ πολλά· ὀλίγων δέ ἐστι χρεία ἢ ἑνός. Μαρία δὲ τὴν ἀγαθὴν μερίδα ἐξελέξατο, ἥτις οὐκ ἀφαιρεθήσεται ἀπ᾽ αὐτῆς. [369]

ΟΡΟΣ ΛΘ΄.

[39.1] Ὅτι οὐ δεῖ εὐμετάθετον εἶναι, ἀλλὰ ἑδραῖον ἐν τῇ πίστει, καὶ ἀμετάθετον ἀπὸ τῶν ἐν Κυρίῳ καλῶν.

Κεφάλ. α΄.

ΜΑΤΘΑΙΟΣ. Ὁ δὲ ἐπὶ τὰ πετρώδη σπαρείς, οὗτός ἐστιν ὁ τὸν λόγον ἀκούων, καὶ εὐθὺς μετὰ χαρᾶς λαμβάνων αὐτόν. Οὐκ ἔχει δὲ ῥίζαν ἐν ἑαυτῷ, ἀλλὰ πρόσκαιρός ἐστι· γενομένης δὲ θλίψεως ἢ διωγμοῦ διὰ τὸν λόγον, εὐθὺς σκανδαλίζεται.

ΠΡΟΣ ΚΟΡ. α΄. Ὥστε, ἀδελφοί μου, ἑδραῖοι γίνεσθε, ἀμετακίνητοι, περισσεύοντες ἐν τῷ ἔργῳ τοῦ Κυρίου πάντοτε.

ΠΡΟΣ ΓΑΛΑΤ. Θαυμάζω, ὅτι οὕτω ταχέως μετατίθεσθε ἀπὸ τοῦ καλέσαντος ὑμᾶς ἐν χάριτι Χριστοῦ, εἰς ἕτερον εὐαγγέλιον.

ΟΡΟΣ Μ΄.

[40.1] Ὅτι οὐ δεῖ ἑτεροδιδασκαλούντων ἀνέχεσθαι, κἂν σχηματίζωνται πρὸς ἀπάτην ἢ ἔλεγχον τῶν ἀβεβαίων.

---

¹²Corrected from τυρβάζῃ.

JOHN: One of his disciples, Andrew, *Simon's* brother, said to him, "There is *one* lad here, *and he* has five barley loaves and two fish; but what are they among so many?" Jesus said, "Make the people sit down." Now there was much grass in the place, so the men sat down, in number about five thousand. *Jesus took* the loaves, and when he had given thanks he distributed them to those who were seated; so also the fish, as much as they wanted (6.8–11).

LUKE: Now as they went on their way he entered a village, and a woman named Martha received him into her house. And she had a sister called Mary, who sat at Jesus' feet and listened to his teaching. But Martha was distracted with much serving, and she went to him and said, "Lord, do you not care that my sister has left me to serve alone? Tell her then to help me." But the Lord answered her, "Martha, Martha, you are anxious and troubled about many things; *few things are needful, rather one.* Mary has chosen the good portion, which shall not be taken away from her" (10.38–42).

39.1 That it is necessary not to be easily moved but constant in the faith and immoveable from the good things in the Lord.

MATTHEW: As for what was sown on rocky ground, this is he who hears the word and immediately receives it with joy; yet he has no root in himself, but endures for a while, and when tribulation or persecution arises on account of the word, immediately he falls away (13.20–21).

1 CORINTHIANS: Therefore, *my* brethren, be steadfast, immovable, always abounding in the work of the Lord (15.58).

GALATIANS: I am astonished that you are so quickly deserting him who called you in the grace of Christ and turning to a different gospel (1.6).

40.1 That it is necessary not to tolerate teachers of a different doctrine, though they make a show to deceive or induce the uncertain.

Κεφάλ. αʹ.

ΜΑΤΘΑΙΟΣ. Βλέπετε μή τις ὑμᾶς πλανήσῃ. Πολλοὶ γὰρ ἐλεύσονται ἐπὶ τῷ ὀνόματί μου, λέγοντες, ὅτι ἐγώ εἰμι ὁ Χριστός· καὶ πολλοὺς πλανήσουσιν.

ΛΟΥΚΑΣ. Προσέχετε ἀπὸ τῶν γραμματέων τῶν θελόντων περιπατεῖν ἐν στολαῖς, καὶ φιλούντων ἀσπασμοὺς ἐν ταῖς ἀγοραῖς, καὶ πρωτοκαθεδρίας ἐν ταῖς συναγωγαῖς, καὶ πρωτοκλισίας ἐν τοῖς δείπνοις· οἳ κατεσθίουσι τὰς οἰκίας τῶν χηρῶν, καὶ προφάσει μακρὰ προσεύχονται. Οὗτοι λήψονται περισσότερον κρῖμα.

ΠΡΟΣ ΓΑΛ. Ἀλλὰ καὶ ἐὰν ἡμεῖς, ἢ ἄγγελος ἐξ οὐρανοῦ εὐαγγελίζηται ὑμῖν, παρ' ὃ εὐηγγελισάμεθα ὑμῖν, ἀνάθεμα ἔστω. Ὡς προειρήκαμεν, καὶ ἄρτι πάλιν λέγω· εἴ τις ὑμᾶς εὐαγγελίζεται παρ' ὃ παρελάβετε, ἀνάθεμα ἔστω. [370]

ΟΡΟΣ ΜΑʹ.

[41.1] Ὅτι δεῖ πᾶν τὸ σκανδαλίζον ἐκκόπτειν, κἂν οἰκειότατόν τι καὶ ἀναγκαιότατον εἶναι δοκῇ.

Κεφάλ. αʹ.

ΜΑΤΘΑΙΟΣ. Οὐαὶ τῷ ἀνθρώπῳ ἐκείνῳ δι' οὗ τὸ σκάνδαλον ἔρχεται. Εἰ δὲ ὁ πούς σου ἢ ἡ χείρ σου σκανδαλίζει σε, ἔκκοψον αὐτὰ, καὶ βάλε ἀπὸ σοῦ. Καλόν σοι ἐστὶν εἰσελθεῖν εἰς τὴν ζωὴν χωλὸν, ἢ κυλλὸν, ἢ δύο πόδας ἢ δύο χεῖρας ἔχοντα βληθῆναι εἰς τὸ πῦρ τὸ αἰώνιον. Καὶ εἰ ὁ ὀφθαλμός σου σκανδαλίζει σε, ἔξελε αὐτὸν, καὶ βάλε ἀπὸ σοῦ.

[41.2] Ὅτι τῶν ἀσθενεστέρων ἐν τῇ πίστει φείδεσθαι δεῖ, καὶ ἀνάγειν αὐτοὺς δι' ἐπιμελείας ἐπὶ τὴν τελειότητα· φείδεσθαι δὲ, δηλονότι, χωρὶς τοῦ παριδεῖν ἐντολὴν Θεοῦ.

Κεφάλ. βʹ.

ΜΑΤΘΑΙΟΣ. Κάλαμον συντετριμμένον οὐ κατεάξει, καὶ λίνον τυφόμενον οὐ σβέσει, ἕως ἂν ἐκβάλῃ εἰς νῖκος τὴν κρίσιν, καὶ τῷ ὀνόματι αὐτοῦ ἔθνη ἐλπιοῦσιν.

ΠΡΟΣ ΡΩΜ. Τὸν δὲ ἀσθενοῦντα τῇ πίστει προσλαμβάνεσθε.

MATTHEW: And Jesus answered them, "Take heed that no one leads you astray. For many will come in my name, saying, 'I am the Christ,' and they will lead many astray" (24.4–5).

LUKE: Beware of the scribes who like to go about in long robes and love salutations in the marketplaces and the best seats in the synagogues and the places of honor at feasts, who devour widows' houses and for a pretense make long prayers. They will receive the greater condemnation (20.46–47).

GALATIANS: But even if we or an angel from heaven should preach to you a gospel contrary to that which we preached to you, let him be accursed. As we have said before so now I say again: If anyone is preaching to you a gospel contrary to that which you received, let him be accursed (1.8–9).

41.1 That it is necessary to cut off every cause of scandal even if it might appear to be the most natural and the most necessary thing.

MATTHEW: Woe to the man by whom the *scandal* comes! And if your *foot or your hand scandalizes you*, cut *them* off and throw *them* away; it is better for you to enter life *lame or maimed* than with *two feet or two hands* to be thrown into the eternal fire. And if your eye *scandalizes you*, pluck it out and throw it away (18.7–9).

41.2 That it is necessary to spare those weaker in the faith and to lead them up through careful cultivation to full maturity; that is, of course, to spare them without neglecting the command of God.

MATTHEW: "He will not break a bruised reed or quench a smoldering wick till he *issues judgment unto victory*, and in his name will the Gentiles hope"[18] (12.20–21).

ROMANS: As for the man who is weak in faith, welcome him (14.1).

---

[18]Quoting Is 42.3–4

ΠΡΟΣ ΓΑΛ. Ἐὰν καὶ προληφθῇ ἄνθρωπος ἔν τινι παραπτώματι, ὑμεῖς οἱ πνευματικοὶ καταρτίζετε τὸν τοιοῦτον ἐν πνεύματι πραό-τητος, σκοπῶν σεαυτόν, μὴ καὶ σὺ πειρασθῇς. Ἀλλήλων τὰ βάρη βαστάζετε, καὶ οὕτως ἀναπληρώσατε τὸν νόμον τοῦ Χριστοῦ.

ΟΡΟΣ ΜΒ'.

[42.1] Ὅτι οὐ δεῖ νομίζειν ἐπὶ καταλύσει τοῦ νόμου καὶ τῶν προφητῶν τὸν Κύριον ἐληλυθέναι, ἀλλ' ἐπὶ πληρώσει καὶ προσθήκῃ τῶν τελειοτέρων.

Κεφάλ. α'.

ΜΑΤΘΑΙΟΣ. Μὴ νομίσητε ὅτι ἦλθον καταλῦσαι τὸν νόμον, ἢ τοὺς προφήτας· οὐκ ἦλθον καταλῦσαι, ἀλλὰ πληρῶσαι. ΠΡΟΣ ΡΩΜ. Νόμον οὖν καταργοῦμεν διὰ τῆς πίστεως; Μὴ γένοιτο, ἀλλὰ νόμον ἱστῶμεν. [371]

ΟΡΟΣ ΜΓ'.

[43.1] Ὅτι ὡς νόμος τὰς πράξεις ἀπαγορεύει τὰς φαύλας, οὕτω τὸ εὐαγγέλιον αὐτὰ τὰ κεκρυμμένα πάθη τῆς ψυχῆς.

Κεφάλ. α'.

ΜΑΤΘΑΙΟΣ. Ἠκούσατε, ὅτι ἐρρέθη τοῖς ἀρχαίοις, οὐ φονεύσεις· ὃς δ' ἂν φονεύσῃ, ἔνοχος ἔσται τῇ κρίσει. Ἐγὼ δὲ λέγω ὑμῖν, ὅτι πᾶς ὁ ὀργιζόμενος τῷ ἀδελφῷ αὐτοῦ εἰκῆ, ἔνοχος ἔσται τῇ κρίσει. ΠΡΟΣ ΡΩΜ. Οὐ γὰρ ὁ ἐν τῷ φανερῷ Ἰουδαῖός ἐστιν, οὐδὲ ἡ ἐν τῷ φανερῷ ἐν σαρκὶ περιτομή· ἀλλ' ὁ ἐν τῷ κρυπτῷ Ἰουδαῖος, καὶ περιτομὴ καρδίας ἐν πνεύματι, οὐ γράμματι, οὗ ὁ ἔπαινος οὐκ ἐξ ἀνθρώπων, ἀλλ' ἐκ τοῦ Θεοῦ.

[43.2] Ὅτι ὡς ὁ νόμος τὸ ἐκ μέρους, οὕτω τὸ εὐαγγέλιον τὸ ὁλόκληρον ἐφ' ἑκάστῳ τῶν κατορθουμένων ἐπιζητεῖ.

Κεφάλ. β'.

ΛΟΥΚΑΣ. Πάντα ὅσα ἔχεις πώλησον, καὶ διάδος πτωχοῖς, καὶ ἕξεις θησαυρὸν ἐν οὐρανῷ, καὶ δεῦρο, ἀκολούθει μοι. ΠΡΟΣ ΚΟΛ. Ἐν ᾧ καὶ περιετμήθητε περιτομῇ ἀχειροποιήτῳ ἐν τῇ ἀπεκδύσει τοῦ σώματος τῶν ἁμαρτιῶν τῆς σαρκὸς, ἐν τῇ περιτομῇ τοῦ Χριστοῦ.

GALATIANS: If a man is overtaken in any trespass, you who are spiritual should restore him in a spirit of gentleness. Look to yourself, lest you too be tempted. Bear one another's burdens, and so fulfill the law of Christ (6.1–2).

42.1   That it is necessary not to think that the Lord came to dissolve the law and the prophets, but for their fulfillment and completion.

MATTHEW: Think not that I have come to abolish the law and the prophets; I have come not to abolish them but to fulfill them (5.17).

ROMANS: Do we then overthrow the law by this faith? By no means! On the contrary, we uphold the law (3.31).

43.1   That as the law forbids base acts, so the Gospel, in like manner, the hidden passions of the soul.

MATTHEW: You have heard that it was said to the men of old, "You shall not kill, and whoever kills shall be liable to judgment." But I say to you that everyone who is angry with his brother *without cause* shall be liable to judgment (5.21–22).

ROMANS: For he is not a real Jew who is one outwardly, nor is true circumcision something external and physical. He is a Jew who is one inwardly, and real circumcision is a matter of the heart, spiritual and not literal. His praise is not from men but from God (2.28–29).

43.2   That as the law seeks after a part, so the Gospel seeks the fullness of every kind of righteousness.

LUKE: Sell all that you have and distribute to the poor, and you will have treasure in heaven, and come follow me (18.22).

COLOSSIANS: In him also you were circumcised with a circumcision made without hands by putting off the body *of the sins* of the flesh in the circumcision of Christ (2.11).

[43.3] Ὅτι ἀδύνατον καταξιωθῆναι βασιλείας οὐρανῶν τοὺς μὴ πλείονα τῆς ἐν τῷ νόμῳ τὴν κατὰ τὸ εὐαγγέλιον δικαιοσύνην ἐπιδεικνυμένους.

Κεφάλ. γ'.

ΜΑΤΘΑΙΟΣ. Ἐὰν μὴ περισσεύῃ ἡ δικαιοσύνη ὑμῶν πλεῖον τῶν γραμματέων καὶ Φαρισαίων, οὐ μὴ εἰσέλθητε εἰς τὴν βασιλείαν τῶν οὐρανῶν.

ΠΡΟΣ ΦΙΛΙΠ. Εἴ τις δοκεῖ ἄλλος πεποιθέναι ἐν σαρκὶ, ἐγὼ μᾶλλον, περιτομὴ ὀκταήμερος· ἐκ γένους Ἰσραὴλ· φυλῆς Βενιαμίν· Ἑβραῖος ἐξ Ἑβραίων· κατὰ νόμον Φαρισαῖος· κατὰ ζῆλον διώκων τὴν [372] Ἐκκλησίαν· κατὰ δικαιοσύνην τὴν ἐν νόμῳ γενόμενος ἄμεμπτος. Ἀλλ' ἅτινα ἦν μοι κέρδη, ταῦτα ἥγημαι διὰ τὸν Χριστὸν ζημίαν.

Ἀλλὰ μὲν οὖν καὶ ἡγοῦμαι ζημίαν πάντα εἶναι διὰ τὸ ὑπερέχον τῆς γνώσεως Ἰησοῦ Χριστοῦ τοῦ Κυρίου ἡμῶν, δι' ὃν τὰ πάντα ἐζημιώθην, καὶ ἡγοῦμαι σκύβαλα εἶναι, ἵνα Χριστὸν κερδήσω, καὶ εὑρεθῶ[13] ἐν αὐτῷ μὴ ἔχων ἐμὴν δικαιοσύνην τὴν ἐκ νόμου, ἀλλὰ τὴν διὰ πίστεως Χριστοῦ, τὴν ἐκ Θεοῦ δικαιοσύνην.

ΟΡΟΣ ΜΔ'.

[44.1] Ὅτι ὁ ζυγὸς τοῦ Χριστοῦ χρηστὸς, καὶ τὸ φορτίον αὐτοῦ ἐλαφρόν ἐστιν εἰς ἀνάπαυσιν τῶν καταδεχομένων· πάντα δὲ τὰ ἀλλότρια τῆς κατὰ τὸ εὐαγγέλιον διδασκαλίας, βαρέα καὶ φορτικά.

Κεφάλ. α'.

ΜΑΤΘΑΙΟΣ. Δεῦτε πάντες πρός με οἱ κοπιῶντες καὶ πεφορτισμένοι, κἀγὼ ἀναπαύσω ὑμᾶς. Ἄρατε τὸν ζυγόν μου ἐφ' ὑμᾶς, καὶ μάθετε ἀπ' ἐμοῦ, ὅτι πρᾶός εἰμι καὶ ταπεινὸς τῇ καρδίᾳ, καὶ εὑρήσετε ἀνάπαυσιν ταῖς ψυχαῖς ὑμῶν. Ὁ γὰρ ζυγός μου χρηστὸς, καὶ τὸ φορτίον μου ἐλαφρόν ἐστιν.

ΟΡΟΣ ΜΕ'.

[45.1] Ὅτι ἀδύνατον καταξιωθῆναι βασιλείας οὐρανῶν τοὺς μὴ παιδίων πρὸς ἄλληλα ἰσοτιμίαν ἐν ἀλλήλοις μιμουμένους.

Κεφάλ. α'.

ΜΑΤΘΑΙΟΣ. Ἀμὴν λέγω ὑμῖν, ἐὰν μὴ στραφῆτε, καὶ γένησθε ὡς τὰ παιδία, οὐ μὴ εἰσέλθητε εἰς τὴν βασιλείαν τῶν οὐρανῶν.

---

[13]Corrected from εὑρεθῷ.

43.3 That those who do not manifest righteousness according to the Gospel, which is greater than that according to the law, cannot be found worthy of the kingdom of heaven.

MATTHEW: Unless your righteousness exceeds that of the scribes and Pharisees, you will never enter the kingdom of heaven (5.20).

PHILIPPIANS: If any other man thinks he has reason for confidence in the flesh, I have more: circumcised on the eighth day, of the people of Israel, of the tribe of Benjamin, a Hebrew born of Hebrews; as to the law a Pharisee, as to zeal a persecutor of the church, as to righteousness under the law blameless. But whatever gain I had I counted as loss for the sake of Christ. Indeed I count everything as loss because of the surpassing worth of knowing *Jesus Christ our Lord.* For his sake I have suffered the loss of all things and count them as refuse, in order that I may gain Christ and be found in him, not having a righteousness of my own based on law but that which is through faith in Christ, the righteousness from God (3.4–9).

44.1 That the yoke of Christ is favorable, and his burden is light, unto the respite of those who receive it; and that everything foreign to the teaching of the Gospel is heavy and burdensome.

MATTHEW: Come to me all who labor and are heavy laden, and I will give you rest. Take my yoke upon you and learn from me, for I am gentle and lowly in heart, and you will find rest for your souls. For my yoke is easy, and my burden is light (11.28–30).

45.1 That those who do not imitate little children among one another, sharing equal honor, cannot be found worthy of the kingdom of heaven.

MATTHEW: Truly I say to you, unless you turn and become like children, you will never enter the kingdom of heaven (18.3).

[45.2] Ὅτι δεῖ τὸν ἐπιθυμοῦντα μείζονος δόξης καταξιωθῆναι ἐν τῇ βασιλείᾳ τῶν οὐρανῶν τὸ ἐνταῦθα ταπεινὸν καὶ ἔσχατον ἀγαπᾶν.

Κεφάλ. β'.

ΜΑΤΘΑΙΟΣ. Ὅστις οὖν ταπεινώσει ἑαυτὸν, ὡς [373] τὸ παιδίον τοῦτο, οὗτός ἐστιν ὁ μείζων ἐν τῇ βασιλείᾳ τῶν οὐρανῶν.

ΜΑΡΚΟΣ.[14] Ἀλλ' ὃς ἐὰν θέλῃ γενέσθαι μέγας ἐν ὑμῖν, ἔσται ὑμῶν διάκονος· καὶ ὃς ἐὰν θέλῃ γενέσθαι πρῶτος ὑμῶν, ἔσται πάντων δοῦλος.

ΠΡΟΣ ΦΙΛΙΠ. Μηδὲν κατ' ἐριθείαν[15] ἢ κενοδοξίαν, ἀλλὰ τῇ ταπεινοφροσύνῃ ἀλλήλους ἡγούμενοι ὑπερέχοντας ἑαυτῶν.

ΟΡΟΣ Μς'.

[46.1] Ὅτι ἐξ ἀντιπαραθέσεως τῆς ἐπὶ τοῖς ἐλάττοσι φυλαττομένης ἀκολουθίας τὴν ἐπὶ τοῖς μείζοσι σπουδὴν ἀπαιτούμεθα.

Κεφάλ. α'.

ΛΟΥΚΑΣ. Ἕκαστος ὑμῶν τῷ σαββάτῳ οὐ λύει τὸν βοῦν αὐτοῦ, ἢ τὸν ὄνον ἀπὸ τῆς φάτνης, καὶ ἀπαγαγὼν ποτίζει; Ταύτην δὲ θυγατέρα Ἀβραὰμ οὖσαν, ἣν ἔδησεν ὁ σατανᾶς ἰδοὺ δέκα καὶ ὀκτὼ ἔτη, οὐκ ἔδει λυθῆναι ἀπὸ τοῦ δεσμοῦ τούτου τῇ ἡμέραι τοῦ σαββάτου; Ἔλεγε δὲ παραβολὴν αὐτοῖς, πρὸς τὸ δεῖν πάντοτε προσεύχεσθαι καὶ μὴ ἐκκακεῖν. Κριτής τις ἦν ἔν τινι πόλει, τὸν Θεὸν μὴ φοβούμενος, καὶ ἄνθρωπον μὴ ἐντρεπόμενος. Χήρα δὲ ἦν ἐν τῇ πόλει ἐκείνῃ, καὶ ἤρχετο πρὸς αὐτὸν λέγουσα· ἐκδίκησόν με ἀπὸ τοῦ ἀντιδίκου μου. Καὶ οὐκ ἤθελεν ἐπὶ χρόνον. Μετὰ δὲ ταῦτα εἶπεν ἐν ἑαυτῷ· εἰ καὶ τὸν Θεὸν οὐ φοβοῦμαι, καὶ ἄνθρωπον οὐκ ἐντρέπομαι, διά γε τὸ παρέχειν μοι κόπον τὴν χήραν ταύτην, ἐκδικήσω αὐτὴν, ἵνα μὴ εἰς τέλος ἐρχομένη ὑπωπιάζῃ με. Εἶπε δὲ ὁ Κύριος· ἀκούσατε, τί ὁ κριτὴς τῆς ἀδικίας λέγει· ὁ δὲ Θεὸς οὐ μὴ ποιήσῃ τὴν ἐκδίκησιν τῶν ἐκλεκτῶν αὐτοῦ, τῶν βοώντων πρὸς αὐτὸν ἡμέρας καὶ νυκτός;

ΠΡΟΣ ΤΙΜ. β'. Οὐδεὶς στρατευόμενος ἐμπλέκεται ταῖς τοῦ βίου πραγματείαις, ἵνα τῷ στρατολογήσαντι ἀρέσῃ. Ἐὰν δὲ καὶ ἀθλῇ τις, οὐ στεφανοῦται, ἐὰν μὴ νομίμως ἀθλήσῃ. [374]

---

[14]The attribution has been corrected.
[15]Corrected from ἐρίθειαν.

45.2 That it is necessary for the one who desires to be found worthy of greater glory in the kingdom of heaven, now to love humility and last place.

MATTHEW: Whoever humbles himself like this child, he is the greatest in the kingdom of heaven (18.4).

MARK: But whoever would be great among you must be your servant, and whoever would be first among you must be slave of all (10.43–44).

PHILIPPIANS: Do nothing from selfishness or conceit, but in humility count others better than yourselves (2.3).

46.1 That by comparison with the manner in which lesser things are pursued is zeal demanded in greater things.

LUKE: Does not each of you on the Sabbath untie his ox or his ass from the manger and lead it away to water it? And ought not this woman, a daughter of Abraham whom Satan bound for eighteen years, be loosed from this bond on the Sabbath day? (13.15–16).

LUKE: And he told them a parable to the effect that *one* ought always to pray and not lose heart. He said, "In a certain city there was a judge who neither feared God nor regarded man, and there was a widow in that city who kept coming to him and saying, 'Vindicate me against my adversary.' For a while he refused, but afterward he said to himself, 'Though I neither fear God nor regard man, yet because this widow bothers me I will vindicate her, or she will wear me out by her continual coming.'" And the Lord said, "Hear what the unrighteous judge says. And will not God vindicate his elect, who cry to him day and night?" (18.1–7).

2 TIMOTHY: No soldier on service gets entangled in civilian pursuits, since his aim is to satisfy the one who enlisted him. An athlete is not crowned unless he competes according to the rules (2.4–5).

[46.2]   Ὅτι ἐξ ἀντιπαραθέσεως τῶν ἐπὶ τοῖς ἐλάττοσιν ἐκ πίστεως
φόβον, καὶ ἐξ ἐπιθυμίας ἀξιολόγου σπουδὴν ἐπιδειξαμένων, οἱ ἐπὶ
τοῖς μείζοσι καταφρονηταὶ ἢ ἀμελεῖς ἁλόντες σφοδροτέραν ἔχουσι
τὴν κατάκρισιν.

Κεφάλ. β΄.

ΛΟΥΚΑΣ. Βασίλισσα Νότου ἐγερθήσεται ἐν τῇ κρίσει μετὰ τῶν
ἀνδρῶν τῆς γενεᾶς ταύτης, καὶ κατακρινεῖ αὐτούς, ὅτι ἦλθεν ἐκ τῶν
περάτων τῆς γῆς, ἀκοῦσαι τὴν σοφίαν Σολομῶντος, καὶ ἰδοὺ πλεῖον
Σολομῶντος ὧδε.

ΜΑΤΘΑΙΟΣ. Ἄνδρες Νινευῖται ἀναστήσονται ἐν τῇ κρίσει μετὰ
τῆς γενεᾶς ταύτης, καὶ κατακρινοῦσιν αὐτήν, ὅτι μετενόησαν εἰς τὸ
κήρυγμα Ἰωνᾶ, καὶ ἰδοὺ πλεῖον Ἰωνᾶ ὧδε.

[46.3]   Ὅτι οὐ δεῖ καταφρονεῖν τῶν μειζόνων, ἐπὶ τοῖς ἐλάττοσι
σπουδὴν ἐνδεικνύμενον. Προηγουμένως δὲ τὰ μείζονα τῶν
προσταγμάτων ποιοῦντα, συγκατορθοῦν καὶ τὰ ἐλάττονα.

Κεφάλ. γ΄.

ΜΑΤΘΑΙΟΣ. Οὐαὶ ὑμῖν, γραμματεῖς καὶ Φαρισαῖοι, ὑποκριταὶ,
ὅτι ἀποδεκατοῦτε τὸ ἡδύοσμον, καὶ τὸ ἄνηθον, καὶ τὸ κύμινον, καὶ
ἀφήκατε τὰ βαρύτερα τοῦ νόμου, τὴν κρίσιν, καὶ τὸν ἔλεον, καὶ τὴν
πίστιν. Ταῦτα ἔδει ποιῆσαι, κἀκεῖνα μὴ ἀφιέναι. Ὁδηγοὶ τυφλοί, οἱ
διυλίζοντες τὸν κώνωπα, τὴν δὲ κάμηλον καταπίνοντες.

ΟΡΟΣ ΜΖ΄.

[47.1]   Ὅτι οὐ δεῖ θησαυρίζειν ἑαυτῷ ἐπὶ τῆς γῆς, ἀλλ᾽ ἐν οὐρανῷ·
καὶ τίς ὁ τρόπος τοῦ ἐν οὐρανῷ θησαυρίζειν.

Κεφάλ. α΄.

ΜΑΤΘΑΙΟΣ. Μὴ θησαυρίζετε ὑμῖν θησαυροὺς ἐπὶ τῆς γῆς,
ὅπου σὴς καὶ βρῶσις ἀφανίζει, καὶ ὅπου κλέπται διορύσσουσι καὶ
κλέπτουσι. Θησαυρίζετε [375] δὲ ὑμῖν θησαυροὺς ἐν οὐρανῷ, ὅπου
οὔτε σὴς, οὔτε βρῶσις ἀφανίζει, καὶ ὅπου κλέπται οὐ διορύσσουσιν,
οὐδὲ κλέπτουσιν.

ΛΟΥΚΑΣ. Πωλήσατε τὰ ὑπάρχοντα ὑμῶν, καὶ δότε ἐλεημοσύνην.
Ποιήσατε ἑαυτοῖς βαλάντια μὴ παλαιούμενα· θησαυρὸν ἀνέκλει-
πτον ἐν τοῖς οὐρανοῖς.

46.2   That by comparison with those manifesting in lesser things fear born of faith and zeal from a praiseworthy desire are those more vehemently condemned who are found disdainful or heedless of the greater things.

LUKE: The queen of the South will arise at the judgment with the men of this generation and condemn them; for she came from the ends of the earth to hear the wisdom of Solomon,[19] and behold, something greater than Solomon is here (11.31).

MATTHEW: The men of Nineveh will arise at the judgment with this generation and condemn it; for they repented at the preaching of Jonah,[20] and behold, something greater than Jonah is here (12.41).

46.3   That it is necessary not to disdain the greater things, showing zeal for the lesser, but, first doing the greater commands, to cooperate also in maintaining the lesser.

MATTHEW: Woe to you scribes and Pharisees, hypocrites! For you tithe mint and dill and cumin and have neglected the weightier matters of the law, justice and mercy and faith; these you ought to have done without neglecting the others. You blind guides, straining out a gnat and swallowing a camel (23.23–24)!

47.1   That it is necessary not to store up for yourself upon the earth, but in heaven; and what the way is to store up in heaven.

MATTHEW: Do not lay up for yourselves treasures on earth, where moth and rust consume and where thieves break in and steal, but lay up for yourselves treasures in heaven, where neither moth nor rust consumes and where thieves do not break in and steal (6.19–20).

LUKE: Sell your possessions and give alms; provide yourselves with purses that do not grow old, with a treasure in the heavens that does not fail (12.33).

[19]Cf. 1 Kg (LXX 3 Kingdoms) 10.1; 2 Chr 2.9
[20]Cf. Jon 3.4–5

ΛΟΥΚΑΣ. Πάντα ὅσα ἔχεις πώλησον, καὶ διάδος πτωχοῖς, καὶ ἕξεις θησαυρὸν ἐν οὐρανοῖς.

ΠΡΟΣ ΤΙΜ. α΄. Εὐμεταδότους εἶναι, κοινωνικούς, ἀποθησαυρίζοντας ἑαυτοῖς θεμέλιον καλὸν εἰς τὸ μέλλον, ἵνα ἐπιλάβωνται τῆς ὄντως ζωῆς.

ΟΡΟΣ ΜΗ΄.

[48.1] Ὅτι δεῖ ἐλεήμονα καὶ εὐμετάδοτον εἶναι· κατηγοροῦνται γὰρ οἱ μὴ τοιοῦτοι.

Κεφάλ. α΄.

ΜΑΤΘΑΙΟΣ. Μακάριοι οἱ ἐλεήμονες, ὅτι αὐτοὶ ἐλεηθήσονται.

ΛΟΥΚΑΣ.[16] Παντὶ τῷ αἰτοῦντί σε, δίδου.

ΠΡΟΣ ΡΩΜ. Ἀστόργους, ἀνελεήμονας, οἵτινες τὸ δικαίωμα τοῦ Θεοῦ ἐπιγνόντες, ὅτι οἱ τὰ τοιαῦτα πράσσοντες ἄξιοι θανάτου εἰσίν.

ΠΡΟΣ ΤΙΜ. α΄. Εὐμεταδότους εἶναι, κοινωνικούς.

[48.2] Ὅτι πᾶν ὅπερ ἂν ἔχῃ τις πλέον τοῦ ἐπιδεομένου τῶν πρὸς τὸ ζῆν ἀναγκαίων, ὀφειλέτης ἐστὶν ἐκεῖνον εὐεργετῆσαι, κατ᾽ ἐντολὴν τοῦ Κυρίου τοῦ καὶ δεδωκότος ἃ ἔχομεν.

Κεφάλ. β΄.

ΛΟΥΚΑΣ. Ὁ ἔχων δύο χιτῶνας, μεταδότω τῷ μὴ ἔχοντι· καὶ ὁ ἔχων βρώματα, ὁμοίως ποιείτω.

ΠΡΟΣ ΚΟΡ. α΄. Τί γὰρ ἔχεις, ὃ οὐκ ἔλαβες;

ΠΡΟΣ ΚΟΡ. β΄. Τὸ ὑμῶν περίσσευμα, εἰς τὸ ἐκείνων ὑστέρημα· ἵνα καὶ τὸ ἐκείνων περίσσευμα γένηται εἰς τὸ ὑμῶν ὑστέρημα, ὅπως γένηται ἰσότης, καθὼς γέγραπται· «Ὁ τὸ πολύ, οὐκ ἐπλεόνασε· καὶ ὁ τὸ ὀλίγον οὐκ ἠλαττόνησεν.» [376]

[48.3] Ὅτι οὐ δεῖ πλουτεῖν, ἀλλὰ πτωχεύειν, κατὰ τὸν τοῦ Κυρίου λόγον.

Κεφάλ. γ΄.

ΛΟΥΚΑΣ. Μακάριοι οἱ πτωχοί, ὅτι ὑμετέρα ἐστὶν ἡ βασιλεία τοῦ Θεοῦ. Οὐαὶ ὑμῖν τοῖς πλουσίοις, ὅτι ἀπέχετε τὴν παράκλησιν ὑμῶν.

---

[16]The attribution has been corrected.

LUKE: Sell all that you have and distribute to the poor, and you will have treasure in heaven (18.22).

1 TIMOTHY: They are to be liberal and generous, thus laying up for themselves a good foundation for the future, so that they may take hold of the life which is life indeed (6.18–19).

48.1 That it is necessary to be merciful and generous; for they who are not are accused.

MATTHEW: Blessed are the merciful, for they shall obtain mercy (5.7).

LUKE: Give to everyone who begs from you (6.30).

ROMANS: Heartless, ruthless; though they know God's decree that those who do such things deserve to die (1.31–32).

1 TIMOTHY: They are to be liberal and generous (6.18).

48.2 That with everything someone might possess beyond the requirements of life's necessities one is obliged to do good, according to the commandment of the Lord who gave us what we have.

LUKE: He who has two coats, let him share with him who has none, and he who has food, let him do likewise (3.11).

1 CORINTHIANS: *For* what have you that you did not receive (4.7)?

2 CORINTHIANS: Your abundance should supply their want, so that their abundance may supply your want, that there may be equality. As it is written, "He who gathered much had nothing over, and he who gathered little had no lack"[21] (8.14–15).

48.3 That it is necessary not to be rich but to be poor, according to the word of the Lord.

LUKE: Blessed are you poor, for yours is the kingdom of God (6.20). But woe to you that are rich, for you have received your consolation (6.24).

[21]Ex 16.18

ΠΡΟΣ ΚΟΡ. β΄. Ἡ κατὰ βάθους πτωχεία αὐτῶν ἐπερίσσευσεν εἰς τὸν πλοῦτον τῆς ἁπλότητος αὐτῶν.

ΠΡΟΣ ΤΙΜ. α΄. Οἱ δὲ βουλόμενοι πλουτεῖν, ἐμπίπτουσιν εἰς πειρασμὸν καὶ παγίδα, καὶ ἐπιθυμίας πολλὰς ἀνοήτους καὶ βλαβερὰς, αἵτινες βυθίζουσι τοὺς ἀνθρώπους εἰς ὄλεθρον καὶ ἀπώλειαν. Ῥίζα γὰρ πάντων τῶν κακῶν ἐστιν ἡ φιλαργυρία, ἧς τινες ὀρεγόμενοι, ἀπεπλανήθησαν ἀπὸ τῆς πίστεως, καὶ ἑαυτοὺς περιέπειραν ὀδύναις πολλαῖς.

[48.4] Ὅτι οὐ δεῖ φροντίζειν τοῦ περισσεύεσθαι ἐν τοῖς πρὸς τὸ ζῆν· οὔτε περὶ τὴν πλησμονὴν, οὔτε περὶ τὴν πολυτέλειαν σπουδὴν ἔχειν· καθαρεύειν δὲ παντὸς εἴδους πλεονεξίας καὶ καλλωπισμοῦ.

Κεφάλ. δ΄.

ΛΟΥΚΑΣ. Ὁρᾶτε, καὶ φυλάσσεσθε ἀπὸ πάσης πλεονεξίας, ὅτι οὐκ ἐν τῷ περισσεύειν τινὶ ἡ ζωὴ αὐτοῦ ἐστιν ἐκ τῶν ὑπαρχόντων αὐτῷ.

ΠΡΟΣ ΤΙΜ. α΄. Κοσμεῖν ἑαυτὰς μὴ ἐν πλέγμασιν, ἢ χρυσῷ, ἢ μαργαρίταις, ἢ ἱματισμῷ πολυτελεῖ. Ἔχοντες διατροφὰς καὶ σκεπάσματα, τούτοις ἀρκεσθησόμεθα.

[48.5] Ὅτι οὐ δεῖ μεριμνᾶν τῆς ἰδίας ἕνεκεν χρείας, οὐδὲ τοῖς ἡτοιμασμένοις πρὸς τὴν παροῦσαν ζωὴν ἐπελπίζειν, ἀλλὰ τῷ Θεῷ ἀποδιδόναι τὰ καθ᾽ ἑαυτόν.

Κεφάλ. ε΄.

ΜΑΤΘΑΙΟΣ. Οὐ δύνασθε Θεῷ δουλεύειν καὶ μαμμωνᾷ. Διὰ τοῦτο λέγω ὑμῖν, μὴ μεριμνᾶτε τῇ ψυχῇ ὑμῶν τί φάγητε, καὶ τί πίητε, μηδὲ τῷ σώματι ὑμῶν τί ἐνδύσησθε. Οὐχὶ ἡ ψυχὴ πλεῖόν ἐστι τῆς τροφῆς, καὶ τὸ σῶμα τοῦ ἐνδύματος; Ἐμβλέψατε [377] εἰς τὰ πετεινὰ τοῦ οὐρανοῦ, ὅτι οὐ σπείρουσιν, οὐδὲ θερίζουσιν, οὐδὲ συνάγουσιν εἰς ἀποθήκας· καὶ ὁ Πατὴρ ὑμῶν ὁ οὐράνιος τρέφει αὐτά. Οὐχ ὑμεῖς μᾶλλον διαφέρετε αὐτῶν; Τίς δὲ ἐξ ὑμῶν μεριμνῶν δύναται προσθεῖναι ἐπὶ τὴν ἡλικίαν αὐτοῦ πῆχυν ἕνα; Καὶ περὶ ἐνδύματος τί μεριμνᾶτε; Καταμάθετε τὰ κρίνα τοῦ ἀγροῦ πῶς αὐξάνει· οὐ κοπιᾷ, οὐδὲ νήθει. Λέγω δὲ ὑμῖν· οὐδὲ Σολομὼν ἐν πάσῃ τῇ

2 CORINTHIANS: Their extreme poverty has overflowed in a wealth of liberality on their part (8.2).

1 TIMOTHY: But those who desire to be rich fall into temptation, into a snare, into many senseless and hurtful desires that plunge men into ruin and destruction. For the love of money is the root of all evils; it is through this craving that some have wandered away from the faith and pierced *themselves* with many pangs (6.9–10).

48.4 That it is necessary neither to set one's mind on acquiring a surplus of the things of this life nor to be zealous after abundance or extravagance, but to be clean of every kind of covetousness and display.

LUKE: Take heed and beware of all covetousness, for a man's life does not consist in the abundance of his possessions (12.15).

1 TIMOTHY: Women should adorn themselves not with braided hair or gold or pearls or costly attire (2.9).

1 TIMOTHY: If we have food and clothing, with these we shall be content (6.8).

48.5 That it is necessary not to be anxious about one's own needs nor to set one's hope on arrangements made for the present life, but to deliver one's cares over to God.

MATTHEW: You cannot serve God and mammon. Therefore I tell you, do not be anxious about your life, what you shall eat *and* what you shall drink, nor about your body, what you shall put on. Is not life more than food and the body more than clothing? Look at the birds of the air: they neither sow nor reap nor gather into barns, and yet your heavenly Father feeds them. Are you not of more value than they? And which of you by being anxious can add one cubit to his span of life? And why are you anxious about clothing? Consider the lilies of the field, how they grow; they neither toil nor spin, yet I tell you, even Solomon in all his glory was not arrayed like one

δόξῃ αὐτοῦ περιεβάλετο ὡς ἓν τούτων. Εἰ δὲ τὸν χόρτον τοῦ ἀγροῦ, σήμερον ὄντα, καὶ αὔριον εἰς κλίβανον βαλλόμενον, ὁ Θεὸς οὕτως ἀμφιέννυσιν, οὐ πολλῷ μᾶλλον ὑμᾶς, ὀλιγόπιστοι; Μὴ οὖν μεριμνήσητε λέγοντες· τί φάγωμεν, ἢ τί πίωμεν, ἢ τί περιβαλώμεθα; Ταῦτα γὰρ πάντα τὰ ἔθνη ἐπιζητεῖ. Οἶδε γὰρ ὁ Πατὴρ ὑμῶν ὁ οὐράνιος, ὅτι χρῄζετε τούτων πάντων. Ζητεῖτε δὲ πρῶτον τὴν βασιλείαν τοῦ Θεοῦ, καὶ τὴν δικαιοσύνην αὐτοῦ, καὶ ταῦτα πάντα προστεθήσεται ὑμῖν. Μὴ οὖν μεριμνήσητε εἰς τὴν αὔριον· ἡ γὰρ αὔριον μεριμνήσει τὰ ἑαυτῆς· ἀρκετὸν τῇ ἡμέρᾳ ἡ κακία αὐτῆς.

ΛΟΥΚΑΣ. Ἀνθρώπου τινὸς πλουσίου εὐφόρησεν ἡ χώρα, καὶ διελογίζετο ἐν ἑαυτῷ λέγων· τί ποιήσω; ὅτι οὐκ ἔχω ποῦ συνάξω τοὺς καρπούς μου. Καὶ εἶπε· τοῦτο ποιήσω· καθελῶ μου τὰς ἀποθήκας, καὶ μείζονας οἰκοδομήσω, καὶ συνάξω ἐκεῖ πάντα τὰ γεννήματά μου καὶ τὰ ἀγαθά μου· καὶ ἐρῶ τῇ ψυχῇ μου· ψυχή, ἔχεις πολλὰ ἀγαθὰ κείμενα εἰς ἔτη πολλά· ἀναπαύου, φάγε, πίε, εὐφραίνου, καὶ τὰ ἑξῆς.

ΠΡΟΣ ΤΙΜ. α΄. Τοῖς πλουσίοις τοῦ νῦν αἰῶνος παράγγελλε, μὴ ὑψηλοφρονεῖν, μηδὲ ἠλπικέναι ἐπὶ πλούτου ἀδηλότητι, ἀλλ᾿ ἐπὶ τῷ Θεῷ τῷ παρέχοντι ἡμῖν τὰ πάντα πλουσίως εἰς ἀπόλαυσιν.

[48.6] Ὅτι δεῖ φροντίζειν καὶ μεριμνᾶν περὶ τῆς τῶν ἀδελφῶν χρείας κατὰ τὸ θέλημα τοῦ Κυρίου.

Κεφάλ. ς΄.

ΜΑΤΘΑΙΟΣ. Δεῦτε, οἱ εὐλογημένοι τοῦ Πατρός μου, κληρονομήσατε τὴν ἡτοιμασμένην ὑμῖν βασιλείαν ἀπὸ καταβολῆς κόσμου· ἐπείνασα γάρ, καὶ ἐδώκατέ μοι φαγεῖν· ἐδίψησα, καὶ ἐποτίσατέ με· ξένος ἤμην, καὶ συνηγάγετέ με· γυμνός, καὶ περιεβάλετέ [378] με· ἠσθένησα, καὶ ἐπεσκέψασθέ με· ἐν φυλακῇ ἤμην, καὶ ἤλθετε πρός με. Καὶ μετ᾿ ὀλίγα· Ἀμὴν λέγω ὑμῖν, ἐφ᾿ ὅσον ἐποιήσατε ἑνὶ τούτων τῶν ἀδελφῶν μου τῶν ἐλαχίστων, ἐμοὶ ἐποιήσατε.

ΙΩΑΝΝΗΣ. Ἐπάρας οὖν τοὺς ὀφθαλμοὺς ὁ Ἰησοῦς, καὶ θεασάμενος ὅτι πολὺς ὄχλος ἔρχεται πρὸς αὐτόν, λέγει πρὸς τὸν Φίλιππον· πόθεν ἀγοράσομεν ἄρτους, ἵνα φάγωσιν οὗτοι; καὶ τὰ ἑξῆς.

of these. But if God so clothes the grass of the field, which today is alive and tomorrow is thrown into the oven, will he not much more clothe you, O men of little faith? Therefore do not be anxious, saying, "What shall we eat?" or "What shall we drink?" or "What shall we wear?" for the Gentiles seek all these things, and your heavenly Father knows that you need them all. But seek first *the kingdom of God* and his righteousness, and all these things shall be yours as well. Therefore do not be anxious about tomorrow, for tomorrow will be anxious for *its own things*. Let the day's own trouble be sufficient for the day (6.24–34).

LUKE: The land of a rich man brought forth plentifully, and he thought to himself, "What shall I do, for I have nowhere to store my crops?" And he said, "I will do this: I will pull down my barns and build larger ones, and there I will store all my *produce* and my goods. And I will say to my soul, 'Soul, you have ample goods laid up for many years; take your ease, eat, drink, be merry'" (12.16–19), *and what follows*.

1 TIMOTHY: As for the rich *of* this world, charge them not to be haughty nor to set their hopes on uncertain riches but on God who richly furnishes us with everything to enjoy (6.17).

48.6 That it is necessary to set one's mind upon and be anxious about the needs of the brethren, according to the will of the Lord.

MATTHEW: Come, O blessed of my Father, inherit the kingdom prepared for you from the foundation of the world, for I was hungry and you gave me food; I was thirsty and you gave me drink; I was a stranger and you welcomed me; I was naked and you clothed me; I was sick and you visited me; I was in prison and you came to me (25.34–36). *And a little further*: Truly I say to you, as you did it to one of the least of these my brethren you did it to me (25.40).

JOHN: Lifting up his eyes then and seeing that a multitude was coming to him, Jesus said to Philip, "How *will we* buy bread, so that these people may eat?" (6.5). *and what follows*.

ΠΡΟΣ ΚΟΡ. α΄. Περὶ δὲ τῆς λογίας τῆς εἰς τοὺς ἁγίους, ὥσπερ διέταξα ταῖς Ἐκκλησίαις τῆς Γαλατίας, οὕτω καὶ ὑμεῖς ποιήσατε. Κατὰ μίαν σαββάτων ἕκαστος ὑμῶν παρ᾽ ἑαυτῷ τιθέτω, θησαυρίζων ὅ τι ἂν εὐοδῶται· ἵνα μὴ ὅταν ἔλθω, τότε λογίαι γίνωνται.

[48.7] Ὅτι δεῖ τὸν δυνατῶς ἔχοντα ἐργαζόμενον μεταδιδόναι τοῖς χρείαν ἔχουσιν. Ὁ γὰρ μὴ θέλων ἐργάζεσθαι οὐδὲ τοῦ φαγεῖν ἄξιος ἐκρίθη.

Κεφάλ. ζ΄.

ΜΑΤΘΑΙΟΣ. Ἄξιος ὁ ἐργάτης τῆς τροφῆς αὐτοῦ.

ΠΡΑΞΕΙΣ. Πάντα ὑπέδειξα ὑμῖν, ὅτι οὕτω κοπιῶντας δεῖ ἀντιλαμβάνεσθαι τῶν ἀσθενούντων, μνημονεύειν τε τῶν λόγων τοῦ Κυρίου, ὅτι αὐτὸς εἶπε· μακάριόν ἐστι διδόναι μᾶλλον ἢ λαμβάνειν.

ΠΡΟΣ ΕΦΕΣ. Ὁ κλέπτων μηκέτι κλεπτέτω· μᾶλλον δὲ κοπιάτω, ἐργαζόμενος τὸ ἀγαθὸν ταῖς χερσὶν, ἵνα ἔχῃ μεταδιδόναι τῷ χρείαν ἔχοντι.

ΠΡΟΣ ΘΕΣΣ. β΄. Ὅτε ἦμεν πρὸς ὑμᾶς, τοῦτο παρηγγέλλομεν ὑμῖν, ὅτι εἴ τις οὐ θέλει ἐργάζεσθαι, μηδὲ ἐσθιέτω.

ΟΡΟΣ ΜΘ΄.

[49.1] Ὅτι οὐ χρὴ δικάζεσθαι οὐδὲ περὶ αὐτῶν τῶν πρὸς τὴν ἀναγκαίαν σκέπην τῷ σώματι περικειμένων.

Κεφάλ. α΄.

ΛΟΥΚΑΣ. Τῷ τύπτοντί σε ἐπὶ τὴν δεξιὰν σιαγόνα, πάρεχε καὶ τὴν ἄλλην· καὶ ἀπὸ τοῦ αἴροντός σου τὸ ἱμάτιον, καὶ τὸν χιτῶνα μὴ κωλύσῃς. Παντὶ δὲ τῷ αἰτοῦντί σε, δίδου· καὶ ἀπὸ τοῦ αἴροντος τὰ σὰ, μὴ ἀπαίτει.

ΠΡΟΣ ΚΟΡ. α΄. Τολμᾷ τις, πρᾶγμα [379] ἔχων πρὸς τὸν ἕτερον, κρίνεσθαι ἐπὶ τῶν ἀδίκων, καὶ οὐχὶ ἐπὶ τῶν ἁγίων; Καὶ μετ᾽ ὀλίγα· Ἤδη μὲν οὖν ὅλως ἥττημα ὑμῖν ἐστιν, ὅτι κρίματα ἔχετε μεθ᾽ ἑαυτῶν. Διὰ τί οὐχὶ μᾶλλον ἀδικεῖσθε; διὰ τί οὐχὶ μᾶλλον ἀποστερεῖσθε; Ἀλλὰ ὑμεῖς ἀδικεῖτε καὶ ἀποστερεῖτε, καὶ ταῦτα ἀδελφούς.

1 CORINTHIANS: Now concerning the contribution for the saints: as I directed the churches of Galatia, so you also are to do. On the first day of every week, each of you is to put something aside and store it up, as he may prosper, so that contributions need not be made when I come (16.1–2).

48.7   That it is necessary, for the one who is able, to work and to give to those in need, for the one who chooses not to work was judged worthy neither of eating.

MATTHEW: The laborer deserves his food (10.10).

ACTS: In all things I have shown you that by so toiling one must help the weak, remembering the words of *the Lord*, how he said, "It is more blessed to give than to receive" (20.35).

EPHESIANS: Let the thief no longer steal, but rather let him labor, doing honest work with his hands, so that he may be able to give to those in need (4.28).

2 THESSALONIANS: When we were with you we gave you this command: If anyone will not work, let him not eat (3.10).

49.1   That it is necessary not to go to law even over the very clothes one needs for covering one's body.

LUKE: To him who strikes you on the *right* cheek offer the other also, and from him who takes away your coat do not withhold even your shirt. Give to everyone who begs from you, and of him who takes away your goods do not ask them again (6.29–30).

1 CORINTHIANS: When one of you has a grievance against a brother does he dare go to law before the unrighteous instead of the saints (6.1)? *And a little further*: To have lawsuits at all with one another is defeat for you. Why not rather suffer wrong? Why not rather be defrauded? But you yourselves wrong and defraud, and that even your own brethren (6.7–8).

[49.2] Ὅτι οὐ δεῖ μάχεσθαι, ἢ ἑαυτὸν ἐκδικεῖν· πρὸς πάντας δὲ, εἰ δυνατὸν, εἰρηνεύειν, κατὰ τὴν ἐντολὴν τοῦ Κυρίου.

Κεφάλ. β΄.

ΜΑΤΘΑΙΟΣ. Ἠκούσατε, ὅτι ἐρρέθη, ὀφθαλμὸν ἀντὶ ὀφθαλμοῦ, καὶ ὀδόντα ἀντὶ ὀδόντος. Ἐγὼ δὲ λέγω ὑμῖν, μὴ ἀντιστῆναι τῷ πονηρῷ· ἀλλ᾽ ὅστις σε ῥαπίσῃ εἰς τὴν δεξιὰν σιαγόνα, στρέψον αὐτῷ καὶ τὴν ἄλλην, καὶ τὰ ἑξῆς.

ΜΑΡΚΟΣ. Ἔχετε ἐν ἑαυτοῖς ἅλα καὶ εἰρηνεύετε ἐν ἀλλήλοις.¹⁷

ΠΡΟΣ ΡΩΜ. Μηδενὶ κακὸν ἀντὶ κακοῦ ἀποδιδόντες, προνοού-μενοι καλὰ ἐνώπιον πάντων ἀνθρώπων. Εἰ δυνατὸν, τὸ ἐξ ὑμῶν μετὰ πάντων ἀνθρώπων εἰρηνεύοντες· μὴ ἑαυτοὺς ἐκδικοῦντες, ἀγαπητοί· ἀλλὰ δότε τόπον τῇ ὀργῇ.

ΠΡΟΣ ΤΙΜ. β΄. Δοῦλον δὲ Κυρίου οὐ δεῖ μάχεσθαι, ἀλλὰ ἤπιον εἶναι πρὸς πάντας.

[49.3] Ὅτι οὐ δεῖ οὔτε εἰς ἐκδίκησιν ἀδικουμένου ἑτέρου ἀμύ-νασθαι τὸν ἀδικοῦντα.

Κεφάλ. γ΄.

ΜΑΤΘΑΙΟΣ. Τότε προσελθόντες, ἐπέβαλον τὰς χεῖρας ἐπὶ τὸν Ἰησοῦν, καὶ ἐκράτησαν αὐτόν. Καὶ ἰδοὺ εἷς τῶν μετὰ Ἰησοῦ, ἐκτείνας τὴν χεῖρα, ἀπέσπασε τὴν μάχαιραν αὐτοῦ, καὶ πατάξας τὸν δοῦλον τοῦ ἀρχιερέως, ἀφεῖλεν αὐτοῦ τὸ ὠτίον. Λέγει δὲ αὐτῷ ὁ Ἰησοῦς· ἀπόστρεψον τὴν μάχαιράν σου εἰς τὸν τόπον αὐτῆς, ὅτι πάντες οἱ λαβόντες μάχαιραν, ἐν μαχαίρᾳ ἀπολοῦνται.

ΛΟΥΚΑΣ. Καὶ ἀπέστειλεν ἀγγέλους πρὸ προσώπου αὐτοῦ· καὶ [380] πορευθέντες ἦλθον εἰς κώμην Σαμαρειτῶν, ὥστε ἑτοιμάσα αὐτῷ. Καὶ οὐκ ἐδέξαντο αὐτὸν, ὅτι τὸ πρόσωπον αὐτοῦ ἦν

---

¹⁷Garnier: Ἀγάπην ἔχετε ἐν ἑαυτοῖς, ἀλλὰ καὶ εἰρηνεύετε ἐν ἀλλήλοις. What I have printed is the usual reading of Mk 9.50, which is not attested in Garnier's appa-ratus, but I have observed it in Vat. Gr. 413. Garnier's mss as well as Vat. Gr. 425 and BL Add MS 10069 agree on reading ἀλλὰ in place of ἅλα, but they disagree consider-ably concerning the direct object added to the front of the verse to make up for the loss of ἅλα, while Vat. Gr. 428 has ἀλλὰ but adds no new direct object. I suggest that Vat. Gr. 413 represents the original reading, which was first corrupted in the reading of Vat. Gr. 428 and further corrupted variously as scribes attempted to resolve the obvious deficiency.

49.2 That it is necessary not to fight nor to avenge oneself, but to be at peace with everyone if possible, according to the commandment of the Lord.

MATTHEW: You have heard that it was said, "An eye for an eye and a tooth for a tooth." But I say to you, "Do not resist one who is evil. But if anyone strikes you on the right cheek, turn to him the other also" (5.38–39), *and what follows.*

MARK: Have salt in yourselves and be at peace with one another (9.50).

ROMANS: Repay no one evil for evil, but take thought for what is noble in the sight of all. If possible, so far as it depends upon you, live peaceably with all. Beloved, never avenge yourselves but leave it to the wrath of God (12.17–19).

2 TIMOTHY: And the Lord's servant must not be quarrelsome but kindly to everyone (2.24).

49.3 That it is necessary not to exact vengeance on a wrongdoer even to avenge another who has been wronged.

MATTHEW: Then they came up and laid hands on Jesus and seized him. And behold, one of those who were with Jesus stretched out his hand and drew his sword and struck the slave of the high priest and cut off his ear. *Jesus* said to him, "Put your sword back into its place, for all who take the sword will perish by the sword" (26.50–52).

LUKE: And he sent messengers ahead of him who went and entered a village of the Samaritans to make ready for him, but the people would not receive him because his face was set toward Jerusa-

πορευόμενον εἰς Ἰερουσαλήμ. Ἰδόντες δὲ οἱ μαθηταὶ αὐτοῦ Ἰάκωβος
καὶ Ἰωάννης, εἶπον· Κύριε, θέλεις εἴπωμεν πῦρ καταβῆναι ἐκ τοῦ
οὐρανοῦ καὶ ἀναλῶσαι αὐτούς, ὡς καὶ Ἡλίας ἐποίησε; Στραφεὶς δὲ
ἐπετίμησεν αὐτοῖς, καὶ ἐπορεύθησαν εἰς ἑτέραν κώμην.

ΟΡΟΣ Ν΄.

[50.1] Ὅτι δεῖ συμβιβάζειν καὶ ἑτέρους εἰς εἰρήνην τὴν ἐν Χριστῷ.

Κεφάλ. α΄.

ΜΑΤΘΑΙΟΣ. Μακάριοι οἱ εἰρηνοποιοί, ὅτι αὐτοὶ υἱοὶ Θεοῦ
κληθήσονται.

ΙΩΑΝΝΗΣ. Εἰρήνην ἀφίημι ὑμῖν· εἰρήνην τὴν ἐμὴν δίδωμι ὑμῖν.

ΟΡΟΣ ΝΑ΄.

[51.1] Ὅτι δεῖ πρότερον ἑαυτὸν διορθοῦσθαι ἐφ᾽ ᾧτινιοῦν
ἐλαττώματι, καὶ τότε ἑτέρῳ ἐγκαλεῖν.

Κεφάλ. α΄.

ΜΑΤΘΑΙΟΣ. Τί δὲ βλέπεις τὸ κάρφος τὸ ἐν τῷ ὀφθαλμῷ τοῦ
ἀδελφοῦ σου, τὴν δὲ δοκὸν τὴν ἐν τῷ σῷ ὀφθαλμῷ οὐ κατανοεῖς; Ἢ
πῶς ἐρεῖς τῷ ἀδελφῷ σου· ἄφες ἐκβάλω τὸ κάρφος ἐκ τοῦ ὀφθαλμοῦ
σου· καὶ ἰδοὺ ἡ δοκὸς ἐν τῷ ὀφθαλμῷ σου; Ὑποκριτά, ἔκβαλε πρῶτον
τὴν δοκὸν ἐκ τοῦ ὀφθαλμοῦ σου, καὶ τότε διαβλέψεις ἐκβαλεῖν τὸ
κάρφος ἐκ τοῦ ὀφθαλμοῦ τοῦ ἀδελφοῦ σου.

ΠΡΟΣ ΡΩΜ. Διὸ ἀναπολόγητος εἶ, ἄνθρωπε, πᾶς ὁ κρίνων. Ἐν ᾧ
γὰρ κρίνεις τὸν ἕτερον, σεαυτὸν κατακρίνεις· τὰ γὰρ αὐτὰ πράσσεις
ὁ κρίνων. Οἴδαμεν δὲ ὅτι τὸ κρίμα τοῦ Θεοῦ ἐστι κατὰ ἀλήθειαν, ἐπὶ
τοὺς τὰ τοιαῦτα πράσσοντας. Λογίζῃ δὲ τοῦτο, ὦ ἄνθρωπε, ὁ κρίνων
τοὺς τὰ τοιαῦτα πράσσοντας, καὶ ποιῶν τὰ αὐτά, ὅτι σὺ ἐκφεύξῃ τὸ
κρῖμα τοῦ Θεοῦ; [381]

ΟΡΟΣ ΝΒ΄.

[52.1] Ὅτι οὐ χρὴ ἀδιαφορεῖν ἐπὶ τοῖς ἁμαρτάνουσι, λυπεῖσθαι δὲ
καὶ πενθεῖν ἐπ᾽ αὐτοῖς.

Κεφάλ. α΄.

ΛΟΥΚΑΣ. Καὶ ὡς ἤγγισεν, ἰδὼν τὴν πόλιν, ἔκλαυσεν ἐπ᾽ αὐτήν,
λέγων· ὅτι, εἰ ἔγνως καὶ σύ, καί γε ἐν τῇ ἡμέρᾳ ταύτῃ τὰ πρὸς εἰρήνην
σου· νῦν δὲ ἐκρύβη ἀπὸ ὀφθαλμῶν σου.

lem. And when his disciples James and John saw it, they said, "Lord, do you want us to bid fire come down from heaven and consume them *even as Elijah did*?" But he turned and rebuked them. And they went on to another village (9.52–56).

50.1 That it is necessary to bring others also into the peace that is in Christ.

MATTHEW: Blessed are the peacemakers, for they shall be called sons of God (5.9).

JOHN: Peace I leave with you; my peace I give to you (14.27).

51.1 That it is necessary first to correct oneself in the littlest thing whatsoever and then to call out another.

MATTHEW: Why do you see the speck that is in your brother's eye but do not notice the log that is in your own eye? Or how can you say to your brother, "Let me take the speck out of your eye," when there is the log in your own eye? You hypocrite, first take the log out of your own eye, and then you will see clearly to take the speck out of your brother's eye (7.3–5).

ROMANS: Therefore you have no excuse, you man, whoever you are, when you judge another; for in passing judgment upon him you condemn yourself because you, the judge, are doing the very same things. We know that the judgment of God rightly falls upon those who do such things. Do you suppose, O man, that when you judge those who do such things and yet do them yourself you will escape the judgment of God (2.1–3)?

52.1 That it is necessary not to be indifferent to sinners but to be grieved and to mourn for them.

LUKE: And when he drew near and saw the city he wept over it, saying, "*If only you knew, even this very day,* the things that make for *your* peace! But now they are hid from your eyes" (19.41–42).

ΠΡΟΣ ΚΟΡ. α΄. Ὅλως ἀκούεται ἐν ὑμῖν πορνεία, καὶ τοιαύτη πορνεία, ἥτις οὐδὲ ἐν τοῖς ἔθνεσιν ὀνομάζεται· ὥστε γυναῖκά τινα τοῦ πατρὸς ἔχειν. Καὶ ὑμεῖς πεφυσιωμένοι ἐστὲ, καὶ οὐχὶ μᾶλλον ἐπενθήσατε, ἵνα ἐξαρθῇ ἐκ μέσου ὑμῶν ὁ τὸ ἔργον τοῦτο ποιήσας. ΠΡΟΣ ΚΟΡ. β΄. Μὴ πάλιν ἐλθόντα με πρὸς ὑμᾶς ταπεινώσῃ με ὁ Θεός μου, καὶ πενθήσω πολλοὺς τῶν προημαρτηκότων, καὶ μὴ μετανοησάντων.

[52.2]   Ὅτι οὐ δεῖ ἐφησυχάζειν τοῖς ἁμαρτάνουσιν.
Κεφάλ. β΄.
ΛΟΥΚΑΣ. Ἐὰν δὲ ἁμάρτῃ ὁ ἀδελφός σου, ἐπιτίμησον αὐτῷ· καὶ τὰ ἑξῆς.
ΠΡΟΣ ΕΦΕΣ. Καὶ μὴ συγκοινωνεῖτε τοῖς ἔργοις τοῖς ἀκάρποις τοῦ σκότους, μᾶλλον δὲ καὶ ἐλέγχετε.

[52.3]   Ὅτι δεῖ τὴν πρὸς τοὺς ἁμαρτάνοντας συντυχίαν καταδέχεσθαι, οὐκ ἄλλου τινὸς ἕνεκεν, ἢ τοῦ εἰς μετάνοιαν αὐτοὺς ἀνακαλέσασθαι, ᾧπερ ἂν τρόπῳ δυνατὸν ᾖ χωρὶς ἁμαρτίας.
Κεφάλ. γ΄.
ΜΑΤΘΑΙΟΣ. Καὶ ἰδοὺ πολλοὶ τελῶναι καὶ ἁμαρτωλοὶ ἐλθόντες συνανέκειντο τῷ Ἰησοῦ, καὶ τοῖς μαθηταῖς αὐτοῦ. Καὶ ἰδόντες οἱ Φαρισαῖοι, εἶπον [382] τοῖς μαθηταῖς αὐτοῦ· διὰ τί μετὰ τῶν τελωνῶν καὶ ἁμαρτωλῶν ἐσθίει ὁ διδάσκαλος ὑμῶν; Ὁ δὲ Ἰησοῦς ἀκούσας, εἶπεν αὐτοῖς· οὐ χρείαν ἔχουσιν οἱ ἰσχύοντες ἰατροῦ, ἀλλ᾽ οἱ κακῶς ἔχοντες. Πορευθέντες δὲ μάθετε τί ἐστιν, ἔλεον θέλω καὶ οὐ θυσίαν. Οὐ γὰρ ἦλθον καλέσαι δικαίους, ἀλλὰ ἁμαρτωλοὺς εἰς μετάνοιαν.
ΛΟΥΚΑΣ. Ἦσαν δὲ αὐτῷ ἐγγίζοντες πάντες οἱ τελῶναι καὶ ἁμαρτωλοὶ ἀκούειν αὐτοῦ. Καὶ διεγόγγυζον οἱ γραμματεῖς καὶ οἱ Φαρισαῖοι, λέγοντες ὅτι[18] οὗτος ἁμαρτωλοὺς προσδέχεται, καὶ συνεσθίει αὐτοῖς. Εἶπε δὲ πρὸς αὐτοὺς τὴν παραβολὴν ταύτην, λέγων· τίς ἐξ ὑμῶν ἔχων ἑκατὸν πρόβατα, καὶ ἀπολέσας ἕν ἐξ αὐτῶν, οὐ καταλείπει τὰ ἐνενηκονταεννέα ἐν τῇ ἐρήμῳ, καὶ πορεύεται ἐπὶ τὸ ἀπολωλὸς, ἕως οὗ εὕρῃ αὐτό; καὶ τὰ ἑξῆς.

---

[18]Corrected from λέγοντες. Ὅτι.

1 CORINTHIANS: It is actually reported that there is immorality among you, and of a kind that is not *named* even among pagans; for a man is living with his father's wife. And you are arrogant *when you should be lamenting, so that he who has done this might* be removed from among you (5.1–2).

2 CORINTHIANS: I fear that when I come again my God may humble me before you, and I may have to mourn over many of those who sinned before and have not repented (12.21).

52.2 That it is necessary not to remain silent when sin is committed.

LUKE: If your brother sins, rebuke him (17.3), *and what follows*.

EPHESIANS: Take no part in the unfruitful works of darkness, but instead expose them (5.11).

52.3 That it is necessary to allow meeting with sinners for no other reason than to call them back to repentance in whatever way might be possible, barring sin.

MATTHEW: And behold, many tax collectors and sinners came and sat down with Jesus and his disciples. And when the Pharisees saw this they said to his disciples, "Why does your teacher eat with tax collectors and sinners?" But when *Jesus* heard it he said *to them*, "Those who are well have no need of a physician, but those who are sick. Go and learn what this means, 'I desire mercy and not sacrifice.' For I came not to call the righteous but sinners *to repentance*" (9.10–13).

LUKE: Now the tax collectors and sinners were all drawing near to hear him. And *the scribes and the Pharisees* murmured, saying, "This man receives sinners and eats with them." So he told them this parable: "What man of you, having a hundred sheep, if he has lost one of them, does not leave the ninety–nine in the wilderness and go after the one which is lost until he finds it?" (15.1–4), *and what follows*.

ΠΡΟΣ ΘΕΣΣ. β΄. Εἰ δέ τις οὐχ ὑπακούει τῷ λόγῳ ἡμῶν, διὰ τῆς ἐπιστολῆς τοῦτον σημειοῦσθε, καὶ μὴ συναναμίγνυσθε αὐτῷ, ἵνα ἐντραπῇ. Καὶ μὴ ὡς ἐχθρὸν ἡγεῖσθε, ἀλλὰ νουθετεῖτε ὡς ἀδελφόν. ΠΡΟΣ ΚΟΡ. β΄. Εἰ δέ τις λελύπηκεν, οὐκ ἐμὲ λελύπηκεν, ἀλλὰ ἀπὸ μέρους, ἵνα μὴ ἐπιβαρῶ πάντας ὑμᾶς. Ἱκανὸν τῷ τοιούτῳ ἡ ἐπιτιμία αὕτη, ἡ ὑπὸ τῶν πλειόνων· ὥστε τοὐναντίον ὑμᾶς μᾶλλον χαρίσασθαι, καὶ παρακαλέσαι, μή πως τῇ περισσοτέρᾳ λύπῃ καταποθῇ ὁ τοιοῦτος.

[52.4] Ὅτι δεῖ τοὺς, μετὰ τὸ πληρωθῆναι πάντα τρόπον τῆς εἰς αὐτοὺς ἐπιμελείας, ἐπιμένοντας τῇ ἰδίᾳ κακίᾳ ἀποστρέφεσθαι.

Κεφάλ. δ΄.

ΜΑΤΘΑΙΟΣ. Ἐὰν ἁμάρτῃ εἰς σὲ ὁ ἀδελφός σου, ὕπαγε, ἔλεγξον αὐτὸν μεταξὺ σοῦ καὶ αὐτοῦ μόνου. Ἐάν σου ἀκούσῃ, ἐκέρδησας τὸν ἀδελφόν σου· ἐὰν δὲ μὴ ἀκούσῃ, παράλαβε μετὰ σοῦ ἕνα ἢ δύο, ἵνα ἐπὶ στόματος δύο ἢ τριῶν μαρτύρων σταθῇ πᾶν ῥῆμα. Ἐὰν δὲ παρακούσῃ αὐτῶν, εἰπὲ τῇ ἐκκλησίᾳ· ἐὰν δὲ καὶ τῆς ἐκκλησίας παρακούσῃ, ἔστω σοι ὥσπερ ὁ ἐθνικὸς καὶ ὁ τελώνης. [383]

ΟΡΟΣ ΝΓ΄.

[53.1] Ὅτι οὐ δεῖ τὸν Χριστιανὸν μνησικακεῖν, ἀλλ᾽ ἀπὸ καρδίας ἀφιέναι τοῖς εἰς αὐτὸν ἡμαρτηκόσιν.

Κεφάλ. α΄.

ΜΑΤΘΑΙΟΣ. Ἐὰν μὴ ἀφῆτε τοῖς ἀνθρώποις τὰ παραπτώματα αὐτῶν, οὐδὲ ὁ Πατὴρ ὑμῶν ὁ οὐράνιος ἀφήσει τὰ παραπτώματα ὑμῶν· ἐὰν δὲ ἀφῆτε τοῖς ἀνθρώποις τὰ παραπτώματα αὐτῶν, ἀφήσει καὶ ὑμῖν ὁ Πατὴρ ὑμῶν ὁ οὐράνιος.

ΟΡΟΣ ΝΔ΄.

[54.1] Ὅτι οὐ δεῖ κρίνειν ἀλλήλους ἐπὶ τοῖς ὑπὸ τῆς Γραφῆς συγκεχωρημένοις.

Κεφάλ. α΄.

ΜΑΤΘΑΙΟΣ. Μὴ κρίνετε, ἵνα μὴ κριθῆτε. Ἐν ᾧ γὰρ κρίματι κρίνετε, κριθήσεσθε.

ΛΟΥΚΑΣ. Μὴ κρίνετε, καὶ οὐ μὴ κριθῆτε· μὴ καταδικάζετε, καὶ οὐ μὴ καταδικασθῆτε.

2 THESSALONIANS: If anyone refuses to obey what we say in this letter, note that man and have nothing to do with him, that he may be ashamed. Do not look on him as an enemy but warn him as a brother (3.14–15).

2 CORINTHIANS: But if anyone has caused pain, he has caused it not to me but in some measure—not to put it too severely—to you all. For such a one this punishment by the majority is enough; so you should rather turn to forgive and comfort him, or he may be overwhelmed by excessive sorrow (2.5–7).

52.4 That it is necessary to turn away from those persisting in their evil after every means of care for them has been exercised.

MATTHEW: If your brother *should sin* against you, go and tell him his fault between you and him alone. If he listens to you, you have gained your brother. But if he does not listen, take one or two others along with you, that every word may be confirmed by the evidence of two or three witnesses. If he refuses to listen to them, tell it to the church; and if he refuses to listen even to the church, let him be to you as a Gentile and a tax collector (18.15–17).

53.1 That it is necessary for the Christian not to hold grudges but to forgive from the heart those who sin against him.

MATTHEW: *If you do not forgive men their trespasses, neither will your heavenly Father forgive your trespasses; but if you forgive men their trespasses, your heavenly Father also will forgive you* (6.14–15).

54.1 That it is necessary not to judge one another for things allowed by the Scriptures.

MATTHEW: Judge not, that you be not judged. For with the judgment you pronounce you will be judged (7.1–2).

LUKE: Judge not, and you will not be judged; condemn not, and you will not be condemned (6.37).

ΠΡΟΣ ΡΩΜ. Ὃς μὲν πιστεύει φαγεῖν πάντα, ὁ δὲ ἀσθενῶν λάχανα ἐσθίει. Ὁ ἐσθίων, τὸν μὴ ἐσθίοντα μὴ ἐξουθενείτω, καὶ ὁ μὴ ἐσθίων, τὸν ἐσθίοντα μὴ κρινέτω. Ὁ Θεὸς γὰρ αὐτὸν προσελάβετο. Σὺ τίς εἶ ὁ κρίνων ἀλλότριον οἰκέτην; Τῷ ἰδίῳ Κυρίῳ στήκει, ἢ πίπτει· σταθήσεται δέ· δυνατὸς γάρ ἐστιν ὁ Θεὸς στῆσαι αὐτόν. Ὃς μὲν γὰρ κρίνει ἡμέραν παρ' ἡμέραν, ὃς δὲ κρίνει πᾶσαν ἡμέραν, ἕκαστος ἐν τῷ ἰδίῳ νοῖ πληροφορείσθω. Ὁ φρονῶν τὴν ἡμέραν, Κυρίῳ φρονεῖ· καὶ ὁ μὴ φρονῶν τὴν ἡμέραν, Κυρίῳ οὐ φρονεῖ. Καὶ ὁ ἐσθίων, Κυρίῳ ἐσθίει· εὐχαριστεῖ γὰρ τῷ Θεῷ. Καὶ ὁ μὴ ἐσθίων, Κυρίῳ οὐκ ἐσθίει, καὶ εὐχαριστεῖ τῷ Θεῷ. Καὶ μετ' ὀλίγα· Ἄρα οὖν ἕκαστος ἡμῶν περὶ ἑαυτοῦ λόγον δώσει τῷ Θεῷ. Μηκέτι οὖν ἀλλήλους κρίνωμεν.

ΠΡΟΣ ΚΟΛ. [384] Μὴ οὖν τις ὑμᾶς κρινέτω ἐν βρώσει, ἢ ἐν πόσει, ἢ ἐν μέρει ἑορτῆς, ἢ νουμηνίας, ἢ σαββάτων, ἅ ἐστι σκιὰ τῶν μελλόντων.

[54.2] Ὅτι οὐ δεῖ διακρίνεσθαι ἐπὶ τοῖς ὑπὸ τῆς Γραφῆς συγκεχωρημένοις.

Κεφάλ. β'.

ΠΡΟΣ ΡΩΜ. Μακάριος ὁ μὴ κρίνων ἑαυτὸν ἐν ᾧ δοκιμάζει. Ὁ δὲ διακρινόμενος, ἐὰν φάγῃ, κατακέκριται, ὅτι οὐκ ἐκ πίστεως. Πᾶν δὲ ὃ οὐκ ἐκ πίστεως, ἁμαρτία ἐστίν.

ΠΡΟΣ ΚΟΛ. Εἰ ἀπεθάνετε σὺν Χριστῷ ἀπὸ τῶν στοιχείων τοῦ κόσμου, τί ὡς ζῶντες ἐν κόσμῳ δογματίζεσθε; Μὴ ἅψῃ, μηδὲ γεύσῃ, μηδὲ θίγῃς· ἅ ἐστι πάντα εἰς φθορὰν τῇ ἀποχρήσει, κατὰ τὰ ἐντάλματα καὶ διδασκαλίας τῶν ἀνθρώπων.

[54.3] Ὅτι οὐ δεῖ κρίνειν περὶ τῶν ἀδήλων.

Κεφάλ. γ'.

ΠΡΟΣ ΚΟΡ. α'. Ὥστε μὴ πρὸ καιροῦ τι κρίνετε, ἕως ἂν ἔλθῃ ὁ Κύριος, ὃς καὶ φωτίσει τὰ κρυπτὰ τοῦ σκότους, καὶ φανερώσει τὰς βουλὰς τῶν καρδιῶν· καὶ τότε ὁ ἔπαινος γενήσεται ἑκάστῳ ἀπὸ τοῦ Θεοῦ.

ROMANS: One believes he may eat anything, while the weak man eats only vegetables. Let not him who eats despise him who abstains, and let not him who abstains pass judgment on him who eats, for God has welcomed him. Who are you to pass judgment on the servant of another? It is before his own master that he stands or falls. And he will be upheld, for the Master is able to make him stand. *For* one man esteems one day as better than another, while another man esteems all days alike. Let everyone be fully convinced in his own mind. He who observes the day observes it *for* the Lord, *and he who does not observe the day observes it not for the Lord*. He also who eats, eats *for* the Lord, since he gives thanks to God, while he who abstains, abstains *for* the Lord and gives thanks to God (14.2–6). *And a little further*: So each of us shall give account of himself to God. Then let us no more pass judgment on one another (14.12–13).

COLOSSIANS: Therefore let no one pass judgment on you in questions of food and drink or with regard to a festival or a new moon or a Sabbath. These are only a shadow of what is to come (2.16–17).

54.2 That it is necessary not to vacillate over things allowed by Scripture.

ROMANS: Happy is he who has no reason to judge himself for what he approves. But he who has doubts is condemned if he eats, because he does not act from faith, for whatever does not proceed from faith is sin (14.22–23).

COLOSSIANS: If with Christ you died to the elemental spirits of the universe, why do you live as if you still belonged to the world? Why do you submit to regulations, "Do not handle; do not taste; do not touch" (referring to things which all perish as they are used), according to human precepts and doctrines (2.20–22)?

54.3 That it is necessary not to judge concerning uncertain matters.

1 CORINTHIANS: Therefore do not pronounce judgment before the time, before the Lord comes, who will bring to light the things now hidden in darkness and will disclose the purposes of the heart. Then every man will receive his commendation from God (4.5).

[54.4] Ὅτι οὐ δεῖ ἐν προσωποληψία κρίνειν.

Κεφάλ. δ'.

ΙΩΑΝΝΗΣ. Εἰ περιτομὴν λαμβάνει ἄνθρωπος ἐν σαββάτῳ, ἵνα μὴ λυθῇ ὁ νόμος Μωσέως, ἐμοὶ τί χολᾶτε, ὅτι ὅλον ἄνθρωπον ὑγιῆ ἐποίησα ἐν σαββάτῳ; Μὴ κρίνετε κατ' ὄψιν, ἀλλὰ τὴν δικαίαν κρίσιν κρίνατε. [385]

[54.5] Ὅτι οὐ δεῖ κατακρίνειν τινὰ, μὴ πρότερον ἐπὶ παρουσίᾳ αὐτοῦ τὰ κατ' αὐτὸν ἀκριβώσαντες, κἂν πολλοὶ ὦσιν οἱ κατηγοροῦντες.

Κεφάλ. ε'.

ΙΩΑΝΝΗΣ. Λέγει Νικόδημος, ὁ ἐλθὼν πρὸς αὐτὸν νυκτὸς, εἷς ὢν ἐξ αὐτῶν· μὴ ὁ νόμος ἡμῶν κρίνει τὸν ἄνθρωπον, ἐὰν μὴ ἀκούσῃ παρ' αὐτοῦ πρότερον, καὶ γνῷ τί ποιεῖ;

ΠΡΑΞΕΙΣ. Ὡς δὲ πλείους ἡμέρας διέτριβον ἐκεῖ, ὁ Φῆστος τῷ βασιλεῖ ἀνέθετο τὰ κατὰ τὸν Παῦλον, λέγων· ἀνήρ τίς ἐστι καταλελειμμένος ὑπὸ Φήλικος δέσμιος, περὶ οὗ γενομένου μου εἰς Ἱεροσόλυμα ἐνεφάνισαν οἱ ἀρχιερεῖς καὶ οἱ πρεσβύτεροι τῶν Ἰουδαίων αἰτούμενοι κατ' αὐτοῦ καταδίκην· πρὸς οὓς ἀπεκρίθην, ὅτι οὐκ ἔστιν ἔθος Ῥωμαίοις χαρίζεσθαί τινα ἄνθρωπον, πρὶν ἢ ὁ κατηγορούμενος κατὰ πρόσωπον ἔχῃ τοὺς κατηγόρους, τόπον τε ἀπολογίας λάβῃ περὶ τοῦ ἐγκλήματος.

ΟΡΟΣ ΝΕ'.

[55.1] Ὅτι δεῖ εἰδέναι καὶ ὁμολογεῖν παντὸς ἀγαθοῦ τὴν χάριν, καὶ αὐτῶν τῶν ὑπὲρ Χριστοῦ παθημάτων τὴν ὑπομονὴν παρὰ Θεοῦ ὑπάρχειν.

Κεφάλ. α'.

ΙΩΑΝΝΗΣ. Οὐ δύναται ἄνθρωπος λαμβάνειν οὐδὲν, ἐὰν μὴ ᾖ δεδομένον αὐτῷ ἐκ τοῦ οὐρανοῦ.

ΠΡΟΣ ΚΟΡ. α'. Τί δὲ ἔχεις, ὃ οὐκ ἔλαβες;

ΠΡΟΣ ΕΦΕΣ. Τῇ γὰρ χάριτί ἐστε σεσωσμένοι διὰ τῆς πίστεως· καὶ τοῦτο οὐκ ἐξ ὑμῶν· Θεοῦ τὸ δῶρον· οὐκ ἐξ ἔργων, ἵνα μή τις καυχήσηται.

54.4   That it is necessary not to judge with respect to persons.

JOHN: If on the Sabbath a man receives circumcision so that the law of Moses may not be broken, are you angry with me because on the Sabbath I made a man's whole body well? Do not judge by appearances but judge with right judgment (7.23–24).

54.5   That it is necessary not to condemn a person without first examining closely in his presence the case against him, no matter how numerous his accusers may be.

JOHN: Nicodemus, who had gone to him *at night* and who was one of them, *said*, "Does our law judge a man *before* giving him a hearing and learning what he does?" (7.50–51).

ACTS: And as they stayed there many days, Festus laid Paul's case before the king, saying, "There is a man left prisoner by Felix, and when I was at Jerusalem, the chief priests and the elders of the Jews gave information about him, asking for sentence against him. I answered them that it was not the custom of the Romans to give up anyone before the accused met the accusers face to face and had opportunity to make his defense concerning the charge laid against him" (25.14–16).

55.1   That it is necessary to recognize and to confess that the grace of every good and the endurance of sufferings for Christ's sake are from God.

JOHN: No one can receive anything except what is given him from heaven (3.27).

1 CORINTHIANS: What have you that you did not receive (4.7)?

EPHESIANS: For by grace you have been saved through faith, and this is not your own doing; it is the gift of God—not because of works, lest any man should boast (2.8–9).

ΠΡΟΣ ΦΙΛΙΠ. Καὶ τοῦτο ἀπὸ Θεοῦ, ὅτι ὑμῖν ἐχαρίσθη τὸ ὑπὲρ Χριστοῦ, οὐ μόνον τὸ εἰς αὐτὸν πιστεύειν, ἀλλὰ καὶ τὸ ὑπὲρ αὐτοῦ πάσχειν, τὸν αὐτὸν ἀγῶνα ἔχοντες, καὶ τὰ ἑξῆς. [386]

[55.2]   Ὅτι οὐ δεῖ σιωπᾶν τὰς εὐεργεσίας τοῦ Θεοῦ, ἀλλ᾿ εὐχαριστεῖν ἐπ᾿ αὐταῖς.

Κεφάλ. β΄.

ΛΟΥΚΑΣ. Ἐδέετο δὲ αὐτοῦ ὁ ἀνὴρ, ἀφ᾿ οὗ ἐξεληλύθει τὰ δαιμόνια, εἶναι σὺν αὐτῷ. Ἀπέλυσε δὲ αὐτὸν ὁ Ἰησοῦς, λέγων· ὑπόστρεφε εἰς τὸν οἶκόν σου, καὶ διηγοῦ ὅσα ἐποίησέ σοι ὁ Θεός. Καὶ ἀπῆλθεν εἰς ὅλην τὴν πόλιν κηρύσσων ὅσα ἐποίησεν αὐτῷ ὁ Ἰησοῦς.

ΛΟΥΚΑΣ. Καὶ εἰσερχομένου αὐτοῦ εἴς τινα κώμην, ὑπήντησαν αὐτῷ δέκα λεπροὶ ἄνδρες, οἳ ἔστησαν πόρρωθεν. Καὶ αὐτοὶ ἦραν φωνὴν, λέγοντες· Ἰησοῦ ἐπιστάτα, ἐλέησον ἡμᾶς. Καὶ ἰδὼν, εἶπεν αὐτοῖς· πορευθέντες, ἐπιδείξατε ἑαυτοὺς τοῖς ἱερεῦσι. Καὶ ἐγένετο ἐν τῷ ὑπάγειν αὐτοὺς, ἐκαθαρίσθησαν. Εἷς δέ τις ἐξ αὐτῶν ἰδὼν ὅτι ἰάθη, ὑπέστρεψε μετὰ φωνῆς μεγάλης δοξάζων τὸν Θεόν. Καὶ ἔπεσεν ἐπὶ πρόσωπον ἐπὶ τοὺς πόδας αὐτοῦ, εὐχαριστῶν αὐτῷ· καὶ αὐτὸς ἦν Σαμαρείτης. Ἀποκριθεὶς δὲ ὁ Ἰησοῦς εἶπεν· οὐχὶ οἱ δέκα ἐκαθαρίσθησαν; Οἱ δὲ ἐννέα ποῦ; Οὐχ εὑρέθησαν ὑποστρέψαντες δοῦναι δόξαν τῷ Θεῷ, εἰ μὴ ὁ ἀλλογενὴς οὗτος. Καὶ εἶπεν αὐτῷ· ἀναστὰς πορεύου· ἡ πίστις σου σέσωκέ σε.

ΠΡΟΣ ΚΟΡ. α΄. Χάριτι δὲ Θεοῦ εἰμι ὅ εἰμι.

ΠΡΟΣ ΤΙΜ. α΄. Πᾶν κτίσμα Θεοῦ καλὸν, καὶ οὐδὲν ἀπόβλητον, μετ᾿ εὐχαριστίας λαμβανόμενον.

ΟΡΟΣ Νς΄.

[56.1]   Ὅτι δεῖ προσκαρτερεῖν ταῖς προσευχαῖς καὶ ταῖς ἀγρυπνίαις.

Κεφάλ. α΄.

ΜΑΤΘΑΙΟΣ. Αἰτεῖτε, καὶ δοθήσεται ὑμῖν· ζητεῖτε, καὶ εὑρήσετε· κρούετε, καὶ ἀνοιγήσεται ὑμῖν. Πᾶς γὰρ ὁ αἰτῶν λαμβάνει· καὶ ὁ ζητῶν εὑρίσκει· καὶ τῷ κρούοντι ἀνοιγήσεται· καὶ τὰ ἑξῆς.

PHILIPPIANS: And this is from God, for it has been granted to you that for the sake of Christ you should not only believe in him but also suffer for his sake, engaged in the same conflict (1.28–30), *and what follows.*

55.2 That it is necessary not to be silent concerning the good works of God but to give thanks for them.

LUKE: The man from whom the demons had gone begged that he might be with him, but *Jesus* sent him away, saying, "Return to your home and declare how much God has done for you." And he went away, proclaiming *to* the whole city how much Jesus had done for him (8.38–39).

LUKE: And as he entered a village he was met by ten lepers, who stood at a distance and lifted up their voices and said, "Jesus, Master, have mercy on us." When he saw them he said to them, "Go and show yourselves to the priests." And as they went they were cleansed. Then one of them, when he saw that he was healed, turned back, praising God with a loud voice; and he fell on his face at Jesus' feet, giving him thanks. Now he was a Samaritan. Then said Jesus, "Were not ten cleansed? Where are the nine? Was no one found to return and give praise to God except this foreigner?" And he said to him, "Rise and go your way; your faith has made you well" (17.12–19).

1 CORINTHIANS: But by the grace of God I am what I am (15.10).

1 TIMOTHY: For everything created by God is good, and nothing is to be rejected if it is received with thanksgiving (4.4).

56.1 That it is necessary to persevere in prayers and vigils.

MATTHEW: Ask, and it will be given you; seek, and you will find; knock, and it will be opened to you. For everyone who asks receives, and he who seeks finds, and to him who knocks it will be opened (7.7–8), *and what follows.*

ΛΟΥΚΑΣ. Ἔλεγε δὲ καὶ παραβολὴν αὐτοῖς, πρὸς τὸ [387] δεῖν πάντοτε προσεύχεσθαι, καὶ μὴ ἐκκακεῖν, λέγων· Κριτὴς ἦν ἔν τινι πόλει· καὶ τὰ λοιπά.

ΛΟΥΚΑΣ. Προσέχετε δὲ ἑαυτοῖς, μήποτε βαρυνθῶσιν ὑμῶν αἱ καρδίαι ἐν κραιπάλῃ, καὶ μέθῃ, καὶ μερίμναις βιωτικαῖς, καὶ αἰφνιδίως ἐφ᾽ ὑμᾶς ἐπιστῇ ἡ ἡμέρα ἐκείνη. Ὡς παγὶς γὰρ ἐπελεύσεται ἐπὶ πάντας τοὺς καθημένους ἐπὶ πρόσωπον πάσης τῆς γῆς. Ἀγρυπνεῖτε οὖν, ἐν παντὶ καιρῷ δεόμενοι, ἵνα καταξιωθῆτε ἐκφυγεῖν πάντα τὰ μέλλοντα γενέσθαι, καὶ σταθῆναι ἔμπροσθεν τοῦ Υἱοῦ τοῦ ἀνθρώπου.

ΠΡΟΣ ΚΟΛ. Τῇ προσευχῇ προσκαρτερεῖτε, γρηγοροῦντες ἐν αὐτῇ, ἐν εὐχαριστίᾳ.

ΠΡΟΣ ΘΕΣΣ. α΄. Πάντοτε χαίρετε, ἀδιαλείπτως προσεύχεσθε.

[56.2]   Ὅτι δεῖ καὶ ὑπὲρ αὐτῶν τῶν πρὸς τὴν καθημερινὴν χρείαν τοῦ σώματος εὐχαριστεῖν πρότερον τῷ Θεῷ, καὶ οὕτως μεταλαμβάνειν.

Κεφάλ. β΄.

ΜΑΤΘΑΙΟΣ. Καὶ λαβὼν τοὺς πέντε ἄρτους, καὶ τοὺς δύο ἰχθύας, εὐχαριστήσας, ἔκλασε καὶ ἔδωκε τοῖς μαθηταῖς αὐτοῦ· οἱ δὲ μαθηταὶ τῷ ὄχλῳ.

ΠΡΑΞΕΙΣ. Εἰπὼν δὲ ταῦτα, καὶ λαβὼν ἄρτον, ηὐχαρίστησε τῷ Θεῷ ἐνώπιον πάντων, καὶ κλάσας, ἤρξατο ἐσθίειν.

ΠΡΟΣ ΤΙΜ. α΄. Πᾶν κτίσμα Θεοῦ καλὸν, καὶ οὐδὲν ἀπόβλητον, μετὰ εὐχαριστίας λαμβανόμενον.

[56.3]   Ὅτι οὐ δεῖ βαττολογεῖν προσευχόμενον ἐν τῷ φθαρτὰ καὶ ἀνάξια τοῦ Κυρίου αἰτεῖν.

Κεφάλ. γ΄.

ΜΑΤΘΑΙΟΣ. Προσευχόμενοι δὲ, μὴ βαττολογήσητε, ὥσπερ οἱ ἐθνικοί. Δοκοῦσι γὰρ, ὅτι ἐν τῇ πολυλογίᾳ αὐτῶν εἰσακουσθήσονται. Μὴ οὖν ὁμοιωθῆτε αὐτοῖς· οἶδε γὰρ ὁ Πατὴρ ὑμῶν ὁ οὐράνιος, ὧν χρείαν ἔχετε, πρὸ τοῦ ὑμᾶς αἰτῆσαι αὐτόν.

LUKE: And he *also* told them a parable to the effect that *it is necessary* always to pray and not lose heart. He said, "In a certain city there was a judge" (18.1–2), *and the rest.*

LUKE: But take heed to yourselves lest your hearts be weighed down with dissipation and drunkenness and cares of this life and that day come upon you suddenly like a snare, for it will come upon all who dwell upon the face of the whole earth. *Therefore* watch at all times, praying that you may *be found worthy* to escape *all that* will take place and to stand before the Son of man (21.34–36).

COLOSSIANS: Continue steadfastly in prayer, being watchful in it with thanksgiving (4.2).

1 THESSALONIANS: Rejoice always; pray constantly (5.16–17).

56.2 That it is necessary first to give thanks to God even for the daily necessities of the body before partaking of them.

MATTHEW: And taking the five loaves and the two fish, *he gave thanks* and broke and gave the loaves to *his* disciples, and the disciples gave them to the *crowd* (14.19).

ACTS: And when he had said this he took bread, and, giving thanks to God in the presence of all, he broke it and began to eat (27.35).

1 TIMOTHY: For everything created by God is good, and nothing is to be rejected if it is received with thanksgiving (4.4).

56.3 That it is necessary not to chatter in prayer, asking transient and unworthy things of the Lord.

MATTHEW: And in praying do not heap up empty phrases as the Gentiles do; for they think that they will be heard for their many words. Do not be like them, for your *heavenly* Father knows what you need before you ask him (6.7–8).

ΛΟΥΚΑΣ. Καὶ ὑμεῖς μὴ ζητεῖτε τί φάγητε, καὶ τί πίητε· καὶ μὴ μετεωρίζεσθε. Πάντα γὰρ ταῦτα τὰ ἔθνη τοῦ κόσμου ἐπιζητεῖ. Ὑμῶν δὲ ὁ Πατὴρ οἶδεν ὅτι χρῄζετε τούτων. [388]

[56.4] Πῶς δεῖ προσεύχεσθαι, καὶ ἐν ποίᾳ τῆς ψυχῆς καταστάσει. Κεφάλ. δ΄.

ΜΑΤΘΑΙΟΣ. Πάτερ ἡμῶν ὁ ἐν τοῖς οὐρανοῖς, ἁγιασθήτω τὸ ὄνομά σου, ἐλθέτω ἡ βασιλεία σου, γενηθήτω τὸ θέλημά σου, καὶ τὰ ἑξῆς. ΜΑΤΘΑΙΟΣ. Ζητεῖτε δὲ πρῶτον τὴν βασιλείαν τοῦ Θεοῦ, καὶ τὴν δικαιοσύνην αὐτοῦ. ΜΑΡΚΟΣ. Ὅταν στήκητε προσευχόμενοι, ἀφίετε, εἴ τι ἔχετε κατά τινος. ΠΡΟΣ ΤΙΜ. α΄. Βούλομαι οὖν προσεύχεσθαι τοὺς ἄνδρας ἐν παντὶ τόπῳ, ἐπαίροντας ὁσίας χεῖρας, χωρὶς ὀργῆς καὶ διαλογισμῶν.

[56.5] Ὅτι δεῖ προσεύχεσθαι ὑπὲρ ἀλλήλων, καὶ ὑπὲρ τῶν προεστώτων τοῦ λόγου τῆς ἀληθείας. Κεφάλ. ε΄.

ΛΟΥΚΑΣ. Εἶπε δὲ ὁ Κύριος· Σίμων, Σίμων, ἰδοὺ ὁ σατανᾶς ἐξητήσατο ὑμᾶς, τοῦ σινιάσαι ὡς τὸν σῖτον· ἐγὼ δὲ ἐδεήθην περὶ σοῦ, ἵνα μὴ ἐκλίπῃ ἡ πίστις σου. ΠΡΟΣ ΕΦΕΣ. Προσευχόμενοι ἐν παντὶ καιρῷ ἐν πνεύματι, καὶ εἰς αὐτὸ ἀγρυπνοῦντες πάντοτε ἐν πάσῃ προσκαρτερήσει καὶ δεήσει, περὶ πάντων τῶν ἁγίων, καὶ ὑπὲρ ἐμοῦ, ἵνα μὴ δοθῇ λόγος ἐν ἀνοίξει τοῦ στόματός μου ἐν παρρησίᾳ, γνωρίσαι τὸ μυστήριον τοῦ εὐαγγελίου, ὑπὲρ οὗ πρεσβεύω ἐν ἁλύσει, ἵνα ἐν αὐτῷ παρρησιάσωμαι ὡς δεῖ με λαλῆσαι. ΠΡΟΣ ΘΕΣΣ. β΄. Τὸ λοιπὸν προσεύχεσθε περὶ ἡμῶν, ἵνα ὁ λόγος τοῦ Κυρίου τρέχῃ καὶ δοξάζηται ἐν παντί, καθὼς καὶ πρὸς ὑμᾶς.

[56.6] Ὅτι δεῖ καὶ ὑπὲρ τῶν ἐχθρῶν προσεύχεσθαι. Κεφάλ. ς΄.

LUKE: And do not seek what you are to eat and what you are to drink, nor be of anxious mind. For all the nations of the world seek these things, and your Father knows that you need them (12.29–30).

56.4   The manner in which it is necessary to pray and in what state of soul.

MATTHEW: Our Father who art in heaven, hallowed be thy name. Thy kingdom come. Thy will be done (6.9–10), *and what follows*.

MATTHEW: But seek first *the kingdom of God* and his righteousness (6.33).

MARK: Whenever you stand praying, forgive if you have anything against anyone (11.25).

1 TIMOTHY: I desire then that in every place the men should pray, lifting holy hands without anger or *quarrels* (2.8).

56.5   That it is necessary to pray for one another and for those set over the Word of Truth.

LUKE: *The Lord said,* "Simon, Simon behold, Satan demanded to have you that he might sift you like wheat, but I have prayed for you that your faith may not fail; and when you have turned again, strengthen your brethren" (22.31–32).

EPHESIANS: Pray at all times in the Spirit with all prayer and supplication. To that end keep *always* alert with all perseverance, making supplication for all the saints and also for me, that utterance may be given me in opening my mouth boldly to proclaim the mystery of the gospel, for which I am an ambassador in chains, that I may declare it boldly as I ought to speak (6.18–20).

2 THESSALONIANS: *Finally*, pray for us that the word of the Lord may speed on and triumph *in every way* as it did among you (3.1).

56.6   That it is necessary to pray also for enemies.

ΜΑΤΘΑΙΟΣ. Προσεύχεσθε ὑπὲρ τῶν ἐπηρεαζόντων ὑμᾶς, καὶ διωκόντων ὑμᾶς, ὅπως γένησθε υἱοὶ τοῦ Πατρὸς ὑμῶν τοῦ ἐν τοῖς οὐρανοῖς.

[56.7] Ὅτι οὐ δεῖ ἄνδρα κεκαλυμμένον προσεύχεσθαι, ἢ προφητεύειν, οὔτε γυναῖκα ἀκατακάλυπτον.

Κεφάλ. ζʹ.

ΠΡΟΣ ΚΟΡ. αʹ. Θέλω δὲ ὑμᾶς εἰδέναι, ὅτι [389] παντὸς ἀνδρὸς ἡ κεφαλὴ ὁ Χριστός ἐστι· κεφαλὴ δὲ γυναικὸς ὁ ἀνήρ· κεφαλὴ δὲ Χριστοῦ, ὁ Θεός. Πᾶς ἀνὴρ προσευχόμενος ἢ προφητεύων, κατὰ κεφαλῆς ἔχων, καταισχύνει τὴν κεφαλὴν αὐτοῦ. Πᾶσα δὲ γυνὴ προσευχομένη, ἢ προφητεύουσα ἀκατακαλύπτῳ τῇ κεφαλῇ, καταισχύνει τὴν κεφαλὴν αὐτῆς, καὶ τὰ ἑξῆς.

ΟΡΟΣ ΝΖʹ.

[57.1] Ὅτι οὐ δεῖ μεγαλοφρονεῖν ἐφ' ἑαυτῷ ἐν τοῖς κατορθώμασι, καὶ ἐξουθενεῖν τοὺς λοιπούς.

Κεφάλ. αʹ.

ΛΟΥΚΑΣ. Εἶπε δὲ πρός τινας τοὺς πεποιθότας ἐφ' ἑαυτοῖς, ὅτι εἰσὶ δίκαιοι, καὶ ἐξουθενοῦντας τοὺς λοιπούς, τὴν παραβολὴν ταύτην· Ἄνθρωποι δύο ἀνέβησαν εἰς τὸ ἱερὸν προσεύξασθαι· ὁ εἷς Φαρισαῖος, ὁ δὲ ἕτερος τελώνης. Ὁ Φαρισαῖος σταθεὶς, πρὸς ἑαυτὸν ταῦτα προσηύχετο· ὁ Θεός, εὐχαριστῶ σοι, ὅτι οὐκ εἰμὶ ὥσπερ οἱ λοιποὶ τῶν ἀνθρώπων, ἅρπαγες, ἄδικοι, μοιχοί, ἢ καὶ ὡς οὗτος ὁ τελώνης. Νηστεύω δὶς τοῦ σαββάτου· ἀποδεκατῶ πάντα ὅσα κτῶμαι. Καὶ ὁ τελώνης μακρόθεν ἑστώς, οὐκ ἤθελεν οὐδὲ τοὺς ὀφθαλμοὺς εἰς τὸν οὐρανὸν ἐπᾶραι· ἀλλ' ἔτυπτεν εἰς τὸ στῆθος αὐτοῦ λέγων· ὁ Θεός, ἱλάσθητί μοι τῷ ἁμαρτωλῷ. Λέγω ὑμῖν, κατέβη οὗτος δεδικαιωμένος εἰς τὸν οἶκον αὐτοῦ, ἤπερ ἐκεῖνος· ὅτι πᾶς ὁ ὑψῶν ἑαυτὸν, ταπεινωθήσεται· καὶ ὁ ταπεινῶν ἑαυτὸν, ὑψωθήσεται.

ΟΡΟΣ ΝΗʹ.

[58.1] Ὅτι οὐ δεῖ νομίζειν δωρεὰν Θεοῦ διὰ χρημάτων ἢ καὶ δι' ἄλλης τινὸς ἐπινοίας κτᾶσθαι.

MATTHEW: Pray for those who *abuse you and* persecute you, so that you may be sons of your Father who is in heaven (5.44–45).

56.7   That it is necessary for a man neither to pray nor to prophesy while covered, nor for a woman to do so uncovered.

1 CORINTHIANS: But I want you to understand that the head of every man is Christ, the head of a woman is her husband, and the head of Christ is God. Any man who prays or prophesies with his head covered dishonors his head, but any woman who prays or prophesies with her head unveiled dishonors her head (11.3–5), *and what follows.*

57.1   That it is necessary not to think highly of oneself for one's virtues and to neglect what remains.[22]

LUKE: He also told this parable to some who trusted in themselves, that they were righteous, and despised others: "Two men went up into the temple to pray, one a Pharisee and the other a tax collector. The Pharisee stood and prayed thus with himself, 'God, I thank thee that I am not like other men, extortioners, unjust, adulterers, or even like this tax collector. I fast twice a week; I give tithes of all that I get.' *And* the tax collector, standing far off, would not even lift up his eyes to heaven but beat his breast, saying, 'God, be merciful to me a sinner!' I tell you, this man went down to his house justified rather than the other, for everyone who exalts himself will be humbled, but he who humbles himself will be exalted" (18.9–14).

58.1   That it is necessary not to think that the gift of God is acquired with money or through any other device.

---

[22]That is, to neglect the pursuit of virtues one still lacks.

Κεφάλ. α′.

ΠΡΑΞΕΙΣ. Ἰδὼν δὲ ὁ Σίμων, ὅτι διὰ τῆς ἐπιθέσεως τῶν χειρῶν τῶν ἀποστόλων δίδοται τὸ Πνεῦμα [390] τὸ ἅγιον, προσήνεγκεν αὐτοῖς χρήματα, λέγων· δότε κἀμοὶ τὴν ἐξουσίαν ταύτην, ἵνα ᾧ ἂν ἐπιθῶ τὰς χεῖρας, λαμβάνῃ Πνεῦμα ἅγιον. Πέτρος δὲ εἶπε πρὸς αὐτόν· τὸ ἀργύριόν σου σὺν σοὶ εἴη εἰς ἀπώλειαν, ὅτι τὴν δωρεὰν τοῦ Θεοῦ ἐνόμισας διὰ χρημάτων κτᾶσθαι. Οὐκ ἔστι σοι μερὶς, οὐδὲ κλῆρος ἐν τῷ λόγῳ τούτῳ· ἡ γὰρ καρδία σου οὐκ ἔστιν εὐθεῖα ἐναντίον τοῦ Θεοῦ. Μετανόησον οὖν ἀπὸ τῆς κακίας σου ταύτης, καὶ δεήθητι τοῦ Κυρίου, εἰ ἄρα ἀφεθήσεταί σοι ἡ ἐπίνοια τῆς καρδίας σου. Εἰς γὰρ χολὴν πικρίας, καὶ σύνδεσμον ἀδικίας ὁρῶ σε ὄντα.

[58.2] Ὅτι κατὰ ἀναλογίαν τῆς πίστεως ἑκάστῳ δίδοται παρὰ Θεοῦ χαρίσματα πρὸς τὸ συμφέρον.

Κεφάλ. β′.

ΠΡΟΣ ΡΩΜ. Ἔχοντες δὲ χαρίσματα, κατὰ τὴν χάριν τὴν δοθεῖσαν ἡμῖν, διάφορα, εἴτε προφητείαν κατὰ τὴν ἀναλογίαν τῆς πίστεως.

ΠΡΟΣ ΚΟΡ. α′. Ἑκάστῳ δὲ δίδοται ἡ φανέρωσις τοῦ Πνεύματος πρὸς τὸ συμφέρον· ᾧ μὲν γὰρ διὰ τοῦ Πνεύματος δίδοται λόγος σοφίας· ἄλλῳ δὲ λόγος γνώσεως, κατὰ τὸ αὐτὸ Πνεῦμα· ἑτέρῳ δὲ πίστις, ἐν τῷ αὐτῷ Πνεύματι· ἄλλῳ δὲ χαρίσματα ἰαμάτων· ἄλλῳ προφητεία· ἄλλῳ διακρίσεις πνευμάτων· ἑτέρῳ δὲ γένη γλωσσῶν· ἄλλῳ δὲ ἑρμηνεία γλωσσῶν.

[58.3] Ὅτι δεῖ τὴν χάριν τοῦ Θεοῦ δωρεὰν λαμβάνοντα, δωρεὰν διδόναι, καὶ μὴ πραγματεύεσθαι αὐτὴν πρὸς τὰς ἰδίας ἡδονάς.

Κεφάλ. γ′.

ΜΑΤΘΑΙΟΣ. Ἀσθενοῦντας θεραπεύετε, λεπροὺς καθαρίζετε, δαιμόνια ἐκβάλλετε· δωρεὰν ἐλάβετε, δωρεὰν δότε. Μὴ κτήσησθε χρυσίον, μηδὲ ἀργύριον, μηδὲ χαλκὸν εἰς τὰς ζώνας ὑμῶν.

ΠΡΑΞΕΙΣ. Εἶπε δὲ Πέτρος· Ἀργύριον καὶ χρυσίον οὐχ ὑπάρχει μοι· ὃ δὲ ἔχω, τοῦτό σοι δίδωμι. Ἐν τῷ ὀνόματι Ἰησοῦ Χριστοῦ τοῦ Ναζωραίου ἔγειραι καὶ περιπάτει. Καὶ πιάσας αὐτὸν τῆς δεξιᾶς χειρός, ἤγειρεν αὐτόν.

ACTS: Now when Simon saw that the Spirit was given through the laying on of the apostles' hands, he offered them money, saying, "Give me also this power, that anyone on whom I lay my hands may receive the Holy Spirit." But Peter said to him, "Your silver perish with you, because you thought you could obtain the gift of God with money! You have neither part nor lot in this matter, for your heart is not right before God. Repent therefore of this wickedness of yours and pray to the Lord that, if possible, the intent of your heart may be forgiven you. For I see that you are in the gall of bitterness and in the bond of iniquity" (8.18–23).

58.2   That charisms are given to each by God for succor in proportion to their faith.

ROMANS: Having *charisms* that differ according to the grace given to us, let us use them: if prophecy, in proportion to our faith (12.6).

1 CORINTHIANS: To each is given the manifestation of the Spirit for the common good. To one is given through the Spirit the utterance of wisdom and to another the utterance of knowledge according to the same Spirit, to another faith by the same Spirit, to another *charisms of healing, to another prophecy*, to another the ability to distinguish between spirits, to another various kinds of tongues, to another the interpretation of tongues (12.7–10).

58.3   That it is necessary to give the grace of God freely, as it was received freely, and not to trade on it for one's own pleasure.

MATTHEW: Heal the *sick, cleanse* lepers, cast out demons. You received without paying, give without pay. Take no gold, nor silver, nor copper in your belts (10.8–9).

ACTS: But Peter said, "I have no silver and gold, but I give you what I have; in the name of Jesus Christ of Nazareth, *rise and* walk." And he took him by the right hand and raised him up (3.6–7).

ΠΡΟΣ ΘΕΣΣ. α'. Οὔτε γὰρ ἐν λόγῳ κολακείας ἐγενήθημεν, καθὼς οἴδατε, οὔτε [391] προφάσει πλεονεξίας, Θεὸς μάρτυς· οὔτε ζητοῦντες ἐξ ἀνθρώπων δόξαν, οὔτε ἀφ' ὑμῶν, οὔτε ἀπ' ἄλλων. Δυνάμενοι ἐν βάρει εἶναι, ὡς Χριστοῦ ἀπόστολοι· ἀλλ' ἐγενήθημεν ἤπιοι ἐν μέσῳ ὑμῶν. Ὡς ἐὰν τροφὸς θάλπῃ τὰ ἑαυτῆς τέκνα, οὕτως ἱμειρόμενοι ὑμῶν, εὐδοκοῦμεν μεταδοῦναι ὑμῖν οὐ μόνον τὸ εὐαγγέλιον τοῦ Θεοῦ, ἀλλὰ καὶ τὰς ἑαυτῶν ψυχάς, διότι ἀγαπητοὶ ἡμῖν ἐγενήθητε.

[58.4] Ὅτι ὁ τὴν πρώτην παρὰ Θεοῦ δωρεὰν εὐγνωμόνως δεξά-μενος, καὶ σπουδαίως κατεργασάμενος εἰς τὴν δόξαν τοῦ Θεοῦ, καὶ ἑτέρων καταξιοῦται· ὁ δὲ μὴ τοιοῦτος τήν τε προϋπάρχουσαν ἀφαιρεῖται, καὶ τῆς ἡτοιμασμένης οὐ καταξιοῦται, καὶ τιμωρίᾳ παραδίδοται.

Κεφάλ. δ'.

ΜΑΤΘΑΙΟΣ. Καὶ προσελθόντες οἱ μαθηταὶ εἶπον αὐτῷ· διὰ τί ἐν παραβολαῖς λαλεῖς αὐτοῖς; Ὁ δὲ ἀποκριθεὶς εἶπεν αὐτοῖς· ὅτι ὑμῖν δέδοται γνῶναι τὰ μυστήρια τῆς βασιλείας τῶν οὐρανῶν, ἐκείνοις δὲ οὐ δέδοται. Ὅστις γὰρ ἔχει, δοθήσεται αὐτῷ, καὶ περισσευθήσεται· ὅστις δὲ οὐκ ἔχει, καὶ ὃ ἔχει ἀρθήσεται ἀπ' αὐτοῦ. Διὰ τοῦτο ἐν παραβολαῖς αὐτοῖς λαλῶ, ὅτι βλέποντες, οὐ βλέπουσι, καὶ ἀκούοντες, οὐκ ἀκούουσιν, οὐδὲ συνιοῦσι. Καὶ ἀναπληροῦται αὐτοῖς ἡ προφητεία Ἡσαΐου.

ΜΑΤΘΑΙΟΣ. Ὥσπερ γὰρ ἄνθρωπος ἀποδημῶν ἐκάλεσε τοὺς ἰδίους δούλους, καὶ παρέδωκεν αὐτοῖς τὰ ὑπάρχοντα αὐτοῦ· καὶ ᾧ μὲν ἔδωκε πέντε τάλαντα, ᾧ δὲ δύο, ᾧ δὲ ἕν, ἑκάστῳ κατὰ τὴν ἰδίαν δύναμιν, καὶ ἀπεδήμησεν εὐθέως. Πορευθεὶς δὲ ὁ τὰ πέντε τάλαντα λαβών, εἰργάσατο ἐν αὐτοῖς, καὶ ἐποίησεν ἄλλα πέντε τάλαντα. Ὡσαύτως καὶ ὁ τὰ δύο ἐκέρδησεν ἄλλα δύο. Καὶ μετ' ὀλίγα· Τῷ γὰρ ἔχοντι παντὶ δοθήσεται· ἀπὸ δὲ τοῦ μὴ ἔχοντος, καὶ ὃ ἔχει ἀρθήσεται ἀπ' αὐτοῦ. Καὶ τὸν ἀχρεῖον δοῦλον ἐκβάλλετε εἰς τὸ σκότος τὸ ἐξώτερον· ἐκεῖ ἔσται ὁ κλαυθμὸς, καὶ ὁ βρυγμὸς τῶν ὀδόντων. [392]

1 THESSALONIANS: *For we engaged neither in flattering speech, as you know, nor in a pretext for our gain*, as God is witness; nor did we seek glory from men, whether from you or from others, though we might have made demands as apostles of Christ. But we were gentle among you, like a nurse taking care of her children. So, being affectionately desirous of you, we were ready to share with you not only the gospel of God but also our own selves, because you had become very dear to us (2.5–8).

58.4 That the one who has received the first of God's gifts prudently and worked diligently for God's glory is accounted worthy of others also, but the one who does not do so is robbed of the original gift, accounted unworthy of what was prepared for him and given over to torment.

MATTHEW: Then the disciples came and said to him, "Why do you speak to them in parables?" And he answered them, "To you it has been given to know the secrets of the kingdom of heaven, but to them it has not been given. For to him who has will more be given, and he will have abundance; but from him who has not, even what he has will be taken away. This is why I speak to them in parables: because seeing they do not see, and hearing they do not hear, nor do they understand. With them indeed is fulfilled the prophecy of Isaiah"[23] (13.10–14).

MATTHEW: For it will be as when a man going on a journey called his servants and entrusted to them his property; to one he gave five talents, to another two, to another one, to each according to his ability. Then he went away. He who had received the five talents *went* and traded with them, and he made five talents more. So also he who had the two talents made two talents more (25.14–17). *And a little further*: For to everyone who has will more be *given*, but from him who has not, even what he has will be taken away. And cast the worthless servant into the outer darkness; there *will be weeping and gnashing of teeth* (25.29–30).

[23]See Is 6.9

ΟΡΟΣ ΝΘ'.

[59.1] Ὅτι οὐ δεῖ τὸν Χριστιανὸν προσπάσχειν τῇ ἀπὸ τῶν ἀνθρώπων δόξῃ, οὔτε ἀντέχεσθαι τιμῆς ὑπερβαλλούσης, ἀλλὰ καὶ διορθοῦσθαι τοὺς οὕτω τιμῶντας, ἢ πλέον περὶ αὐτοῦ φρονοῦντας.
Κεφάλ. α'.

ΜΑΤΘΑΙΟΣ. Καὶ ἰδοὺ, εἷς προσελθὼν εἶπεν αὐτῷ· διδάσκαλε
ἀγαθὲ, τί ἀγαθὸν ποιήσας ζωὴν αἰώνιον κληρονομήσω; Ὁ δὲ εἶπεν
αὐτῷ· τί με λέγεις ἀγαθόν; Οὐδεὶς ἀγαθὸς, εἰ μὴ εἷς ὁ Θεός.

ΙΩΑΝΝΗΣ. Δόξαν παρὰ ἀνθρώπων οὐ λαμβάνω. Καὶ μετ' ὀλίγα·
Πῶς δύνασθε ὑμεῖς πιστεῦσαι, δόξαν παρ' ἀλλήλων λαμβάνοντες,
καὶ τὴν δόξαν τὴν παρὰ τοῦ μόνου Θεοῦ οὐ ζητοῦντες;

ΛΟΥΚΑΣ. Οὐαὶ ὑμῖν τοῖς Φαρισαίοις, ὅτι ἀγαπᾶτε τὰς πρωτοκαθεδρίας ἐν ταῖς συναγωγαῖς, καὶ τοὺς ἀσπασμοὺς ἐν ταῖς ἀγοραῖς.

ΠΡΟΣ ΘΕΣΣ. α'. Οὔτε γάρ ποτε ἐν λόγῳ κολακείας ἐγενήθημεν,
καθὼς οἴδατε, οὔτε προφάσει πλεονεξίας, Θεὸς μάρτυς· οὔτε
ζητοῦντες ἐξ ἀνθρώπων δόξαν, οὔτε ἀφ' ὑμῶν, οὔτε ἀπ' ἄλλων.

ΠΡΑΞΕΙΣ. Ὡς δὲ ἐγένετο τοῦ εἰσελθεῖν τὸν Πέτρον, συναντήσας
αὐτῷ ὁ Κορνήλιος, πεσὼν ἐπὶ τοὺς πόδας αὐτοῦ, προσεκύνησεν.
Ὁ δὲ Πέτρος ἤγειρεν αὐτὸν λέγων· ἀνάστηθι· καὶ γὰρ κἀγὼ αὐτὸς
ἄνθρωπός εἰμι.

ΠΡΑΞΕΙΣ. Τακτῇ δὲ ἡμέρᾳ ὁ Ἡρώδης, ἐνδυσάμενος ἐσθῆτα
βασιλικὴν, καὶ καθίσας ἐπὶ τοῦ βήματος, ἐδημηγόρει. Ὁ δὲ δῆμος
ἐπεφώνει· Θεοῦ φωνὴ, καὶ οὐκ ἀνθρώπου. Παραχρῆμα δὲ ἐπάταξεν
αὐτὸν ἄγγελος Κυρίου, ἀνθ' ὧν οὐκ ἔδωκε τὴν δόξαν τῷ Θεῷ· καὶ
γενόμενος σκωληκόβρωτος ἐξέψυξε. [393]

ΟΡΟΣ Ξ'.

[60.1] Ὅτι, τῶν χαρισμάτων τοῦ Πνεύματος διαφόρων ὑπαρχόντων, καὶ οὔτε ἑνὸς δυναμένου τὰ πάντα ὑποδέξασθαι, οὔτε
πάντων τὸ αὐτό, δεῖ σωφρόνως καὶ εὐχαρίστως ἕκαστον ἐμμένειν τῷ
δεδομένῳ, καὶ συμφωνεῖν ἀλλήλοις τοὺς πάντας ἐν ἀγάπῃ Χριστοῦ,
ὥσπερ μέλη ἐν σώματι· ὥστε τὸν ὑποβεβηκότα ἐν τοῖς χαρίσμασι
συγκρίσει τοῦ ὑπερέχοντος, αὐτῷ μὴ ἀπογινώσκειν, μήτε μὴν τὸν
μείζονα καταφρονεῖν τοῦ ἐλάττονος. Οἱ γὰρ διαμεμερισμένοι, καὶ
διαστασιάζοντες, καταλύσεως ἄξιοι.

59.1 That it is necessary for a Christian not to desire glory from human beings nor to lay claim to excessive honor, but even to correct those who honor him thus or who think more of him.

MATTHEW: And behold, one came up to him saying, "*Good teacher, what good deed must I do to inherit eternal life?*" And he said to him, "*Why do you call me good? No one is good except the one God*" (19.16–17).

JOHN: I do not receive glory from men (5.41). *And a little further:* How can you believe, who receive glory from one another and do not seek the glory that comes from the only God (5.44)?

LUKE: Woe to you Pharisees! For you love the best *seats* in the synagogues and salutations in the marketplaces (11.43).

1 THESSALONIANS: *For we engaged neither in flattering speech, as you know, nor in a pretext for our gain*, as God is witness; nor did we seek glory from men, whether from you or from others (2.5–6).

ACTS: When Peter entered, Cornelius met him and fell down at his feet and worshiped him. But Peter lifted him up, saying, "Stand up; for I too am *also* a man" (10.25–26).

ACTS: On an appointed day Herod put on his royal robes, took his seat upon the throne, and made an *oration*. And the people shouted, "The voice of a god, and not of man!" Immediately an angel of the Lord smote him, because he did not give God the glory, and he was eaten by worms and died (12.21–23).

60.1 That since the charisms of the Spirit are diverse and no one is able to receive all nor everyone the same, it is necessary for each person to remain temperately and thankfully in what he has been given and for everyone to be in harmony with one another in the love of Christ as members in a body, so that one inferior in charisms by comparison with one superior does not despair of himself, nor especially does the greater look down on the lesser; for those who are divided and dissenting are worthy of dissolution.

Κεφάλ. α'.

ΜΑΤΘΑΙΟΣ. Πᾶσα βασιλεία, μερισθεῖσα καθ' ἑαυτῆς, ἐρημοῦται· καὶ πᾶσα πόλις ἢ οἰκία, μερισθεῖσα καθ' ἑαυτῆς, οὐ σταθήσεται.

ΠΡΟΣ ΓΑΛ. Εἰ δὲ ἀλλήλους δάκνετε, καὶ κατεσθίετε, βλέπετε μὴ ὑπὸ ἀλλήλων ἀναλωθῆτε.

ΙΩΑΝΝΗΣ. Οὐ περὶ τούτων ἐρωτῶ μόνον, ἀλλὰ καὶ περὶ τῶν πιστευόντων διὰ τοῦ λόγου αὐτῶν εἰς ἐμέ· ἵνα πάντες ἓν ὦσι, καθὼς σὺ, Πάτερ, ἐν ἐμοί, κἀγὼ ἐν σοί· ἵνα καὶ οὗτοι ἐν ἡμῖν ἓν ὦσι.

ΠΡΑΞΕΙΣ. Τοῦ δὲ πλήθους τῶν πιστευσάντων ἦν ἡ καρδία καὶ ἡ ψυχὴ μία, καὶ οὐδὲ εἷς τι τῶν ὑπαρχόντων αὐτῷ ἔλεγεν ἴδιον εἶναι, ἀλλ' ἦν αὐτοῖς ἅπαντα κοινά.

ΠΡΟΣ ΡΩΜ. Λέγω γὰρ, διὰ τῆς χάριτος τῆς δοθείσης μοι, παντὶ τῷ ὄντι ἐν ὑμῖν, μὴ ὑπερφρονεῖν παρ' ὃ δεῖ φρονεῖν· ἀλλὰ φρονεῖν εἰς τὸ σωφρονεῖν· ἑκάστῳ ὡς ὁ Θεὸς ἐμέρισε μέτρον πίστεως. Καθάπερ γὰρ ἐν ἑνὶ σώματι μέλη πολλὰ ἔχομεν, τὰ δὲ μέλη πάντα οὐ τὴν αὐτὴν ἔχει πρᾶξιν· οὕτως οἱ πολλοὶ ἓν σῶμά ἐσμεν ἐν Χριστῷ, ὁ δὲ καθ' εἷς ἀλλήλων μέλη· ἔχοντες δὲ χαρίσματα κατὰ τὴν χάριν τὴν δοθεῖσαν ἡμῖν διάφορα, καὶ τὰ ἑξῆς.

ΠΡΟΣ ΚΟΡ. α'. Παρακαλῶ δὲ ὑμᾶς διὰ τοῦ ὀνόματος τοῦ Κυρίου Ἰησοῦ Χριστοῦ, ἵνα τὸ αὐτὸ λέγητε πάντες, καὶ μὴ ᾖ ἐν ὑμῖν σχίσματα· ἦτε δὲ κατηρτισμένοι ἐν τῷ αὐτῷ νοΐ, καὶ ἐν τῇ αὐτῇ [394] γνώμῃ.

ΠΡΟΣ ΚΟΡ. α'. Καθάπερ γὰρ τὸ σῶμα ἕν ἐστι, μέλη δὲ ἔχει πολλὰ, πάντα δὲ τὰ μέλη τοῦ σώματος τοῦ ἑνὸς πολλὰ ὄντα, ἕν ἐστι σῶμα· οὕτω καὶ ἐν Χριστῷ. Καὶ γὰρ ἐν ἑνὶ Πνεύματι ἡμεῖς πάντες εἰς ἓν σῶμα ἐβαπτίσθημεν, εἴτε Ἰουδαῖοι, εἴτε Ἕλληνες, εἴτε δοῦλοι, εἴτε ἐλεύθεροι, καὶ τὰ ἑξῆς.

ΠΡΟΣ ΦΙΛΙΠ. Ἵνα τὸ αὐτὸ φρονῆτε πάντες, τὴν αὐτὴν ἀγάπην ἔχοντες, σύμψυχοι, τὸ ἓν φρονοῦντες, μηδὲν κατ' ἐριθείαν, ἢ κενοδοξίαν, ἀλλὰ τῇ ταπεινοφροσύνῃ ἀλλήλους ἡγούμενοι ὑπερέχοντας ἑαυτῶν· μὴ τὰ ἑαυτῶν ἕκαστος σκοποῦντες, ἀλλὰ καὶ τὰ ἑτέρων ἕκαστοι.

MATTHEW: Every kingdom divided against itself is laid waste, and no city or house divided against itself will stand (12.25).

GALATIANS: But if you bite and devour one another, take heed that you are not consumed by one another (5.15).

JOHN: I do not pray for these only but also for those who believe in me through their word, that they may all be one even as thou, Father, art in me and I in thee, that *these* also may be *one* in us (17.20–21).

ACTS: Now the company of those who believed were of one heart and soul, and no one said that any of the things which he possessed was his own, but they had everything in common (4.32).

ROMANS: For by the grace given to me I bid everyone among you not to think of himself more highly than he ought to think but to think with sober judgment, each according to the measure of faith which God has *assigned*. For as in one body we have many members, and all the members do not have the same function, so we, though many, are one body in Christ and individually members one of another, having gifts that differ according to the grace given to us (12.3–6), *and what follows.*

1 CORINTHIANS: I appeal to *you* by the name of *the* Lord Jesus Christ that all of you agree and that there be no dissensions among you but that you be united in the same mind and the same judgment (1.10).

1 CORINTHIANS: For just as the body is one and has many members, and all the members of the *one* body, though many, are one body, so it is with Christ. For by one Spirit we were all baptized into one body—Jews or Greeks, slaves or free (12.12–13), *and what follows.*

PHILIPPIANS: *That you all have the same mind*, having the same love, being in full accord and of one mind. Do nothing from selfishness or conceit but in humility count others better than yourselves. Let each of you look not only to his own interests but also to the interests of others (2.2–4).

ΟΡΟΣ ΞΑ'.

[61.1] Ὅτι οὐ δεῖ ἐξουθενεῖν τοὺς συνεργοῦντας τὴν χάριν τοῦ Κυρίου, εἰς τὴν εὐτέλειαν αὐτῶν ἀφορῶντας. Ἐν τούτοις γὰρ μάλιστα εὐδοκεῖ ὁ Θεός.

Κεφάλ. α'.

ΜΑΤΘΑΙΟΣ. Ἐξομολογοῦμαί σοι, Πάτερ, Κύριε τοῦ οὐρανοῦ καὶ τῆς γῆς, ὅτι ἀπέκρυψας ταῦτα ἀπὸ σοφῶν καὶ συνετῶν, καὶ ἀπεκάλυψας αὐτὰ νηπίοις. Ναί, ὁ Πατὴρ, ὅτι οὕτως ἐγένετο εὐδοκία ἔμπροσθέν σου. ΜΑΤΘΑΙΟΣ. Ἐλθὼν εἰς τὴν πατρίδα αὐτοῦ, ἐδίδασκεν αὐτοὺς ἐν τῇ συναγωγῇ αὐτῶν, ὥστε ἐκπλήσσεσθαι αὐτοὺς, καὶ λέγειν· πόθεν ἡ σοφία αὕτη τούτῳ καὶ αἱ δυνάμεις; Οὐχ οὗτός ἐστιν ὁ τοῦ τέκτονος υἱός; Οὐχ ἡ μήτηρ αὐτοῦ λέγεται Μαριάμ; καὶ οἱ ἀδελφοὶ αὐτοῦ Ἰάκωβος, καὶ Ἰωσὴφ,[19] καὶ Σίμων, καὶ Ἰούδας; καὶ αἱ ἀδελφαὶ αὐτοῦ οὐχὶ πᾶσαι πρὸς ἡμᾶς εἰσι; Πόθεν οὖν τούτῳ πάντα ταῦτα; Καὶ ἐσκανδαλίζοντο ἐν αὐτῷ. Ὁ δὲ Ἰησοῦς εἶπεν αὐτοῖς· οὐκ ἔστι προφήτης ἄτιμος εἰ μὴ ἐν τῇ πατρίδι αὐτοῦ καὶ ἐν τῇ οἰκίᾳ αὐτοῦ. Καὶ οὐκ ἐποίησεν ἐκεῖ δυνάμεις πολλὰς διὰ τὴν ἀπιστίαν αὐτῶν. ΠΡΟΣ ΚΟΡ. α'. Βλέπετε γὰρ τὴν κλῆσιν ὑμῶν, ἀδελφοὶ, ὅτι οὐ πολλοὶ σοφοὶ κατὰ σάρκα, οὐ πολλοὶ δυνατοὶ, οὐ πολλοὶ εὐγενεῖς· ἀλλὰ τὰ μωρὰ τοῦ κόσμου ἐξελέξατο ὁ Θεὸς, ἵνα καταισχύνῃ τοὺς σοφούς· καὶ τὰ ἀσθενῆ τοῦ [395] κόσμου ἐξελέξατο ὁ Θεὸς, ἵνα καταισχύνῃ τὰ ἰσχυρά· καὶ τὰ ἀγενῆ τοῦ κόσμου, καὶ τὰ ἐξουθενημένα ἐξελέξατο ὁ Θεὸς, καὶ τὰ μὴ ὄντα, ἵνα τὰ ὄντα καταργήσῃ, ὅπως μὴ καυχήσηται πᾶσα σὰρξ ἐνώπιον τοῦ Θεοῦ.

ΟΡΟΣ ΞΒ'.

[62.1] Ὅτι τοὺς πιστεύσαντας τῷ Θεῷ, καὶ βαπτισθέντας, εὐθὺς παρασκευάζεσθαι δεῖ πρὸς τοὺς πειρασμοὺς, καὶ παρ' αὐτῶν τῶν οἰκείων, μέχρι θανάτου. Ὁ γὰρ μὴ οὕτως ἑτοιμασάμενος, αἰφνίδιον τῆς περιστάσεως καταλαβούσης, εὐκόλως διασαλεύεται.

Κεφάλ. α'.

ΜΑΤΘΑΙΟΣ. Καὶ βαπτισθεὶς ὁ Ἰησοῦς ἀνέβη εὐθὺς ἀπὸ τοῦ ὕδατος. Καὶ ἰδοὺ ἀνεῴχθησαν αὐτῷ οἱ οὐρανοὶ, καὶ εἶδε τὸ Πνεῦμα τοῦ Θεοῦ

---

[19]Corrected from Ἰωσὴς.

61.1 That it is necessary not to disregard those who cooperate with the grace of the Lord, considering only their meagerness, for in these God is especially well pleased.

MATTHEW: I thank thee, Father, Lord of heaven and earth, that thou hast hidden these things from the wise and understanding and revealed them to babes; yea, Father, for such was thy gracious will (11.25–26).

MATTHEW: Coming to his own country, he taught them in their synagogue, so that they were astonished and said, "Where did this man get this wisdom and these mighty works? Is not this the carpenter's son? Is not his mother called Mary? And are not his brothers James and Joseph and Simon and Judas? And are not all his sisters with us? Where then did this man get all this?" And they *were scandalized by* him. But Jesus said to them, "A prophet is not without honor except in his own country and in his own house." And he did not do many mighty works there because of their unbelief (13.54–58).

1 CORINTHIANS: For consider your call, brethren. Not many of you were wise according to worldly standards; not many were powerful; not many were of noble birth, but God chose what is foolish in the world to shame the wise. God chose what is weak in the world to shame the strong. God chose what is low and despised in the world, even things that are not, to bring to nothing things that are, so that no *flesh* might boast in the presence of God (1.26–29).

62.1 That it is necessary for those who have believed in God and been baptized to prepare themselves immediately for trials,[24] even from their own household, until death; for the one who has not readied himself thus is easily shaken when a crisis comes unexpectedly.

MATTHEW: And when Jesus was baptized he went up immediately from the water, and behold, the heavens were opened, and he

[24]Or "temptations." The range of πειρασμός covers both English words, and it has been translated variously in what follows.

καταβαῖνον ὡσεὶ περιστερὰν, καὶ ἐρχόμενον ἐπ' αὐτόν. Καὶ ἰδοὺ φωνὴ ἐκ τῶν οὐρανῶν λέγουσα· οὗτός ἐστιν ὁ Υἱός μου ὁ ἀγαπητὸς, ἐν ᾧ εὐδόκησα. Τότε ὁ Ἰησοῦς ἀνήχθη εἰς τὴν ἔρημον ὑπὸ τοῦ Πνεύματος, πειρασθῆναι ὑπὸ τοῦ διαβόλου. ΜΑΤΘΑΙΟΣ. Ἰδοὺ ἐγὼ ἀποστέλλω ὑμᾶς ὡς πρόβατα ἐν μέσῳ λύκων. Γίνεσθε οὖν φρόνιμοι, ὡς οἱ ὄφεις, καὶ ἀκέραιοι, ὡς αἱ περιστεραί. Προσέχετε δὲ ἀπὸ τῶν ἀνθρώπων. Παραδώσουσι γὰρ ὑμᾶς εἰς συνέδρια, καὶ ἐν ταῖς συναγωγαῖς αὐτῶν μαστιγώσουσιν ὑμᾶς. Καὶ ἐπὶ ἡγεμόνας δὲ καὶ βασιλεῖς ἀχθήσεσθε ἕνεκεν ἐμοῦ, εἰς μαρτύριον αὐτοῖς καὶ τοῖς ἔθνεσι. Καὶ μετ' ὀλίγα· Παραδώσει δὲ ἀδελφὸς ἀδελφὸν εἰς θάνατον, καὶ πατὴρ τέκνον· καὶ ἐπαναστήσονται τέκνα ἐπὶ γονεῖς, καὶ θανατώσουσιν αὐτούς. Καὶ ἔσεσθε μισούμενοι ὑπὸ πάντων διὰ τὸ ὄνομά μου· ὁ δὲ ὑπομείνας εἰς τέλος, οὗτος σωθήσεται. ΜΑΤΘΑΙΟΣ. Καὶ ὃς οὐ λαμβάνει τὸν σταυρὸν αὐτοῦ, καὶ ἀκολουθεῖ ὀπίσω μου, οὐκ ἔστι μου ἄξιος. ΙΩΑΝΝΗΣ. Ταῦτα λελάληκα ὑμῖν, ἵνα μὴ σκανδαλισθῆτε. Ἀποσυναγώγους ποιήσουσιν ὑμᾶς· ἀλλ' ἔρχεται ὥρα, ἵνα πᾶς ὁ ἀποκτείνας ὑμᾶς δόξῃ λατρείαν προσφέρειν τῷ Θεῷ. Καὶ ταῦτα ποιήσουσιν ὑμῖν, ὅτι οὐκ ἔγνωσαν τὸν Πατέρα, οὐδὲ ἐμὲ· καὶ τὰ ἑξῆς. ΛΟΥΚΑΣ. Οἱ δὲ ἐπὶ τῆς πέτρας, οἵ, ὅταν [396] ἀκούσωσι, μετὰ χαρᾶς δέχονται τὸν λόγον, καὶ οὗτοι ῥίζαν οὐκ ἔχουσιν, οἳ πρὸς καιρὸν πιστεύουσι, καὶ ἐν καιρῷ πειρασμῶν ἀφίστανται. ΠΡΟΣ ΚΟΡ. β'. Οὐ θέλω γὰρ ὑμᾶς ἀγνοεῖν, ἀδελφοί, περὶ τῆς θλίψεως ἡμῶν τῆς γενομένης ἡμῖν ἐν τῇ Ἀσίᾳ, ὅτι καθ' ὑπερβολὴν ὑπὲρ δύναμιν ἐβαρήθημεν, ὥστε ἐξαπορηθῆναι ἡμᾶς καὶ τοῦ ζῆν· ἀλλ' αὐτοὶ ἐν ἑαυτοῖς τὸ ἀπόκριμα τοῦ θανάτου ἐσχήκαμεν, ἵνα μὴ πεποιθότες ὦμεν ἐφ' ἑαυτοῖς, ἀλλ' ἐπὶ τῷ Θεῷ τῷ ἐγείροντι τοὺς νεκρούς. ΠΡΟΣ ΤΙΜ. β'. Πάντες δὲ οἱ θέλοντες εὐσεβῶς ζῆν ἐν Χριστῷ Ἰησοῦ, διωχθήσονται.

saw the Spirit of God descending like a dove and alighting on him; and lo, a voice from heaven, saying, "This is my beloved Son, with whom I am well pleased." Then Jesus was led up by the Spirit into the wilderness to be tempted by the devil (3.16–4.1).

MATTHEW: Behold, I send you out as sheep in the midst of wolves, so be wise as serpents and innocent as doves. Beware of men, for they will deliver you up to councils and flog you in their synagogues, and you will be dragged before governors and kings for my sake to bear testimony before them and the Gentiles (10.16–18). *And a little further*: Brother will deliver up brother to death, and the father his child, and children will rise against parents and have them put to death, and you will be hated by all for my name's sake. But he who endures to the end will be saved (10.21–22).

MATTHEW: And he who does not take his cross and follow me is not worthy of me (10.38).

JOHN: I have said all this to you to keep you from falling away. They will put you out of the synagogues; indeed, the hour is coming when whoever kills you will think he is offering service to God. And they will do this *to you* because they have not known the Father nor me (16.1–3), *and what follows*.

LUKE: And the ones on the rock are those who, when they hear the word, receive it with joy, but these have no root; they believe for a while and in time of temptation fall away (8.13).

2 CORINTHIANS: For I do not want you to be ignorant, brethren, of the affliction we experienced in Asia; for we were so utterly, unbearably crushed that we despaired of life itself. Why, we felt that we had received the sentence of death, but that was to make us rely not on ourselves but on God who raises the dead (1.8–9).

2 TIMOTHY: Indeed all who desire to live a godly life in Christ Jesus will be persecuted (3.12).

[62.2]   Ὅτι οὐ δεῖ ἑαυτὸν ἐπιρρίπτειν πειρασμοῖς πρὸ καιροῦ τῆς τοῦ Θεοῦ συγχωρήσεως, ἀλλὰ καὶ προσεύχεσθαι μὴ ἐμπεσεῖν εἰς πειρασμόν.

Κεφάλ. β'.

ΜΑΤΘΑΙΟΣ. Οὕτως οὖν προσεύχεσθε· Πάτερ ἡμῶν, ὁ ἐν τοῖς οὐρανοῖς, ἁγιασθήτω τὸ ὄνομά σου, ἐλθέτω ἡ βασιλεία σου. Καὶ μετ' ὀλίγα· Καὶ μὴ εἰσενέγκῃς ἡμᾶς εἰς πειρασμὸν, ἀλλὰ ῥῦσαι ἡμᾶς ἀπὸ τοῦ πονηροῦ. ΙΩΑΝΝΗΣ. Καὶ περιεπάτει ὁ Ἰησοῦς μετὰ ταῦτα ἐν τῇ Γαλιλαίᾳ· οὐ γὰρ ἤθελεν ἐν τῇ Ἰουδαίᾳ περιπατεῖν, ὅτι ἐζήτουν αὐτὸν οἱ Ἰουδαῖοι ἀποκτεῖναι. Ἦν δὲ ἐγγὺς ἡ ἑορτὴ τῶν Ἰουδαίων, ἡ σκηνοπηγία. Εἶπον οὖν πρὸς αὐτὸν οἱ ἀδελφοὶ αὐτοῦ· μετάβηθι ἐντεῦθεν, καὶ ὕπαγε εἰς τὴν Ἰουδαίαν, ἵνα καὶ οἱ μαθηταί σου θεωρήσωσι τὰ ἔργα ἃ ποιεῖς. Οὐδεὶς γὰρ ἐν κρυπτῷ ποιεῖ τι, καὶ ζητεῖ αὐτὸς ἐν παρρησίᾳ εἶναι. Εἰ ταῦτα ποιεῖς, φανέρωσον σεαυτὸν τῷ κόσμῳ. Οὐδὲ γὰρ οἱ ἀδελφοὶ αὐτοῦ ἐπίστευον εἰς αὐτόν. Λέγει οὖν αὐτοῖς ὁ Ἰησοῦς· ὁ καιρὸς ὁ ἐμὸς οὔπω πάρεστιν· ὁ δὲ καιρὸς ὁ ὑμέτερος πάντοτέ ἐστιν ἕτοιμος. Οὐ δύναται ὁ κόσμος μισεῖν ὑμᾶς· ἐμὲ δὲ μισεῖ, ὅτι ἐγὼ μαρτυρῶ περὶ αὐτοῦ, ὅτι τὰ ἔργα αὐτοῦ πονηρά ἐστιν. Ὑμεῖς ἀνάβητε εἰς τὴν ἑορτήν· ἐγὼ οὔπω ἀναβαίνω εἰς τὴν ἑορτὴν ταύτην, ὅτι ὁ καιρὸς ὁ ἐμὸς οὔπω πεπλήρωται. Ταῦτα δὲ εἰπὼν αὐτοῖς, ἔμεινεν ἐν τῇ Γαλιλαίᾳ. Ὡς δὲ ἀνέβησαν οἱ ἀδελφοὶ αὐτοῦ, τότε καὶ αὐτὸς ἀνέβη εἰς τὴν ἑορτήν, οὐ φανερῶς, ἀλλ' ὡς ἐν κρυπτῷ. ΛΟΥΚΑΣ. Ἀναστάντες δὲ προσεύχεσθε, ἵνα μὴ ἐμπέσητε εἰς πειρασμόν. [397]

[62.3]   Ὅτι δεῖ κατὰ καιρὸν ὑπαναχωρεῖν τῶν ἐπιβουλευόντων, συγχωρηθέντα μέντοι περιπεσεῖν πειρασμῷ, τὴν ἔκβασιν τοῦ δύνασθαι ὑπενεγκεῖν, καὶ τὸ θέλημα τοῦ Θεοῦ διὰ προσευχῆς αἰτεῖν.

Κεφάλ. γ'.

ΜΑΤΘΑΙΟΣ. Ὅταν διώκωσιν ὑμᾶς ἐν τῇ πόλει ταύτῃ, φεύγετε εἰς τὴν ἄλλην. Οἱ δὲ Φαρισαῖοι συμβούλιον ἔλαβον κατ' αὐτοῦ, ἐξελθόντες, ὅπως αὐτὸν ἀπολέσωσιν. Ὁ δὲ Ἰησοῦς γνούς, ἀνεχώρησεν ἐκεῖθεν.

62.2 That it is necessary not to cast oneself upon trials before the time allowed by God, but even to pray not to fall into trial.

MATTHEW: Pray then like this: Our Father, who art in heaven, hallowed be thy name. Thy kingdom come (6.9–10). *And a little further*: And lead us not into temptation, but deliver us from the evil one (6.13).

JOHN: After this Jesus went about in Galilee; he would not go about in Judea, because the Jews sought to kill him. Now the Jews' feast of Tabernacles was at hand, so his brothers said to him, "Leave here and go to Judea, that your disciples may see the works you are doing. For no man works in secret if he seeks to be known openly. If you do these things, show yourself to the world." For even his brothers did not believe in him. Jesus said to them, "My time has not yet come, but your time is always here. The world cannot hate you, but it hates me because I testify of it that its works are evil. Go to the feast yourselves; I am not going up to this feast, for my time has not yet fully come." So saying, he remained in Galilee. But after his brothers had gone up to the feast, then he also went up, not publicly but in private (7.1–10).

LUKE: Rise and pray that you may not enter into temptation (22.46).

62.3 That it is necessary to withdraw in good time from those who lay snares; nevertheless, when allowed to meet with trials, ask in prayer for the fulfillment of the ability to endure and that God's will be done.

MATTHEW: When they persecute you in one town, flee to the next (10.23).

MATTHEW: But the Pharisees went out and took counsel against him, how to destroy him. Jesus, aware of this, withdrew from there (12.14–15).

ΙΩΑΝΝΗΣ. Ἀπ' ἐκείνης οὖν τῆς ἡμέρας συνεβουλεύσαντο, ἵνα ἀποκτείνωσιν αὐτόν. Ἰησοῦς οὖν οὐκέτι παρρησίᾳ περιεπάτει ἐν τοῖς Ἰουδαίοις.

ΛΟΥΚΑΣ. Καὶ θεὶς τὰ γόνατα, προσηύχετο λέγων· Πάτερ, εἰ βούλει παρενεγκεῖν τὸ ποτήριον τοῦτο ἀπ' ἐμοῦ· πλὴν μὴ τὸ θέλημά μου, ἀλλὰ τὸ σὸν γενέσθω. ΠΡΟΣ ΚΟΡ. α'. Πειρασμὸς ὑμᾶς οὐκ εἴληφεν εἰ μὴ ἀνθρώπινος· πιστὸς δὲ ὁ Θεός, ὃς οὐκ ἐάσει ὑμᾶς πειρασθῆναι ὑπὲρ ὃ δύνασθε, ἀλλὰ ποιήσει σὺν τῷ πειρασμῷ καὶ τὴν ἔκβασιν, τοῦ δύνασθαι ὑπενεγκεῖν.

[62.4] Ὅτι δεῖ τὸν Χριστιανὸν ἐν τοῖς πειρασμοῖς ἐφ' ἑκάστῳ τῶν προσαγομένων αὐτῷ, μνημονεύοντα τῶν ἐν τῇ θεοπνεύστῳ Γραφῇ πρὸς τὸ προκείμενον εἰρημένων, οὕτως αὐτόν τε ἀνεπηρέαστον συντηρεῖν, καὶ τοὺς ἐναντίους καταργεῖν.

Κεφάλ. δ'.

ΜΑΤΘΑΙΟΣ. Τότε ὁ Ἰησοῦς ἀνήχθη εἰς τὴν ἔρημον ὑπὸ τοῦ Πνεύματος, πειρασθῆναι ὑπὸ τοῦ διαβόλου. Καὶ νηστεύσας ἡμέρας τεσσαράκοντα, καὶ νύκτας τεσσαράκοντα, ὕστερον ἐπείνασε. Καὶ προσελθὼν αὐτῷ ὁ πειράζων, εἶπεν· εἰ Υἱὸς εἶ τοῦ Θεοῦ, εἰπὲ ἵνα οἱ λίθοι οὗτοι ἄρτοι γένωνται. Ὁ δὲ ἀποκριθεὶς εἶπεν· γέγραπται, ὅτι «οὐκ ἐπ' ἄρτῳ μόνῳ ζήσεται ἄνθρωπος, ἀλλ' ἐπὶ παντὶ ῥήματι ἐκπορευομένῳ διὰ στόματος Θεοῦ,» καὶ τὰ ἑξῆς. [398]

ΟΡΟΣ ΞΓ'.

[63.1] Ὅτι οὐ δεῖ τὸν Χριστιανὸν φοβεῖσθαι, καὶ ἀγωνιᾶν ἐν ταῖς περιστάσεσι, μετεωριζόμενον ἀπὸ τῆς ἐν Θεῷ πεποιθήσεως· θαρρεῖν δέ, ὡς τοῦ Κυρίου παρόντος, καὶ τὰ κατ' αὐτὸν οἰκονομοῦντος, καὶ πρὸς πάντας ἐνδυναμοῦντος, καὶ τοῦ ἁγίου Πνεύματος διδάσκοντος μέχρι καὶ ἀποκρίσεως τῆς πρὸς τοὺς ὑπεναντίους.

Κεφάλ. α'.

ΜΑΤΘΑΙΟΣ. Μὴ φοβεῖσθε ἀπὸ τῶν ἀποκτεινόντων τὸ σῶμα, τὴν δὲ ψυχὴν ἀποκτεῖναι μὴ δυναμένων· φοβήθητε δὲ μᾶλλον τὸν δυνάμενον καὶ ψυχὴν καὶ σῶμα ἀπολέσαι ἐν γεέννῃ. Οὐχὶ δύο στρουθία ἀσσαρίου πωλεῖται; Καὶ ἓν ἐξ αὐτῶν οὐ πεσεῖται ἐπὶ τὴν

JOHN: So from that day on they took counsel *together* how to put him to death. Jesus therefore no longer went about openly among the Jews (11.53–54).

LUKE: And he knelt down and prayed, "Father, if thou art willing, remove this cup from me; nevertheless not my will, but thine be done" (22.41–42).

1 CORINTHIANS: No temptation has overtaken you that is not common to man. God is faithful, and he will not let you be tempted beyond your strength, but with the temptation will also provide the way of escape, that you may be able to endure it (10.13).

62.4 That it is necessary for the Christian, each time temptations confront him, by recalling the things said in the God-breathed Scripture regarding the matter at hand, thus to preserve himself from being maimed and to render harmless the opposition.

MATTHEW: Then Jesus was led up by the Spirit into the wilderness to be tempted by the devil. And he fasted forty days and forty nights, and afterward he was hungry. And the tempter came and said to him, "If you are the Son of God, command these stones to become loaves of bread." But he answered, "It is written, 'A man shall not live by bread alone, but by every word that proceeds from the mouth of God'"[25] (4.1–4), *and what follows*.

63.1 That it is necessary for a Christian not to be fearful and anxious in crises but, being buoyed by his confidence in God, to be courageous, since the Lord is present and ordering his affairs and empowering him for everything, and the Holy Spirit teaches him even what to answer his adversaries.

MATTHEW: Do not fear those who kill the body but cannot kill the soul; rather fear him who can destroy both soul and body in hell. Are not two sparrows sold for a penny? And not one of them will fall

[25]Deut 8.3

γῆν, ἄνευ τοῦ Πατρὸς ὑμῶν. Ὑμῶν δὲ καὶ αἱ τρίχες τῆς κεφαλῆς πᾶσαι ἠριθμημέναι εἰσίν. Μὴ οὖν φοβηθῆτε, πολλῶν στρουθίων διαφέρετε ὑμεῖς.

ΛΟΥΚΑΣ. Ὅταν δὲ προσφέρωσιν ὑμᾶς ἐπὶ τὰς συναγωγὰς, καὶ τὰς ἀρχὰς, καὶ τὰς ἐξουσίας, μὴ μεριμνᾶτε πῶς ἢ τί ἀπολογήσησθε, ἢ τί εἴπητε· τὸ γὰρ ἅγιον Πνεῦμα διδάξει ὑμᾶς ἐν αὐτῇ τῇ ὥρᾳ, ἃ δεῖ εἰπεῖν.

ΜΑΡΚΟΣ. Καὶ γίνεται λαίλαψ ἀνέμου μεγάλη· τὰ δὲ κύματα ἐπέβαλλεν εἰς τὸ πλοῖον, ὥστε αὐτὸ ἤδη γεμίζεσθαι. Καὶ ἦν αὐτὸς ἐπὶ τῇ πρύμνῃ ἐπὶ τὸ προσκεφάλαιον καθεύδων. Καὶ διεγείρουσιν αὐτὸν, καὶ λέγουσιν αὐτῷ· διδάσκαλε, οὐ μέλει σοι ὅτι ἀπολλύμεθα; Καὶ διεγερθεὶς ἐπετίμησε τῷ ἀνέμῳ, καὶ εἶπε τῇ θαλάσσῃ, σιώπα, πεφίμωσο. Καὶ ἐκόπασεν ὁ ἄνεμος, καὶ ἐγένετο γαλήνη μεγάλη. Καὶ εἶπεν αὐτοῖς· τί δειλοί ἐστε οὕτως; Πῶς οὐκ ἔχετε πίστιν;

ΠΡΑΞΕΙΣ. Ἀναστὰς δὲ ὁ ἀρχιερεὺς, καὶ οἱ σὺν αὐτῷ (ἡ οὖσα αἵρεσις τῶν Σαδδουκαίων), ἐπλήσθησαν ζήλου· καὶ ἐπέβαλον τὰς χεῖρας αὐτῶν ἐπὶ τοὺς ἀποστόλους, καὶ ἔθεντο αὐτοὺς ἐν τηρήσει δημοσίᾳ. Ἄγγελος δὲ Κυρίου διὰ τῆς νυκτὸς ἤνοιξε τὰς θύρας τῆς φυλακῆς, ἐξαγαγών τε αὐτοὺς, εἶπε· [399] πορεύεσθε, καὶ σταθέντες λαλεῖτε ἐν τῷ ἱερῷ τῷ λαῷ πάντα τὰ ῥήματα τῆς ζωῆς ταύτης. Ἀκούσαντες δὲ εἰσῆλθον ὑπὸ τὸν ὄρθρον εἰς τὸ ἱερόν, καὶ ἐδίδασκον.

ΠΡΟΣ ΚΟΡ. β′. Οὐ γὰρ θέλομεν ὑμᾶς ἀγνοεῖν, ἀδελφοὶ, περὶ τῆς θλίψεως ἡμῶν, τῆς γενομένης ἡμῖν ἐν τῇ Ἀσίᾳ. Καὶ μετ' ὀλίγα· ὃς ἐκ τηλικούτου θανάτου ἐρρύσατο ἡμᾶς, καὶ ῥύεται· εἰς ὃν ἠλπίκαμεν, ὅτι καὶ ἔτι ῥύσεται.

ΟΡΟΣ ΞΔ′.

[64.1] Ὅτι δεῖ χαίρειν πᾶν ὁτιοῦν πάσχοντα μέχρι θανάτου ἕνεκεν τοῦ ὀνόματος τοῦ Κυρίου καὶ τῶν ἐντολῶν αὐτοῦ.

Κεφάλ. α′.

ΜΑΤΘΑΙΟΣ. Μακάριοι οἱ δεδιωγμένοι ἕνεκεν δικαιοσύνης, ὅτι αὐτῶν ἐστιν ἡ βασιλεία τῶν οὐρανῶν. Μακάριοί ἐστε, ὅταν ὀνειδίσωσιν ὑμᾶς, καὶ διώξωσι, καὶ εἴπωσι πᾶν πονηρὸν ῥῆμα καθ' ὑμῶν ψευδόμενοι, ἕνεκεν ἐμοῦ. Χαίρετε καὶ ἀγαλλιᾶσθε, ὅτι ὁ μισθὸς ὑμῶν πολὺς ἐν τοῖς οὐρανοῖς.

to the ground without your Father's will. But even the hairs of your head are all numbered. Fear not, therefore; you are of more value than many sparrows (10.28–31).

LUKE: And when they bring you before the synagogues and the rulers and the authorities, do not be anxious how or what you are to answer or what you are to say, for the Holy Spirit will teach you in that very hour what you ought to say (12.11–12).

MARK: And a great storm of wind arose, and the waves beat into the boat, so that *it* was already filling. But he was in the stern, asleep on the cushion; and they woke him and said to him, "Teacher, do you not care if we perish?" And he awoke and rebuked the wind and said to the sea, "Peace! Be still!" And the wind ceased, and there was a great calm. He said to them, "Why are you *so* afraid? *How* have you no faith?" (4.37–40).

ACTS: But the high priest rose up and *those* who were with him, that is, the party of the Sadducees, and, filled with jealousy, they arrested the apostles and put them in the common prison. But at night an angel of the Lord opened the prison doors and brought them out and said, "Go and stand in the temple and speak to the people all the words of this Life." And when they heard this they entered the temple at daybreak and taught (5.17–21).

2 CORINTHIANS: For we do not want you to be ignorant, brethren, of the affliction we experienced in Asia (1.8). *And little further*: He delivered us from so deadly a peril, and he will deliver us; on him we have set our hope that he will deliver us again (1.10).

64.1 That it is necessary to rejoice in any suffering whatsoever, even to death, that is for the sake of the name of the Lord and his commandments.

MATTHEW: Blessed are those who are persecuted for righteousness' sake, for theirs is the kingdom of heaven. Blessed are you when *they* revile you and persecute you and utter all kinds of evil *words* against you falsely on my account. Rejoice and be glad, for your reward is great in heaven (5.10–12).

ΛΟΥΚΑΣ. Μακάριοί ἐστε, ὅταν μισήσωσιν ὑμᾶς οἱ ἄνθρωποι, καὶ ὅταν ἀφορίσωσιν ὑμᾶς, καὶ ὀνειδίσωσι, καὶ ἐκβάλωσι τὸ ὄνομα ὑμῶν ὡς πονηρὸν, ἕνεκεν τοῦ Υἱοῦ τοῦ ἀνθρώπου. Χάρητε ἐν ἐκείνῃ τῇ ἡμέρᾳ, καὶ σκιρτήσατε· ἰδοὺ γὰρ ὁ μισθὸς ὑμῶν πολὺς ἐν τοῖς οὐρανοῖς.

ΠΡΑΞΕΙΣ. Καὶ προσκαλεσάμενοι τοὺς ἀποστόλους, δείραντες παρήγγειλαν μὴ λαλεῖν ἐπὶ τῷ ὀνόματι τοῦ Ἰησοῦ, καὶ ἀπέλυσαν αὐτούς. Οἱ μὲν οὖν ἐπορεύοντο χαίροντες ἀπὸ προσώπου τοῦ συνεδρίου, ὅτι κατηξιώθησαν ὑπὲρ τοῦ ὀνόματος τοῦ Κυρίου ἀτιμασθῆναι. Πᾶσάν τε ἡμέραν ἐν τῷ ἱερῷ καὶ κατ᾽ οἶκον οὐκ ἐπαύοντο διδάσκοντες καὶ εὐαγγελιζόμενοι τὸν Χριστὸν Ἰησοῦν.

ΠΡΟΣ ΚΟΛ. Οὗ ἐγενόμην ἐγὼ Παῦλος διάκονος. Νῦν χαίρω ἐν τοῖς παθήμασί μου ὑπὲρ ὑμῶν, καὶ ἀνταναπληρῶ τὰ ὑστερήματα τῶν θλίψεων τοῦ Χριστοῦ, ἐν τῇ σαρκί μου ὑπὲρ τοῦ σώματος αὐτοῦ, ὅ ἐστιν ἡ Ἐκκλησία. [400]

ΟΡΟΣ ΞΕ′.

[65.1]   Ὅτι δεῖ καὶ ἐν αὐτῇ τῇ ἐξόδῳ προσεύχεσθαι τὰ πρέποντα.

Κεφάλ. α′.

ΜΑΤΘΑΙΟΣ. Περὶ δὲ τὴν ἐννάτην ὥραν ἀνεβόησεν ὁ Ἰησοῦς φωνῇ μεγάλῃ, λέγων· Ἠλὶ, ἠλὶ, λαμμὰ σαβαχθανί; τουτέστι· Θεέ μου, Θεέ μου, ἵνα τί με ἐγκατέλιπες; Καὶ φωνήσας φωνῇ μεγάλῃ ὁ Ἰησοῦς εἶπε· Πάτερ, εἰς χεῖράς σου παρατίθημι τὸ πνεῦμά μου. Καὶ τοῦτο εἰπὼν, ἐξέπνευσεν.

ΠΡΑΞΕΙΣ. Καὶ ἐλιθοβόλουν τὸν Στέφανον ἐπικαλούμενον, καὶ λέγοντα· Κύριε, μὴ στήσῃς αὐτοῖς τὴν ἁμαρτίαν ταύτην. Καὶ τοῦτο εἰπὼν, ἐκοιμήθη.

ΟΡΟΣ Ξϛ′.

[66.1]   Ὅτι οὐ δεῖ ἐγκαταλιμπάνειν τοὺς ὑπὲρ εὐσεβείας ἀγωνιζομένους.

Κεφάλ. α′.

ΙΩΑΝΝΗΣ. Ἀπεκρίθη αὐτοῖς ὁ Ἰησοῦς, ἄρτι πιστεύετε; Ἰδοὺ ἔρχεται ὥρα, καὶ νῦν ἐλήλυθεν, ἵνα σκορπισθῆτε ἕκαστος εἰς τὰ ἴδια, καὶ ἐμὲ μόνον ἀφῆτε.

LUKE: Blessed are you when men hate you and when they exclude you and revile you and cast out your name as evil on account of the Son of man! Rejoice in that day and leap for joy, for behold, your reward is great in heaven (6.22–23).

ACTS: And when they had called in the apostles they beat them and charged them not to speak in the name of Jesus, and let them go. Then they left the presence of the council rejoicing that they were counted worthy to suffer dishonor for the name *of the Lord.* And every day in the temple and at home they did not cease teaching and preaching Jesus as the Christ (5.40–42).

COLOSSIANS: Of which I, Paul, became a minister. Now I rejoice in my sufferings for your sake, and in my flesh I complete what is lacking in Christ's afflictions for the sake of his body, that is, the church (1.23–24).

65.1 That it is necessary even in the very moment of departing this life to pray in a fitting manner.

MATTHEW: And about the ninth hour Jesus cried with a loud voice, "Eli, Eli, lama sabachthani? That is, "My God, my God, why hast thou forsaken me?" (27.46).

LUKE: Then Jesus, crying with a loud voice, said, "Father, into thy hands I commit my spirit!" And having said this he breathed his last (23.46).

ACTS: And as they were stoning Stephen he prayed, "Lord, do not hold this sin against them." And when he had said this he fell asleep (7.59–60).

66.1 That it is necessary not to desert those struggling on behalf of piety.

JOHN: Jesus answered them, "Do you now believe? The hour is coming and *now is come* when you will be scattered, every man to his home, and will leave me alone" (16.31–32).

ΠΡΟΣ ΤΙΜ. β'. Οἶδας τοῦτο, ὅτι ἀπεστράφησάν με πάντες οἱ ἐν τῇ Ἀσίᾳ, ὧν ἐστι Φύγελλος καὶ Ἑρμογένης. Δώῃ ὁ Κύριος ἔλεος τῷ Ὀνησιφόρου οἴκῳ, ὅτι πολλάκις με ἀνέψυξε, καὶ τὴν ἅλυσίν μου οὐκ ἐπησχύνθη· ἀλλὰ γενόμενος ἐν Ῥώμῃ, σπουδαίως ἐζήτησέ με, καὶ εὗρε. Δώῃ αὐτῷ ὁ Κύριος εὑρεῖν ἔλεος παρὰ Κυρίου ἐν ἐκείνῃ τῇ ἡμέρᾳ. Καὶ ὅσα ἐν Ἐφέσῳ διηκόνησε, βέλτιον σὺ γινώσκεις.

ΠΡΟΣ ΤΙΜ. β'. Ἐν τῇ πρώτῃ μου ἀπολογίᾳ οὐδείς μοι συμπαρεγένετο, ἀλλὰ πάντες με ἐγκατέλιπον· μὴ αὐτοῖς λογισθείη.

[66.2] Ὅτι δεῖ προσεύχεσθαι ὑπὲρ τῶν ἐν πειρασμοῖς ἐξεταζομένων.

Κεφάλ. β'.

ΛΟΥΚΑΣ. Σίμων, Σίμων, ἰδοὺ ὁ σατανᾶς ἐξῃτήσατο [401] ὑμᾶς, τοῦ σινιάσαι ὡς τὸν σῖτον· ἐγὼ δὲ ἐδεήθην περὶ σοῦ, ἵνα μὴ ἐκλίπῃ ἡ πίστις σου.

ΠΡΑΞΕΙΣ. Ὁ μὲν οὖν Πέτρος ἐτηρεῖτο ἐν τῇ φυλακῇ. Προσευχὴ δὲ ἦν ἐκτενὴς γενομένη ὑπὸ τῆς Ἐκκλησίας πρὸς τὸν Θεὸν ὑπὲρ αὐτοῦ.

ΟΡΟΣ ΞΖ'.

[67.1] Ὅτι τῶν πληροφορίαν ἐχόντων τῆς ἐκ νεκρῶν ἀναστάσεως, ἀλλότριον τὸ λυπεῖσθαι ἐπὶ τοῖς κεκοιμημένοις.

Κεφάλ. α'.

ΛΟΥΚΑΣ. Ἠκολούθει δὲ αὐτῷ πολὺ πλῆθος τοῦ λαοῦ, καὶ γυναικῶν, αἳ καὶ ἐκόπτοντο, καὶ ἐθρήνουν αὐτόν. Στραφεὶς δὲ εἶπεν πρὸς αὐτάς· θυγατέρες Ἱερουσαλήμ, μὴ κλαίετε ἐπ᾽ ἐμέ.

ΠΡΟΣ ΘΕΣΣ. α'. Περὶ δὲ τῶν κεκοιμημένων οὐ θέλω ὑμᾶς ἀγνοεῖν, ἀδελφοί, ἵνα μὴ λυπῆσθε ὡς καὶ οἱ λοιποί, οἱ μὴ ἔχοντες ἐλπίδα. Εἰ γὰρ πιστεύομεν ὅτι Ἰησοῦς ἀπέθανε, καὶ ἀνέστη· οὕτω καὶ ὁ Θεὸς τοὺς κοιμηθέντας διὰ τοῦ Ἰησοῦ ἄξει σὺν αὐτῷ.

ΟΡΟΣ ΞΗ'.

[68.1] Ὅτι οὐ δεῖ τὰ ἰδιώματα τοῦ αἰῶνος τούτου καὶ μετὰ τὴν ἀνάστασιν προσδοκᾶν, ἀλλὰ ἀγγελικὸν καὶ ἀπροσδεῆ βίον εἰδέναι ἐν τῷ μέλλοντι αἰῶνι.

2 TIMOTHY: You are aware that all who are in Asia turned away from me, and among them Phygelus and Hermogenes. May the Lord grant mercy to the household of Onesiphorus, for he often refreshed me; he was not ashamed of my chains, but when he arrived in Rome he searched for me eagerly and found me—may the Lord grant him to find mercy from the Lord on that Day—and you well know all the service he rendered at Ephesus (1.15–18).

2 TIMOTHY: At my first defense no one took my part; all deserted me. May it not be charged against them (4.16).

66.2 That it is necessary to pray for those being tried in temptations.

LUKE: Simon, Simon behold, Satan demanded to have you that he might sift you like wheat, but I have prayed for you that your faith may not fail (22.31–32).

ACTS: So Peter was kept in prison; but *prayer* for him was made *earnestly* to God by the church (12.5).

67.1 That it is foreign to those who are certain of the resurrection of the dead to be grieved over those fallen asleep.

LUKE: And there followed him a great multitude of the people and of women who bewailed and lamented him. But Jesus, *turning, said to them*, "Daughters of Jerusalem, do not weep for me" (23.27–28).

1 THESSALONIANS: But *I* would not have you ignorant, brethren, concerning those who are asleep, that you may not grieve as others do who have no hope. For since we believe that Jesus died and rose again, even so, through Jesus God will bring with him those who have fallen asleep (4.13–14).

68.1 That it is necessary not to look for what belongs to this age to exist also after the resurrection, but to know that life in the age to come is angelic and without necessity.

Κεφάλ. α΄.

ΛΟΥΚΑΣ. Ἀποκριθεὶς ὁ Ἰησοῦς εἶπεν αὐτοῖς· οἱ υἱοὶ τοῦ αἰῶνος τούτου γαμοῦσι καὶ ἐκγαμίζονται· οἱ δὲ καταξιωθέντες τοῦ αἰῶνος ἐκείνου τυχεῖν, καὶ τῆς ἀναστάσεως τῆς ἐκ νεκρῶν, οὔτε γαμοῦσιν, οὔτε ἐκγαμίζονται. Οὔτε γὰρ ἀποθανεῖν ἔτι δύνανται· ἰσάγγελοι γάρ εἰσι, καὶ υἱοί εἰσι τοῦ Θεοῦ, τῆς ἀναστάσεως υἱοὶ ὄντες.

ΠΡΟΣ ΚΟΡ. α΄. Ἀλλ᾽ ἐρεῖ τις, πῶς ἐγείρονται οἱ νεκροί; ποίῳ δὲ σώματι ἔρχονται; Ἄφρον, σὺ ὃ σπείρεις, οὐ ζωοποιεῖται, ἐὰν μὴ ἀποθάνῃ πρῶτον. Καὶ ὃ σπείρεις, οὐ τὸ σῶμα τὸ γενησόμενον [402] σπείρεις, ἀλλὰ γυμνὸν κόκκον, εἰ τύχοι σίτου, ἤ τινος τῶν λοιπῶν. Ὁ δὲ Θεὸς δίδωσιν αὐτῷ σῶμα, καθὼς ἠθέλησε. Καὶ μετ᾽ ὀλίγα· Οὕτω καὶ ἡ ἀνάστασις τῶν νεκρῶν. Σπείρεται ἐν φθορᾷ, ἐγείρεται ἐν ἀφθαρσίᾳ. Σπείρεται ἐν ἀτιμίᾳ, ἐγείρεται ἐν δόξῃ· σπείρεται ἐν ἀσθενείᾳ, ἐγείρεται ἐν δυνάμει· σπείρεται σῶμα ψυχικόν, ἐγείρεται σῶμα πνευματικόν.

[68.2] Ὅτι οὐ δεῖ τοπικὴν ἢ σαρκικὴν ἐκδέχεσθαι τὴν παρουσίαν τοῦ Κυρίου, ἀλλ᾽ ἐν τῇ δόξῃ τοῦ Πατρὸς κατὰ πάσης τῆς οἰκουμένης ἀθρόως προσδοκᾶν.

Κεφάλ. β΄.

ΜΑΤΘΑΙΟΣ. Τότε ἐάν τις ὑμῖν εἴπῃ· ἰδοὺ ὧδε ὁ Χριστὸς, ἢ ὧδε, μὴ πιστεύσητε. Ἐγερθήσονται γὰρ ψευδόχριστοι καὶ ψευδοπροφῆται, καὶ δώσουσι σημεῖα μεγάλα καὶ τέρατα, ὥστε πλανῆσαι, εἰ δυνατὸν, καὶ τοὺς ἐκλεκτούς.

ΜΑΡΚΟΣ. Ὑμεῖς δὲ βλέπετε· ἰδοὺ, προείρηκα ὑμῖν πάντα. Ἀλλ᾽ ἐν ἐκείναις ταῖς ἡμέραις, μετὰ²⁰ τὴν θλίψιν ἐκείνην ὁ ἥλιος σκοτισθήσεται, καὶ ἡ σελήνη οὐ δώσει τὸ φέγγος αὐτῆς, καὶ οἱ ἀστέρες τοῦ οὐρανοῦ ἔσονται ἐκπίπτοντες, καὶ αἱ δυνάμεις αἱ ἐν τοῖς οὐρανοῖς σαλευθήσονται. Καὶ τότε ὄψονται τὸν Υἱὸν τοῦ ἀνθρώπου ἐρχόμενον ἐν νεφέλαις μετὰ δυνάμεως καὶ δόξης πολλῆς.

ΠΡΟΣ ΘΕΣΣ. α΄. Τοῦτο γὰρ ὑμῖν λέγομεν ἐν λόγῳ Κυρίου, ὅτι ἡμεῖς οἱ ζῶντες, οἱ περιλειπόμενοι εἰς τὴν παρουσίαν τοῦ Κυρίου, οὐ μὴ φθάσωμεν τοὺς κοιμηθέντας, ὅτι αὐτὸς ὁ Κύριος ἐν κελεύσματι, ἐν

²⁰Corrected from με τὰ.

LUKE: Jesus said to them, "The sons of this age marry and are given in marriage, but those who are accounted worthy to attain to that age and to the resurrection from the dead neither marry nor are given in marriage, for they cannot die anymore, because they are equal to angels and are sons of God, being sons of the resurrection" (20.34–36).

1 CORINTHIANS: But someone will ask, "How are the dead raised? With what kind of body do they come?" *Fool*! What you sow does not come to life unless it *first* dies. And what you sow is not the body which is to be, but a bare kernel, perhaps of wheat or of some other grain. But God gives it a body as he has chosen (15.35–38). *And a little further*: So is it with the resurrection of the dead. What is sown is perishable; what is raised is imperishable. It is sown in dishonor; it is raised in glory. It is sown in weakness; it is raised in power. It is sown a *soulish* body; it is raised a spiritual body (15.42–44).

68.2 That it is necessary not to expect the coming of the Lord geographically or fleshly, but to look for it in the glory of the Father throughout all the world at once.

MATTHEW: Then if anyone says to you, "Lo, here is the Christ!" or "There he is!" do not believe it. For false Christs and false prophets will arise and show great signs and wonders so as to lead astray, if possible, even the elect (24.23–24).

MARK: But take heed; I have told you all things beforehand. But in those days, after that tribulation, the sun will be darkened, and the moon will not give its light, and the stars *of heaven will be falling*, and the powers in the heavens will be shaken. And then they will see the Son of man coming in clouds with great power and glory (13.23–26).

1 THESSALONIANS: For this we declare to you by the word of the Lord, that we who are alive, who are left until the coming of the Lord, shall not precede those who have fallen asleep. For the Lord himself will descend from heaven with a cry of command, with the

φωνῇ ἀρχαγγέλου, καὶ ἐν σάλπιγγι Θεοῦ καταβήσεται ἀπ᾽ οὐρανοῦ, καὶ οἱ νεκροὶ ἐν Χριστῷ ἀναστήσονται πρῶτον. [403]

ΟΡΟΣ ΞΘ΄.

[69.1]   ὅσα κατὰ συνάφειαν ἀπαγορεύονται, καὶ ἀπόφασιν δέχεται ἀπειλῆς.

Κεφάλ. α΄.

ΜΑΤΘΑΙΟΣ. Ἐκ γὰρ τῆς καρδίας ἐξέρχονται διαλογισμοὶ πονηροί, φόνοι, μοιχεῖαι, πορνεῖαι, κλοπαί, ψευδομαρτυρίαι, βλασφημίαι. Ταῦτά ἐστι τὰ κοινοῦντα τὸν ἄνθρωπον.

ΜΑΤΘΑΙΟΣ. Πορεύεσθε ἀπ᾽ ἐμοῦ, οἱ κατηραμένοι, εἰς τὸ πῦρ τὸ αἰώνιον τὸ ἡτοιμασμένον τῷ διαβόλῳ καὶ τοῖς ἀγγέλοις αὐτοῦ. Ἐπείνασα γὰρ, καὶ οὐκ ἐδώκατέ μοι φαγεῖν· ἐδίψησα, καὶ οὐκ ἐποτίσατέ με· ξένος ἤμην, καὶ οὐ συνηγάγετέ με· γυμνὸς, καὶ οὐ περιεβάλετέ με· ἀσθενὴς, καὶ ἐν φυλακῇ, καὶ οὐκ ἐπεσκέψασθέ με.

ΛΟΥΚΑΣ. Οὐαὶ ὑμῖν τοῖς πλουσίοις, ὅτι ἀπέχετε τὴν παράκλησιν ὑμῶν· οὐαὶ οἱ ἐμπεπλησμένοι, ὅτι πεινάσετε· οὐαὶ ὑμῖν οἱ γελῶντες νῦν, ὅτι πενθήσετε καὶ κλαύσετε· οὐαὶ ὅταν καλῶς εἴπωσιν ὑμᾶς πάντες οἱ ἄνθρωποι.

ΛΟΥΚΑΣ. Προσέχετε δὲ ἑαυτοῖς, μήποτε βαρηθῶσιν ὑμῶν αἱ καρδίαι ἐν κραιπάλῃ, καὶ μέθῃ, καὶ μερίμναις βιωτικαῖς, καὶ αἰφνιδίως ἐπιστῇ ἐφ᾽ ὑμᾶς ἡ ἡμέρα ἐκείνη.

ΠΡΟΣ ΡΩΜ. Καὶ καθὼς οὐκ ἐδοκίμασαν τὸν Θεὸν ἔχειν ἐν ἐπιγνώσει, παρέδωκεν αὐτοὺς ὁ Θεὸς εἰς ἀδόκιμον νοῦν, ποιεῖν τὰ μὴ καθήκοντα, πεπληρωμένους πάσῃ ἀδικίᾳ, πορνείᾳ, πλεονεξίᾳ, κακίᾳ, καὶ τὰ ἑξῆς. Τὸ γὰρ, Οὐ μοιχεύσεις, οὐ φονεύσεις, οὐ κλέψεις, οὐκ ἐπιθυμήσεις, καὶ εἴ τις ἑτέρα ἐντολὴ, καὶ τὰ ἑξῆς.

ΠΡΟΣ ΚΟΡ. α΄. Μὴ πλανᾶσθε· οὔτε πόρνοι, οὔτε εἰδωλολάτραι, οὔτε μοιχοὶ, οὔτε μαλακοὶ, οὔτε ἀρσενοκοῖται, οὔτε πλεονέκται, οὔτε μέθυσοι, οὐ λοίδοροι, οὐχ ἅρπαγες, βασιλείαν Θεοῦ οὐ κληρονομήσουσιν.

ΠΡΟΣ ΚΟΡ. β΄. Μήπως ἔρις, ζῆλοι, θυμοὶ, ἐριθεῖαι, καταλαλιαὶ, ψιθυρισμοὶ, φυσιώσεις, ἀκαταστασίαι. [404]

archangel's call, and with the sound of the trumpet of God. And the dead in Christ will rise first (4.15–16).

69.1   All of those things that are conjointly forbidden and are associated explicitly with threats:

MATTHEW: For out of the heart come evil thoughts, murder, adultery, fornication, theft, false witness, slander. These are what defile a man, but to eat with unwashed hands does not defile a man (15.19–20).

MATTHEW: Depart from me, you cursed, into the eternal fire prepared for the devil and his angels, for I was hungry and you gave me no food; I was thirsty and you gave me no drink; I was a stranger and you did not welcome me, naked and you did not clothe me, sick and in prison and you did not visit me (25.41–43).

LUKE: But woe to you that are rich, for you have received your consolation. Woe to you that are *full*, for you shall hunger. Woe to you that laugh now, for you shall mourn and weep. Woe to you when all men speak well of you (6.24–26).

LUKE: But take heed to yourselves lest your hearts be weighed down with dissipation and drunkenness and cares of this life and that day come upon you suddenly like a snare (21.34).

ROMANS: And since they did not see fit to acknowledge God, God gave them up to a base mind and to improper conduct. They were filled with all manner of wickedness, *fornication*, covetousness, malice (1.28–29), *and what follows.*

ROMANS: The commandments, "You shall not commit adultery; you shall not kill; you shall not steal; you shall not covet," and any other commandment (13.9), *and what follows.*

1 CORINTHIANS: Do not be deceived; neither *fornicators*, nor idolaters, nor adulterers, nor *those lacking self-control, nor those who lie with men*, nor the greedy, nor drunkards, nor revilers, nor robbers will inherit the kingdom of God (6.9–10).

2 CORINTHIANS: Lest there be quarreling, jealousy, anger, selfishness, slander, gossip, conceit, and disorder (12.20).

ΠΡΟΣ ΓΑΛ. Φανερὰ δέ ἐστι τὰ ἔργα τῆς σαρκὸς, ἅτινά ἐστι μοιχεία, πορνεία, ἀκαθαρσία, ἀσέλγεια, εἰδωλολατρεία, φαρμακεία, ἔχθραι, ἔρις, ζῆλοι, θυμοὶ, ἐριθεῖαι, διχοστασίαι, αἱρέσεις, φθόνοι, φόνοι, μέθαι, κῶμοι, καὶ τὰ ὅμοια τούτοις, ἃ προλέγω ὑμῖν, καθὼς καὶ προεῖπον, ὅτι οἱ τὰ τοιαῦτα πράσσοντες βασιλείαν Θεοῦ οὐ κληρονομήσουσιν.

ΠΡΟΣ ΓΑΛ. Μὴ γενώμεθα κενόδοξοι, ἀλλήλους προσκαλούμενοι, ἀλλήλοις φθονοῦντες.

ΠΡΟΣ ΕΦΕΣ. Πᾶσα πικρία, καὶ θυμὸς, καὶ ὀργὴ, καὶ κραυγὴ, καὶ βλασφημία ἀρθήτω ἀφ᾽ ὑμῶν, σὺν πάσῃ κακίᾳ. Πορνεία δὲ, καὶ πᾶσα ἀκαθαρσία, ἢ πλεονεξία, μηδὲ ὀνομαζέσθω ἐν ὑμῖν, καθὼς πρέπει ἁγίοις· καὶ αἰσχρότης, ἢ μωρολογία, εὐτραπελία, τὰ οὐκ ἀνήκοντα.

ΠΡΟΣ ΚΟΛ. Νεκρώσατε οὖν τὰ μέλη ὑμῶν τὰ ἐπὶ τῆς γῆς· πορνείαν, ἀκαθαρσίαν, πάθος, ἐπιθυμίαν κακὴν, καὶ τὴν πλεονεξίαν, ἥτις ἐστὶν εἰδωλολατρεία· δι᾽ ἃ ἔρχεται ἡ ὀργὴ τοῦ Θεοῦ ἐπὶ τοὺς υἱοὺς τῆς ἀπειθείας. Νυνὶ δὲ ἀπόθεσθε καὶ ὑμεῖς τὰ πάντα, ὀργὴν, θυμὸν, κακίαν, βλασφημίαν, αἰσχρολογίαν ἐκ τοῦ στόματος ὑμῶν. Μὴ ψεύδεσθε εἰς ἀλλήλους.

ΠΡΟΣ ΤΙΜ. α΄. Ἀνόμοις δὲ καὶ ἀνυποτάκτοις, ἀσεβέσι, καὶ ἁμαρτωλοῖς, ἀνοσίοις, καὶ βεβήλοις, πατρολώαις, καὶ μητρολώαις, ἀνδροφόνοις, πόρνοις, ἀρσενοκοίταις, ἀνδραποδισταῖς, ψεύσταις, ἐπιόρκοις, καὶ εἴ τι ἕτερον τῇ ὑγιαινούσῃ διδασκαλίᾳ[21] ἀντίκειται, τῇ κατὰ τὸ εὐαγγέλιον τῆς δόξης τοῦ μακαρίου Θεοῦ, ὃ ἐπιστεύθην ἐγώ.

ΠΡΟΣ ΤΙΜ. α΄. Ἐν ὑστέροις καιροῖς ἀποστήσονταί τινες τῆς πίστεως, προσέχοντες πνεύμασι πλάνης, καὶ διδασκαλίαις δαιμονίων, ἐν ὑποκρίσει ψευδολόγων, κεκαυτηριασμένων τὴν ἰδίαν συνείδησιν, κωλυόντων γαμεῖν· ἀπέχεσθαι βρωμάτων, ἃ ὁ Θεὸς ἔκτισεν εἰς μετάληψιν μετ᾽ εὐχαριστίας τοῖς πιστοῖς, καὶ ἐπεγνωκόσι τὴν ἀλήθειαν.

ΠΡΟΣ ΤΙΜ. α΄. Εἴ τις ἑτεροδιδασκαλεῖ, καὶ μὴ προσέρχεται ὑγιαίνουσι λόγοις τοῖς τοῦ Κυρίου ἡμῶν Ἰησοῦ Χριστοῦ, καὶ τῇ κατ᾽

---

[21]Corrected from διδασκαλία.

GALATIANS: Now the works of the flesh are plain: *adultery,* fornication, impurity, licentiousness, idolatry, sorcery, enmity, strife, jealousy, anger, selfishness, dissension, party spirit, envy, *murder,* drunkenness, carousing, and the like. I warn you as I warned you before that those who do such things shall not inherit the kingdom of God (5.19–21).

GALATIANS: Let us have no self–conceit, no provoking of one another, no envy of one another (5.26).

EPHESIANS: Let all bitterness and wrath and anger and clamor and slander be put away from you, with all malice. But fornication and all impurity or covetousness must not even be named among you, as is fitting among saints, *and filthiness or silly talk or levity, which are not proper* (4.31; 5.3–4).

COLOSSIANS: Put to death therefore what is earthly in you: fornication, impurity, passion, evil desire, and covetousness, which is idolatry. On account of these the wrath of God is coming *upon the sons of disobedience* (3.5–6). But now put them all away: anger, wrath, malice, slander, and foul talk from your mouth. Do not lie to one another (3.8–9).

1 TIMOTHY: For the unholy and profane, for *those who strike their fathers and those their mothers,* for manslayers, fornicators, *those who lie with men,* kidnappers,[26] liars, perjurers, and whatever else is contrary to sound doctrine, in accordance with the glorious gospel of the blessed God with which I have been entrusted (1.9–11).

1 TIMOTHY: In later times some will depart from the faith by giving heed to deceitful spirits and doctrines of demons, through the pretensions of liars whose consciences are seared, who forbid marriage and enjoin abstinence from foods which God created to be received with thanksgiving by those who believe and know the truth (4.1–3).

1 TIMOTHY: If anyone teaches otherwise and does not agree with the sound words of our Lord Jesus Christ and the teaching which accords with godliness, he is puffed up with conceit; he knows nothing; he has a morbid craving for controversy and for disputes about

---

[26]Specifically, those who kidnap free persons and sell them into slavery.

εὐσέβειαν διδασκαλίᾳ, τετύφωται, μηδὲν ἐπιστάμενος, ἀλλὰ νοσῶν περὶ ζητήσεις καὶ λογομαχίας, ἐξ ὧν γίνεται φθόνος, ἔρις, βλασφημίαι, ὑπόνοιαι πονηραί, διαπαρατριβαὶ διεφθαρμένων ἀνθρώπων τὸν νοῦν, καὶ [405] ἀπεστερημένων τῆς ἀληθείας, νομιζόντων πορισμὸν εἶναι τὴν εὐσέβειαν. Ἀφίστασο ἀπὸ τῶν τοιούτων.

ΠΡΟΣ ΤΙΜ. β΄. Ἐν ἐσχάταις ἡμέραις ἐνστήσονται καιροὶ χαλεποί.
Ἔσονται γὰρ οἱ ἄνθρωποι φίλαυτοι, φιλάργυροι, ἀλαζόνες, ὑπερήφανοι, βλάσφημοι, γονεῦσιν ἀπειθεῖς, ἀχάριστοι, ἀνόσιοι, ἄστοργοι, ἄσπονδοι, διάβολοι, ἀκρατεῖς, ἀνήμεροι, ἀφιλάγαθοι, προδόται, προπετεῖς, τετυφωμένοι, φιλήδονοι μᾶλλον ἢ φιλόθεοι, ἔχοντες μόρφωσιν εὐσεβείας, τὴν δὲ δύναμιν αὐτῆς ἠρνημένοι· καὶ τούτους ἀποτρέπου.

ΠΡΟΣ ΤΙΤ. Ἦμεν γάρ ποτε καὶ ἡμεῖς ἀνόητοι, ἀπειθεῖς, πλανώμενοι δουλεύοντες ἐπιθυμίαις καὶ ἡδοναῖς ποικίλαις, ἐν κακίᾳ καὶ φθόνῳ διάγοντες, στυγητοί, μισοῦντες ἀλλήλους.

[69.2] ὅσα κατὰ συνάφειαν ἐγκρίνεται, ἢ καὶ εὐλογίας ἐπαγγελίαν ἔχει.

Κεφάλ. β΄.

ΜΑΤΘΑΙΟΣ. Μακάριοι οἱ πτωχοὶ τῷ πνεύματι, ὅτι αὐτῶν ἐστιν ἡ βασιλεία τῶν οὐρανῶν. Μακάριοι οἱ πενθοῦντες, ὅτι αὐτοὶ παρακληθήσονται. Μακάριοι οἱ πραεῖς, ὅτι αὐτοὶ κληρονομήσουσι τὴν γῆν. Μακάριοι οἱ πεινῶντες καὶ διψῶντες τὴν δικαιοσύνην, ὅτι αὐτοὶ χορτασθήσονται. Μακάριοι οἱ ἐλεήμονες, ὅτι αὐτοὶ ἐλεηθήσονται. Μακάριοι οἱ καθαροὶ τῇ καρδίᾳ, ὅτι αὐτοὶ τὸν Θεὸν ὄψονται. Μακάριοι οἱ εἰρηνοποιοί, ὅτι αὐτοὶ υἱοὶ Θεοῦ κληθήσονται. Μακάριοι οἱ δεδιωγμένοι ἕνεκεν δικαιοσύνης, ὅτι αὐτῶν ἐστιν ἡ βασιλεία τῶν οὐρανῶν. Μακάριοί ἐστε, ὅταν ὀνειδίσωσιν ὑμᾶς, καὶ διώξωσι, καὶ εἴπωσι πᾶν πονηρὸν ῥῆμα καθ᾽ ὑμῶν ψευδόμενοι, ἕνεκεν ἐμοῦ. Χαίρετε καὶ ἀγαλλιᾶσθε, ὅτι ὁ μισθὸς ὑμῶν πολὺς ἐν τοῖς οὐρανοῖς.

ΜΑΤΘΑΙΟΣ. Δεῦτε, οἱ εὐλογημένοι τοῦ Πατρός μου, κληρονομήσατε τὴν ἡτοιμασμένην ὑμῖν βασιλείαν ἀπὸ καταβολῆς κόσμου. Ἐπείνασα γάρ, καὶ ἐδώκατέ μοι φαγεῖν· ἐδίψησα, καὶ ἐποτίσατέ με·

words, which produce envy, dissension, slander, base suspicions, and wrangling among men who are depraved in mind and bereft of the truth, imagining that godliness is a means of gain. *Keep away from such as these* (6.3–5).

2 TIMOTHY: In the last days there will come times of stress. For men will be lovers of self, lovers of money, proud, arrogant, *blasphemous*, disobedient to their parents, ungrateful, unholy, *heartless*, implacable, slanderers, profligates, fierce, haters of good, treacherous, reckless, swollen with conceit, lovers of pleasure rather than lovers of God, holding the form of religion but denying the power of it. Avoid such people (3.1–5).

TITUS: For we ourselves were once foolish, disobedient, led astray, slaves to various passions and pleasures, passing our days in malice and envy, *hated*, and hating one another (3.3).

69.2   All of those things that are conjointly approved which also have a promise of blessing.

MATTHEW: Blessed are the poor in spirit, for theirs is the kingdom of heaven. Blessed are those who mourn, for they shall be comforted. Blessed are the meek, for they shall inherit the earth. Blessed are those who hunger and thirst for righteousness, for they shall be satisfied. Blessed are the merciful, for they shall obtain mercy. Blessed are the pure in heart, for they shall see God. Blessed are the peacemakers, for they shall be called sons of God. Blessed are those who are persecuted for righteousness' sake, for theirs is the kingdom of heaven. Blessed are you when *they* revile you and persecute you and utter all kinds of evil *words* against you falsely on my account. Rejoice and be glad, for your reward is great in heaven (5.3–12).

MATTHEW: Come, O blessed of my Father, inherit the kingdom prepared for you from the foundation of the world; for I was hungry, and you gave me food; I was thirsty, and you gave me drink; I was a stranger, and you welcomed me; I was naked, and you clothed me;

ξένος ἤμην, καὶ συνηγάγετέ με· γυμνὸς, καὶ περιεβάλετέ με· ἠσθένησα, καὶ ἐπεσκέψασθέ με· ἐν φυλακῇ ἤμην, καὶ ἤλθετε πρός με.
ΠΡΟΣ ΡΩΜ. Εἴτε ὁ διακονῶν ἐν τῇ διακονίᾳ, εἴτε ὁ διδάσκων ἐν
τῇ διδασκαλίᾳ, ὁ παρακαλῶν ἐν τῇ παρακλήσει, ὁ μεταδιδοὺς ἐν
ἁπλότητι· [406] ὁ προϊστάμενος ἐν σπουδῇ, ὁ ἐλεῶν ἐν ἱλαρότητι,
ἡ ἀγάπη ἀνυπόκριτος· ἀποστυγοῦντες τὸ πονηρὸν, κολλώμενοι τῷ
ἀγαθῷ· τῇ φιλαδελφίᾳ εἰς ἀλλήλους φιλόστοργοι· τῇ τιμῇ ἀλλήλους
προηγούμενοι· τῇ σπουδῇ μὴ ὀκνηροί· τῷ πνεύματι ζέοντες· τῷ
Κυρίῳ δουλεύοντες· τῇ ἐλπίδι χαίροντες· τῇ θλίψει ὑπομένοντες· τῇ
προσευχῇ προσκαρτεροῦντες· ταῖς χρείαις τῶν ἁγίων κοινωνοῦντες·
τὴν φιλοξενίαν διώκοντες. Εὐλογεῖτε τοὺς διώκοντας ὑμᾶς·
εὐλογεῖτε, καὶ μὴ καταρᾶσθε. Χαίρειν μετὰ χαιρόντων, καὶ κλαίειν
μετὰ κλαιόντων. Τὸ αὐτὸ εἰς ἀλλήλους φρονοῦντες· μὴ τὰ ὑψηλὰ
φρονοῦντες, ἀλλὰ τοῖς ταπεινοῖς συναπαγόμενοι. Μὴ γίνεσθε
φρόνιμοι παρ' ἑαυτοῖς· μηδενὶ κακὸν ἀντὶ κακοῦ ἀποδιδόντες·
προνοούμενοι καλὰ ἐνώπιον πάντων ἀνθρώπων. Εἰ δυνατὸν,
τὸ ἐξ ὑμῶν, μετὰ πάντων ἀνθρώπων εἰρηνεύοντες· μὴ ἑαυτοὺς
ἐκδικοῦντες, ἀγαπητοὶ, ἀλλὰ δότε τόπον τῇ ὀργῇ· γέγραπται γάρ·
«ἐμοὶ ἐκδίκησις, ἐγὼ ἀνταποδώσω,²² λέγει Κύριος.» Ἀλλὰ «ἐὰν
πεινᾷ ὁ ἐχθρός σου, ψώμιζε αὐτόν· ἐὰν δὲ διψᾷ, πότιζε αὐτόν.» Μὴ
νικῶ ὑπὸ τοῦ κακοῦ, ἀλλὰ νίκα ἐν τῷ ἀγαθῷ τὸ κακόν.
ΠΡΟΣ ΚΟΡ. β'. Μηδεμίαν ἐν μηδενὶ διδόντες προσκοπὴν, ἵνα
μὴ μωμηθῇ ἡ διακονία· ἀλλ' ἐν παντὶ συνιστῶντες ἑαυτοὺς, ὡς
Θεοῦ διάκονοι, ἐν ὑπομονῇ πολλῇ, ἐν θλίψεσιν, ἐν ἀνάγκαις,
ἐν στενοχωρίαις, ἐν πληγαῖς, ἐν φυλακαῖς, ἐν ἀκαταστασίαις,
ἐν κόποις, ἐν ἀγρυπνίαις, ἐν νηστείαις, ἐν ἁγνότητι, ἐν γνώσει,
ἐν μακροθυμίᾳ, ἐν χρηστότητι, ἐν Πνεύματι ἁγίῳ, ἐν ἀγάπῃ
ἀνυποκρίτῳ, ἐν λόγῳ ἀληθείας, ἐν δυνάμει Θεοῦ, διὰ τῶν ὅπλων
τῆς δικαιοσύνης, τῶν δεξιῶν καὶ ἀριστερῶν, διὰ δόξης καὶ
ἀτιμίας, διὰ δυσφημίας καὶ εὐφημίας, ὡς πλάνοι, καὶ ἀληθεῖς· ὡς
ἀγνοούμενοι, καὶ ἐπιγινωσκόμενοι· ὡς ἀποθνήσκοντες, καὶ ἰδοὺ
ζῶμεν· ὡς παιδευόμενοι, καὶ μὴ θανατούμενοι· ὡς λυπούμενοι,

---

²²Corrected from ἀνταποδόσω.

I was sick, and you visited me; I was in prison, and you came to me (25.34–36).

ROMANS: He who serves, *in serving*; he who teaches, in *teaching*; he who exhorts, in *exhortation*; he who contributes, in liberality; he who gives aid, with zeal; he who does acts of mercy, with cheerfulness. Let love be genuine; hate what is evil; hold fast to what is good; love one another with brotherly affection; outdo one another in showing honor. Never flag in zeal; be aglow with the Spirit; serve the Lord. Rejoice in your hope; be patient in tribulation; be constant in prayer. Contribute to the needs of the saints; practice hospitality. Bless those who persecute you; bless and do not curse them. Rejoice with those who rejoice, *and* weep with those who weep. Live in harmony with one another; do not be haughty, but associate with the lowly; never be conceited. Repay no one evil for evil, but take thought for what is noble in the sight of all. If possible, so far as it depends upon you, live peaceably with all. Beloved, never avenge yourselves, but leave it to the wrath of God, for it is written, "Vengeance is mine, I will repay, says the Lord."[27] *But* "if your enemy is hungry, feed him; if he is thirsty, give him *drink*."[28] Do not be overcome by evil, but overcome evil with good (12.7–21).

2 CORINTHIANS: We put no obstacle in anyone's way, so that no fault may be found with our ministry, but as servants of God we commend ourselves in every way: through great endurance, in afflictions, hardships, calamities, beatings, imprisonments, tumults, labors, watching, hunger, by purity, knowledge, forbearance, kindness, the Holy Spirit, genuine love, truthful speech, and the power of God, with the weapons of righteousness for the right hand and for the left, in honor and dishonor, in ill repute and good repute. We are treated as impostors and yet are true, as unknown and yet well known, as dying and behold, we live, as punished and yet not killed, as sorrowful yet always rejoicing, as poor yet making many rich, as having nothing and yet possessing everything (6.3–10).

[27]Deut 32.35
[28]Prov 25.21

ἀεὶ δὲ χαίροντες· ὡς πτωχοί, πολλοὺς δὲ πλουτίζοντες· ὡς μηδὲν ἔχοντες, καὶ πάντα κατέχοντες.

ΠΡΟΣ ΚΟΡ. β'. Λοιπόν, ἀδελφοί, χαίρετε, καταρτίζεσθε, παρακαλεῖσθε, τὸ αὐτὸ φρονεῖτε, εἰρηνεύετε.

ΠΡΟΣ ΓΑΛ. Ὁ δὲ καρπὸς τοῦ Πνεύματός ἐστιν ἀγάπη, χαρά, εἰρήνη, μακροθυμία, χρηστότης, ἀγαθοσύνη, πίστις, πραότης, ἐγκράτεια, ἀγνεία.

ΠΡΟΣ ΕΦΕΣ. Παρακαλῶ οὖν ὑμᾶς ἐγὼ ὁ δέσμιος ἐν Κυρίῳ, ἀξίως περιπατῆσαι τῆς κλήσεως ἧς ἐκλήθητε, μετὰ πάσης ταπεινοφροσύνης καὶ πραότητος, μετὰ μακροθυμίας ἀνεχόμενοι ἀλλήλων ἐν ἀγάπῃ, σπουδάζοντες τηρεῖν [407] τὴν ἑνότητα τοῦ Πνεύματος ἐν τῷ συνδέσμῳ τῆς εἰρήνης. Ἓν σῶμα καὶ ἓν Πνεῦμα, καθὼς καὶ ἐκλήθητε ἐν μιᾷ ἐλπίδι τῆς κλήσεως ὑμῶν.

ΠΡΟΣ ΕΦΕΣ. Γίνεσθε οὖν εἰς ἀλλήλους χρηστοί, εὔσπλαγχνοι, χαριζόμενοι ἑαυτοῖς, καθὼς καὶ ὁ Θεὸς ἐν Χριστῷ ἐχαρίσατο ὑμῖν. Γίνεσθε οὖν μιμηταὶ τοῦ Θεοῦ, ὡς τέκνα ἀγαπητά, καὶ περιπατεῖτε ἐν ἀγάπῃ, καθὼς καὶ ὁ Χριστὸς ἠγάπησεν ἡμᾶς, καὶ παρέδωκεν ἑαυτὸν ὑπὲρ ἡμῶν προσφορὰν καὶ θυσίαν τῷ Θεῷ εἰς ὀσμὴν εὐωδίας.

ΠΡΟΣ ΦΙΛ. Εἴ τις οὖν παράκλησις ἐν Χριστῷ, εἴ τι παραμύθιον ἀγάπης, εἴ τις κοινωνία πνεύματος, εἴ τινα σπλάγχνα καὶ οἰκτιρμοί, πληρώσατέ μου τὴν χαράν, ἵνα τὸ αὐτὸ φρονῆτε πάντες, τὴν αὐτὴν ἀγάπην ἔχοντες, σύμψυχοι, τὸ ἓν φρονοῦντες, μηδὲν κατ' ἐριθείαν,²³ ἢ κενοδοξίαν.

ΠΡΟΣ ΦΙΛ. Τὸ λοιπόν, ἀδελφοί, ὅσα ἐστὶν ἀληθῆ, ὅσα σεμνά, ὅσα δίκαια, ὅσα ἁγνά, ὅσα προσφιλῆ, ὅσα εὔφημα, εἴ τις ἀρετὴ, καὶ εἴ τις ἔπαινος, ταῦτα λογίζεσθε. Ἃ καὶ ἐμάθετε, καὶ παρελάβετε, καὶ ἠκούσατε, καὶ εἴδετε ἐν ἐμοί, ταῦτα πράσσετε.

ΠΡΟΣ ΚΟΛ. Εἰ οὖν συνηγέρθητε τῷ Χριστῷ, τὰ ἄνω ζητεῖτε, οὗ ὁ Χριστός ἐστιν ἐν δεξιᾷ τοῦ Θεοῦ καθήμενος· τὰ ἄνω φρονεῖτε, μὴ τὰ ἐπὶ τῆς γῆς. Ἀπεθάνετε γάρ, καὶ ἡ ζωὴ ὑμῶν κέκρυπται σὺν τῷ Χριστῷ ἐν τῷ Θεῷ. Ἐνδύσασθε οὖν, ὡς ἐκλεκτοὶ τοῦ Θεοῦ, ἅγιοι καὶ ἠγαπημένοι, σπλάγχνα οἰκτιρμῶν, χρηστότητα, ταπεινοφροσύνην, πραότητα, μακροθυμίαν.

²³Corrected from ἐρίθειαν.

2 CORINTHIANS: Finally, brethren, farewell. Mend your ways; heed my appeal; agree with one another; live in peace (13.11).

GALATIANS: But the fruit of the Spirit is love, joy, peace, patience, kindness, goodness, faithfulness, gentleness, self-control, *purity* (5.22).

EPHESIANS: I therefore, a prisoner for the Lord, beg you to lead a life worthy of the calling to which you have been called with all lowliness and meekness, with patience, forbearing one another in love, eager to maintain the unity of the Spirit in the bond of peace. There is one body and one Spirit, just as you were called to the one hope that belongs to your call (4.1–4).

EPHESIANS: *Therefore* be kind to one another, tenderhearted, forgiving one another, as God in Christ forgave you. Therefore be imitators of God as beloved children. And walk in love as Christ loved us and gave himself up for us, a fragrant offering and sacrifice to God (4.32–5.2).

PHILIPPIANS: So if there is any encouragement in Christ, any incentive of love, any participation in the Spirit, any affection and sympathy, complete my joy by being *all* of the same mind, having the same love, being in full accord and of one mind. Do nothing from selfishness or conceit (2.1–3).

PHILIPPIANS: Finally, brethren, whatever is true, whatever is honorable, whatever is just, whatever is pure, whatever is lovely, whatever is gracious, if there is any excellence, if there is anything worthy of praise, think about these things. What you have learned and received and heard and seen in me, do (4.8–9).

COLOSSIANS: If then you have been raised with Christ, seek the things that are above, where Christ is, seated at the right hand of God. Set your minds on things that are above, not on things that are on earth. For you have died, and your life is hid with Christ in God (3.1–3). Put on then, as God's chosen ones, holy and beloved, compassion, kindness, lowliness, meekness, and patience (3.12).

ΠΡΟΣ ΘΕΣΣ. α'. Νουθετεῖτε τοὺς ἀτάκτους, παραμυθεῖσθε τοὺς ὀλιγοψύχους, ἀντέχεσθε τῶν ἀσθενῶν, μακροθυμεῖτε πρὸς πάντας. Ὁρᾶτε μή τις κακὸν ἀντὶ κακοῦ τινι ἀποδῷ, ἀλλὰ πάντοτε τὸ ἀγαθὸν διώκετε καὶ εἰς ἀλλήλους καὶ εἰς πάντας. Πάντοτε χαίρετε, ἀδιαλείπτως προσεύχεσθε. Ἐν παντὶ εὐχαριστεῖτε· τοῦτο γὰρ θέλημα Θεοῦ ἐν Χριστῷ Ἰησοῦ, εἰς ὑμᾶς. Τὸ Πνεῦμα μὴ σβέννυτε, προφητείας μὴ ἐξουθενεῖτε. Πάντα δὲ δοκιμάζοντες, τὸ καλὸν κατέχετε· ἀπὸ παντὸς εἴδους πονηροῦ ἀπέχεσθε.

ΠΡΟΣ ΤΙΤ. Πρεσβύτας νηφαλίους εἶναι, σεμνούς, σώφρονας, ὑγιαίνοντας τῇ πίστει, τῇ ἀγάπῃ, τῇ ὑπομονῇ. Πρεσβύτιδας ὡσαύτως, ἐν καταστήματι ἱεροπρεπεῖ, μὴ διαβόλους, [408] μὴ οἴνῳ πολλῷ δεδουλωμένας, καλοδιδασκάλους, ἵνα σωφρονίζωσι τὰς νέας, φιλάνδρους εἶναι, φιλοτέκνους, σώφρονας, ἁγνάς, οἰκουρούς, ἀγαθάς, ὑποτασσομένας τοῖς ἰδίοις ἀνδράσιν, ἵνα μὴ ὁ λόγος τοῦ Θεοῦ βλασφημῆται.

ΠΡΟΣ ΤΙΤ. Ὑπομίμνησκε αὐτοὺς ἀρχαῖς καὶ ἐξουσίαις ὑποτάσσεσθαι, πειθαρχεῖν, πρὸς πᾶν ἔργον ἀγαθὸν ἑτοίμους εἶναι, μηδένα βλασφημεῖν, ἀμάχους εἶναι, ἐπιεικεῖς, πᾶσαν ἐνδεικνυμένους πραότητα πρὸς πάντας ἀνθρώπους.

ΠΡΟΣ ΕΒΡ. Ἡ φιλαδελφία μενέτω, τῆς φιλοξενίας μὴ ἐπιλανθάνεσθε· διὰ ταύτης γὰρ ἔλαθόν τινες ξενίσαντες ἀγγέλους. Μιμνήσκεσθε τῶν δεσμίων, ὡς συνδεδεμένοι· τῶν κακουχουμένων, ὡς καὶ αὐτοὶ ὄντες ἐν σώματι. Τίμιος ὁ γάμος ἐν πᾶσι, καὶ ἡ κοίτη ἀμίαντος· πόρνους δὲ καὶ μοιχοὺς κρινεῖ ὁ Θεός. Ἀφιλάργυρος ὁ τρόπος· ἀρκούμενοι τοῖς παροῦσιν.

ΟΡΟΣ Ο'.

[70.1] Ὅτι δεῖ τοὺς ἐγκεχειρισμένους τὸ κήρυγμα τοῦ εὐαγγελίου μετὰ δεήσεως καὶ εὐχῆς καθίστασθαι, εἴτε διακόνους, εἴτε πρεσβυτέρους, ἀνεγκλήτους, καὶ δοκίμους τὸν πρότερον βίον.

Κεφάλ. α'.

ΜΑΤΘΑΙΟΣ. Τότε λέγει τοῖς μαθηταῖς αὐτοῦ· ὁ μὲν θερισμὸς πολύς, οἱ δὲ ἐργάται ὀλίγοι. Δεήθητε οὖν τοῦ Κυρίου τοῦ θερισμοῦ, ὅπως ἐκβάλῃ²⁴ ἐργάτας εἰς τὸν θερισμόν.

²⁴Corrected from ἐκβάλη.

1 THESSALONIANS: Admonish the idlers; encourage the faint-hearted; help the weak; be patient with them all. See that none of you repays evil for evil, but always seek to do good *both* to one another and to all. Rejoice always; pray constantly; give thanks in all circumstances, for this is the will of God in Christ Jesus for you. Do not quench the Spirit; do not despise prophesying, but test everything; hold fast what is good; abstain from every form of evil (5.14–22).

TITUS: Bid the older men be temperate, serious, sensible, sound in faith, in love, and in steadfastness. Bid the older women likewise to be reverent in behavior, not to be slanderers or slaves to drink; they are to teach what is good, and so train the young women to love their husbands and children, to be sensible, chaste, domestic, kind, and submissive to their husbands, that the word of God may not be discredited (2.2–5).

TITUS: Remind them to be submissive to rulers and authorities, to be obedient, to be ready for any honest work, to speak evil of no one, to avoid quarreling, to be gentle, and to show perfect courtesy toward all men (3.1–2).

HEBREWS: Let brotherly love continue. Do not neglect to show hospitality to strangers, for thereby some have entertained angels unawares. Remember those who are in prison as though in prison with them and those who are ill-treated, since you also are in the body. Let marriage be held in honor among all, and let the marriage bed be undefiled, for God will judge the immoral and adulterous. Keep your life free from love of money, and be content with what you have (13.1–5).

70.1 That it is necessary for those entrusted with the preaching of the Gospel, with prayer and supplication to ordain deacons or presbyters who are blameless and esteemed for their former life.

MATTHEW: Then he said to his disciples, "The harvest is plentiful, but the laborers are few; pray therefore the Lord of the harvest to send out laborers into *the* harvest" (9.37–38).

ΛΟΥΚΑΣ. Καὶ ὅτε ἐγένετο ἡμέρα, προσεφώνησε τοὺς μαθητὰς αὐτοῦ, καὶ ἐκλεξάμενος ἀπ᾽ αὐτῶν δώδεκα, οὓς καὶ ἀποστόλους ὠνόμασε, Σίμωνα, ὃν καὶ ὠνόμασε Πέτρον, καὶ Ἀνδρέαν τὸν ἀδελφὸν αὐτοῦ, καὶ Ἰάκωβον, καὶ Ἰωάννην, Φίλιππον, καὶ Βαρθολομαῖον, καὶ Ματθαῖον, καὶ Θωμᾶν, Ἰάκωβον τὸν τοῦ Ἀλφαίου, καὶ Σίμωνα τὸν καλούμενον Ζηλωτὴν, καὶ Ἰούδαν Ἰακώβου, καὶ Ἰούδαν Ἰσκαριώτην, ὃς καὶ ἐγένετο προδότης.

ΛΟΥΚΑΣ. Μετὰ δὲ ταῦτα ἀνέδειξεν ὁ Κύριος καὶ ἑτέρους ἑβδο-μήκοντα, καὶ ἀπέστειλεν αὐτοὺς ἀνὰ δύο πρὸ προσώπου αὐτοῦ, εἰς πᾶσαν πόλιν καὶ τόπον, οὗ ἔμελλεν αὐτὸς ἔρχεσθαι. Ἔλεγεν οὖν πρὸς αὐτούς· ὁ μὲν θερισμὸς πολὺς, οἱ δὲ ἐργάται ὀλίγοι. Δεήθητε οὖν τοῦ Κυρίου τοῦ θερισμοῦ, ὅπως ἐκβάλῃ ἐργάτας εἰς τὸν θερισμὸν αὐτοῦ.

ΠΡΑΞΕΙΣ. [409] Τὸν μὲν πρῶτον λόγον ἐποιησάμην περὶ πάντων, ὦ Θεόφιλε, ὧν ἤρξατο ὁ Ἰησοῦς ποιεῖν τε καὶ διδάσκειν, ἄχρι ἧς ἡμέρας ἐντειλάμενος τοῖς ἀποστόλοις διὰ Πνεύματος ἁγίου, οὓς ἐξελέξατο, ἀνελήφθη.

ΠΡΑΞΕΙΣ. Καὶ ἔστησαν δύο, Ἰωσὴφ τὸν καλούμενον Βαρσαβᾶν, ὃς ἐπεκλήθη Ἰοῦστος, καὶ Ματθίαν. Καὶ προσευξάμενοι εἶπον· σὺ, Κύριε, καρδιογνῶστα πάντων, ἀνάδειξον ὃν ἐξελέξω ἐκ τούτων τῶν δύο ἕνα, λαβεῖν τὸν κλῆρον τῆς διακονίας ταύτης καὶ ἀποστολῆς, ἀφ᾽ ἧς παρέβη Ἰούδας πορευθῆναι εἰς τὸν τόπον τὸν ἴδιον. Καὶ ἔδωκαν κλήρους αὐτῶν, καὶ ἔπεσεν ὁ κλῆρος ἐπὶ Ματθίαν, καὶ συγκατεψηφίσθη μετὰ τῶν ἕνδεκα ἀποστόλων.

ΠΡΟΣ ΤΙΜ. α´. Εἴ τις ἐπισκοπῆς ὀρέγεται, καλοῦ ἔργου ἐπιθυμεῖ. Δεῖ οὖν τὸν ἐπίσκοπον ἀνεπίληπτον εἶναι, μιᾶς γυναικὸς ἄνδρα, νηφάλιον, σώφρονα, κόσμιον, φιλόξενον, διδακτικὸν, μὴ πάροινον, μὴ πλήκτην, μὴ αἰσχροκερδῆ· ἀλλ᾽ ἐπιεικῆ, ἄμαχον, ἀφιλάργυρον, τοῦ ἰδίου οἴκου καλῶς προϊστάμενον, τέκνα ἔχοντα ἐν ὑποταγῇ μετὰ πάσης σεμνότητος· (εἰ δέ τις τοῦ ἰδίου οἴκου προστῆναι οὐκ οἶδε, πῶς Ἐκκλησίας Θεοῦ ἐπιμελήσεται;) μὴ νεόφυτον, ἵνα μὴ τυφωθεὶς εἰς κρῖμα ἐμπέσῃ καὶ παγίδα τοῦ διαβόλου. Δεῖ δὲ αὐτὸν καὶ μαρτυρίαν καλὴν ἔχειν ἀπὸ τῶν ἔξωθεν, ἵνα μὴ εἰς ὀνειδισμὸν ἐμπέσῃ καὶ παγίδα τοῦ διαβόλου. Διακόνους ὡσαύτως, σεμνοὺς, μὴ

LUKE: And when it was day he called his disciples and chose from them twelve, whom he named apostles: Simon, whom he named Peter, and Andrew his brother, and James and *John*, Philip and Bartholomew and Matthew and *Thomas*, James the son of Alphaeus and Simon, who was called the Zealot, and Judas the son of James and Judas Iscariot, who *also* became a traitor (6.13–16).

LUKE: After this the Lord appointed seventy others and sent them on ahead of him, two by two, into every town and place where he himself was about to come. *So* he said to them, "The harvest is plentiful, but the laborers are few; pray therefore the Lord of the harvest to send out laborers into his harvest" (10.1–2).

ACTS: In the first book, O Theophilus, I have dealt with all that Jesus began to do and teach until the day when he was taken up, after he had given commandment through the Holy Spirit to the apostles whom he had chosen (1.1–2).

ACTS: And they put forward two: Joseph called Barsabbas, who was surnamed Justus, and Matthias. And they prayed and said, "Lord, who knowest the hearts of all men, show which one of these two thou hast chosen to take the *lot* in this ministry and apostleship from which Judas turned aside to go to his own place." And they cast lots for them, and the lot fell on Matthias, and he was enrolled with the eleven apostles (1.23–26).

1 TIMOTHY: If anyone aspires to the office of bishop, he desires a noble task. Now a bishop must be above reproach, the husband of one wife, temperate, sensible, dignified, hospitable, an apt teacher, no drunkard, not violent but gentle, not quarrelsome, and no lover of money. He must manage his own household well, keeping his children submissive and respectful in every way, for if a man does not know how to manage his own household, how can he care for God's church? He must not be a recent convert, or he may be puffed up with conceit and fall into the condemnation of the devil; moreover, he must be well thought of by outsiders, or he may fall into reproach and the snare of the devil. Deacons likewise must be serious, not double-tongued, not addicted to much wine, not greedy for gain;

διλόγους, μὴ οἴνῳ πολλῷ προσέχοντας, μὴ αἰσχροκερδεῖς, ἔχοντας τὸ μυστήριον τῆς πίστεως ἐν καθαρᾷ συνειδήσει. Καὶ οὗτοι δὲ δοκιμαζέσθωσαν πρῶτον, εἶτα διακονείτωσαν, ἀνέγκλητοι ὄντες. ΠΡΟΣ ΤΙΤ. Τούτου χάριν κατέλιπόν σε ἐν Κρήτῃ, ἵνα τὰ λείποντα ἐπιδιορθώσῃ, καὶ καταστήσῃς πρεσβυτέρους κατὰ πόλιν, ὡς ἐγώ σοι διεταξάμην. Εἴ τίς ἐστιν ἀνέγκλητος, μιᾶς γυναικὸς ἀνήρ, τέκνα ἔχων πιστά, μὴ ἐν κατηγορίᾳ ἀσωτίας, ἢ ἀνυπότακτα. Δεῖ γὰρ τὸν ἐπίσκοπον ἀνέγκλητον εἶναι, ὡς Θεοῦ οἰκονόμον, μὴ αὐθάδη, μὴ ὀργίλον, μὴ πάροινον, μὴ πλήκτην, μὴ αἰσχροκερδῆ, ἀλλὰ φιλόξενον, φιλάγαθον, σώφρονα, δίκαιον, ὅσιον, ἐγκρατῆ, ἀντεχόμενον τοῦ κατὰ τὴν διδαχὴν πιστοῦ λόγου, ἵνα δυνατὸς ᾖ καὶ παρακαλεῖν ἐν τῇ ὑγιαινούσῃ διδασκαλίᾳ, καὶ τοὺς ἀντιλέγοντας ἐλέγχειν. [410]

[70.2] Ὅτι οὐ δεῖ περὶ τὰς χειροτονίας εὐχερῆ εἶναι, οὔτε ἀπερισκέπτως ἐπ' αὐτὰς ἔρχεσθαι· οὐ γὰρ ἀκίνδυνον τὸ ἀδόκιμον· τὸν δὲ ἁλόντα ἐπί τινι φανεροῦν, ἵνα μήτε αὐτὸς κοινωνήσῃ τῇ ἁμαρτίᾳ, μήτε οἱ λοιποὶ προσκόπτωσιν, ἀλλὰ μᾶλλον φοβεῖσθαι μάθωσιν.

Κεφάλ. β'.

ΠΡΟΣ ΤΙΜ. α'. Χεῖρας ταχέως μηδενὶ ἐπιτίθει, μηδὲ κοινώνει ἁμαρτίαις ἀλλοτρίαις.

ΠΡΟΣ ΤΙΜ. α'. Κατὰ πρεσβυτέρου κατηγορίαν μὴ παραδέχου, ἐκτὸς εἰ μὴ ἐπὶ δύο ἢ τριῶν μαρτύρων. Τοὺς δὲ ἁμαρτάνοντας ἐνώπιον πάντων ἔλεγχε, ἵνα καὶ οἱ λοιποὶ φόβον ἔχωσιν.

[70.3] Ὅτι οὐ δεῖ τὸν ἐκλεγέντα, ἀφ' ἑαυτοῦ παρεῖναι ἐπὶ τὸ κήρυγμα, ἀναμένειν δὲ τὸν καιρὸν τῆς τοῦ Θεοῦ εὐδοκίας, καὶ ἄρχεσθαι μὲν τοῦ κηρύγματος ὅταν ἐπιτραπῇ· κηρύσσειν δὲ ἐκείνοις πρὸς οὓς ἂν ἀποσταλῇ.

Κεφάλ. γ'.

ΜΑΤΘΑΙΟΣ. Τούτους τοὺς δώδεκα ἀπέστειλεν ὁ Ἰησοῦς, παραγγείλας αὐτοῖς, λέγων· εἰς ὁδὸν ἐθνῶν μὴ ἀπέλθητε, καὶ εἰς πόλιν Σαμαρειτῶν μὴ εἰσέλθητε· πορεύεσθε δὲ μᾶλλον πρὸς τὰ

they must hold the mystery of the faith with a clear conscience. And let them also be tested first; then, if they prove themselves blameless, let them serve as deacons (3.1–10).

TITUS: This is why I left you in Crete, that you might amend what was defective and appoint *presbyters* in every town as I directed you, if any man is blameless, the husband of one wife, and his children are believers and not open to the charge of being profligate or insubordinate. For a bishop, as God's steward, must be blameless; he must not be arrogant or quick–tempered or a drunkard or violent or greedy for gain, but hospitable, a lover of goodness, master of himself, upright, holy, and self–controlled; he must hold firm to the sure word as taught, so that he may be able to give instruction in sound doctrine and also to confute those who contradict it (1.5–9).

70.2   That it is necessary not to be reckless in ordinations or to approach them heedlessly (for what is untested is not without danger), and to expose the one convicted of anything, so that one does not commune with the sin and others do not stumble into it but rather learn to fear it.

1 TIMOTHY: Do not be hasty in the laying on of hands, nor *commune with* another's sins (5.22).

1 TIMOTHY: Never admit any charge against a *presbyter* except on the evidence of two or three witnesses. As for those who persist in sin, rebuke them in the presence of all, so that the rest may stand in fear (5.19–20).

70.3   That it is necessary for the one chosen not to present himself for preaching on his own initiative but to await the timing of the good pleasure of God and to make a beginning of preaching when commissioned and to preach to those to whom he has been sent.

MATTHEW: These twelve Jesus sent out, charging them, "Go nowhere among the Gentiles, and enter no town of the Samaritans, but go rather to the lost sheep of the house of Israel" (10.5–6).

πρόβατα τὰ ἀπολωλότα οἴκου Ἰσραήλ.

ΜΑΤΘΑΙΟΣ. Καὶ ἰδοὺ γυνὴ Χαναναία, ἀπὸ τῶν ὁρίων ἐκείνων ἐξελθοῦσα, ἐκραύγασεν, αὐτῷ λέγουσα· ἐλέησόν με, Κύριε, υἱὸς Δαβίδ· ἡ θυγάτηρ μου κακῶς δαιμονίζεται· ὁ δὲ οὐκ ἀπεκρίθη αὐτῇ λόγον. Καὶ προσελθόντες οἱ μαθηταὶ αὐτοῦ, ἠρώτων αὐτὸν λέγοντες· ἀπόλυσον αὐτήν, ὅτι κράζει ὄπισθεν ἡμῶν. Ὁ δὲ ἀποκριθεὶς εἶπεν· οὐκ ἀπεστάλην εἰ μὴ εἰς τὰ πρόβατα τὰ ἀπολωλότα οἴκου Ἰσραήλ.

ΙΩΑΝΝΗΣ. Ἐγὼ γὰρ ἐκ τοῦ Θεοῦ ἐξῆλθον καὶ ἥκω· οὔτε γὰρ ἀπ' ἐμαυτοῦ ἐλήλυθα, ἀλλ' ἐκεῖνός με ἀπέστειλεν.

ΠΡΑΞΕΙΣ. Οἱ μὲν οὖν διασπαρέντες ἀπὸ τῆς θλίψεως τῆς γενομένης ἐπὶ Στεφάνῳ, διῆλθον ἕως Φοινίκης καὶ Κύπρου καὶ Ἀντιοχείας, μηδενὶ λαλοῦντες τὸν λόγον, εἰ μὴ μόνον Ἰουδαίοις.

ΠΡΟΣ ΡΩΜ. Παῦλος δοῦλος Ἰησοῦ Χριστοῦ, κλητὸς ἀπόστολος, ἀφωρισμένος εἰς εὐαγγέλιον Θεοῦ.

ΠΡΟΣ ΡΩΜ. Πῶς δὲ ἀκούσονται χωρὶς κηρύσσοντος; πῶς δὲ κηρύξουσιν, [411] ἐὰν μὴ ἀποσταλῶσιν;

ΠΡΟΣ ΤΙΜ. α'. Παῦλος ἀπόστολος Ἰησοῦ Χριστοῦ κατ' ἐπιταγὴν Θεοῦ Σωτῆρος ἡμῶν, καὶ Χριστοῦ Ἰησοῦ τῆς ἐλπίδος ἡμῶν.

[70.4]   Ὅτι δεῖ τὸν κληθέντα εἰς τὸ κήρυγμα τοῦ εὐαγγελίου εὐθὺς ὑπακούειν, καὶ μὴ ἀναβάλλεσθαι.

Κεφάλ. δ'.

ΛΟΥΚΑΣ. Εἶπε δὲ πρὸς ἕτερον, ἀκολούθει μοι. Ὁ δὲ εἶπε· Κύριε, ἐπίτρεψόν μοι ἀπελθόντι πρῶτον θάψαι τὸν πατέρα μου. Εἶπε δὲ αὐτῷ ὁ Κύριος· ἄφες τοὺς νεκροὺς θάψαι τοὺς ἑαυτῶν νεκρούς· σὺ δὲ ἀπελθών, διάγγελλε τὴν βασιλείαν τοῦ Θεοῦ.

ΠΡΟΣ ΓΑΛ. Ὅτε δὲ εὐδόκησεν ὁ Θεὸς ὁ ἀφορίσας με ἐκ κοιλίας μητρός μου, καὶ καλέσας με διὰ τῆς χάριτος αὐτοῦ, ἀποκαλύψαι τὸν Υἱὸν αὐτοῦ ἐν ἐμοί, ἵνα εὐαγγελίζωμαι αὐτὸν ἐν τοῖς ἔθνεσιν· εὐθέως οὐ προσανεθέμην σαρκὶ καὶ αἵματι, οὐδὲ ἀπῆλθον εἰς Ἱεροσόλυμα πρὸς τοὺς πρὸ ἐμοῦ ἀποστόλους· ἀλλὰ ἀπῆλθον εἰς Ἀραβίαν, καὶ πάλιν ὑπέστρεψα εἰς Δαμασκόν.

MATTHEW: And behold, a Canaanite woman from that region came out and cried *to him*, "Have mercy on me, O Lord, Son of David; my daughter is severely possessed by a demon." But he did not answer her a word. And his disciples came and begged him, saying, "Send her away, for she is crying after us." He answered, "I was sent only to the lost sheep of the house of Israel" (15.22–24).

JOHN: For I proceeded and came forth from God; I came not of my own accord, but he sent me (8.42).

ACTS: Now those who were scattered because of the persecution that arose over Stephen traveled as far as Phoenicia and Cyprus and Antioch, speaking the word to none except Jews (11.19).

ROMANS: Paul, a servant of Jesus Christ, called to be an apostle, set apart for the gospel of God (1.1).

ROMANS: *How will they* hear without a preacher? And how *will they* preach unless they are sent (10.14–15)?

1 TIMOTHY: Paul, an apostle of Christ Jesus by command of God our Savior and of Christ Jesus our hope (1.1).

70.4   That it is necessary for the one called to preach the Gospel to obey immediately and not delay.

LUKE: To another he said, "Follow me." But he said, "Lord, let me first go and bury my father." But *the Lord* said to him, "Leave the dead to bury their own dead, but as for you, go and proclaim the kingdom of God" (9.59–60).

GALATIANS: But when *God*, who had set me apart before I was born and had called me through his grace, was pleased to reveal his Son to me in order that I might preach him among the Gentiles, I did not confer with flesh and blood nor did I go up to Jerusalem to those who were apostles before me, but I went away into Arabia, and again I returned to Damascus (1.15–17).

[70.5]   Ὅτι οὐ δεῖ ἑτεροδιδασκαλεῖν.

Κεφάλ. ε΄.

ΙΩΑΝΝΗΣ. Ἀμὴν ἀμὴν λέγω ὑμῖν, ὁ μὴ εἰσερχόμενος διὰ τῆς θύρας εἰς τὴν αὐλὴν τῶν προβάτων, ἀλλὰ ἀναβαίνων ἀλλαχόθεν, ἐκεῖνος κλέπτης ἐστὶ καὶ λῃστής. Ὁ δὲ εἰσερχόμενος διὰ τῆς θύρας, ποιμήν ἐστι τῶν προβάτων. Καὶ μετ᾽ ὀλίγα· Ἐγώ εἰμι ἡ θύρα τῶν προβάτων. Πάντες ὅσοι ἦλθον, κλέπται εἰσὶ καὶ λῃσταί· ἀλλ᾽ οὐκ ἤκουσαν αὐτῶν τὰ πρόβατα.

ΠΡΟΣ ΓΑΛ. Ἀλλὰ καὶ ἐὰν ἡμεῖς ἢ ἄγγελος ἐξ οὐρανοῦ εὐαγγελίζηται παρ᾽ ὃ εὐηγγελισάμεθα ὑμῖν, ἀνάθεμα ἔστω. Ὡς προειρήκαμεν, καὶ ἄρτι πάλιν λέγω· εἴ τις ὑμᾶς εὐαγγελίζεται παρ᾽ ὃ παρελάβετε, ἀνάθεμα ἔστω.

ΠΡΟΣ ΤΙΜ. α΄. Εἴ τις ἑτεροδιδασκαλεῖ, καὶ μὴ προσέρχεται ὑγιαίνουσι λόγοις τοῖς τοῦ Κυρίου ἡμῶν Ἰησοῦ Χριστοῦ, καὶ τῇ κατ᾽ εὐσέβειαν διδασκαλίᾳ, τετύφωται, μηδὲν ἐπιστάμενος, καὶ τὰ ἑξῆς. [412]

[70.6]   Ὅτι δεῖ πάντα τὰ προστεταγμένα ὑπὸ τοῦ Κυρίου ἐν τῷ εὐαγγελίῳ καὶ διὰ τῶν ἀποστόλων διδάσκειν τοὺς πεπιστευμένους, καὶ ὅσα τούτοις ἀκόλουθα.

Κεφάλ. ϛ΄.

ΜΑΤΘΑΙΟΣ. Πορευθέντες, μαθητεύσατε πάντα τὰ ἔθνη, βαπτίζοντες αὐτοὺς εἰς τὸ ὄνομα τοῦ Πατρὸς, καὶ τοῦ Υἱοῦ, καὶ τοῦ ἁγίου Πνεύματος, διδάσκοντες αὐτοὺς τηρεῖν πάντα, ὅσα ἐνετειλάμην ὑμῖν.

ΠΡΑΞΕΙΣ. Ὡς δὲ διεπορεύοντο τὰς πόλεις, παρεδίδουν αὐτοῖς φυλάσσειν τὰ δόγματα τὰ κεκριμένα ὑπὸ τῶν ἀποστόλων καὶ πρεσβυτέρων ἐν Ἱερουσαλήμ.

ΠΡΟΣ ΤΙΜ. α΄. Ταῦτα δίδασκε, καὶ παρακάλει.

ΠΡΟΣ ΤΙΤ. Σὺ δὲ λάλει ἃ πρέπει τῇ ὑγιαινούσῃ διδασκαλίᾳ.

[70.7]   Ὅτι ὁ πιστευθεὶς τὸν λόγον τῆς τοῦ Κυρίου διδασκαλίας, ἐὰν σιωπήσῃ τι τῶν ἀναγκαίων εἰς τὴν πρὸς Θεὸν εὐαρέστησιν, ἔνοχός ἐστι τοῦ αἵματος τῶν κινδυνευόντων, ἤτοι ὑπὸ τῆς ἐργασίας

70.5   That it is necessary not to teach strange doctrine.

JOHN: Truly, truly I say to you, he who does not enter the sheep-fold by the door but climbs in by another way, that man is a thief and a robber, but he who enters by the door is the shepherd of the sheep (10.1–2). *And a little further*: I am the door of the sheep. All who *have come* are thieves and robbers, but the sheep did not heed them (10.7–8).

GALATIANS: But even if we or an angel from heaven should *preach* a gospel contrary to that which we preached to you, let him be accursed. As we have said before so now I say again: if anyone is preaching to you a gospel contrary to that which you received, let him be accursed (1.8–9).

1 TIMOTHY: If anyone teaches otherwise and does not agree with the sound words of our Lord Jesus Christ and the teaching which accords with godliness, he is puffed up with conceit; he knows nothing (6.3–4), *and what follows*.

70.6   That it is necessary to teach those entrusted to one all that is prescribed by the Lord in the Gospel and through the apostles and whatever follows from these.

MATTHEW: Go and make disciples of all nations, baptizing them in the name of the Father and of the Son and of the Holy Spirit, teaching them to observe all that I have commanded you (28.19–20).

ACTS: As they went on their way through the cities, they delivered to them for observance the decisions which had been reached by the apostles and *presbyters in* Jerusalem (16.4).

1 TIMOTHY: Teach and urge these duties (6.2).

TITUS: But as for you, teach what befits sound doctrine (2.1).

70.7   That if the one entrusted with the Word of the Lord's teaching is silent concerning anything necessary for pleasing God, he is liable for the blood of those endangered by doing what is forbidden or by failing to do the good that is expected of them.

τῶν ἀπηγορευμένων, ἢ καὶ ὑπὲρ τῆς ἐλλείψεως τῶν κατορθωθῆναι ὀφειλόντων.

Κεφάλ. ζ'.

ΛΟΥΚΑΣ. Οὐαὶ ὑμῖν τοῖς νομικοῖς, ὅτι ἤρατε τὴν κλεῖδα τῆς γνώσεως· αὐτοὶ οὐκ εἰσήλθετε, καὶ τοὺς εἰσερχομένους ἐκωλύσατε.

ΠΡΑΞΕΙΣ. Ὡς δὲ κατῆλθον ἀπὸ τῆς Μακεδονίας, ὅ τε Σίλας, καὶ ὁ Τιμόθεος, συνείχετο τῷ λόγῳ ὁ Παῦλος, διαμαρτυρόμενος τοῖς Ἰουδαίοις εἶναι τὸν Χριστὸν Ἰησοῦν. Ἀντιτασσομένων δὲ αὐτῶν, καὶ βλασφημούντων, ἐκτιναξάμενος τὸ ἱμάτιον, εἶπε πρὸς αὐτούς· τὸ αἷμα ὑμῶν ἐπὶ τὴν κεφαλὴν ὑμῶν· καθαρὸς ἐγώ· ἀπὸ τοῦ νῦν εἰς τὰ ἔθνη πορεύσομαι.

ΠΡΑΞΕΙΣ. Διὸ μαρτύρομαι ὑμῖν ἐν τῇ σήμερον ἡμέρᾳ, ὅτι καθαρός εἰμι ἀπὸ τοῦ αἵματος ὑμῶν. Οὐ γὰρ ὑπεστειλάμην τοῦ μὴ ἀναγγεῖλαι ὑμῖν πᾶσαν τὴν βουλὴν τοῦ Θεοῦ. [413]

[70.8] Ὅτι δεῖ καὶ ἐπὶ τῶν μὴ κατ᾽ ἐπιταγὴν ὑπὸ τῆς Γραφῆς ὡρισμένων προτρέπειν ἕκαστον πρὸς τὸ κρεῖττον.

Κεφάλ. η'.

ΜΑΤΘΑΙΟΣ. Εἰσὶν εὐνοῦχοι, οἵτινες ἐκ κοιλίας μητρὸς ἐγεννήθησαν οὕτως· καὶ εἰσὶν εὐνοῦχοι, οἵτινες εὐνουχίσθησαν ὑπὸ τῶν ἀνθρώπων· καὶ εἰσὶν εὐνοῦχοι, οἵτινες εὐνούχισαν ἑαυτοὺς διὰ τὴν βασιλείαν τῶν οὐρανῶν. Ὁ δυνάμενος χωρεῖν, χωρείτω.

ΠΡΟΣ ΚΟΡ. α'. Περὶ δὲ τῶν παρθένων ἐπιταγὴν Κυρίου οὐκ ἔχω· γνώμην δὲ δίδωμι, ὡς ἠλεημένος ὑπὸ Κυρίου πιστὸς εἶναι. Νομίζω οὖν τοῦτο καλὸν ὑπάρχειν, διὰ τὴν ἐνεστῶσαν ἀνάγκην, ὅτι καλὸν ἀνθρώπῳ τὸ οὕτως εἶναι. Δέδεσαι γυναικί; Μὴ ζήτει λύσιν. Λέλυσαι ἀπὸ γυναικός; Μὴ ζήτει γυναῖκα, καὶ τὰ ἑξῆς.

[70.9] Ὅτι οὐκ ἔξεστιν ἑτέροις ἀνάγκην ἐπιτιθέναι ὧν αὐτὸς οὐ κατώρθωσεν.

Κεφάλ. θ'.

ΛΟΥΚΑΣ. Καὶ ὑμῖν τοῖς νομικοῖς οὐαί, ὅτι φορτίζετε τοὺς ἀνθρώπους φορτία δυσβάστακτα, καὶ αὐτοὶ ἑνὶ τῶν δακτύλων ὑμῶν οὐ προσψαύετε τοῖς φορτίοις.

LUKE: Woe to you lawyers! For you have taken away the key of knowledge; you did not enter yourselves, and you hindered those who were entering (11.52).

ACTS: When Silas and Timothy arrived from Macedonia, Paul was occupied with preaching, testifying to the Jews that the Christ was Jesus. And when they opposed and reviled him, he shook out his garments and said to them, "Your blood be upon your heads! I am innocent. From now on I will go to the Gentiles" (18.5–6).

ACTS: Therefore I testify to you this day that I am innocent of *your blood*, for I did not shrink from declaring to you the whole counsel of God (20.26–27).

70.8 That it is necessary, even for cases not determined by the prescription of the Scriptures, to convince each person of the better course.

MATTHEW: There are eunuchs who have been so from birth, and there are eunuchs who have been made eunuchs by men, and there are eunuchs who have made themselves eunuchs for the sake of the kingdom of heaven. He who is able to receive this, let him receive it (19.12).

1 CORINTHIANS: Now concerning the unmarried, I have no command of the Lord, but I give my opinion as one who by the Lord's mercy is trustworthy. I think that in view of the present distress it is well for a person *so to be*. Are you bound to a wife? Do not seek to be free. Are you free from a wife? Do not seek marriage (7.25–27), *and what follows*.

70.9 That it is not permitted to lay upon others a requirement which one has not met oneself.

LUKE: Woe to you lawyers also! For you load men with burdens hard to bear, and you yourselves do not touch the burdens with one of your fingers (11.46).

[70.10] Ὅτι δεῖ τὸν προεστῶτα τοῦ λόγου τύπον προκεῖσθαι τοῖς ἄλλοις παντὸς καλοῦ, κατορθοῦντα πρότερον ἃ διδάσκει.

Κεφάλ. ι'.

ΜΑΤΘΑΙΟΣ. Δεῦτε πρὸς μὲ, πάντες οἱ κοπιῶντες καὶ πεφορτισμένοι, κἀγὼ ἀναπαύσω ὑμᾶς. Ἄρατε τὸν ζυγόν μου ἐφ' ὑμᾶς, καὶ μάθετε ἀπ' ἐμοῦ, ὅτι πρᾷός εἰμι, καὶ ταπεινὸς τῇ καρδίᾳ.

ΙΩΑΝΝΗΣ. Ὅτε οὖν ἔνιψε τοὺς πόδας τῶν μαθητῶν αὐτοῦ, καὶ ἔλαβε τὰ ἱμάτια αὐτοῦ, ἀναπεσὼν πάλιν εἶπεν αὐτοῖς· γινώσκετε τί πεποίηκα ὑμῖν; Ὑμεῖς φωνεῖτέ με, ὁ διδάσκαλος, καὶ ὁ Κύριος, καὶ καλῶς λέγετε, εἰμὶ γάρ. Εἰ οὖν ἐγὼ ἔνιψα ὑμῶν τοὺς πόδας, ὁ Κύριος, καὶ ὁ διδάσκαλος, καὶ ὑμεῖς ὀφείλετε ἀλλήλων νίπτειν τοὺς πόδας. [414] Ὑπόδειγμα γὰρ ἔδωκα ὑμῖν, ἵνα, καθὼς ἐγὼ ἐποίησα ὑμῖν, καὶ ὑμεῖς ποιῆτε ἀλλήλοις.

ΠΡΑΞΕΙΣ. Πάντα ὑπέδειξα ὑμῖν, ὅτι οὕτω κοπιῶντας δεῖ ἀντιλαμβάνεσθαι τῶν ἀσθενούντων.

ΠΡΟΣ ΚΟΡ. α'. Μιμηταί μου γίνεσθε, καθὼς κἀγὼ Χριστοῦ.

ΠΡΟΣ ΤΙΜ. α'. Μηδείς σου τῆς νεότητος καταφρονείτω, ἀλλὰ τύπος γίνου τῶν πιστῶν ἐν λόγῳ, ἐν ἀναστροφῇ, καὶ τὰ ἑξῆς.

[70.11] Ὅτι δεῖ τὸν προεστῶτα τοῦ λόγου μὴ τοῖς ἑαυτοῦ κατορθώμασιν ἐπαμεριμνεῖν, ἴδιον δὲ καὶ ἐξαίρετον τῆς ἐγχειρισθείσης αὐτῷ φροντίδος ἔργον εἰδέναι τὴν τῶν πεπιστευμένων βελτίωσιν.

Κεφάλ. ια'.

ΜΑΤΘΑΙΟΣ. Ὑμεῖς ἐστε τὸ ἅλας τῆς γῆς. Ἐὰν δὲ τὸ ἅλας μωρανθῇ, ἐν τίνι ἁλισθήσεται; Εἰς οὐδὲν ἰσχύει ἔτι, εἰ μὴ βληθῆναι ἔξω, καὶ καταπατεῖσθαι ὑπὸ τῶν ἀνθρώπων.

ΙΩΑΝΝΗΣ. Πᾶν ὃ δίδωσί μοι ὁ Πατὴρ, πρὸς ἐμὲ ἥξει, καὶ τὸν ἐρχόμενον πρός με οὐ μὴ ἐκβάλω ἔξω. Ὅτι καταβέβηκα ἐκ τοῦ οὐρανοῦ, οὐχ ἵνα ποιῶ τὸ θέλημα τὸ ἐμὸν, ἀλλὰ τὸ θέλημα τοῦ πέμψαντός με Πατρός. Τοῦτο δέ ἐστι τὸ θέλημα τοῦ πέμψαντός με, ἵνα πᾶς ὁ θεωρῶν τὸν Υἱὸν καὶ πιστεύων εἰς αὐτὸν ἔχῃ ζωὴν αἰώνιον.

70.10 That it is necessary for the one set over the Word to set an example for others of every good, first practicing what he teaches.

MATTHEW: Come to me all who labor and are heavy laden, and I will give you rest. Take my yoke upon you and learn from me, for I am gentle and lowly in heart (11.28–29).

JOHN: When he had washed *his disciples'* feet and taken his garments and resumed his place, he said to them, "Do you know what I have done to you? You call me Teacher and Lord, and you are right, for so I am. If I then, your Lord and Teacher, have washed your feet, you also ought to wash one another's feet. For I have given you an example, that you also should do *to one another* as I have done to you" (13.12–15).

ACTS: In all things I have shown you that by so toiling one must help the weak (20.35).

1 CORINTHIANS: Be imitators of me, as I am of Christ (11.1).

1 TIMOTHY: Let no one despise your youth, but set the believers an example in speech and conduct (4.12), *and what follows.*

70.11 That it is necessary for the one set over the Word not to be lackadaisical in his duty, but to recognize that it is the proper and particular work of the office he has been given to improve those entrusted to him.

MATTHEW: You are the salt of the earth, but if salt has lost its taste, how shall its saltiness be restored? It is no longer good for anything except to be thrown out and trodden under foot by men (5.13).

JOHN: All that the Father gives me will come to me, and he who comes to me I will not cast out. For I have come down from heaven not to do my own will but the will of *the Father* who sent me, and this is the will of him who sent me: that I should lose nothing of all that he has given me but raise it up at the last day. For this is the will of my Father: that everyone who sees the Son and believes in him should have eternal life (6.37–40).

ΠΡΟΣ ΘΕΣΣ. α΄. Τίς γὰρ ἡμῶν ἐλπὶς, ἢ χαρὰ, ἢ στέφανος καυχήσεως; ἢ οὐχὶ καὶ ὑμεῖς ἔμπροσθεν τοῦ Κυρίου ἡμῶν Ἰησοῦ Χριστοῦ, ἐν τῇ αὐτοῦ παρουσίᾳ; Ὑμεῖς γάρ ἐστε ἡ δόξα ἡμῶν, καὶ ἡ χαρά.

[70.12]   Ὅτι δεῖ τὸν προεστῶτα τοῦ λόγου περιάγειν τὰς κώμας καὶ τὰς πόλεις πάσας τὰς ἐγκεχειρισμένας αὐτῷ.

Κεφάλ. ιβ΄.

ΜΑΤΘΑΙΟΣ. Καὶ περιῆγεν ὅλην τὴν Γαλιλαίαν ὁ Ἰησοῦς, διδάσκων ἐν ταῖς συναγωγαῖς, καὶ κηρύσσων τὸ εὐαγγέλιον τῆς βασιλείας, καὶ θεραπεύων πᾶσαν νόσον καὶ πᾶσαν μαλακίαν.

ΛΟΥΚΑΣ. Καὶ αὐτὸς διώδευε κατὰ πόλιν καὶ κώμην κηρύσσων τὴν βασιλείαν τοῦ Θεοῦ, καὶ εὐαγγελιζόμενος· καὶ οἱ δώδεκα σὺν αὐτῷ. [415]

[70.13]   Ὅτι δεῖ πάντας προσκαλεῖσθαι πρὸς ὑπακοὴν τοῦ εὐαγγελίου, καὶ μετὰ πάσης παρρησίας καταγγέλλειν τὸν λόγον, καὶ μαρτυρεῖν τῇ ἀληθείᾳ, κἄν τινες κωλύωσι, καὶ διώκωσιν οἵῳ δήποτε τρόπῳ μέχρι θανάτου.

Κεφάλ. ιγ΄.

ΜΑΤΘΑΙΟΣ. Ὃ λέγω ὑμῖν ἐν τῇ σκοτίᾳ, εἴπατε ἐν τῷ φωτί· καὶ ὃ πρὸς τὸ οὖς ἠκούσατε, κηρύξατε ἐπὶ τῶν δωμάτων. Καὶ μὴ φοβεῖσθε ἀπὸ τῶν ἀποκτεινόντων τὸ σῶμα, τὴν δὲ ψυχὴν μὴ δυναμένων ἀποκτεῖναι.

ΜΑΤΘΑΙΟΣ. Ὁ μὲν γάμος ἕτοιμός ἐστιν, οἱ δὲ κεκλημένοι οὐκ ἦσαν ἄξιοι. Πορεύεσθε οὖν ἐπὶ τὰς διεξόδους τῶν ὁδῶν, καὶ ὅσους ἂν εὕρητε, καλέσατε εἰς τοὺς γάμους.

ΙΩΑΝΝΗΣ. Ἀπεκρίθη αὐτῷ ὁ Ἰησοῦς, ἐγὼ παρρησίᾳ ἐλάλησα τῷ κόσμῳ· ἐγὼ πάντοτε ἐδίδαξα ἐν τῇ συναγωγῇ καὶ ἐν τῷ ἱερῷ, ὅπου πάντες οἱ Ἰουδαῖοι συνέρχονται, καὶ ἐν κρυπτῷ ἐλάλησα οὐδέν.

ΠΡΑΞΕΙΣ. Ἀγαγόντες δὲ αὐτοὺς ἔστησαν ἐν τῷ συνεδρίῳ, καὶ ἐπηρώτησεν αὐτοὺς ὁ ἀρχιερεὺς, λέγων· οὐ παραγγελίᾳ παρηγγείλαμεν ὑμῖν μὴ διδάσκειν ἐπὶ τῷ ὀνόματι τούτῳ; Καὶ ἰδοὺ πεπληρώκατε τὴν Ἱερουσαλὴμ τῆς διδαχῆς ὑμῶν, καὶ βούλεσθε ἐπαγαγεῖν ἐφ᾽ ἡμᾶς τὸ αἷμα τοῦ ἀνθρώπου τούτου. Ἀποκριθεὶς

1 THESSALONIANS: For what is our hope or joy or crown of boasting before our Lord Jesus *Christ* at his coming? Is it not you? For you are our glory and joy (2.19–20).

70.12   That it is necessary for the one set over the Word to go around to all of the villages and cities that have been placed in his hands.

MATTHEW: And *Jesus* went about all Galilee teaching in *the* synagogues and preaching the gospel of the kingdom and healing every disease and every infirmity (4.23).
LUKE: And he went on through cities and villages preaching *the kingdom of God and bringing the good news, and the twelve with him* (8.1).

70.13   That it is necessary to call everyone to obey the Gospel and to proclaim the Word most frankly and to testify to the truth even if some would hinder you or even persecute you—indeed, even to the point of death.

MATTHEW: What I tell you in the dark utter in the light, and what you hear whispered proclaim upon the housetops. And do not fear those who kill the body but cannot kill the soul (10.27–28).
MATTHEW: The wedding is ready, but those invited were not worthy. Go therefore to the thoroughfares and invite to the marriage feast as many as you find (22.8–9).
JOHN: Jesus answered him, "I have spoken openly to the world; I have always taught in synagogues and in the temple, where all Jews come together; I have said nothing secretly" (18.20).
ACTS: And when they had brought them, they set them before the council. And the high priest questioned them, saying, "*Did we not strictly charge* you not to teach in this name? Yet here you have filled Jerusalem with your teaching, and you intend to bring this man's

δὲ Πέτρος καὶ οἱ ἀπόστολοι εἶπον· πειθαρχεῖν δεῖ μᾶλλον Θεῷ ἢ ἀνθρώποις.

ΠΡΑΞΕΙΣ. Πλὴν ὅτι τὸ Πνεῦμά μοι τὸ ἅγιον κατὰ πόλιν διαμαρτύρεται, λέγον, ὅτι δεσμὰ καὶ θλίψεις με μένουσιν. Ἀλλ' οὐδενὸς λόγον ποιοῦμαι, οὐδὲ ἔχω τὴν ψυχήν μου τιμίαν ἐμαυτῷ, ὡς τελειῶσαι τὸν δρόμον μου μετὰ χαρᾶς, καὶ τὴν διακονίαν ἣν ἔλαβον παρὰ τοῦ Κυρίου Ἰησοῦ, διαμαρτύρασθαι τὸ εὐαγγέλιον τῆς χάριτος τοῦ Θεοῦ.

ΠΡΟΣ ΘΕΣΣ. α'. Αὐτοὶ γὰρ οἴδατε, ἀδελφοί, τὴν εἴσοδον ἡμῶν τὴν πρὸς ὑμᾶς, ὅτι οὐ κενὴ γέγονεν· ἀλλὰ προπαθόντες καὶ ὑβρισθέντες, καθὼς οἴδατε, ἐν Φιλίπποις, ἐπαρρησιασάμεθα ἐν τῷ Θεῷ ἡμῶν λαλῆσαι πρὸς ὑμᾶς τὸ εὐαγγέλιον τοῦ Θεοῦ ἡμῶν ἐν πολλῷ ἀγῶνι. [416]

[70.14] Ὅτι δεῖ προσεύχεσθαι ὑπὲρ τῆς προκοπῆς τῶν πεπιστευκότων, καὶ ἐπ' αὐτῇ εὐχαριστεῖν.
Κεφάλ. ιδ'.

ΙΩΑΝΝΗΣ. Οὐ περὶ τούτων δὲ ἐρωτῶ μόνον, ἀλλὰ καὶ περὶ τῶν πιστευόντων διὰ τοῦ λόγου αὐτῶν εἰς ἐμέ, ἵνα πάντες ἓν ὦσι, καθὼς σύ, Πάτερ, ἐν ἐμοὶ, κἀγὼ ἐν σοί, ἵνα καὶ αὐτοὶ ἐν ἡμῖν ἓν ὦσι. Καὶ πάλιν· Πάτερ, οὓς δέδωκάς μοι, θέλω ἵνα ὅπου εἰμὶ ἐγώ, κἀκεῖνοι ὦσι μετ' ἐμοῦ.

ΛΟΥΚΑΣ. Ἐν αὐτῇ τῇ ὥρᾳ ἠγαλλιάσατο τῷ πνεύματι ὁ Ἰησοῦς, καὶ εἶπεν· ἐξομολογοῦμαί σοι, Πάτερ, Κύριε τοῦ οὐρανοῦ καὶ τῆς γῆς, ὅτι ἀπέκρυψας ταῦτα ἀπὸ σοφῶν καὶ συνετῶν, καὶ ἀπεκάλυψας αὐτὰ νηπίοις. Ναί, ὁ Πατὴρ, ὅτι οὕτως ἐγένετο εὐδοκία ἔμπροσθέν σου.

ΠΡΟΣ ΡΩΜ. Πρῶτον μὲν εὐχαριστῶ τῷ Θεῷ μου διὰ Ἰησοῦ Χριστοῦ ὑπὲρ πάντων ὑμῶν, ὅτι ἡ πίστις ὑμῶν καταγγέλλεται ἐν ὅλῳ τῷ κόσμῳ. Μάρτυς γάρ μού ἐστιν ὁ Θεός, ᾧ λατρεύω ἐν τῷ πνεύματί μου, ἐν τῷ εὐαγγελίῳ τοῦ Υἱοῦ αὐτοῦ, ὡς ἀδιαλείπτως μνείαν ὑμῶν ποιοῦμαι ἐπὶ τῶν προσευχῶν μου.

ΠΡΟΣ ΦΙΛ. Μάρτυς γάρ μού ἐστιν ὁ Θεός, ὡς ἐπιποθῶ πάντας ὑμᾶς ἐν σπλάγχνοις Ἰησοῦ Χριστοῦ. Καὶ τοῦτο προσεύχομαι, ἵνα

blood upon us." But Peter and the apostles answered, "We must obey God rather than men" (5.27–29).

ACTS: Except that the Holy Spirit testifies to me in every city that imprisonment and afflictions await me. But I do not account my life of any value nor as precious to myself, if only I may accomplish my course and the ministry which I received from the Lord Jesus, to testify to the gospel of the grace of God (20.23–24).

1 THESSALONIANS: For you yourselves know, brethren, that our visit to you was not in vain; but though we had already suffered and been shamefully treated at Philippi, as you know, we had courage in our God to declare to you the gospel of *our* God in the face of great opposition (2.1–2).

70.14 That it is necessary to pray for the progress of the faithful and to give thanks for it.

JOHN: I do not pray for these only but also for those who believe in me through their word, that they may all be one; even as thou, Father, art in me and I in you, that they also may be *one* in us (17.20–21). *And again*: Father, I desire that they also, whom thou hast given me, may be with me where I am (17.24).

LUKE: In that same hour he rejoiced in the *Spirit* and said, "I thank thee, Father, Lord of heaven and earth, that thou hast hidden these things from the wise and understanding and revealed them to babes; yea, Father, for such was thy gracious will" (10.21).

ROMANS: First, I thank my God through Jesus Christ for all of you, because your faith is proclaimed in all the world. For God is my witness, whom I serve with my spirit in the gospel of his Son, that without ceasing I mention you always in my prayers (1.8–9).

PHILIPPIANS: For God is my witness how I yearn for you all with the affection of Christ Jesus. And it is my prayer that your love may abound more and more with knowledge and all discernment, so that you may approve what is excellent and may be pure and blameless

ἡ ἀγάπη ὑμῶν ἔτι μᾶλλον καὶ μᾶλλον περισσεύῃ ἐν ἐπιγνώσει καὶ πάσῃ αἰσθήσει, εἰς τὸ δοκιμάζειν ὑμᾶς τὰ διαφέροντα, ἵνα ἦτε εἰλικρινεῖς καὶ ἀπρόσκοποι εἰς ἡμέραν Χριστοῦ, πεπληρωμένοι καρπῶν δικαιοσύνης τῶν διὰ Ἰησοῦ Χριστοῦ εἰς δόξαν καὶ ἔπαινον Θεοῦ.

[70.15] Ὅτι δεῖ τὰ Θεοῦ χάριτι κατορθούμενα γνώριμα ποιεῖν καὶ ἑτέροις εἰς δόξαν Θεοῦ.

Κεφάλ. ιε΄.

ΛΟΥΚΑΣ. Καὶ ὑποστρέψαντες οἱ ἀπόστολοι διηγήσαντο αὐτῷ, ὅσα ἐποίησαν.

ΠΡΑΞΕΙΣ. Παραγενόμενοι δὲ καὶ συναγαγόντες τὴν ἐκκλησίαν, ἀπήγγειλαν ὅσα ὁ Θεὸς ἐποίησε μετ᾽ αὐτῶν.

ΠΡΟΣ ΕΦΕΣ. Ἵνα δὲ εἰδῆτε καὶ ὑμεῖς τὰ κατ᾽ ἐμὲ, τί [417] πράσσω, πάντα ὑμῖν γνωρίσει Τυχικὸς ὁ ἀγαπητὸς ἀδελφὸς, καὶ πιστὸς διάκονος ἐν Κυρίῳ, ὃν ἔπεμψα πρὸς ὑμᾶς εἰς αὐτὸ τοῦτο, ἵνα γνῶτε τὰ περὶ ἡμῶν.

[70.16] Ὅτι δεῖ μὴ μόνον τῶν παρόντων ἐπιμελεῖσθαι, ἀλλὰ καὶ τῶν ἀπόντων· καὶ πάντα ποιεῖν ὡς ἂν ἀπαιτῇ ἡ χρεία τῆς οἰκοδομῆς.

Κεφάλ. ις΄.

ΙΩΑΝΝΗΣ. Καὶ ἄλλα πρόβατα ἔχω, ἃ οὐκ ἔστιν ἐκ τῆς αὐλῆς ταύτης· κἀκεῖνά με δεῖ ἀγαγεῖν· καὶ τῆς φωνῆς μου ἀκούσουσι· καὶ γενήσεται μία ποίμνη, εἷς ποιμήν.

ΠΡΟΣ ΘΕΣΣ. α΄. Διὸ μηκέτι στέγοντες ηὐδοκήσαμεν καταλειφθῆναι ἐν Ἀθήναις μόνοι, καὶ ἐπέμψαμεν τὸν ἀδελφὸν ἡμῶν Τιμόθεον, καὶ διάκονον τοῦ Θεοῦ ἐν τῷ εὐαγγελίῳ τοῦ Χριστοῦ, εἰς τὸ στηρίξαι ὑμᾶς καὶ παρακαλέσαι ὑπὲρ τῆς πίστεως ὑμῶν.

[70.17] Ὅτι δεῖ τῶν προσκαλουμένων ἐπ᾽ εὐεργεσίᾳ ἀνέχεσθαι.

Κεφάλ. ιζ΄.

ΜΑΤΘΑΙΟΣ. Ταῦτα αὐτοῦ λαλοῦντος, ἰδοὺ ἄρχων εἰσελθὼν προσεκύνει αὐτῷ, λέγων, ὅτι ἡ θυγάτηρ μου ἄρτι ἐτελεύτησεν· ἀλλὰ ἐλθὼν, ἐπίθες τὴν χεῖρά σου ἐπ᾽ αὐτὴν, καὶ ζήσεται. Καὶ ἐγερθεὶς ὁ Ἰησοῦς, ἠκολούθησεν αὐτῷ.

for the day of Christ, filled with the fruits of righteousness which come through Jesus Christ, to the glory and praise of God (1.8–11).

70.15   That it is necessary, for God's glory, to make known to others also the good things done by the grace of God.

LUKE: On their return the apostles told him what they had done (9.10).

ACTS: And when they arrived they gathered the church together and declared all that God had done with them (14.26).

EPHESIANS: Now, that you also may know how I am and what I am doing, Tychicus the beloved brother and faithful minister in the Lord will tell you everything. I have sent him to you for this very purpose, that you may know how we are (6.21–22).

70.16   That it is necessary to care not only for those present but also for those absent and to do everything required by the need for edification.

JOHN: And I have other sheep that are not of this fold; I must bring them also, and they will heed my voice. So there shall be one flock, one shepherd (10.16).

1 THESSALONIANS: Therefore when we could bear it no longer, we were willing to be left behind at Athens alone, and we sent Timothy, our brother and God's servant in the gospel of Christ, to establish you in your faith and to exhort you (3.1–2).

70.17   That it is necessary to bear with those who request a service.

MATTHEW: While he was thus speaking to them, behold, a ruler came in and knelt before him, saying, "My daughter has just died, but come and lay your hand on her, and she will live." And Jesus rose and followed him (9.18–19).

ΠΡΑΞΕΙΣ. Ἐγγὺς δὲ οὔσης Λύδδης τῇ Ἰόππῃ, οἱ μαθηταὶ ἀκούσαντες ὅτι Πέτρος ἐστὶν ἐν αὐτῇ, ἀπέστειλαν δύο ἄνδρας πρὸς αὐτὸν, παρακαλοῦντες, μὴ ὀκνῆσαι διελθεῖν ἕως αὐτῶν. Ἀναστὰς δὲ ὁ Πέτρος, συνῆλθεν αὐτοῖς.

[70.18] Ὅτι δεῖ τοὺς ὑποδεχομένους τὸν λόγον τῆς ἀληθείας ἐπιστηρίζειν δι᾽ ἐπισκέψεως.

Κεφάλ. ιη΄.

ΠΡΑΞΕΙΣ. Μετὰ δέ τινας ἡμέρας εἶπε Παῦλος πρὸς Βαρνάβαν· ἐπιστρέψαντες δὴ ἐπισκεψώμεθα τοὺς ἀδελφοὺς ἡμῶν κατὰ πᾶσαν πόλιν, ἐν αἷς κατηγγείλαμεν τὸν λόγον τοῦ Κυρίου, πῶς ἔχουσιν.

ΠΡΟΣ ΘΕΣΣ. α΄. Ἡμεῖς δὲ, ἀδελφοὶ, ἀπορφανισθέντες ἀφ᾽ ὑμῶν πρὸς καιρὸν ὥρας, προσώπῳ, [418] οὐ καρδίᾳ, περισσοτέρως ἐσπουδάσαμεν τὸ πρόσωπον ὑμῶν ἰδεῖν ἐν πολλῇ ἐπιθυμίᾳ. Διὸ ἐθελήσαμεν ἐλθεῖν πρὸς ὑμᾶς, ἐγὼ μὲν Παῦλος, καὶ ἅπαξ καὶ δὶς, καὶ ἐνέκοψεν ἡμᾶς ὁ σατανᾶς. Καὶ μετ᾽ ὀλίγα· Διὸ μηκέτι στέγοντες ηὐδοκήσαμεν καταλειφθῆναι ἐν Ἀθήναις μόνοι· καὶ ἐπέμψαμεν Τιμόθεον τὸν ἀδελφὸν ἡμῶν, καὶ διάκονον τοῦ Θεοῦ ἐν τῷ εὐαγγελίῳ τοῦ Χριστοῦ, εἰς τὸ στηρίξαι ὑμᾶς καὶ παρακαλέσαι ὑπὲρ τῆς πίστεως ὑμῶν, τὸ μηδένα σαίνεσθαι ἐν ταῖς θλίψεσι ταύταις· αὐτοὶ γὰρ οἴδατε ὅτι εἰς τοῦτο κείμεθα.

[70.19] Ὅτι ἴδιον τοῦ ἀγαπῶντος τὸν Κύριον τὸ, ἐν πολλῇ φιλοστοργίᾳ, τῇ περὶ τοὺς διδασκομένους, μετὰ πάσης σπουδῆς ἐπιμελεῖσθαι αὐτῶν παντὶ τρόπῳ, κἂν μέχρι θανάτου δέῃ προσκαρτεροῦντα τῇ διδασκαλίᾳ ἔν τε τῷ κοινῷ καὶ κατ᾽ ἰδίαν.

Κεφάλ. ιθ΄.

ΙΩΑΝΝΗΣ. Ὁ ποιμὴν ὁ καλὸς τὴν ψυχὴν αὐτοῦ τίθησιν ὑπὲρ τῶν προβάτων.

ΙΩΑΝΝ. Ὅτε δὲ ἠρίστησαν, λέγει τῷ Σίμωνι Πέτρῳ ὁ Ἰησοῦς· Σίμων Ἰωνᾶ, ἀγαπᾷς με πλεῖον τούτων; Λέγει αὐτῷ· ναὶ, Κύριε· σὺ οἶδας ὅτι φιλῶ σε. Λέγει αὐτῷ· βόσκε τὰ ἀρνία μου. Λέγει αὐτῷ πάλιν δεύτερον· Σίμων Ἰωνᾶ, ἀγαπᾷς με; Λέγει αὐτῷ· ναὶ, Κύριε· σὺ οἶδας ὅτι φιλῶ σε. Λέγει αὐτῷ· ποίμαινε τὰ πρόβατά μου. Λέγει

ACTS: Since Lydda was near Joppa, the disciples, hearing that Peter was there, sent two men to him entreating him *to come to them without delay*. So Peter rose and went with them (9.38–39).

70.18 That it is necessary to establish by visitation those who receive the Word of truth.

ACTS: And after some days Paul said to Barnabas, "Come, let us return and visit the brethren in every city where we proclaimed the word of the Lord and see how they are" (15.36).

1 THESSALONIANS: But since we were bereft of you, brethren, for a short time (in person, not in heart), we endeavored the more eagerly and with great desire to see you face to face; because we wanted to come to you—I, Paul, again and again—but Satan hindered us (2.17–18). *And a little further*: Therefore when we could bear it no longer, we were willing to be left behind at Athens alone, and we sent Timothy, our brother and God's servant in the gospel of Christ, to establish you in your faith and to exhort you, that no one be moved by these afflictions. You yourselves know that this is to be our lot (3.1–3).

70.19 That the mark of one who loves the Lord is that, having great affection for those he teaches, he cares for them in every way with all zeal, even unto death if necessary, persevering in teaching both collectively and individually.

JOHN: The good shepherd lays down his life for the sheep (10.11).

JOHN: When they had finished breakfast, Jesus said to Simon Peter, "Simon, son of *Jonah*, do you love me more than these?" He said to him, "Yes, Lord; you know that I love you." He said to him, "Feed my lambs." A second time he said to him, "Simon, son of *Jonah*, do you love me?" He said to him, "Yes, Lord; you know that I love you." He said to him, "Tend my sheep." He said to him the third

αὐτῷ τὸ τρίτον· Σίμων Ἰωνᾶ, φιλεῖς με; Ἐλυπήθη ὁ Πέτρος, ὅτι εἶπεν αὐτῷ τὸ τρίτον, φιλεῖς με; Καὶ εἶπεν αὐτῷ· Κύριε, σὺ πάντα οἶδας· σὺ γινώσκεις ὅτι φιλῶ σε. Λέγει αὐτῷ ὁ Ἰησοῦς· βόσκε τὰ πρόβατά μου.

ΠΡΑΞΕΙΣ. Ἐν δὲ τῇ μιᾷ τῶν σαββάτων,[25] συνηγμένων τῶν μαθητῶν κλάσαι ἄρτον, ὁ Παῦλος διελέγετο αὐτοῖς, μέλλων ἐξιέναι τῇ ἐπαύριον· παρέτεινε δὲ τὸν λόγον μέχρι μεσονυκτίου. Καὶ μετ' ὀλίγα· Ἀναβὰς δὲ, καὶ κλάσας ἄρτον, καὶ γευσάμενος, ἐφ' ἱκανόν τε ὁμιλήσας μέχρις αὐγῆς, ἐξῆλθεν.

ΠΡΑΞΕΙΣ. Ὡς οὐδὲν ὑπεστειλάμην τῶν συμφερόντων τοῦ μὴ ἀναγγεῖλαι ὑμῖν, καὶ διδάξαι ὑμᾶς δημοσίᾳ καὶ κατ' οἴκους, διαμαρτυρόμενος Ἰουδαίοις τε καὶ Ἕλλησι τὴν εἰς τὸν Θεὸν μετάνοιαν, καὶ πίστιν τὴν εἰς τὸν Κύριον ἡμῶν Ἰησοῦν.

ΠΡΑΞΕΙΣ. Διὸ γρηγορεῖτε, μνημονεύοντες ὅτι τριετίαν νύκτα καὶ ἡμέραν οὐκ ἐπαυσάμην μετὰ δακρύων νουθετῶν ἕνα ἕκαστον ὑμῶν.

ΠΡΟΣ [419] ΘΕΣΣ. α'. Αὐτοὶ γὰρ οἴδατε, ἀδελφοὶ, τὸν κόπον ἡμῶν, καὶ τὸν μόχθον· νυκτὸς καὶ ἡμέρας ἐργαζόμενοι πρὸς τὸ μὴ ἐπιβαρῆσαί τινα ὑμῶν, ἐκηρύξαμεν τὸ εὐαγγέλιον τοῦ Θεοῦ, καὶ τὰ ἑξῆς.

[70.20] Ὅτι δεῖ τὸν προεστῶτα τοῦ λόγου ἐλεήμονα καὶ εὔσπλαγχνον εἶναι, καὶ μάλιστα ἐπὶ τῶν κεκακωμένων τὰς ψυχάς.

Κεφάλ. κ'.

ΜΑΤΘΑΙΟΣ. Καὶ ἰδόντες οἱ Φαρισαῖοι, εἶπον τοῖς μαθηταῖς αὐτοῦ· διὰ τί μετὰ τῶν τελωνῶν καὶ ἁμαρτωλῶν ἐσθίει ὁ διδάσκαλος ὑμῶν; Ὁ δὲ Ἰησοῦς ἀκούσας, εἶπεν· οὐ χρείαν ἔχουσιν οἱ ὑγιαίνοντες ἰατροῦ, ἀλλ' οἱ κακῶς ἔχοντες. Πορευθέντες δὲ, μάθετε τί ἐστιν· ἔλεον θέλω, καὶ οὐ θυσίαν· οὐ γὰρ ἦλθον καλέσαι δικαίους, ἀλλὰ ἁμαρτωλοὺς εἰς μετάνοιαν.

ΜΑΤΘΑΙΟΣ. Ἰδὼν δὲ τοὺς ὄχλους, εὐσπλαγχνίσθη περὶ αὐτῶν, ὅτι ἦσαν ἐσκυλμένοι, ὡς πρόβατα μὴ ἔχοντα ποιμένα.

---

[25]Corrected from συββάτων.

time, "Simon, son of *Jonah*, do you love me?" Peter was grieved because he said to him the third time, "Do you love me?" And he said to him, "Lord, you know everything; you know that I love you." Jesus said to him, "Feed my sheep" (21.15–17).

ACTS: On the first day of the week, when we were gathered together to break bread, Paul talked with them, intending to depart on the morrow; and he prolonged his speech until midnight (20.7). *And a little further*: And when Paul had gone up and had broken bread and eaten, he conversed with *them until* daybreak, and so departed (20.11).

ACTS: I did not shrink from declaring to you anything that was profitable and teaching you in public and from house to house testifying both to Jews and to Greeks of repentance to God and of faith in our Lord Jesus Christ (20.20–21).

ACTS: Therefore be alert, remembering that for three years I did not cease night or day to admonish *every one of* you with tears (20.31).

1 THESSALONIANS: For you *yourselves know* our labor and toil, brethren; we worked night and day that we might not burden any of you while we *preached* the gospel of God (2.9), *and what follows*.

70.20 That it is necessary for the one set over the Word to be merciful and compassionate, especially to those disfigured in soul.

MATTHEW: And when the Pharisees saw this, they said to his disciples, "Why does your teacher eat with tax collectors and sinners?" But when *Jesus* heard it, he said, "Those who are well have no need of a physician but those who are sick. Go and learn what this means: 'I desire mercy and not sacrifice.' For I came not to call the righteous, but sinners *to repentance*" (9.11–13).

MATTHEW: When he saw the crowds he had compassion for them, because they were harassed and helpless like sheep without a shepherd (9.36).

[70.21]   Ὅτι δεῖ καὶ ἐν ταῖς τοῦ σώματος χρείαις σπλαγχνίζεσθαι ἐπὶ τοῖς πεπιστευμένοις, καὶ φροντίζειν αὐτῶν.

Κεφάλ. κα΄.

ΜΑΤΘΑΙΟΣ. Σπλαγχνίζομαι ἐπὶ τὸν ὄχλον, ὅτι ἤδη ἡμέραι τρεῖς προσμένουσί μοι, καὶ οὐκ ἔχουσι τί φάγωσι, καὶ ἀπολῦσαι αὐτοὺς νήστεις οὐ θέλω, μήποτε ἐκλυθῶσιν ἐν τῇ ὁδῷ.

ΜΑΡΚΟΣ. Καὶ ἔρχεται πρὸς αὐτὸν λεπρὸς, παρακαλῶν αὐτὸν, καὶ γονυπετῶν αὐτὸν, καὶ λέγων αὐτῷ, ὅτι ἐὰν θέλῃς, δύνασαί με καθαρίσαι. Ὁ δὲ Ἰησοῦς σπλαγχνισθεὶς, ἐκτείνας τὴν χεῖρα αὐτοῦ, ἥψατο αὐτοῦ, καὶ λέγει αὐτῷ· θέλω, καθαρίσθητι.

ΠΡΑΞΕΙΣ. Ἐν δὲ ταῖς ἡμέραις ταύταις πληθυνόντων τῶν μαθητῶν, ἐγένετο γογγυσμὸς τῶν Ἑλληνιστῶν πρὸς τοὺς Ἑβραίους, ὅτι παρεθεωροῦντο ἐν τῇ διακονίᾳ τῇ καθημερινῇ αἱ χῆραι αὐτῶν. Προσκαλεσάμενοι δὲ οἱ δώδεκα τὸ πλῆθος τῶν μαθητῶν, εἶπον· οὐκ ἀρεστόν ἐστι καταλιπόντας ἡμᾶς τὸν λόγον τοῦ Θεοῦ, διακονεῖν ταῖς τραπέζαις. Ἐπισκέψασθε, ἀδελφοὶ, ἄνδρας ἐξ ὑμῶν μαρτυρουμένους ἑπτὰ, πλήρεις Πνεύματος ἁγίου καὶ σοφίας, οὓς καταστήσομεν ἐπὶ τῆς χρείας ταύτης. [420]

[70.22]   Ὅτι οὐ δεῖ τὸν προεστῶτα τοῦ λόγου ἐν τοῖς ἐλάττοσιν αὐτουργεῖν φιλοτιμούμενον τῆς ὀφειλομένης περὶ τὰ μείζω σπουδῆς ἀπολείπεσθαι.

Κεφάλ. κβ΄.

ΠΡΑΞΕΙΣ.[26] Προσκαλεσάμενοι δὲ οἱ δώδεκα τὸ πλῆθος τῶν μαθητῶν, εἶπον· οὐκ ἀρεστόν ἐστι καταλιπόντας ἡμᾶς τὸν λόγον τοῦ Θεοῦ, διακονεῖν τραπέζαις. Καὶ μετ᾽ ὀλίγα· Ἡμεῖς δὲ τῇ προσευχῇ καὶ τῇ διακονίᾳ τοῦ λόγου προσκαρτερήσωμεν.

[70.23]   Ὅτι οὐ δεῖ ἐπιδεικτιᾶν, οὐδὲ ἐμπορεύεσθαι τὸν λόγον τῆς διδασκαλίας ἐν κολακείᾳ τῶν ἀκουόντων, εἰς πληροφορίαν τῶν ἰδίων ἡδονῶν, ἤτοι χρειῶν· ἀλλὰ τοιούτους εἶναι, ὡς εἰς δόξαν Θεοῦ ἐνώπιον αὐτοῦ λαλοῦντας.

---

[26]I have supplied the missing attribution in Garnier.

70.21 That it is necessary also with respect to bodily necessities to show compassion for those entrusted to one and to care for them.

MATTHEW: I have compassion on the crowd, because they have been with me now three days and have nothing to eat, and I am unwilling to send them away hungry, lest they faint on the way (15.32).

MARK: And a leper came to him beseeching him, and kneeling said to him, "If you will, you can make me clean." Moved with *compassion, Jesus* stretched out his hand and touched him and said to him, "I will; be clean" (1.40–41).

ACTS: Now in these days, when the disciples were increasing in number, the Hellenists murmured against the Hebrews because their widows were neglected in the daily distribution. And the twelve summoned the body of the disciples and said, "It is not right that we should give up preaching the word of God to serve tables. *Brethren*, pick out from among you seven men of good repute, full of the Spirit and of wisdom, whom we may appoint to this duty" (6.1–3).

70.22 That it is necessary for the one set over the Word not to neglect the zeal due to greater things because he is earnest to work, himself, at the lesser.

ACTS: And the twelve summoned the body of the disciples and said, "It is not right that we should give up preaching the word of God to serve tables" (6.2). *And a little further*: "But we will devote ourselves to prayer and to the ministry of the word" (6.4).

70.23 That it is necessary not to make a display of or put on a show with the Word of teaching, flattering the listeners for the satisfaction of one's own desires or needs, but to be such as speak for the glory of God in his very presence.

Κεφάλ. κγ΄.

ΜΑΤΘΑΙΟΣ. Πάντα δὲ τὰ ἔργα αὐτῶν ποιοῦσι πρὸς τὸ θεαθῆναι τοῖς
ἀνθρώποις· πλατύνουσι δὲ τὰ φυλακτήρια αὐτῶν, καὶ μεγαλύνουσι
τὰ κράσπεδα τῶν ἱματίων αὐτῶν· φιλοῦσί τε τὰς πρωτοκλισίας ἐν
τοῖς δείπνοις, καὶ τὰς πρωτοκαθεδρίας ἐν ταῖς συναγωγαῖς, καὶ τοὺς
ἀσπασμοὺς ἐν ταῖς ἀγοραῖς, καὶ καλεῖσθαι ὑπὸ τῶν ἀνθρώπων, ῥαββὶ,
ῥαββί. Ὑμεῖς δὲ μὴ κληθῆτε ῥαββί· εἷς γάρ ἐστιν ὑμῶν ὁ καθηγητής·
πάντες δὲ ὑμεῖς ἀδελφοί ἐστε. Καὶ πατέρα μὴ καλέσητε ὑμῶν ἐπὶ τῆς
γῆς· εἷς γάρ ἐστιν ὁ Πατὴρ ὑμῶν, ὁ ἐν τοῖς οὐρανοῖς· μηδὲ κληθῆτε
καθηγηταί, εἷς γάρ ἐστιν ὁ καθηγητὴς ὑμῶν, ὁ Χριστός.

ΙΩΑΝΝΗΣ. Ἡ ἐμὴ διδαχὴ οὐκ ἔστιν ἐμὴ, ἀλλὰ τοῦ πέμψαντός με.
Ἐάν τις τὸ θέλημα αὐτοῦ ποιῇ, γνώσεται περὶ τῆς διδαχῆς, πότερον
ἐκ τοῦ Θεοῦ ἐστιν, ἢ ἐγὼ ἀπ᾽ ἐμαυτοῦ λαλῶ. Ὁ ἀφ᾽ ἑαυτοῦ λαλῶν,
τὴν δόξαν τὴν ἰδίαν ζητεῖ· ὁ δὲ ζητῶν τὴν δόξαν τοῦ πέμψαντος
αὐτὸν, οὗτος ἀληθής ἐστι, καὶ ἀδικία ἐν αὐτῷ οὐκ ἔστιν.

ΠΡΟΣ ΚΟΡ. β΄. Οὐ γάρ ἐσμεν, ὡς οἱ πολλοὶ, καπηλεύοντες τὸν λόγον
τοῦ Θεοῦ, ἀλλ᾽ ὡς ἐξ εἰλικρινείας, ἀλλ᾽ ὡς ἐκ Θεοῦ, κατενώπιον
Θεοῦ ἐν Χριστῷ λαλοῦμεν.

ΠΡΟΣ ΘΕΣΣ. α΄. Ἡ γὰρ παράκλησις ἡμῶν οὐκ ἐκ πλάνης, οὐδὲ
ἐξ ἀκαθαρσίας, οὐδὲ ἐν δόλῳ, ἀλλὰ καθὼς δεδοκιμάσμεθα ὑπὸ
τοῦ [421] Θεοῦ πιστευθῆναι τὸ εὐαγγέλιον, οὕτω λαλοῦμεν· οὐχ
ὡς ἀνθρώποις ἀρέσκοντες, ἀλλὰ τῷ Θεῷ τῷ δοκιμάζοντι τὰς
καρδίας ἡμῶν. Οὔτε γάρ ποτε ἐν λόγῳ κολακείας ἐγενήθημεν πρὸς
ὑμᾶς, καθὼς οἴδατε, οὔτε προφάσει πλεονεξίας, Θεὸς μάρτυς, οὔτε
ζητοῦντες ἐξ ἀνθρώπων δόξαν, οὔτε ἀφ᾽ ὑμῶν, οὔτε ἀπὸ ἄλλων,
δυνάμενοι ἐν βάρει εἶναι, ὡς Χριστοῦ ἀπόστολοι.

[70.24] Ὅτι οὐ δεῖ τὸν προεστῶτα τοῦ λόγου εἰς τὴν κατὰ τῶν
ὑποκειμένων ὕβριν ἀποκεχρῆσθαι τῇ ἐξουσίᾳ· οὐ μὴν οὐδὲ κατε-
παίρεσθαι αὐτῶν· ἀλλὰ μᾶλλον ὑπόθεσιν τῆς πρὸς αὐτοὺς ταπεινοφροσύνης τὸν βαθμὸν ἔχειν.

Κεφάλ. κδ΄.

ΜΑΤΘΑΙΟΣ. Τίς ἄρα ἐστὶν ὁ πιστὸς δοῦλος καὶ φρόνιμος, ὃν
κατέστησεν ὁ κύριος ἐπὶ τῆς οἰκίας αὐτοῦ, τοῦ δοῦναι αὐτοῖς ἐν

MATTHEW: They do all their deeds to be seen by men; *they* make their phylacteries broad and *the fringes of their garments* long, and they love the *places* of honor at feasts and the best seats in the syna-gogues and salutations in the market places and being called *by men* *"Rabbi, rabbi!"* But you are not to be called rabbi, for you have one teacher, and you are all brethren. And call no man your father on earth, for you have one Father, who is in heaven. *Do not be called teachers, for you have one teacher,* the Christ (23.5–10).

JOHN: My teaching is not mine but his who sent me; *if anyone does his will,* he shall know whether the teaching is from God or whether I am speaking on my own authority. He who speaks on his own authority seeks his own glory, but he who seeks the glory of him who sent him is true, and in him there is no falsehood (7.16–18).

2 CORINTHIANS: For we are not, like so many, peddlers of God's word; but as *from* sincerity, as *from* God, in the sight of God we speak in Christ (2.17).

1 THESSALONIANS: For our appeal does not spring from error or uncleanness, nor is it made with guile; but just as we have been approved by God to be entrusted with the gospel, so we speak—not to please men, but to please God who tests our hearts. *For we engaged neither in flattering speech among you, as you know, nor in a pretext for our gain,* as God is witness; nor did we seek glory from men, whether from you or from others, though we might have made demands as apostles of Christ (2.3–6).

70.24   That it is necessary for the one set over the Word not to misuse his authority to abuse those under him nor, of course, to lord it over them, but rather to make his rank an occasion for humbling himself before them.

MATTHEW: Who then is the faithful and wise servant, whom his master has set over his household to give them their food at the proper time? Blessed is that servant whom his master, when he comes, will find so doing. Truly I say to you, he will set him over all

καιρῷ τὴν τροφήν; Μακάριος ὁ δοῦλος ἐκεῖνος, ὃν ἐλθὼν ὁ κύριος αὐτοῦ, εὑρήσει ποιοῦντα οὕτως. Ἀμὴν λέγω ὑμῖν, ὅτι ἐπὶ πᾶσι τοῖς ὑπάρχουσιν αὐτοῦ καταστήσει αὐτόν. Ἐὰν δὲ εἴπῃ ὁ κακὸς δοῦλος ἐκεῖνος ἐν τῇ καρδίᾳ αὐτοῦ· χρονίζει ὁ κύριός μου ἔρχεσθαι, καὶ ἄρξηται τύπτειν τοὺς συνδούλους αὐτοῦ, ἐσθίῃ τε καὶ πίνῃ μετὰ τῶν μεθυόντων· ἥξει ὁ κύριος τοῦ δούλου ἐκείνου ἐν ἡμέρᾳ ᾗ οὐ προσδοκᾷ, καὶ ἐν ὥρᾳ ᾗ οὐ γινώσκει· καὶ διχοτομήσει αὐτὸν, καὶ τὸ μέρος αὐτοῦ μετὰ τῶν ὑποκριτῶν θήσει. Ἐκεῖ ἔσται ὁ κλαυθμὸς, καὶ ὁ βρυγμὸς τῶν ὀδόντων.

ΙΩΑΝΝΗΣ. Ὑμεῖς φωνεῖτέ με, ὁ Κύριος, καὶ ὁ διδάσκαλος, καὶ ἀληθῶς λέγετε· εἰμὶ γάρ. Εἰ οὖν ἐγὼ ἔνιψα τοὺς πόδας ὑμῶν, ὁ Κύριος, καὶ ὁ διδάσκαλος, καὶ ὑμεῖς ὀφείλετε ἀλλήλων νίπτειν τοὺς πόδας.

ΛΟΥΚΑΣ. Ἐγένετο δὲ καὶ φιλονεικία ἐν αὐτοῖς, τὸ, τίς αὐτῶν μείζων δοκεῖ εἶναι. Ὁ δὲ Ἰησοῦς εἶπεν αὐτοῖς· οἱ βασιλεῖς τῶν ἐθνῶν κυριεύουσιν αὐτῶν, καὶ οἱ ἐξουσιάζοντες αὐτῶν εὐεργέται καλοῦνται· ὑμεῖς δὲ οὐχ οὕτως, ἀλλ᾽ ὁ μείζων ἐν ὑμῖν γενέσθω ὡς ὁ νεώτερος, καὶ ὁ ἡγούμενος, ὡς ὁ διακονῶν. Τίς γὰρ μείζων, ὁ ἀνακείμενος ἢ ὁ διακονῶν; Οὐχ ὁ ἀνακείμενος; Ἐγὼ δέ εἰμι ἐν μέσῳ ὑμῶν, ὡς ὁ διακονῶν.

ΠΡΑΞΕΙΣ. Ἀπὸ δὲ τῆς Μιλήτου πέμψας εἰς Ἔφεσον, μετεκαλέσατο τοὺς πρεσβυτέρους τῆς Ἐκκλησίας· ὡς δὲ παρεγένοντο πρὸς αὐτὸν, εἶπεν [422] αὐτοῖς· ὑμεῖς ἐπίστασθε, ἀπὸ πρώτης ἡμέρας ἀφ᾽ ἧς ἐπέβην εἰς τὴν Ἀσίαν, πῶς μεθ᾽ ὑμῶν τὸν πάντα χρόνον ἐγενόμην, δουλεύων τῷ Κυρίῳ μετὰ πάσης ταπεινοφροσύνης, καὶ πολλῶν δακρύων καὶ πειρασμῶν, τῶν συμβάντων μοι ἐν ταῖς ἐπιβουλαῖς τῶν Ἰουδαίων.

ΠΡΟΣ ΚΟΡ. β΄. Ἡδέως γὰρ ἀνέχεσθε τῶν ἀφρόνων, φρόνιμοι ὄντες. Ἀνέχεσθε γὰρ, εἴ τις ὑμᾶς καταδουλοῖ, εἴ τις κατεσθίει, εἴ τις λαμβάνει, εἴ τις ἐπαίρεται, εἴ τις εἰς πρόσωπον ὑμᾶς δέρει. Κατὰ ἀτιμίαν λέγω, ὡς ὅτι ἡμεῖς ἠσθενήσαμεν ἐν τῷ μέρει τούτῳ.

[70.25]   Ὅτι οὐ δεῖ κατ᾽ ἔριν, ἢ φθόνον, ἢ φιλονεικίαν τὴν πρός τινας, κηρύσσειν τὸ εὐαγγέλιον.

his possessions. But if that wicked servant says to himself, "My master *delays his coming*," and begins to beat his fellow servants and eats and drinks with the drunken, the master of that servant will come on a day when he does not expect him and at an hour he does not know and will punish him and put him with the hypocrites; there *will be weeping and gnashing of teeth* (24.45–51).

JOHN: You call me *Lord and Teacher*, and you are right, for so I am. If I then, your Lord and Teacher, have washed your feet, you also ought to wash one another's feet (13.13–14).

LUKE: A dispute also arose among them, which of them was to be regarded as the greatest. And *Jesus* said to them, "The kings of the Gentiles exercise lordship over them, and those in authority over them are called benefactors. But not so with you; rather let the greatest among you become as the youngest and the leader as one who serves. For which is the greater, one who sits at table or one who serves? Is it not the one who sits at table? But I am among you as one who serves" (22.24–27).

ACTS: And from Miletus he sent to Ephesus and called to him the elders of the church. And when they came to him, he said to them, "You yourselves know how I lived among you all the time from the first day that I set foot in Asia, serving the Lord with all humility and with *many tears and trials* which befell me through the plots of the Jews" (20.17–19).

2 CORINTHIANS: For you gladly bear with fools, being wise yourselves. For you bear it if a man makes slaves of you or preys upon you or takes advantage of you or puts on airs or strikes you in the face. *To my dishonor I speak, as though we were weak in this regard* (11.19–21).

70.25 That it is necessary not to preach the Gospel out of contention or envy or rivalry with anyone.

Κεφάλ. κε΄.

ΜΑΤΘΑΙΟΣ. Ἰδοὺ ὁ παῖς μου, ὃν ᾑρέτισα, ὁ ἀγαπητός μου, εἰς ὃν ηὐδόκησεν ἡ ψυχή μου. Θήσω τὸ Πνεῦμά μου ἐπ' αὐτὸν, καὶ κρίσιν τοῖς ἔθνεσιν ἀπαγγελεῖ. Οὐκ ἐρίσει, οὐδὲ κραυγάσει, οὐδὲ ἀκούσει τις ἐν ταῖς πλατείαις τὴν φωνὴν αὐτοῦ.

ΠΡΟΣ ΦΙΛΙΠ. Τινὲς μὲν καὶ διὰ φθόνον καὶ ἔριν, τινὲς δὲ καὶ δι' εὐδοκίαν τὸν Χριστὸν κηρύσσουσιν· οἱ μὲν ἐξ ἀγάπης, εἰδότες ὅτι εἰς ἀπολογίαν τοῦ εὐαγγελίου κεῖμαι· οἱ δὲ ἐξ ἐριθείας τὸν Χριστὸν καταγγέλλουσιν, οὐχ ἁγνῶς, οἰόμενοι θλίψιν ἐπιφέρειν τοῖς δεσμοῖς μου.

[70.26]   Ὅτι οὐ δεῖ τοῖς ἀνθρωπίνοις πλεονεκτήμασι κεχρῆσθαι εἰς τὸ κήρυγμα τοῦ εὐαγγελίου, ἵνα μὴ ἐγκρύπτηται αὐτοῖς ἡ τοῦ Θεοῦ χάρις.

Κεφάλ. κς΄.

ΜΑΤΘΑΙΟΣ. Ἐξομολογοῦμαί σοι, Πάτερ, Κύριε τοῦ οὐρανοῦ καὶ τῆς γῆς, ὅτι ἀπέκρυψας ταῦτα ἀπὸ σοφῶν καὶ συνετῶν, καὶ ἀπεκάλυψας αὐτὰ νηπίοις.

ΠΡΟΣ ΚΟΡ. α΄. Οὐ γὰρ ἀπέστειλέ με ὁ Χριστὸς βαπτίζειν, ἀλλ' εὐαγγελίζεσθαι· οὐκ ἐν σοφίᾳ λόγου, ἵνα μὴ κενωθῇ ὁ σταυρὸς τοῦ Χριστοῦ.

ΠΡΟΣ ΚΟΡ. α΄. Κἀγὼ ἐλθὼν πρὸς ὑμᾶς, ἀδελφοὶ, ἦλθον οὐ καθ' ὑπεροχὴν λόγου, ἢ σοφίας, καταγγέλλων ὑμῖν τὸ μαρτύριον τοῦ Θεοῦ. Οὐ γὰρ ἔκρινά τι εἰδέναι ἐν ὑμῖν, εἰ μὴ Ἰησοῦν Χριστὸν, [423] καὶ τοῦτον ἐσταυρωμένον. Κἀγὼ ἐν ἀσθενείᾳ, καὶ ἐν φόβῳ, καὶ ἐν τρόμῳ πολλῷ ἐγενόμην πρὸς ὑμᾶς· καὶ ὁ λόγος μου, καὶ τὸ κήρυγμά μου οὐκ ἐν πειθοῖς ἀνθρωπίνης σοφίας λόγοις, ἀλλ' ἐν ἀποδείξει Πνεύματος καὶ δυνάμεως· ἵνα ἡ πίστις ἡμῶν μὴ ᾖ ἐν σοφίᾳ ἀνθρώπων, ἀλλ' ἐν δυνάμει Θεοῦ.

[70.27]   Ὅτι οὐ δεῖ οἴεσθαι τὴν εὐοδίαν τοῦ κηρύγματος ἐν ἰδίαις ἐπινοίαις κατεργάζεσθαι· τὸ δὲ ὅλον ἐπὶ τῷ Θεῷ πεποιθέναι.

MATTHEW: "Behold, my *child* whom I have chosen, my beloved with whom my soul is well pleased. I will put my Spirit upon him, and he shall proclaim justice to the Gentiles. He will not wrangle or cry aloud, nor will anyone hear his voice in the streets"[29] (12.18–19).

PHILIPPIANS: Some indeed preach Christ from envy and rivalry, but others from good will. The latter do it out of love, knowing that I am put here for the defense of the gospel; the former proclaim Christ out of partisanship, not sincerely but thinking to afflict me in my imprisonment (1.15–17).

70.26 That it is necessary not to make use of human excellences in the preaching of the Gospel, that the grace of God might not be hidden by them.

MATTHEW: I thank thee Father, Lord of heaven and earth, that thou hast hidden these things from the wise and understanding and revealed them to babes (11.25).

1 CORINTHIANS: For Christ did not send me to baptize but to preach the gospel, and not with eloquent wisdom, lest the cross of Christ be emptied of its power (1.17).

1 CORINTHIANS: When I came to you, brethren, I did not come proclaiming to you the testimony of God in lofty words or wisdom, for I decided to know nothing among you except Jesus Christ and him crucified. And I was with you in weakness and in much fear and trembling, and my speech and my message were not in plausible words of *human* wisdom but in demonstration of the Spirit and of power, that *our* faith might not rest in the wisdom of men but in the power of God (2.1–5).

70.27 That it is necessary not to suppose that success in preaching is attained by our own contrivances, but to rely wholly upon God.

[29]Quoting Is 42.1–2

Κεφάλ. κζ'.

ΠΡΟΣ ΚΟΡ. β'. Πεποίθησιν δὲ τοιαύτην ἔχομεν διὰ τοῦ Χριστοῦ πρὸς τὸν Θεὸν, οὐχ ὅτι ἱκανοί ἐσμεν ἀφ' ἑαυτῶν λογίσασθαί τι, ὡς ἐξ ἑαυτῶν· ἀλλ' ἡ ἱκανότης ἡμῶν ἐκ τοῦ Θεοῦ, ὃς καὶ ἱκάνωσεν ἡμᾶς γενέσθαι διακόνους καινῆς διαθήκης.
ΠΡΟΣ ΚΟΡ. β'. Ἔχομεν δὲ τὸν θησαυρὸν τοῦτον ἐν ὀστρακίνοις σκεύεσιν, ἵνα ἡ ὑπερβολὴ τῆς δυνάμεως ᾖ τοῦ Θεοῦ, καὶ μὴ ἐξ ἡμῶν.

[70.28]   Ὅτι οὐ δεῖ τὸν ἐγκεχειρισμένον τὸ κήρυγμα τοῦ εὐαγγελίου κτᾶσθαί τι πλέον τῶν πρὸς τὴν παρ' αὐτοῦ ἀναγκαίαν χρείαν.
Κεφάλ. κη'.
ΜΑΤΘΑΙΟΣ. Μὴ κτήσησθε χρυσὸν, μήτε ἄργυρον, μήτε χαλκὸν εἰς τὰς ζώνας ὑμῶν· μὴ πήραν εἰς ὁδὸν, μηδὲ δύο χιτῶνας, μηδὲ ὑποδήματα, μηδὲ ῥάβδον· ἄξιος γὰρ ὁ ἐργάτης τῆς τροφῆς αὐτοῦ ἐστι.
ΛΟΥΚΑΣ. Μηδὲν αἴρετε εἰς ὁδὸν, μήτε ῥάβδους, μήτε πήραν, μήτε ἄρτον, μήτε ἀργύριον, μήτε ἀνὰ δύο χιτῶνας ἔχειν.
ΠΡΑΞΕΙΣ. Ἀργυρίου ἢ χρυσίου ἢ ἱματισμοῦ οὐδενὸς ἐπεθύμησα, αὐτοὶ γινώσκετε.
ΠΡΟΣ ΤΙΜ. β'. Οὐδεὶς στρατευόμενος ἐμπλέκεται ταῖς τοῦ βίου πραγματείαις, ἵνα τῷ στρατολογήσαντι ἀρέσῃ. [424]

[70.29]   Ὅτι οὐ δεῖ κιχρᾶν ἑαυτὸν εἰς τὴν περὶ τῶν βιωτικῶν φροντίδα τοῖς κατὰ προσπάθειαν περὶ ταῦτα ἀσχολουμένοις.
Κεφάλ. κθ'.
ΛΟΥΚΑΣ. Εἶπε δέ τις αὐτῷ ἐκ τοῦ ὄχλου· διδάσκαλε, εἰπὲ τῷ ἀδελφῷ μου μερίσασθαι μετ' ἐμοῦ τὴν κληρονομίαν. Ὁ δὲ εἶπεν· ἄνθρωπε, τίς με κατέστησε δικαστὴν ἢ μεριστὴν ἐφ' ὑμᾶς;
ΠΡΟΣ ΤΙΜ. β'. Οὐδεὶς στρατευόμενος ἐμπλέκεται ταῖς τοῦ βίου πραγματείαις, καὶ τὰ ἑξῆς.

[70.30]   Ὅτι οἱ διὰ τὴν πρὸς τοὺς ἀκούοντας ἀρέσκειαν ἀμελοῦντες τῆς παρρησίας τῶν τοῦ Θεοῦ θελημάτων, ἐκείνοις ἑαυτοὺς

2 CORINTHIANS: Such is the confidence that we have through Christ toward God—not that we are competent of ourselves to claim anything as coming from us; our competence is from God, who has made us competent to be ministers of a new covenant (3.4–6).

2 CORINTHIANS: But we have this treasure in earthen vessels to show that the transcendent power belongs to God and not to us (4.7).

70.28 That it is necessary for the one charged with preaching the Gospel not to acquire anything more than what he requires to meet his needs.

MATTHEW: Take no gold nor silver nor copper in your belts, no bag for your journey nor two tunics nor sandals nor a staff, for the laborer deserves his food (10.9–10).

LUKE: Take nothing for your journey: no *staves* nor bag nor bread nor money, and do not have two tunics *apiece* (9.3).

ACTS: I coveted no one's silver or gold or apparel, you yourselves know (20.33–34).

2 TIMOTHY: No soldier on service gets entangled in civilian pursuits, since his aim is to satisfy the one who enlisted him (2.4).

70.29 That it is necessary not to lend one's mind to dwelling on the things of this life with those preoccupied with an attachment to them.

LUKE: One of the multitude said to him, "Teacher, bid my brother divide the inheritance with me." But he *said*, "Man, who made me a judge or divider over you?" (12.13–14).

2 TIMOTHY: No soldier on service gets entangled in civilian pursuits (2.4), *and what follows.*

70.30 That those who are heedless in proclaiming the unadulterated will of God in order to please their listeners enslave

δουλοῦντες, οἷς ἀρέσκειν θέλουσι, τῆς τοῦ Κυρίου δεσποτείας ἐκπίπτουσιν.

Κεφάλ. λ΄.

ΙΩΑΝΝΗΣ. Πῶς δύνασθε ὑμεῖς πιστεύειν, δόξαν παρὰ ἀλλήλων λαμβάνοντες, καὶ τὴν δόξαν τὴν παρὰ τοῦ μόνου Θεοῦ οὐ ζητοῦντες; ΠΡΟΣ ΓΑΛ. Εἰ ἔτι ἀνθρώποις ἤρεσκον, Χριστοῦ δοῦλος οὐκ ἂν ἤμην.

[70.31] Ὅτι δεῖ σκοπὸν προκεῖσθαι τῷ διδάσκοντι, πάντας μὲν εἰς ἄνδρα τέλειον, εἰς μέτρον ἡλικίας τοῦ πληρώματος τοῦ Χριστοῦ καταρτίσαι, ἕκαστον δὲ ἐν τῷ ἰδίῳ τάγματι.

Κεφάλ. λα΄.

ΜΑΤΘΑΙΟΣ. Ἔσεσθε οὖν ὑμεῖς τέλειοι, ὥσπερ ὁ Πατὴρ ὑμῶν ὁ ἐν τοῖς οὐρανοῖς τέλειός ἐστιν.

ΙΩΑΝΝΗΣ. Οὐ περὶ τούτων δὲ ἐρωτῶ μόνον, ἀλλὰ καὶ περὶ τῶν πιστευόντων διὰ τοῦ λόγου αὐτῶν εἰς ἐμέ· ἵνα πάντες ἓν ὦσιν, καθὼς σύ, Πάτερ, ἐν ἐμοὶ, κἀγὼ ἐν σοὶ, ἵνα καὶ αὐτοὶ ἐν ἡμῖν ἓν ὦσιν. ΠΡΟΣ ΕΦΕΣ. Καὶ αὐτὸς ἔδωκε τοὺς μὲν ἀποστόλους, τοὺς δὲ προφήτας, τοὺς δὲ ποιμένας καὶ διδασκάλους πρὸς τὸν καταρτισμὸν τῶν ἁγίων, εἰς ἔργον διακονίας, εἰς οἰκοδομὴν τοῦ σώματος τοῦ Χριστοῦ, μέχρι καταντήσωμεν οἱ πάντες εἰς τὴν [425] ἑνότητα τῆς πίστεως, καὶ τῆς ἐπιγνώσεως τοῦ Υἱοῦ τοῦ Θεοῦ, εἰς ἄνδρα τέλειον, εἰς μέτρον ἡλικίας τοῦ πληρώματος τοῦ Χριστοῦ.

[70.32] Ὅτι δεῖ ἐν ἀνεξικακίᾳ καὶ πραότητι παιδεύειν τοὺς ἀντιδιατιθεμένους, προσδοκῶντα αὐτῶν τὴν μετάνοιαν, ἕως ἂν πληρώσῃ τὸ μέτρον τῆς εἰς αὐτοὺς ἐπιμελείας.

Κεφάλ. λβ΄.

ΜΑΤΘΑΙΟΣ. Οὐκ ἐρίσει, οὐδὲ κραυγάσει, οὔτε ἀκούσει τις ἐν ταῖς πλατείαις τὴν φωνὴν αὐτοῦ. Κάλαμον συντετριμμένον οὐ κατεάξει, καὶ λίνον τυφόμενον οὐ σβέσει, ἕως ἂν ἐκβάλῃ εἰς νῖκος τὴν κρίσιν.

themselves to those they seek to please and lose the Lord for their master.

JOHN: How can you believe, who receive glory from one another and do not seek the glory that comes from the only God (5.44)?

GALATIANS: If I were still pleasing men, I should not be a servant of Christ (1.10).

70.31 That it is necessary for a teacher to have the goal of establishing everyone as a perfect man in the measure of the stature of the fullness of Christ, each in his own manner.

MATTHEW: You therefore must be perfect, *just* as your heavenly Father is perfect (5.48).

JOHN: I do not pray for these only but also for those who believe in me through their word, that they may all be one; even as thou, Father, art in me and I in thee, that they also may be *one* in us (17.20–21).

EPHESIANS: And his gifts were that some should be apostles, some *prophets, some* pastors and teachers, to equip the saints for the work of ministry, for building up the body of Christ until we all attain to the unity of the faith and of the knowledge of the Son of God, to *a perfect man*, to the measure of the stature of the fullness of Christ (4.11–13).

70.32 That it is necessary to teach one's adversaries in forbearance and gentleness, awaiting their repentance, until one has fulfilled the measure of care for them.

MATTHEW: "He will not wrangle or cry aloud, nor will any one hear his voice in the streets; he will not break a bruised reed or quench a smoldering wick till he *issues judgment unto victory*"[30] (12.19–20).

[30]Quoting Is 42.2–3

ΠΡΟΣ ΤΙΜ. β'. Δοῦλον δὲ Κυρίου οὐ δεῖ μάχεσθαι, ἀλλ᾽ ἤπιον εἶναι πρὸς πάντας, διδακτικόν, ἀνεξίκακον, ἐν πραΰτητι παιδεύοντα τοὺς ἀντιδιατιθεμένους, μήποτε δῷ αὐτοῖς ὁ Θεὸς μετάνοιαν εἰς ἐπίγνωσιν ἀληθείας, καὶ ἀνανήψωσιν ἐκ τῆς τοῦ διαβόλου παγίδος.

[70.33] Ὅτι δεῖ τοῖς διὰ φόβον καὶ εὐλάβειαν παραιτουμένοις τὴν παρουσίαν τοῦ κηρύσσοντος τὸν λόγον εἴκειν, καὶ μὴ φιλονείκως ἐγκεῖσθαι.
Κεφάλ. λγ'.
ΛΟΥΚΑΣ. Καὶ ἠρώτησαν αὐτὸν ἅπαν τὸ πλῆθος τῆς περιχώρου τῶν Γαδαρηνῶν, ἀπελθεῖν ἀπ᾽ αὐτῶν, ὅτι φόβῳ μεγάλῳ συνείχοντο. Αὐτὸς δὲ ἐμβὰς εἰς τὸ πλοῖον, ὑπέστρεψεν.

[70.34] Ὅτι δεῖ καὶ τῶν διὰ ἀγνωμοσύνην μὴ καταδεχομένων τὸ κήρυγμα τοῦ εὐαγγελίου ἀναχωρεῖν, μηδὲ τὰ πρὸς τὴν ἀναγκαίαν τοῦ σώματος χρείαν παρ᾽ αὐτῶν εὐεργετηθῆναι ἀνεχομένους.
Κεφάλ. λδ'.
ΜΑΤΘΑΙΟΣ. Καὶ ὃς ἂν μὴ δέξηται ὑμᾶς, μηδὲ ἀκούσῃ τῶν λόγων ὑμῶν, ἐξερχόμενοι τῆς οἰκίας ἐκείνης, ἢ τῆς πόλεως, ἐκτινάξατε τὸν κονιορτὸν ἀπὸ τῶν ποδῶν ὑμῶν.
ΛΟΥΚΑΣ. Εἰς ἣν δ᾽ ἂν πόλιν εἰσέρχησθε, καὶ μὴ δέξωνται ὑμᾶς, ἐξελθόντες εἰς τὰς πλατείας αὐτῆς, εἴπατε· καὶ τὸν [426] κονιορτὸν τὸν κολληθέντα ἡμῖν ἀπὸ τῆς πόλεως ὑμῶν ἀποματτόμεθα ὑμῖν· πλὴν τοῦτο γινώσκετε, ὅτι ἤγγικεν ἐφ᾽ ὑμᾶς ἡ βασιλεία τοῦ Θεοῦ.
ΠΡΑΞΕΙΣ. Ὡς δὲ κατῆλθον ἀπὸ τῆς Μακεδονίας ὅ τε Σίλας καὶ ὁ Τιμόθεος, συνείχετο τῷ λόγῳ ὁ Παῦλος, διαμαρτυρόμενος τοῖς Ἰουδαίοις εἶναι τὸν Χριστὸν Ἰησοῦν. Ἀντιτασσομένων δὲ αὐτῶν, καὶ βλασφημούντων, ἐκτιναξάμενος τὰ ἱμάτια, εἶπε πρὸς αὐτούς· τὸ αἷμα ὑμῶν ἐπὶ τὴν κεφαλὴν ὑμῶν· ἀθῷος ἐγώ· ἀπὸ τοῦ νῦν εἰς τὰ ἔθνη πορεύσομαι.

[70.35] Ὅτι δεῖ τῶν μετὰ τὸ πληρωθῆναι εἰς αὐτοὺς πάντα τρόπον ἐπιμελείας ἀπειθούντων ἀναχωρεῖν.

2 TIMOTHY: And the Lord's servant must not be quarrelsome but kindly to everyone, an apt teacher, forbearing, correcting his opponents with gentleness. God may perhaps grant that they will repent and come to know the truth and they may escape from the snare of the devil (2.24–26).

70.33 That it is necessary to yield to those who on account of fear and piety beg off the presence of the one preaching the Word, and not to obstinately intrude.

LUKE: Then all the people of the surrounding country of the *Gadarenes* asked him to depart from them, for they were seized with great fear, so he got into the boat and returned (8.37).

70.34 That it is necessary also to withdraw from those who, for want of sense, do not receive the preaching of the Gospel and not even to accept from them bodily necessities.

MATTHEW: And if anyone will not receive you or listen to your words, shake off the dust from your feet as you leave that house or town (10.14).

LUKE: But whenever you enter a town and they do not receive you, go into its streets and say, "Even the dust of your town that clings to *us* we wipe off against you; nevertheless know this: that the kingdom of God has come near *to you*" (10.10–11).

ACTS: When Silas and Timothy arrived from Macedonia, Paul was occupied with preaching, testifying to the Jews that the Christ was Jesus. And when they opposed and reviled him, he shook out his garments and said to them, "Your blood be upon your heads! I am innocent. From now on I will go to the Gentiles" (18.5–6).

70.35 That it is necessary to withdraw from those persisting in disobedience after every manner of care has been exercised for them.

Κεφάλ. λε'.

ΜΑΤΘΑΙΟΣ. Ἱερουσαλήμ, Ἱερουσαλήμ, ἡ ἀποκτείνουσα τοὺς προφήτας, καὶ λιθοβολοῦσα τοὺς ἀπεσταλμένους πρὸς αὐτήν, ποσάκις ἠθέλησα ἐπισυναγαγεῖν τὰ τέκνα σου, ὃν τρόπον ὄρνις ἐπισυνάγει τὰ νοσσία ἑαυτῆς ὑπὸ τὰς πτέρυγας αὐτῆς, καὶ οὐκ ἠθελήσατε; Ἰδοὺ ἀφίεται ὑμῖν ὁ οἶκος ὑμῶν ἔρημος.

ΠΡΑΞΕΙΣ. Ὑμῖν ἦν ἀναγκαῖον λαληθῆναι τὸν λόγον τοῦ Θεοῦ· ἐπειδὴ δὲ ἀπωθεῖσθε αὐτόν, καὶ οὐκ ἀξίους κρίνετε ἑαυτοὺς τῆς αἰωνίου ζωῆς, ἰδοὺ στρεφόμεθα εἰς τὰ ἔθνη. Οὕτω γὰρ ἐντέταλται ἡμῖν ὁ Κύριος· «τέθεικά σε εἰς φῶς ἐθνῶν, τοῦ εἶναί σε εἰς σωτηρίαν ἕως ἐσχάτου τῆς γῆς.»

ΠΡΟΣ ΤΙΤ. Αἱρετικὸν ἄνθρωπον μετὰ μίαν καὶ δευτέραν νουθεσίαν παραιτοῦ, εἰδὼς ὅτι ἐξέστραπται ὁ τοιοῦτος, καὶ ἁμαρτάνει, ὢν αὐτοκατάκριτος.

[70.36] Ὅτι πρὸς πάντας ἐν παντὶ πράγματι φυλάσσειν δεῖ τὴν ἀκρίβειαν τῶν τοῦ Κυρίου ῥημάτων, μηδὲν ποιοῦντα κατὰ πρόσκλισιν.

Κεφάλ. λς'.

ΠΡΟΣ ΤΙΜ. α'. Διαμαρτύρομαι ἐνώπιον τοῦ Θεοῦ καὶ Χριστοῦ Ἰησοῦ, καὶ τῶν ἐκλεκτῶν ἀγγέλων, ἵνα ταῦτα φυλάξῃς χωρὶς προκρίματος, μηδὲν ποιῶν κατὰ πρόσκλισιν. [427]

[70.37] Ὅτι δεῖ τὸν προεστῶτα τοῦ λόγου μετὰ περισκέψεως καὶ δοκιμασίας πολλῆς, κατὰ σκοπὸν τῆς πρὸς Θεὸν εὐαρεστήσεως, ἕκαστον ποιεῖν τε καὶ λέγειν, ὡς ὀφείλοντα καὶ ὑπ' αὐτῶν τῶν πεπιστευμένων αὐτῷ δοκιμάζεσθαί τε καὶ μαρτυρεῖσθαι.

Κεφάλ. λζ'.

ΠΡΑΞΕΙΣ. Ὑμεῖς ἐπίστασθε ἀπὸ πρώτης ἡμέρας, ἀφ' ἧς ἐπέβην εἰς τὴν Ἀσίαν, πῶς μεθ' ὑμῶν τὸν πάντα χρόνον ἐγενόμην, δουλεύων τῷ Κυρίῳ μετὰ πάσης ταπεινοφροσύνης, καὶ πολλῶν δακρύων καὶ πειρασμῶν. Καὶ μετ' ὀλίγα· Ἀργυρίου, ἢ χρυσίου, ἢ ἱματισμοῦ οὐδενὸς ἐπεθύμησα. Αὐτοὶ γινώσκετε, ὅτι ταῖς χρείαις μου καὶ τοῖς οὖσι μετ' ἐμοῦ ὑπηρέτησαν αἱ χεῖρες αὗται.

MATTHEW: O Jerusalem, Jerusalem, killing the prophets and stoning those who are sent to you! How often would I have gathered your children together as a hen gathers her brood under her wings, and you would not! Behold, your house is forsaken and desolate (23.37–38).

ACTS: It was necessary that the word of God should be *spoken* to you. Since you thrust it from you and judge yourselves unworthy of eternal life, behold, we turn to the Gentiles. For so the Lord has commanded us, saying, "I have set you to be a light for the Gentiles, that you may bring salvation to the uttermost parts of the earth"[31] (13.46–47).

TITUS: As for a man who is factious, after admonishing him once or twice have nothing more to do with him, knowing that such a person is perverted and sinful; he is self-condemned (3.10–11).

70.36 That in all our dealings with anyone it is necessary to maintain the rigor of the Lord's words and not to show partiality.

1 TIMOTHY: In the presence of God and of Christ Jesus and of the elect angels I charge you to keep these rules without favor, doing nothing from partiality (5.21).

70.37 That it is necessary for the one set over the Word in every instance to act and to speak with circumspection and all consideration with the aim of pleasing God, since he is also accountable to the approbation and testimony of the very ones entrusted to him.

ACTS: You yourselves know how I lived among you all the time from the first day that I set foot in Asia, serving the Lord with all humility and with *many tears and trials* (20.18–19). *And a little further*: I coveted no one's silver or gold or apparel. You yourselves know that these hands ministered to my necessities and to those who were with me (20.33–34).

[31]Is 49.6

ΠΡΟΣ ΘΕΣΣ. α΄. Ὑμεῖς μάρτυρες, καὶ ὁ Θεὸς, ὡς ὁσίως, καὶ δικαίως, καὶ ἀμέμπτως ὑμῖν τοῖς πιστεύουσιν ἐγενήθημεν, καθάπερ ὑμεῖς οἴδατε.

ΟΡΟΣ ΟΑ΄.

[71.1] ὅσα κατὰ συνάφειαν εἴρηται περὶ ἐπισκόπων καὶ πρεσβυτέρων.

Κεφάλ. α΄.

ΠΡΟΣ ΤΙΜ. α΄. Εἴ τις ἐπισκοπῆς ὀρέγεται, καλοῦ ἔργου ἐπιθυμεῖ. Ἀλλὰ δεῖ τὸν ἐπίσκοπον ἀνεπίληπτον εἶναι, καὶ τὰ ἑξῆς.

ΠΡΟΣ ΤΙΜ. α΄. Πρεσβυτέρῳ μὴ ἐπιπλήξῃς, ἀλλὰ παρακάλει ὡς πατέρα, νεωτέρους ὡς ἀδελφούς· πρεσβυτέρας ὡς μητέρας· νεωτέρας ὡς ἀδελφὰς, ἐν πάσῃ ἁγνείᾳ.

ΠΡΟΣ ΤΙΜ. β΄. Τὰς δὲ νεωτερικὰς ἐπιθυμίας φεῦγε, δίωκε δὲ δικαιοσύνην, πίστιν, ἀγάπην, εἰρήνην μετὰ τῶν ἐπικαλουμένων τὸν Κύριον ἐκ καθαρᾶς καρδίας. Τὰς δὲ μωρὰς καὶ ἀπαιδεύτους ζητήσεις παραιτοῦ, εἰδὼς ὅτι γεννῶσι μάχας. Δοῦλον δὲ Κυρίου οὐ δεῖ μάχεσθαι, ἀλλ᾽ ἤπιον εἶναι πρὸς πάντας, καὶ τὰ ἑξῆς.

ΠΡΟΣ ΤΙΜ. β΄. Σὺ δὲ παρηκολούθηκάς μου τῇ πίστει, τῇ διδασκαλίᾳ, τῇ ἀγωγῇ, τῇ προθέσει, τῇ ὑπομονῇ, τοῖς διωγμοῖς, τοῖς παθήμασιν.

ΠΡΟΣ ΤΙΤ. Τούτου χάριν κατέλιπόν σε ἐν Κρήτῃ, ἵνα τὰ λείποντα ἐπιδιορθώσῃς,[27] καὶ καταστήσῃς κατὰ πόλιν πρεσβυτέρους, ὡς ἐγώ σοι διεταξάμην, εἴ τίς ἐστιν ἀνέγκλητος, καὶ τὰ ἑξῆς. [428]

[71.2] Περὶ διακόνων.

Κεφάλ. β΄.

ΠΡΑΞΕΙΣ. Καὶ ἐξελέξαντο Στέφανον ἄνδρα πλήρη πίστεως καὶ Πνεύματος ἁγίου, καὶ Φίλιππον, καὶ Πρόχορον, καὶ Νικάνορα, καὶ τοὺς λοιπούς, οὓς ἔστησαν ἐνώπιον τῶν ἀποστόλων· καὶ προσευξάμενοι ἐπέθηκαν αὐτοῖς τὰς χεῖρας.

ΠΡΟΣ ΤΙΜ. α΄. Διακόνους ὡσαύτως σεμνούς, μὴ διλόγους, μὴ οἴνῳ πολλῷ προσέχοντας, μὴ αἰσχροκερδεῖς, καὶ τὰ ἑξῆς.

---

[27]Corrected from ἐπιδιορθώσῃ.

1 THESSALONIANS: You are witnesses, and God also, how holy and righteous and blameless was our behavior to you believers, *just as you know* (2.10–11).

71.1   Whatever is said conjointly of bishops and presbyters.

1 TIMOTHY: If anyone aspires to the office of bishop, he desires a noble task. *But* a bishop must be above reproach (3.1–2), *and what follows*.

1 TIMOTHY: Do not rebuke an older man[32] but exhort him as you would a father; treat younger men like brothers, older women like mothers, younger women like sisters, in all purity (5.1–2).

2 TIMOTHY: So shun youthful passions and aim at righteousness, faith, love, and peace along with those who call upon the Lord from a pure heart. Have nothing to do with stupid, senseless controversies; you know that they breed quarrels. And the Lord's servant must not be quarrelsome but kindly to everyone (2.22–24), *and what follows*.

2 TIMOTHY: Now you have observed *my faith*, my teaching, my conduct, my aim in life, *my steadfastness*, my persecutions, my sufferings (3.10–11).

TITUS: This is why I left you in Crete, that you might amend what was defective and appoint *presbyters* in every town as I directed you, if any man is blameless (1.5–6), *and what follows*.

71.2   Concerning deacons.

ACTS: And they chose Stephen, a man full of faith and of the Holy Spirit, and Philip and Prochorus and Nicanor and the rest (6.5). These they set before the apostles, and they prayed and laid their hands upon them (6.6).

1 TIMOTHY: Deacons likewise must be serious, not double–tongued, not addicted to much wine, not greedy for gain (3.8), *and what follows*.

[32]Lit. "presbyter."

ΟΡΟΣ ΟΒ΄.

[72.1]   Περὶ ἀκροατῶν.

Ὅτι δεῖ τῶν ἀκροατῶν τοὺς πεπαιδευμένους τὰς Γραφὰς,
δοκιμάζειν τὰ παρὰ τῶν διδασκάλων λεγόμενα· καὶ τὰ μὲν σύμφωνα
ταῖς Γραφαῖς δέχεσθαι, τὰ δὲ ἀλλότρια ἀποβάλλειν· καὶ τοὺς
τοιούτοις διδάγμασιν ἐπιμένοντας ἀποστρέφεσθαι σφοδρότερον.

Κεφάλ. α΄.

ΜΑΤΘΑΙΟΣ. Οὐαὶ τῷ ἀνθρώπῳ ἐκείνῳ, δι᾽ οὗ τὸ σκάνδαλον
ἔρχεται. Καὶ εἰ ὁ ὀφθαλμός σου σκανδαλίζει σε, ἔξελε αὐτόν· ὁμοίως
καὶ περὶ χειρὸς καὶ ποδός.

ΙΩΑΝΝΗΣ. Ἀμὴν ἀμὴν λέγω ὑμῖν· ὁ μὴ εἰσερχόμενος διὰ τῆς
θύρας εἰς τὴν αὐλὴν τῶν προβάτων, ἀλλὰ ἀναβαίνων ἀλλαχόθεν,
ἐκεῖνος κλέπτης ἐστὶ καὶ λῃστής. Καὶ μετ᾽ ὀλίγα· Ἀλλοτρίῳ δὲ οὐ
μὴ ἀκολουθήσωσιν, ἀλλὰ φεύξονται ἀπ᾽ αὐτοῦ, ὅτι οὐκ οἴδασι τῶν
ἀλλοτρίων τὴν φωνήν.

ΠΡΟΣ ΓΑΛ. Ἀλλὰ καὶ ἐὰν ἡμεῖς, ἢ ἄγγελος ἐξ οὐρανοῦ εὐαγγελίζηται ὑμῖν παρ᾽ ὃ παρελάβετε, ἀνάθεμα ἔστω.

ΠΡΟΣ ΘΕΣΣ. α΄. Προφητείας μὴ ἐξουθενεῖτε. Πάντα δοκιμάζετε· τὸ
καλὸν κατέχετε. Ἀπὸ παντὸς εἴδους πονηροῦ ἀπέχεσθε. [429]

[72.2]   Ὅτι δεῖ τοὺς μὴ πολλὴν ἔχοντας τὴν τῶν Γραφῶν γνῶσιν,
ἐν τοῖς καρποῖς τοῦ Πνεύματος γνωρίζειν τὸν χαρακτῆρα τῶν
ἁγίων· καὶ τοὺς μὲν τοιούτους δέχεσθαι, τοὺς δὲ ἄλλως ἔχοντας
ἀποστρέφεσθαι.

Κεφάλ. β΄.

ΜΑΤΘΑΙΟΣ. Προσέχετε δὲ ἀπὸ τῶν ψευδοπροφητῶν, οἵτινες
ἔρχονται πρὸς ὑμᾶς ἐν ἐνδύμασι προβάτων, ἔσωθεν δέ εἰσι λύκοι
ἅρπαγες. Ἀπὸ τῶν καρπῶν αὐτῶν ἐπιγνώσεσθε αὐτούς.

ΠΡΟΣ ΦΙΛΙΠ. Συμμιμηταί μου γίνεσθε, ἀδελφοί, καὶ σκοπεῖτε τοὺς
οὕτω περιπατοῦντας, καθὼς ἔχετε τύπον ἡμᾶς.

[72.3]   Ὅτι δεῖ τῶν ὀρθοτομούντων τὸν λόγον τῆς ἀληθείας οὕτως
ἀνέχεσθαι, ὡς τοῦ Κυρίου, εἰς δόξαν αὐτοῦ τοῦ ἀποστείλαντος
Ἰησοῦ Χριστοῦ τοῦ Κυρίου ἡμῶν.

72.1   Concerning hearers.

That it is necessary for those hearers who have been instructed in the Scriptures to examine what the teachers say and to accept what agrees with the Scriptures and reject what is foreign and to turn away vehemently from those who persist in such teachings.

MATTHEW: Woe to the man by whom the *scandal* comes! (18.7) And if your eye *scandalizes you*, pluck it out (18.9); *likewise also your hand and your foot.*[33]

JOHN: Truly, truly I say to you, he who does not enter the sheep-fold by the door but climbs in by another way, that man is a thief and a robber (10.1). *And a little further:* A stranger they will not follow, but they will flee from him, for they do not know the voice of strangers (10.5).

GALATIANS: But even if we or an angel from heaven should preach to you a gospel contrary to that which *you received*, let him be accursed (1.8).

1 THESSALONIANS: Do not despise prophesying, but test everything; hold fast what is good; abstain from every form of evil (5.20–22).

72.2   That it is necessary for those without much knowledge of the Scriptures to recognize the character of those who are holy in the fruits of the Spirit and to receive such as bear them but to turn away from those who bear otherwise.

MATTHEW: Beware of false prophets who come to you in sheep's clothing but inwardly are ravenous wolves. You will know them by their fruits (7.15–16).

PHILIPPIANS: Brethren, join in imitating me, and mark those who so live as you have an example in us (3.17).

72.3   That it is necessary to receive as the Lord those who rightly administer the Word of truth, to the glory of the one who sends them, Jesus Christ our Lord.

[33]See Mt 18.8

Κεφάλ. γ΄.

ΜΑΤΘΑΙΟΣ. Ὁ δεχόμενος ὑμᾶς, ἐμὲ δέχεται.

ΙΩΑΝΝΗΣ. Ὁ λαμβάνων ἐάν τινα πέμψω, ἐμὲ λαμβάνει.

ΛΟΥΚΑΣ. Ὁ ἀκούων ὑμῶν, ἐμοῦ ἀκούει.

ΠΡΟΣ ΓΑΛ. Καὶ τὸν πειρασμὸν, τὸν ἐν τῇ σαρκί μου, οὐκ ἐξου-
θενήσατε, οὐδὲ ἐξεπτύσατε, ἀλλ᾽ ὡς ἄγγελον Θεοῦ ἐδέξασθέ με, ὡς
Χριστὸν Ἰησοῦν.

[72.4] Ὅτι οἱ ἀπειθοῦντες τοῖς παρὰ τοῦ Κυρίου ἀποστελλομένοις,
τὴν ἀτιμίαν οὐ μέχρι τούτων ἱστῶσιν, ἀλλὰ ἀνάγουσιν ἐπὶ τὸν
ἀποστείλαντα, καὶ κρῖμα ἑαυτοῖς χεῖρον τῶν ἐν Σοδόμοις καὶ
Γομόρροις ἐπισπῶνται.

Κεφάλ. δ΄.

ΜΑΤΘΑΙΟΣ. Καὶ ὃς ἐὰν μὴ δέξηται ὑμᾶς, μηδὲ ἀκούσῃ τοὺς λόγους
ὑμῶν, ἐξερχόμενοι τῆς πόλεως ἢ τῆς οἰκίας ἐκείνης, ἐκτινάξατε τὸν
κονιορτὸν τῶν ποδῶν ὑμῶν. Ἀμὴν λέγω ὑμῖν, ἀνεκτότερον ἔσται γῇ
Σοδόμων καὶ Γομόρρας ἐν ἡμέρᾳ κρίσεως, ἢ τῇ πόλει ἐκείνῃ.

ΛΟΥΚΑΣ. Ὁ ἀθετῶν ὑμᾶς, ἐμὲ ἀθετεῖ.

ΠΡΟΣ ΘΕΣΣ. α΄. Τοιγαροῦν ὁ ἀθετῶν, οὐκ ἄνθρωπον ἀθετεῖ, ἀλλὰ
τὸν Θεὸν, τὸν καὶ δόντα τὸ Πνεῦμα αὐτοῦ τὸ ἅγιον εἰς ἡμᾶς. [430]

[72.5] Ὅτι δεῖ τὴν διδασκαλίαν τῶν ἐντολῶν τοῦ Κυρίου οὕτως
δέχεσθαι, ὡς ζωῆς αἰωνίου καὶ βασιλείας οὐρανῶν περιποιητικήν·
καὶ προθύμως ἐνεργεῖν αὐτὴν, κἂν ἐπίπονος εἶναι δοκῇ.

Κεφάλ. ε΄.

ΙΩΑΝΝΗΣ. Ἀμὴν ἀμὴν λέγω ὑμῖν, ὅτι ὁ τὸν λόγον μου ἀκούων,
καὶ πιστεύων τῷ πέμψαντί με, ἔχει ζωὴν αἰώνιον, καὶ εἰς κρίσιν οὐκ
ἔρχεται, ἀλλὰ μεταβέβηκεν ἐκ τοῦ θανάτου εἰς τὴν ζωήν.

ΠΡΑΞΕΙΣ. Εὐαγγελισάμενοί τε τὴν πόλιν ἐκείνην, καὶ μαθητεύ-
σαντες ἱκανοὺς, ὑπέστρεψαν εἰς τὴν Λύστραν, καὶ Ἰκόνιον, καὶ
Ἀντιόχειαν, ἐπιστηρίζοντες τὰς ψυχὰς τῶν μαθητῶν, παρακαλοῦντες
ἐμμένειν τῇ πίστει· καὶ ὅτι διὰ πολλῶν θλίψεων δεῖ ἡμᾶς εἰσελθεῖν
εἰς τὴν βασιλείαν τῶν οὐρανῶν.

MATTHEW: He who receives you receives me (10.40).

JOHN: He who receives anyone whom I send receives me (13.20).

LUKE: He who hears you hears me (10.16).

GALATIANS: *And you did not scorn or despise the trial in my flesh* but received me as an angel of God, as Christ Jesus (4.14).[34]

72.4   That those who are unreceptive to the ones the Lord has sent show dishonor not only to them, but they cast it also on the one who sent them and pursue a sentence for themselves worse than that given to Sodom and Gomorrah.

MATTHEW: And if anyone will not receive you or listen to your words, shake off the dust from your feet as you leave *the town or that house.* Truly I say to you, it shall be more tolerable on the day of judgment for the land of Sodom and Gomorrah than for that town (10.14–15).

LUKE: He who rejects you rejects me (10.16).

1 THESSALONIANS: Therefore whoever disregards this disregards not man but God, who gives *even* his Holy Spirit to you (4.8).

72.5   That it is necessary to consider the teaching of the commandments of the Lord to be productive of eternal life and of the kingdom of heaven and to work at it eagerly, even if it seems wearisome.

JOHN: Truly, truly I say to you, he who hears my word and believes him who sent me has eternal life; he does not come into judgment but has passed from death to life (5.24).

ACTS: When they had preached the gospel to that city and had made many disciples, they returned to Lystra *and Iconium and Antioch*, strengthening the souls of the disciples, exhorting them to continue in the faith, and saying that through many tribulations we must enter the kingdom of *heaven* (14.21–22).

[34]For Paul's "trial in the flesh" see the surrounding verses; also 2 Cor 12.7–10.

[72.6] Ὅτι δεῖ τὸν ἔλεγχον καὶ τὴν ἐπιτίμησιν οὕτως δέχεσθαι, ὡς φάρμακον ἀναιρετικὸν πάθους, καὶ ὑγείας κατασκευαστικόν. Ἐξ οὗ δῆλόν ἐστιν, ὅτι οἱ ἐν πάθει ἀνθρωπαρεσκείας ἐπιείκειαν ὑποκρινόμενοι, καὶ μὴ ἐλέγχοντες τοὺς ἁμαρτάνοντας, τὸ ὅλον ζημιοῦσι, καὶ εἰς αὐτὴν τὴν ἀληθινὴν ζωὴν ἐπιβουλεύουσιν.

Κεφάλ. ς'.

ΜΑΤΘΑΙΟΣ. Ἐὰν δὲ ἁμάρτῃ εἰς σὲ ἀδελφός σου, ὕπαγε, ἔλεγξον αὐτὸν μεταξὺ σοῦ καὶ αὐτοῦ μόνου· ἐάν σου ἀκούσῃ, ἐκέρδησας τὸν ἀδελφόν σου.

ΠΡΟΣ ΚΟΡ. α'. Συναχθέντων ὑμῶν καὶ τοῦ ἐμοῦ πνεύματος σὺν τῇ δυνάμει τοῦ Κυρίου ἡμῶν Ἰησοῦ Χριστοῦ, παραδοῦναι τὸν τοιοῦτον τῷ σατανᾷ εἰς ὄλεθρον τῆς σαρκὸς, ἵνα τὸ πνεῦμα σωθῇ ἐν τῇ ἡμέρᾳ τοῦ Κυρίου Ἰησοῦ.

ΠΡΟΣ ΚΟΡ. β'. Ὅτι ἡ ἐπιστολὴ ἐκείνη, εἰ καὶ πρὸς ὥραν ἐλύπησεν ὑμᾶς, νῦν χαίρω, οὐχ ὅτι ἐλυπήθητε, ἀλλ᾽ ὅτι ἐλυπήθητε εἰς μετάνοιαν. Ἐλυπήθητε γὰρ κατὰ Θεόν, ἵνα ἐν μηδενὶ ζημιωθῆτε ἐξ ἡμῶν. Ἡ γὰρ κατὰ Θεὸν λύπη, μετάνοιαν εἰς σωτηρίαν ἀμεταμέλητον κατεργάζεται.

ΠΡΟΣ ΤΙΤ. Δι᾽ ἣν αἰτίαν ἔλεγχε αὐτοὺς ἀποτόμως, ἵνα ὑγιαίνωσιν ἐν τῇ πίστει. [431]

ΟΡΟΣ ΟΓ'.

[73.1] Ὅτι οὐ δεῖ ἄνδρα ἀπὸ γυναικὸς, ἢ γυναῖκα ἀπὸ ἀνδρὸς χωρίζεσθαι, εἰ μή τις ἂν ἐπὶ πορνείᾳ ἁλῷ, ἢ εἰς τὴν θεοσέβειαν κωλύηται.

Κεφάλ. α'.

ΜΑΤΘΑΙΟΣ. Ἐρρήθη δὲ, ὅτι ὃς ἐὰν ἀπολύσῃ τὴν γυναῖκα αὐτοῦ, δότω αὐτῇ ἀποστάσιον. Ἐγὼ δὲ λέγω ὑμῖν, ὅτι ὃς ἐὰν ἀπολύσῃ τὴν γυναῖκα αὐτοῦ, παρεκτὸς λόγου πορνείας, ποιεῖ αὐτὴν μοιχᾶσθαι· καὶ ὃς ἐὰν ἀπολελυμένην γαμήσῃ, μοιχᾶται.

ΛΟΥΚΑΣ. Εἴ τις ἔρχεται πρός με, καὶ οὐ μισεῖ τὸν πατέρα, καὶ τὴν μητέρα, καὶ τὴν γυναῖκα, καὶ τὰ τέκνα, καὶ τοὺς ἀδελφοὺς, καὶ τὰς ἀδελφὰς, ἔτι δὲ καὶ τὴν ἑαυτοῦ ψυχὴν, οὐ δύναταί μου εἶναι μαθητής.

72.6 That it is necessary to accept reproach and rebuke as medicine that destroys passions and induces health, from which it is clear that those in the habit of people-pleasing through a facade of clemency and who do not reproach sinners are altogether destructive and contrive against true life itself.

MATTHEW: If your brother sins against you, go and tell him his fault between you and him alone. If he listens to you, you have gained your brother (18.15).

1 CORINTHIANS: *When you and my spirit are assembled* with the power of our Lord Jesus *Christ,* you are to deliver *such a one* to Satan for the destruction of the flesh, that his spirit may be saved in the day of the Lord Jesus (5.4–5).

2 CORINTHIANS: For even if I made you sorry with my letter, I do not regret it (though I did regret it), for I see that that letter grieved you, though only for a while. As it is I rejoice—not because you were grieved, but because you were grieved into repenting; for you felt a godly grief, so that you suffered no loss through us. For godly grief produces a repentance that leads to salvation and brings no regret (7.8–10).

TITUS: Therefore rebuke them sharply, that they may be sound in the faith (1.13).

73.1 That it is necessary for a husband not to be divorced from his wife nor a wife from her husband unless one of them should fall into sexual immorality or be a hindrance to godly piety.

MATTHEW: It was also said, "Whoever divorces his wife, let him give her a certificate of divorce." But I say to you that *whoever* divorces his wife, except on the ground of unchastity, makes her an adulteress; and whoever marries a divorced woman commits adultery (5.31–32).

LUKE: If anyone comes to me and does not hate *his* father and mother and wife and children and brothers and sisters—yes, and even his own life, he cannot be my disciple (14.26).

ΜΑΤΘΑΙΟΣ. Λέγω δὲ ὑμῖν, ὅτι ὃς ἂν ἀπολύσῃ τὴν γυναῖκα αὐτοῦ, εἰ μὴ ἐπὶ πορνείᾳ, καὶ γαμήσῃ ἄλλην, μοιχᾶται· καὶ ὁ ἀπολελυμένην γαμήσας, μοιχᾶται. [432]

ΠΡΟΣ ΚΟΡ. α΄. Τοῖς δὲ γεγαμηκόσι παραγγέλλω, οὐκ ἐγὼ, ἀλλ᾿ ὁ Κύριος, γυναῖκα ἀπὸ ἀνδρὸς μὴ χωρίζεσθαι· ἐὰν δὲ καὶ χωρισθῇ, μενέτω ἄγαμος, ἢ τῷ ἀνδρὶ καταλλαγήτω· καὶ ἄνδρα γυναῖκα μὴ ἀφιέναι.

[73.2]   Ὅτι οὐκ ἔξεστι τῷ ἀπολύσαντι τὴν ἑαυτοῦ γυναῖκα, γαμεῖν ἄλλην, οὔτε τὴν ἀπολελυμένην ἀπὸ ἀνδρὸς, ἑτέρῳ γαμεῖσθαι.
Κεφάλ. β΄.
ΜΑΤΘΑΙΟΣ. Λέγω δὲ ὑμῖν, ὅτι ὃς ἂν ἀπολύσῃ τὴν γυναῖκα αὐτοῦ, εἰ μὴ ἐπὶ πορνείᾳ, καὶ γαμήσῃ ἄλλην, μοιχᾶται· καὶ ὁ ἀπολελυμένην γαμήσας, μοιχᾶται.

[73.3]   Ὅτι δεῖ τοὺς ἄνδρας ἀγαπᾶν τὰς ἑαυτῶν γυναῖκας, ἀγάπην ἣν ὁ Χριστὸς ἠγάπησε τὴν Ἐκκλησίαν, παραδοὺς ἑαυτὸν ὑπὲρ αὐτῆς, ἵνα αὐτὴν ἁγιάσῃ.
Κεφάλ. γ΄.
ΠΡΟΣ ΕΦΕΣ. Οἱ ἄνδρες, ἀγαπᾶτε τὰς γυναῖκας ἑαυτῶν, καθὼς καὶ ὁ Χριστὸς τὴν Ἐκκλησίαν ἠγάπησε, καὶ ἑαυτὸν παρέδωκεν ὑπὲρ αὐτῆς, ἵνα αὐτὴν ἁγιάσῃ, καθαρίσας τῷ λουτρῷ τοῦ ὕδατος ἐν ῥήματι. Καὶ μετ᾿ ὀλίγα· Οὕτως ὀφείλουσιν οἱ ἄνδρες ἀγαπᾶν τὰς ἑαυτῶν γυναῖκας, ὡς τὰ ἑαυτῶν σώματα, καὶ τὰ ἑξῆς.

[73.4]   Ὅτι δεῖ τὰς γυναῖκας ὑποτάσσεσθαι τοῖς ἰδίοις ἀνδράσιν, ὡς καὶ ἡ Ἐκκλησία τῷ Χριστῷ, ποιούσας τὸ θέλημα τοῦ Θεοῦ.
Κεφάλ. δ΄.
ΠΡΟΣ ΕΦΕΣ. Αἱ γυναῖκες τοῖς ἰδίοις ἀνδράσιν ὑποτασσέσθωσαν, ὡς τῷ Κυρίῳ· ὅτι ὁ ἀνὴρ κεφαλή ἐστι τῆς γυναικὸς, ὡς καὶ ὁ Χριστὸς κεφαλὴ τῆς Ἐκκλησίας· καὶ αὐτός ἐστιν ὁ σωτὴρ τοῦ σώματος. Ἀλλ᾿ ὥσπερ ἡ Ἐκκλησία ὑποτάσσεται τῷ Χριστῷ, οὕτω αἱ γυναῖκες τοῖς ἰδίοις ἀνδράσιν ἐν παντί.

MATTHEW: And I say to you: whoever divorces his wife, except for unchastity, and marries another commits adultery (19.9).

1 CORINTHIANS: To the married I give charge, not I but the Lord, that the wife should not separate from her husband (but if she does, let her remain single or else be reconciled to her husband) and that the husband should not divorce his wife (7.10–11).

73.2   That neither is the one who has divorced himself from his wife permitted to marry another nor the one divorced from her husband to marry someone else.

MATTHEW: And I say to you: whoever divorces his wife, except for unchastity, and marries another commits adultery. *And he who marries a divorced woman commits adultery* (19.9).

73.3   That it is necessary for men to love their own wives with the love with which Christ loves the Church, giving himself for her that he might make her holy.

EPHESIANS: Husbands, love your *own* wives as Christ loved the church and gave himself up for her, that he might sanctify her, having cleansed her by the washing of water with the word (5.25–26). *And a little further*: Even so husbands should love their wives as their own bodies (5.28), *and what follows*.

73.4   That it is necessary for wives to be subject to their own husbands as the Church is to Christ, accomplishing the will of God.

EPHESIANS: Wives, be subject to your husbands as to the Lord. For the husband is the head of the wife as Christ is the head of the church *and is himself the Savior of the body*. But *just as* the church is subject to Christ so let wives also be subject in everything to their husbands (5.22–24).

ΠΡΟΣ ΤΙΤ. Ἵνα σωφρονίζωσι τὰς νέας, φιλάνδρους εἶναι, φιλοτέκνους, σώφρονας, ἁγνὰς, οἰκουρούς, ἀγαθὰς, ὑποτασσομένας
τοῖς ἰδίοις ἀνδράσιν, ἵνα μὴ ὁ λόγος τοῦ Θεοῦ βλασφημῆται.

[73.5] Ὅτι οὐ δεῖ τὰς γυναῖκας πρὸς ὡραϊσμὸν κοσμεῖσθαι, ἀλλὰ
τὴν πᾶσαν σπουδὴν καὶ μέριμναν ἔχειν περὶ τὰ ἀγαθὰ ἔργα, καὶ
τοῦτον ἡγεῖσθαι ἀληθῆ καὶ πρέποντα Χριστιαναῖς κόσμον.
Κεφάλ. ε΄.
ΠΡΟΣ. ΤΙΜ. α΄. Ὡσαύτως γυναῖκας ἐν καταστολῇ κοσμίῳ μετὰ
αἰδοῦς καὶ σωφροσύνης κοσμεῖν ἑαυτάς· μὴ ἐν πλέγμασιν, ἢ χρυσῷ,
ἢ μαργαρίταις, ἢ ἱματισμῷ πολυτελεῖ, ἀλλ᾽, ὃ πρέπει γυναιξὶν,
ἐπαγγελλομέναις θεοσέβειαν, δι᾽ ἔργων ἀγαθῶν. [433]

[73.6] Ὅτι δεῖ τὰς γυναῖκας σιγᾶν ἐν ἐκκλησίᾳ, κατ᾽ οἶκον δὲ
σπουδαιολογεῖσθαι περὶ τῆς εἰς Θεὸν εὐαρεστήσεως.
Κεφάλ. ς΄.
ΠΡΟΣ ΚΟΡ. α΄. Αἱ γυναῖκες ὑμῶν ἐν ταῖς ἐκκλησίαις σιγάτωσαν· οὐ
γὰρ ἐπιτέτραπται αὐταῖς λαλεῖν, ἀλλ᾽ ὑποτάσσεσθαι. Εἰ δέ τι μαθεῖν
θέλουσιν, ἐν οἴκῳ τοὺς ἰδίους ἄνδρας ἐπερωτάτωσαν. Αἰσχρὸν γάρ
ἐστι γυναιξὶν ἐν ἐκκλησίᾳ λαλεῖν.
ΠΡΟΣ ΤΙΜ. α΄. Γυνὴ ἐν ἡσυχίᾳ μανθανέτω ἐν πάσῃ ὑποταγῇ.
Διδάσκειν δὲ γυναικὶ οὐκ ἐπιτρέπω, οὐδὲ αὐθεντεῖν ἀνδρός, ἀλλ᾽
εἶναι ἐν ἡσυχίᾳ. Ἀδὰμ γὰρ πρῶτος ἐπλάσθη, εἶτα Εὔα. Καὶ ὁ
Ἀδὰμ οὐκ ἠπατήθη, ἡ δὲ γυνὴ ἐξαπατηθεῖσα ἐν παραβάσει γέγονε.
Σωθήσεται δὲ διὰ τῆς τεκνογονίας, ἐὰν μείνωσιν ἐν τῇ πίστει, καὶ
ἀγάπῃ, καὶ ἁγιασμῷ, μετὰ σωφροσύνης.
ΟΡΟΣ ΟΔ΄.
[74.1] Ὅτι δεῖ τὴν χήραν, τὴν ἰσχυροτέρῳ τῷ σώματι χρωμένην, ἐν
φροντίδι καὶ σπουδῇ διάγειν, μεμνημένην τῶν ὑπὸ τοῦ ἀποστόλου
εἰρημένων, καὶ τῇ Δορκάδι μεμαρτυρημένων.
Κεφάλ. α΄.
ΠΡΑΞΕΙΣ. Ἐν Ἰόππῃ δέ τις ἦν μαθήτρια, ὀνόματι Ταβιθὰ, ἢ
διερμηνευομένη λέγεται Δορκάς. Αὕτη ἦν πλήρης ἔργων ἀγαθῶν,
καὶ ἐλεημοσυνῶν ὧν ἐποίει. Καὶ μετ᾽ ὀλίγα· Καὶ περιέστησαν αὐτῷ

TITUS: So train the young women to love their husbands and children, to be sensible, chaste, domestic, kind, and submissive to their husbands, that the word of God may not be discredited (2.4–5).

73.5   That it is necessary for women not to be cosmetically adorned but to show all zeal and care for good works and to regard this as the true and properly Christian adornment.

1 TIMOTHY: *Likewise* women should adorn themselves modestly and sensibly in seemly apparel, not with braided hair or gold or pearls or costly attire but by good deeds, as befits women who profess religion (2.9–10).

73.6   That it is necessary for women to keep silent in church, but at home to discuss zealously those things that please God.

1 CORINTHIANS: *Your wives* should keep silence in the churches. *For they are not commissioned to speak but to be subordinate.* If there is anything they desire to know, let them ask their husbands at home. For it is shameful for *women* to speak in church (14.34–35).

1 TIMOTHY: Let a woman learn in silence with all submissiveness. I permit no woman to teach or to have authority over men; she is to keep silent. For Adam was formed first, then Eve; and Adam was not deceived, but the woman was deceived and became a transgressor. Yet *she* will be saved through *childbearing*, if *they continue* in faith and love and holiness, with *discretion* (2.11–15).

74.1   That it is necessary for a widow possessed of a stronger body to continue in care and zeal, remembering the words of the Apostle and the witness of Dorcas.

ACTS: Now there was at Joppa a disciple named Tabitha, which means Dorcas. She was full of good works and acts of charity (9.36). *And a little further*: And all the widows stood *around* him weeping

πᾶσαι αἱ χῆραι κλαίουσαι, καὶ ἐπιδεικνύμεναι χιτῶνας καὶ ἱμάτια ὅσα ἐποίει μετ᾽ αὐτῶν οὖσα ἡ Δορκάς.

ΠΡΟΣ ΤΙΜ. α΄. Χήρα καταλεγέσθω, μὴ ἐλάττων ἐτῶν ἑξήκοντα, γεγονυῖα ἑνὸς ἀνδρὸς γυνή· ἐν ἔργοις καλοῖς μαρτυρουμένη, εἰ ἐτεκνοτρόφησεν, εἰ ἐξενοδόχησεν, εἰ ἁγίων πόδας ἔνιψεν, εἰ θλιβομένοις ἐπήρκεσεν, εἰ παντὶ ἔργῳ ἀγαθῷ ἐπηκολούθησεν. [434]

[74.2] Ὅτι δεῖ τὴν χήραν τὴν εὐδοκιμήσασαν ἐν τοῖς ὑπὸ τοῦ ἀποστόλου εἰρημένοις κατορθώμασι, καὶ φθάσασαν εἰς τὸ τάγμα τῶν ὄντως χηρῶν, προσκαρτερεῖν ταῖς δεήσεσι καὶ ταῖς προσευχαῖς μετὰ νηστειῶν νυκτὸς καὶ ἡμέρας.
Κεφάλ. β΄.
ΛΟΥΚΑΣ. Καὶ ἦν Ἄννα προφῆτις, θυγάτηρ Φανουὴλ, ἐκ φυλῆς Ἀσήρ· αὕτη προβεβηκυῖα ἐν ἡμέραις πολλαῖς, ζήσασα μετὰ ἀνδρὸς ἔτη ἑπτὰ ἀπὸ τῆς παρθενίας αὐτῆς. Καὶ αὕτη χήρα ὡς ἐτῶν ὀγδοηκοντατεσσάρων, ἣ οὐκ ἀφίστατο ἀπὸ τοῦ ἱεροῦ, νηστείαις καὶ δεήσεσι λατρεύουσα νύκτα καὶ ἡμέραν.
ΠΡΟΣ ΤΙΜ. α΄. Ἡ δὲ ὄντως χήρα καὶ μεμονωμένη ἤλπικεν ἐπὶ τὸν Θεὸν, καὶ προσμένει ταῖς δεήσεσι καὶ ταῖς προσευχαῖς νυκτὸς καὶ ἡμέρας· ἡ δὲ σπαταλῶσα, ζῶσα τέθνηκεν.

ΟΡΟΣ ΟΕ΄.

[75.1] Ὅτι χρὴ τοὺς δούλους ὑπακούειν τοῖς κατὰ σάρκα κυρίοις εἰς δόξαν Θεοῦ μετὰ πάσης εὐνοίας ἐν οἷς ἂν ἐντολὴ Θεοῦ οὐ λύηται.
Κεφάλ. α΄.
ΠΡΟΣ ΕΦΕΣ. Οἱ δοῦλοι, ὑπακούετε τοῖς κατὰ σάρκα κυρίοις μετὰ φόβου καὶ τρόμου ἐν ἁπλότητι καρδίας ὑμῶν, ὡς τῷ Χριστῷ· μὴ κατ᾽ ὀφθαλμοδουλείαν, ὡς ἀνθρωπάρεσκοι, ἀλλ᾽ ὡς δοῦλοι Χριστοῦ, ποιοῦντες τὸ θέλημα τοῦ Θεοῦ ἐκ ψυχῆς, μετ᾽ εὐνοίας δουλεύοντες, ὡς τῷ Κυρίῳ, καὶ οὐκ ἀνθρώποις· εἰδότες, ὅτι ἕκαστος ὃ ἐὰν ποιήσῃ ἀγαθὸν, τοῦτο κομιεῖται παρὰ τοῦ Κυρίου, εἴτε δοῦλος, εἴτε ἐλεύθερος.

and showing tunics and other garments which Dorcas made while she was with them (9.39).

1 TIMOTHY: Let a widow be enrolled if she is not less than sixty years of age, having been the wife of one husband; and she must be well attested for her good deeds, as one who has brought up children, shown hospitality, washed the feet of the saints, relieved the afflicted, and devoted herself to doing good in every way (5.9–10).

74.2   That it is necessary for the widow who is well known for keeping the words of the Apostle and who has been counted among the order of true widows to persevere in supplications and prayers with fasting night and day.

LUKE: And there was a prophetess, Anna, the daughter of Phanuel of the tribe of Asher; she was of a great age, having lived with her husband seven years from her virginity, and as a widow till she was eighty–four. She did not depart from the temple, worshiping with fasting and prayer night and day (2.36–37).

1 TIMOTHY: She who is a real widow and is left all alone has set her hope on God and continues in supplications and prayers night and day; whereas she who is self-indulgent is dead even while she lives (5.5–6).

75.1   That it is necessary for slaves to obey their earthly lords unto God's glory with all good will in whatever does not break a commandment of God.

EPHESIANS: Slaves, be obedient to those who are your earthly masters, with fear and trembling, in singleness of heart, as to Christ, not in the way of eye-service as men-pleasers but as servants of Christ, doing the will of God from the heart, rendering service with a good will as to the Lord and not to men, knowing that whatever good anyone does, he will receive the same again from the Lord whether he is a slave or free (6.5–8).

ΠΡΟΣ ΤΙΜ. α'. Ὅσοι εἰσὶν ὑπὸ ζυγὸν δοῦλοι, τοὺς ἰδίους δεσπότας πάσης τιμῆς ἀξίους ἡγείσθωσαν, ἵνα μὴ τὸ ὄνομα τοῦ Θεοῦ καὶ ἡ διδασκαλία βλασφημῆται. Οἱ δὲ πιστοὺς ἔχοντες δεσπότας, μὴ καταφρονείτωσαν, ὅτι ἀδελφοί εἰσιν, ἀλλὰ μᾶλλον δουλευέτωσαν, ὅτι πιστοί εἰσι καὶ ἀγαπητοί, οἱ τῆς εὐεργεσίας ἀντιλαμβανόμενοι. ΠΡΟΣ ΤΙΤ. Δούλους ἰδίοις δεσπόταις ὑποτάσσεσθαι,[28] ἐν πᾶσιν εὐαρέστους εἶναι, μὴ ἀντιλέγοντας, μὴ νοσφιζομένους, ἀλλὰ πᾶσαν πίστιν ἐπιδεικνυμένους ἀγαθήν· ἵνα τὴν διδασκαλίαν τοῦ Σωτῆρος ἡμῶν Θεοῦ κοσμῶσιν ἐν πᾶσιν. [435]

[75.2]   Ὅτι δεῖ τοὺς κυρίους μνημονεύοντας τοῦ ἀληθινοῦ Κυρίου, ὧν ἂν ἀπολαύσωσι παρὰ τῶν δούλων, ταῦτα καὶ ποιεῖν αὐτοῖς κατὰ δύναμιν, ἐν φόβῳ Θεοῦ, καὶ ἐπιεικείᾳ τῇ πρὸς αὐτοὺς, κατὰ μίμησιν τοῦ Κυρίου.

Κεφάλ. β'.

ΙΩΑΝΝΗΣ. Εἰδὼς ὁ Ἰησοῦς, ὅτι πάντα δέδωκεν αὐτῷ ὁ Πατὴρ εἰς τὰς χεῖρας, καὶ ὅτι ἀπὸ Θεοῦ ἐξῆλθε, καὶ πρὸς τὸν Θεὸν ὑπάγει, ἐγείρεται ἐκ τοῦ δείπνου, καὶ τίθησι τὰ ἱμάτια αὐτοῦ, καὶ λαβὼν λέντιον, διέζωσεν ἑαυτόν. Εἶτα βάλλει ὕδωρ εἰς τὸν νιπτῆρα, καὶ ἤρξατο νίπτειν τοὺς πόδας τῶν μαθητῶν, καὶ ἐκμάσσειν τῷ λεντίῳ ᾧ ἦν διεζωσμένος. Καὶ μετ' ὀλίγα· Ὑμεῖς φωνεῖτέ με, ὁ διδάσκαλος, καὶ ὁ Κύριος, καὶ καλῶς λέγετε· εἰμὶ γάρ. Εἰ οὖν ἐγὼ ἔνιψα ὑμῶν τοὺς πόδας ὁ Κύριος καὶ ὁ διδάσκαλος, καὶ ὑμεῖς ὀφείλετε ἀλλήλων νίπτειν τοὺς πόδας. Ὑπόδειγμα γὰρ δέδωκα ὑμῖν, ἵνα καθὼς ἐποίησα ὑμῖν, καὶ ὑμεῖς ποιῆτε.

ΠΡΟΣ ΕΦΕΣ. Οἱ κύριοι, τὰ αὐτὰ ποιεῖτε πρὸς αὐτοὺς, ἀνιέντες τὴν ἀπειλήν· εἰδότες ὅτι καὶ ὑμῶν αὐτῶν Κύριός ἐστιν ἐν οὐρανοῖς, καὶ προσωποληψία οὐκ ἔστι παρ' αὐτῷ.

ΟΡΟΣ Ος'.

[76.1]   Ὅτι δεῖ τὰ τέκνα τιμᾶν τοὺς γονεῖς, καὶ ὑπακούειν ἐν πᾶσιν αὐτοῖς, ἐν οἷς ἂν ἐντολὴ Θεοῦ μὴ ἐμποδίζηται.

---

[28]Corrected from ὑποτάσσεθα.

1 TIMOTHY: Let all who are under the yoke of slavery regard their masters as worthy of all honor, so that the name of God and the teaching may not be defamed. Those who have believing masters must not be disrespectful on the ground that they are brethren; rather they must serve all the better since those who benefit by their service are believers and beloved (6.1–2).

TITUS: Bid slaves to be submissive to their masters and to give satisfaction in every respect; they are not to be refractory nor to pilfer, but to show entire and true fidelity, so that in everything they may adorn the doctrine of God our Savior (2.9–10).

75.2 That it is necessary for lords, remembering the true Lord, to do for their slaves, as they are able, the very things they enjoy from them, in the fear of God and in service to them, imitating the Lord.

JOHN: Jesus, knowing that the Father had given all things into his hands and that he had come from God and was going to God, rose from supper, laid aside his garments, and girded himself with a towel. Then he poured water into a basin and began to wash the disciples' feet and to wipe them with the towel with which he was girded (13.3–5). *And a little further*: You call me Teacher and Lord, and you are right, for so I am. If I then, your Lord and Teacher, have washed your feet, you also ought to wash one another's feet. For I have given you an example, that you also should do as I have done to you (13.13–15).

EPHESIANS: *Lords*, do the same to them and forbear threatening, knowing that *your Lord and theirs* is in heaven and that there is no partiality with him (6.9).

76.1 That it is necessary for children to honor their parents and to obey them in everything that will not compromise the commandment of God.

Κεφάλ. α΄.

ΛΟΥΚΑΣ. Καὶ πρὸς αὐτὸν ἡ μήτηρ αὐτοῦ εἶπε· τέκνον, τί ἐποίησας ἡμῖν οὕτως; Ἰδοὺ ὁ πατήρ σου κἀγὼ ὀδυνώμενοι ἐζητοῦμέν σε. Καὶ μετ᾽ ὀλίγα· Καὶ μετέβη μετ᾽ αὐτῶν, καὶ ἦλθεν εἰς Ναζαρὲτ, καὶ ἦν ὑποτασσόμενος αὐτοῖς. ΠΡΟΣ ΕΦΕΣ. Τὰ τέκνα, ὑπακούετε τοῖς γονεῦσιν ὑμῶν ἐν Κυρίῳ· τοῦτο γάρ ἐστι δίκαιον. «Τίμα τὸν πατέρα καὶ τὴν μητέρα,» ἥτις ἐστὶν ἐντολὴ πρώτη ἐν ἐπαγγελίαις, «ἵνα εὖ σοι γένηται, καὶ ἔσῃ μακροχρόνιος ἐπὶ τῆς γῆς.» [436]

[76.2] Ὅτι δεῖ τοὺς γονεῖς ἐν παιδείᾳ καὶ νουθεσίᾳ Κυρίου ἐκτρέφειν τὰ τέκνα μετὰ πραότητος καὶ μακροθυμίας· μηδεμίαν δὲ πρόφασιν, τὸ ὅσον ἐπ᾽ αὐτοῖς, διδόναι ὀργῆς καὶ λύπης.

Κεφάλ. β΄.

ΠΡΟΣ ΕΦΕΣ. Καὶ οἱ πατέρες, μὴ παροργίζετε τὰ τέκνα ὑμῶν, ἀλλ᾽ ἐκτρέφετε αὐτὰ ἐν παιδείᾳ καὶ νουθεσίᾳ Κυρίου. ΠΡΟΣ ΚΟΛ. Οἱ πατέρες, μὴ ἐρεθίζετε τὰ τέκνα ὑμῶν, ἵνα μὴ ἀθυμῶσιν.

ΟΡΟΣ ΟΖ΄.

[77.1] Ὅτι δεῖ τὰς παρθένους ἀπηλλάχθαι πάσης μερίμνης τοῦ ἐνεστῶτος αἰῶνος, πρὸς τὸ δύνασθαι ἀπερισπάστως τῷ Θεῷ εὐχαριστεῖν, κατά τε νοῦν καὶ σῶμα, ἐπ᾽ ἐλπίδι τῆς βασιλείας τῶν οὐρανῶν.

Κεφάλ. α΄.

ΜΑΤΘΑΙΟΣ. Εἰσὶν εὐνοῦχοι, οἵτινες εὐνούχισαν ἑαυτοὺς διὰ τὴν βασιλείαν τῶν οὐρανῶν. Ὁ δυνάμενος χωρεῖν, χωρείτω. ΠΡΟΣ ΚΟΡ. α΄. Θέλω δὲ ὑμᾶς ἀμερίμνους εἶναι. Ὁ ἄγαμος μεριμνᾷ τὰ τοῦ Κυρίου, πῶς ἀρέσει τῷ Κυρίῳ· ὁ δὲ γαμήσας μεριμνᾷ τὰ τοῦ κόσμου, πῶς ἀρέσει τῇ γυναικί. Μεμέρισται καὶ ἡ γυνὴ καὶ ἡ παρθένος. Ἡ ἄγαμος μεριμνᾷ τὰ τοῦ Κυρίου, ἵνα ᾖ ἁγία καὶ τῷ σώματι καὶ τῷ πνεύματι. Ἡ δὲ γαμήσασα μεριμνᾷ τὰ τοῦ κόσμου, πῶς ἀρέσει τῷ ἀνδρί. Τοῦτο δὲ πρὸς τὸ ὑμῶν αὐτῶν συμφέρον

LUKE: And his mother said to him, "Son, why have you treated us so? Behold, your father and I have been looking for you anxiously" (2.48). *And a little further*: And he went down with them and came to Nazareth and was obedient to them (2.51).

EPHESIANS: Children, obey your parents in the Lord, for this is right. "Honor *father* and mother" (this is the first commandment with a promise) "that it may be well with you and that you may live long on the earth"[35] (6.1–3).

76.2   That it is necessary for parents to rear their children in the instruction and admonishment of the Lord with gentleness and patience and, as much as they can, to give no cause for anger or grief.

EPHESIANS: Fathers, do not provoke your children to anger but bring them up in the discipline and instruction of the Lord (6.4).

COLOSSIANS: Fathers, do not provoke your children, lest they become discouraged (3.21).

77.1   That it is necessary for virgins to be released from all the cares of this present age in order to be able to give thanks to God in mind and body without distraction in the hope of the kingdom of heaven.

MATTHEW: There are eunuchs who have made themselves eunuchs for the sake of the kingdom of heaven. He who is able to receive this, let him receive it (19.12).

1 CORINTHIANS: I want you to be free from anxieties. The unmarried man is anxious about the affairs of the Lord, how to please the Lord, but the married man is anxious about worldly affairs, how to please his wife. *The wife and the virgin are likewise divided. The unmarried woman* is anxious about the affairs of the Lord, how to be holy in body and spirit, but the married woman is anxious about

[35]Deut 5.16

λέγω· οὐχ ἵνα βρόχον ὑμῖν ἐπιβάλω, ἀλλὰ πρὸς τὸ εὔσχημον καὶ εὐπάρεδρον τῷ Κυρίῳ ἀπερισπάστως. [437]

ΟΡΟΣ ΟΗ΄.

[78.1]   Ὅτι οὐκ ἔξεστι τοῖς στρατευομένοις διασείειν ἢ συκοφαντεῖν.

Κεφάλ. α΄.

ΛΟΥΚΑΣ. Ἐπηρώτων δὲ αὐτὸν καὶ στρατευόμενοι, λέγοντες· καὶ ἡμεῖς τί ποιήσομεν; Καὶ εἶπε πρὸς αὐτούς· μηδένα διασείσητε, μηδὲ συκοφαντήσητε· καὶ ἀρκεῖσθε τοῖς ὀψωνίοις ὑμῶν.

ΟΡΟΣ ΟΘ΄.

[79.1]   Ὅτι δεῖ τοὺς ἄρχοντας ἐκδίκους εἶναι τῶν δικαιωμάτων τοῦ Θεοῦ.

Κεφάλ. α΄.

ΠΡΟΣ ΡΩΜ. Οἱ γὰρ ἄρχοντες οὐκ εἰσὶ φόβος τῶν ἀγαθῶν ἔργων, ἀλλὰ τῶν κακῶν. Θέλεις δὲ μὴ φοβεῖσθαι τὴν ἐξουσίαν; τὸ ἀγαθὸν ποίει· καὶ ἕξεις ἔπαινον ἐξ αὐτῆς. Θεοῦ γὰρ διάκονός ἐστί σοι εἰς τὸ ἀγαθόν. Ἐὰν δὲ τὸ κακὸν ποιῇς, φοβοῦ· οὐ γὰρ εἰκῆ τὴν μάχαιραν φορεῖ. Θεοῦ γὰρ διάκονός ἐστιν, ἔκδικος εἰς ὀργὴν τῷ τὸ κακὸν πράσσοντι.

[79.2]   Ὅτι δεῖ ἐξουσίαις ὑπερεχούσαις ὑποτάσσεσθαι ἐν αἷς ἂν ἐντολὴ Θεοῦ μὴ ἐμποδίζηται.

Κεφάλ. β΄.

ΠΡΟΣ ΡΩΜ. Πᾶσα ψυχὴ ἐξουσίαις ὑπερεχούσαις ὑποτασσέσθω. Οὐ γάρ ἐστιν ἐξουσία, εἰ μὴ ὑπὸ Θεοῦ· αἱ δὲ οὖσαι ἐξουσίαι ὑπὸ τοῦ Θεοῦ τεταγμέναι εἰσίν, ὥστε ὁ ἀντιτασσόμενος τῇ ἐξουσίᾳ, τῇ τοῦ Θεοῦ διαταγῇ ἀνθέστηκεν· οἱ δὲ ἀνθεστηκότες ἑαυτοῖς κρίμα λήψονται. Οἱ γὰρ ἄρχοντες οὐκ εἰσὶ φόβος τῶν ἀγαθῶν ἔργων, ἀλλὰ τῶν κακῶν, καὶ τὰ ἑξῆς.

ΠΡΑΞΕΙΣ. Πειθαρχεῖν δεῖ Θεῷ μᾶλλον ἢ ἀνθρώποις.

ΠΡΟΣ ΤΙΤ. Ὑπομίμνησκε [438] αὐτοὺς ἀρχαῖς καὶ ἐξουσίαις ὑποτάσσεσθαι, πειθαρχεῖν, πρὸς πᾶν ἔργον ἀγαθὸν ἑτοίμους εἶναι.

worldly affairs, how to please her husband. I say this for your own benefit, not to lay any restraint upon you but to promote good order and to secure your undivided devotion to the Lord (7.32–35).

78.1 That it is not permitted for soldiers to intimidate or extort.

LUKE: Soldiers also asked him, "And we, what shall we do?" And he said to them, "Rob no one by *intimidation* or by *extortion* and be content with your wages" (3.14).

79.1 That it is necessary for rulers to uphold the righteous statutes of God.

ROMANS: For rulers are not a terror *for* good conduct, but *for* bad. Would you have no fear of *the authority*? Then do what is good, and you will receive his approval, for he is God's servant for your good. But if you do wrong, be afraid, for he does not bear the sword in vain; he is the servant of God to execute *requital* on the wrongdoer (13.3–4).

79.2 That it is necessary to be subject to the authorities so long as the commandment of God is not compromised.

ROMANS: Let every person be subject to the governing authorities. For there is no authority except from God, and *the authorities* that exist have been instituted by God. Therefore he who resists the authorities resists what God has appointed, and those who resist will incur judgment. For rulers are not a terror *for* good conduct, but *for* bad (13.1–3), *and what follows.*

ACTS: We must obey God rather than men (5.29).

TITUS: Remind them to be submissive to rulers and authorities, to be obedient, to be ready for any honest work (3.1).

ΟΡΟΣ Π΄.

[80.1] Ποταποὺς εἶναι βούλεται ὁ λόγος τοὺς Χριστιανούς, ὡς μαθητὰς Χριστοῦ, πρὸς μόνα τυπουμένους, ἃ βλέπουσιν ἐν αὐτῷ, ἢ ἀκούουσι παρ' αὐτοῦ.

Κεφάλ. α΄.

ΜΑΤΘΑΙΟΣ. Ἄρατε τὸν ζυγόν μου ἐφ' ὑμᾶς, καὶ μάθετε ἀπ' ἐμοῦ. ΙΩΑΝΝΗΣ. Ὑμεῖς φωνεῖτέ με, ὁ διδάσκαλος, καὶ ὁ Κύριος· καὶ καλῶς λέγετε· εἰμὶ γάρ. Εἰ οὖν ἐγὼ ἔνιψα ὑμῶν τοὺς πόδας ὁ Κύριος καὶ ὁ διδάσκαλος, καὶ ὑμεῖς ὀφείλετε ἀλλήλων νίπτειν τοὺς πόδας. Ὑπόδειγμα γὰρ δέδωκα ὑμῖν, ἵνα καθὼς ἐγὼ ἐποίησα ὑμῖν, καὶ ὑμεῖς ποιῆτε.

[80.2] Ὡς πρόβατα Χριστοῦ τῆς φωνῆς τοῦ ἰδίου ποιμένος ἀκούοντα μόνου, καὶ αὐτῷ ἀκολουθοῦντας.

Κεφάλ. β΄.

ΙΩΑΝΝΗΣ. Τὰ πρόβατα τὰ ἐμὰ τῆς φωνῆς μου ἀκούει, κἀγὼ γινώσκω αὐτά, καὶ ἀκολουθοῦσί μοι. Καὶ ἀνωτέρω· Ἀλλοτρίῳ δὲ οὐ μὴ ἀκολουθήσωσιν, ἀλλὰ φεύξονται ἀπ' αὐτοῦ, ὅτι οὐκ οἴδασι τῶν ἀλλοτρίων τὴν φωνήν.

[80.3] Ὡς κλήματα Χριστοῦ, ἐν αὐτῷ ἐρριζωμένους, καὶ ἐν αὐτῷ καρποφοροῦντας, καὶ πᾶν ὁτιοῦν οἰκεῖον αὐτοῦ καὶ ἄξιον ποιοῦντας καὶ ἔχοντας.

Κεφάλ. γ΄.

ΙΩΑΝΝΗΣ. Ἐγώ εἰμι ἡ ἄμπελος, ὑμεῖς τὰ κλήματα. [439]

[80.4] Ὡς μέλη Χριστοῦ, ἐν πάσῃ ἐνεργείᾳ τῶν ἐντολῶν τοῦ Κυρίου, ἢ τῶν χαρισμάτων τοῦ ἁγίου Πνεύματος κατηρτισμένους πρὸς ἀξίαν τῆς κεφαλῆς, ἥτις ἐστὶν ὁ Χριστός.

Κεφάλ. δ΄.

ΠΡΟΣ ΚΟΡ. α΄. Οὐκ οἴδατε, ὅτι τὰ σώματα ὑμῶν μέλη Χριστοῦ ἐστιν;

ΠΡΟΣ ΕΦΕΣ. Ἀληθεύοντες δὲ ἐν ἀγάπῃ, αὐξήσωμεν εἰς αὐτὸν τὰ πάντα, ὅς ἐστιν ἡ κεφαλή, Χριστός· ἐξ οὗ πᾶν τὸ σῶμα συναρμολογούμενον καὶ συμβιβαζόμενον διὰ πάσης ἁφῆς τῆς

80.1 Of what sort the Word desires Christians to be: as disciples of Christ, who pattern themselves on only what they see in him or hear from him.

MATTHEW: Take my yoke upon you and learn from me (11.29).

JOHN: You call me Teacher and Lord, and you are right, for so I am. If I then, your Lord and Teacher, have washed your feet, you also ought to wash one another's feet. For I have given you an example, that you also should do as I have done to you (13.13–15).

80.2 As sheep of Christ, who hearken only to the voice of their shepherd and follow him.

JOHN: My sheep hear my voice, and I know them, and they follow me (10.27). *And earlier*: A stranger they will not follow, but they will flee from him, for they do not know the voice of strangers (10.5).

80.3 As cuttings grafted onto Christ, who are rooted in him and bear fruit in him and who do and have everything whatsoever that belongs to him and is worthy of him.

JOHN: I am the vine; you are the branches (15.5).

80.4 As members of Christ, complete in every work whether of the commandments of the Lord or of the charisms of the Holy Spirit, in order to be worthy of their head, who is Christ.

1 CORINTHIANS: Do you not know that your bodies are members of Christ (6.15)?

EPHESIANS: Speaking the truth in love, we are to grow up in every way into him who is the head, into Christ, from whom the whole body, joined and knit together by every joint with which it is supplied, when each part is working properly, makes bodily growth and upbuilds itself in love (4.15–16).

ἐπιχορηγίας, κατ᾽ ἐνέργειαν ἐν μέτρῳ ἑνὸς ἑκάστου μέρους τὴν αὔξησιν τοῦ σώματος ποιεῖται, εἰς οἰκοδομὴν ἑαυτοῦ ἐν ἀγάπῃ.

[80.5]   Ὡς νύμφην Χριστοῦ φυλάσσουσαν τὸ ἁγνὸν, ἐν τῷ μόνοις τοῖς θελήμασι τοῦ νυμφίου στοιχεῖν.

Κεφάλ. ε΄.

ΙΩΑΝΝΗΣ. Ὁ ἔχων τὴν νύμφην νυμφίος ἐστίν.

ΠΡΟΣ ΚΟΡ. β΄. Ἡρμοσάμην γὰρ ὑμᾶς ἑνὶ ἀνδρὶ, παρθένον ἁγνὴν παραστῆσαι τῷ Χριστῷ.

[80.6]   Ὡς ναοὺς Θεοῦ ἁγίους, καθαροὺς, καὶ μόνων πεπληρωμένους τῶν πρὸς λατρείαν Θεοῦ.

Κεφάλ. ϛ΄.

ΙΩΑΝΝΗΣ. Ἐάν τις ἀγαπᾷ με, τὸν λόγον μου τηρήσῃ, καὶ ὁ Πατήρ μου ἀγαπήσει αὐτόν· καὶ πρὸς αὐτὸν ἐλευσόμεθα, καὶ μονὴν παρ᾽ αὐτῷ ποιήσομεν.

ΠΡΟΣ ΚΟΡ. β΄. Ὑμεῖς γὰρ ναὸς Θεοῦ ἐστε ζῶντος. Λέγει γὰρ ἡ Γραφὴ, ὅτι «ἐνοικήσω ἐν αὐτοῖς, καὶ ἐμπεριπατήσω, καὶ ἔσομαι αὐτῶν Θεός.»

[80.7]   Ὡς θυσίαν Θεοῦ ἄμωμον καὶ ἀλώβητον, παντὶ μέλει καὶ μέρει τῆς θεοσεβείας τὸ ὑγιὲς διασώζοντας.

Κεφάλ. ζ΄.

ΠΡΟΣ ΡΩΜ. Παρακαλῶ ὑμᾶς, ἀδελφοὶ, διὰ [440] τῶν οἰκτιρμῶν τοῦ Θεοῦ, παραστῆσαι τὰ σώματα ὑμῶν θυσίαν ζῶσαν, ἁγίαν, εὐάρεστον τῷ Θεῷ, τὴν λογικὴν λατρείαν ὑμῶν.

[80.8]   Ὡς τέκνα Θεοῦ, μεμορφωμένους πρὸς τὴν εἰκόνα τοῦ Θεοῦ, κατὰ τὸ μέτρον τὸ ἀνθρώποις κεχαρισμένον.

Κεφάλ. η΄.

ΙΩΑΝΝΗΣ. Τεκνία, ἔτι μικρὸν μεθ᾽ ὑμῶν εἰμι.

ΠΡΟΣ ΓΑΛ. Τεκνία μου, οὓς πάλιν ὠδίνω, ἄχρις οὗ μορφωθῇ Χριστὸς ἐν ὑμῖν.

[80.9]   Ὡς φῶς ἐν κόσμῳ, ὥστε αὐτούς τε εἶναι ἀνεπιδέκτους κακίας, καὶ τοὺς πλησιάζοντας αὐτοῖς φωτίζειν εἰς ἐπίγνωσιν τῆς

80.5　As a bride of Christ, maintaining chastity, to be content with the desires of the bridegroom alone.

JOHN: He who has the bride is the bridegroom (3.29).

2 CORINTHIANS: For I betrothed you to *one husband*, to present you as a pure bride to *Christ* (11.2).

80.6　As holy temples of God, clean and filled only with what is conducive to God's worship.

JOHN: If a man loves me, he will keep my word, and my Father will love him, and we will come to him and make our home with him (14.23).

2 CORINTHIANS: For we are the temple of the living God, *for the Scripture says*, "I will live in them and move among them, and I will be their God"[36] (6.16).

80.7　As a sacrifice to God, blameless and unblemished, preserving in all our limbs and members the health of godly piety.

ROMANS: I appeal to you therefore, brethren, by the mercies of God, to present your bodies as a living sacrifice, holy and acceptable to God, which is your *rational* worship (12.1).

80.8　As children of God, formed in the image of God according to the measure graced to humanity.

JOHN: Little children, yet a little while I am with you (13.33).

GALATIANS: My little children, with whom I am again in travail until Christ be formed in you (4.19).

80.9　As light in the world: both that they admit of no evil and that they illuminate those who come near them with the full knowledge

---

[36]Cf. Lev 26.12 and Ez 37.27

ἀληθείας, πρὸς τὸ γενέσθαι ὃ δεῖ, ἢ ἐλέγχειν ὅ εἰσιν.

Κεφάλ. θ΄.

ΜΑΤΘΑΙΟΣ. Ὑμεῖς ἐστε τὸ φῶς τοῦ κόσμου.

ΠΡΟΣ ΦΙΛΙΠ. Ἐν οἷς φαίνεσθε ὡς φωστῆρες ἐν κόσμῳ.

[80.10] Ὡς ἅλας ἐν γῇ, ὥστε τοὺς κοινωνοῦντας αὐτοῖς ἀνανεοῦσθαι τῷ πνεύματι πρὸς ἀφθαρσίαν.

Κεφάλ. ι΄.

ΜΑΤΘΑΙΟΣ. Ὑμεῖς ἐστε τὸ ἅλας τῆς γῆς.

[80.11] Ὡς λόγον ζωῆς τῇ πρὸς τὰ παρόντα νεκρώσει πιστουμένους τὴν ἐλπίδα τῆς ὄντως ζωῆς.

Κεφάλ. ια΄.

ΠΡΟΣ ΦΙΛΙΠ. Ἐν οἷς φαίνεσθε ὡς φωστῆρες ἐν κόσμῳ, λόγον ζωῆς ἐπέχοντες, εἰς καύχημα ἐμοὶ εἰς ἡμέραν Χριστοῦ. [441]

[80.12] Ποταποὺς βούλεται εἶναι ὁ λόγος τοὺς πιστευομένους τὸ κήρυγμα τοῦ εὐαγγελίου· ὡς ἀποστόλους, καὶ ὑπηρέτας Χριστοῦ, καὶ οἰκονόμους πιστοὺς μυστηρίων Θεοῦ, μόνα τὰ διατεταγμένα ὑπὸ τοῦ Κυρίου ἀπαραλείπτως ἔργῳ καὶ λόγῳ πληροῦντας.

Κεφάλ. ιβ΄.

ΜΑΤΘΑΙΟΣ. Ἰδοὺ ἐγὼ ἀποστέλλω ὑμᾶς ὡς πρόβατα ἐν μέσῳ λύκων. Πορευθέντες μαθητεύσατε πάντα τὰ ἔθνη.

ΠΡΟΣ ΚΟΡ. α΄. Οὕτως ἡμᾶς λογιζέσθω ἄνθρωπος, ὡς ὑπηρέτας Χριστοῦ, καὶ οἰκονόμους μυστηρίων Θεοῦ· ὃ δὲ λοιπὸν, ζητεῖται ἐν τοῖς οἰκονόμοις, ἵνα πιστός τις εὑρεθῇ.

[80.13] Ὡς κήρυκας βασιλείας οὐρανῶν, ἐπὶ καταλύσει τοῦ ἔχοντος τὸ κράτος τοῦ θανάτου ἐν τῇ ἁμαρτίᾳ.

Κεφάλ. ιγ΄.

ΜΑΤΘΑΙΟΣ. Πορευόμενοι δὲ κηρύσσετε λέγοντες· ὅτι ἤγγικεν ἡ βασιλεία τῶν οὐρανῶν.

of the truth, so that these either become what they must or are exposed for what they are.

MATTHEW: You are the light of the world (5.14).

PHILIPPIANS: Among whom you shine as lights in the world (2.15).

80.10 As salt in the earth, so that those who fellowship with them are revived by the Spirit unto incorruptibility.

MATTHEW: You are the salt of the earth (5.13).

80.11 As word of life, guaranteeing the hope of the true life by being dead to the present one.

PHILIPPIANS: Among whom you shine as lights in the world, holding fast the word of life, so that in the day of Christ I may be proud (2.15–16).

80.12 Of what sort the Word desires those entrusted with preaching the Gospel to be: as apostles and servants of Christ and faithful stewards of the mysteries of God, consistently fulfilling in deed and in word only what the Lord has appointed.

MATTHEW: Behold, I send you out as sheep in the midst of wolves (10.16). Go therefore and make disciples of all nations (28.19).

1 CORINTHIANS: This is how one should regard us: as servants of Christ and stewards of the mysteries of God. Moreover it is required of stewards that they be found trustworthy (4.1–2).

80.13 As heralds of the kingdom of heaven unto the destruction of the one who holds the power of death in sin.

MATTHEW: And preach as you go, saying, "The kingdom of heaven is at hand" (10.7).

ΠΡΟΣ ΤΙΜ. β΄. Διαμαρτύρομαι ἐγὼ ἐνώπιον τοῦ Θεοῦ καὶ Ἰησοῦ Χριστοῦ, τοῦ μέλλοντος κρίνειν ζῶντας καὶ νεκροὺς κατὰ τὴν ἐπιφάνειαν αὐτοῦ καὶ τὴν βασιλείαν αὐτοῦ· κήρυξον τὸν λόγον τοῦ Θεοῦ.

[80.14] Ὡς τύπον ἢ κανόνα τῆς εὐσεβείας εἰς κατόρθωσιν μὲν τῆς ἐν πᾶσιν εὐθύτητος τῶν ἀκολουθούντων τῷ Κυρίῳ, ἔλεγχον δὲ τῆς διαστροφῆς τῶν ἐν οἱῳδηποτοῦν ἀπειθούντων.

Κεφάλ. ιδ΄.

ΠΡΟΣ ΦΙΛΙΠ. Τὰ μὲν ὀπίσω ἐπιλανθανόμενος, τοῖς δὲ ἔμπροσθεν ἐπεκτεινόμενος, κατὰ σκοπὸν διώκω ἐπὶ τὸ βραβεῖον τῆς ἄνω κλήσεως Θεοῦ ἐν Χριστῷ Ἰησοῦ. Ὅσοι οὖν τέλειοι, τοῦτο φρονῶμεν· καὶ εἴ τι ἑτέρως φρονεῖτε, καὶ τοῦτο ὁ Θεὸς ὑμῖν ἀποκαλύψει. Πλὴν εἰς ὃ ἐφθάσαμεν τῷ αὐτῷ στοιχεῖν κανόνι, τὸ αὐτὸ φρονεῖν.

ΠΡΟΣ ΤΙΜ. α΄. Τύπος γίνου τῶν πιστῶν ἐν λόγῳ, ἐν ἀναστροφῇ, ἐν ἀγάπῃ, ἐν πίστει, ἐν ἁγνείᾳ.

ΠΡΟΣ ΤΙΜ. β΄. Σπούδασον σεαυτὸν δόκιμον παραστῆσαι τῷ Θεῷ· [442] ἐργάτην ἀνεπαίσχυντον, ὀρθοτομοῦντα τὸν λόγον τῆς ἀληθείας.

[80.15] Ὡς ὀφθαλμὸν ἐν σώματι, διακριτικοὺς μὲν τῶν ἀγαθῶν καὶ τῶν φαύλων, κατευθύνοντας δὲ τὰ μέλη τοῦ Χριστοῦ, πρὸς τὰ ἑκάστῳ ἐπιβάλλοντα.

Κεφάλ. ιε΄.

ΜΑΤΘΑΙΟΣ. Ὁ λύχνος τοῦ σώματός ἐστιν ὁ ὀφθαλμός· ἐὰν οὖν ᾖ ὁ ὀφθαλμός σου ἁπλοῦς, ὅλον τὸ σῶμά σου φωτεινὸν ἔσται.

[80.16] Ὡς ποιμένας προβάτων Χριστοῦ, μηδὲ τὴν ψυχὴν ὑπὲρ αὐτῶν θεῖναι ἐν καιρῷ παραιτουμένους, ὑπὲρ τοῦ μεταδοῦναι αὐτοῖς τὸ εὐαγγέλιον τοῦ Θεοῦ.

Κεφάλ. ις΄.

ΙΩΑΝΝΗΣ. Ὁ ποιμὴν ὁ καλὸς τὴν ψυχὴν αὐτοῦ τίθησιν ὑπὲρ τῶν προβάτων.

2 TIMOTHY: I charge you in the presence of God and of *Jesus Christ*, who is to judge the living and the dead *according to* his appearing and his kingdom: preach the word *of God* (4.1–2).

80.14   As an example or rule of piety for setting aright in all things those who follow the Lord and a rebuke for the distortions of those who in any way whatsoever defy him.

PHILIPPIANS: Forgetting what lies behind and straining forward to what lies ahead, I press on toward the goal for the prize of the upward call of God in Christ Jesus. Let those of us who are mature be thus minded, and if in anything you are otherwise minded, God will reveal that also to you. *Only, regarding what we have already attained, let us walk by the same rule; let us have the same mind* (3.13–16).

1 TIMOTHY: Set the believers an example in speech and conduct, in love, in faith, in purity (4.12).

2 TIMOTHY: Do your best to present yourself to God as one approved, a workman who has no need to be ashamed, rightly handling the word of truth (2.15).

80.15   As an eye in the body, discerning the good and the bad and conducting the members of Christ to the proper portion of each.

MATTHEW: The eye is the lamp of the body. So, if your eye is sound, your whole body will be full of light (6.22).

80.16   As shepherds of the sheep of Christ, who shrink not even from laying down their life for them if this is called for, for the sake of delivering to them the gospel of God.

JOHN: The good shepherd lays down his life for the sheep (10.11).

ΠΡΑΞΕΙΣ. Προσέχετε οὖν ἑαυτοῖς, καὶ παντὶ τῷ ποιμνίῳ, ἐν ᾧ ὑμᾶς τὸ Πνεῦμα τὸ ἅγιον ἔθετο ἐπισκόπους, ποιμαίνειν τὴν Ἐκκλησίαν τοῦ Θεοῦ.

[80.17]   Ὡς ἰατροὺς, ἐν πολλῇ εὐσπλαγχνίᾳ κατ' ἐπιστήμην τῆς τοῦ Κυρίου διδασκαλίας θεραπεύοντας τὰ πάθη τῶν ψυχῶν, εἰς περιποίησιν τῆς ἐν Χριστῷ ὑγείας καὶ διαμονῆς.

Κεφάλ. ιζ'.

ΜΑΤΘΑΙΟΣ. Οὐ χρείαν ἔχουσιν οἱ ἰσχύοντες ἰατροῦ, ἀλλ' οἱ κακῶς ἔχοντες.

ΠΡΟΣ ΡΩΜ. Ὀφείλομεν δὲ ἡμεῖς οἱ δυνατοὶ τὰ ἀσθενήματα τῶν ἀδυνάτων βαστάζειν.

[80.18]   Ὡς πατέρας καὶ τροφοὺς ἰδίων τέκνων, ἐν πολλῇ διαθέσει τῆς ἐν Χριστῷ ἀγάπης εὐδοκοῦντας μεταδοῦναι αὐτοῖς οὐ μόνον τὸ εὐαγγέλιον τοῦ Θεοῦ, ἀλλὰ καὶ τὰς ἑαυτῶν ψυχάς.

Κεφάλ. ιη'.

ΙΩΑΝΝΗΣ. Τεκνία, ἔτι μικρὸν χρόνον μεθ' ὑμῶν εἰμι.

ΠΡΟΣ ΚΟΡ. α'. Ἐν γὰρ Χριστῷ Ἰησοῦ διὰ τοῦ εὐαγγελίου ἐγὼ ὑμᾶς ἐγέννησα.

ΠΡΟΣ [443] ΘΕΣΣ. α'. Ὡς ἐὰν τροφὸς θάλπῃ τὰ ἑαυτῆς τέκνα, οὕτως ἱμειρόμενοι ὑμῶν, εὐδοκοῦμεν μεταδοῦναι ὑμῖν οὐ μόνον τὸ εὐαγγέλιον τοῦ Θεοῦ, ἀλλὰ καὶ τὰς ἑαυτῶν ψυχάς, διότι ἀγαπητοὶ ἡμῖν ἐγενήθητε.

[80.19]   Ὡς Θεοῦ συνεργοὺς, πρὸς μόνα τὰ ἄξια τοῦ Θεοῦ ἔργα ὅλους ἑαυτοὺς ἀποδεδωκότας ὑπὲρ τῆς Ἐκκλησίας.

Κεφάλ. ιθ'.

ΠΡΟΣ ΚΟΡ. α'. Θεοῦ γάρ ἐσμεν συνεργοί· Θεοῦ γεώργιον, Θεοῦ οἰκοδομή ἐστε.

[80.20]   Ὡς φυτευτὰς κλημάτων Θεοῦ, ἀλλότριον μὲν οὐδὲν τῆς ἀμπέλου, ἥτις ἐστὶν ὁ Χριστὸς, οὔτε μὴν ἄκαρπον ἐναφιέντας· τὰ δὲ οἰκεῖα καὶ καρποφόρα διὰ πάσης ἐπιμελείας βελτιοῦντας.

ACTS: *Therefore* take heed to yourselves and to all the flock in which the Holy Spirit has made you overseers[37] to care for the church of God (20.28).

80.17   As physicians who heal the passions of souls with great compassion and according to their knowledge of the Lord's teachings, so acquiring their health and endurance in Christ.

MATTHEW: Those who are well have no need of a physician, but those who are sick (9.12).

ROMANS: We who are strong ought to bear with the failings of the weak (15.1).

80.18   As fathers and rearers of their own children, who are well disposed out of their love in Christ to deliver to them not only the Gospel of God but even their own souls.

JOHN: Little children, yet a *short time* I am with you (13.33).

1 CORINTHIANS: For I became your father in Christ Jesus through the gospel (4.15).

1 THESSALONIANS: Like a nurse taking care of her children, *so* affectionately desirous of you, we were ready to share with you not only the gospel of God but also our own *souls*, because you had become very dear to us (2.7–8).

80.19   As coworkers with God who give their whole selves up for the Church solely to do the worthy works of God.

1 CORINTHIANS: For we are God's fellow workers; you are God's field, God's building (3.9).

80.20   As planters of the cuttings of God, who allow nothing alien to the vine, which is Christ, nor anything fruitless but who cultivate with all care that which is his and is fruitful.

[37]Or "bishops."

Κεφάλ. κ'.

ΙΩΑΝΝΗΣ.[29] Ἐγώ εἰμι ἡ ἄμπελος ἡ ἀληθινὴ, καὶ ὁ Πατήρ μου ὁ γεωργός ἐστι. Πᾶν κλῆμα, ἐν ἐμοὶ μὴ φέρον καρπὸν, αἴρει αὐτὸ, καὶ πᾶν, τὸ καρπὸν φέρον, καθαίρει αὐτὸ, ἵνα πλείονα καρπὸν φέρῃ. ΠΡΟΣ ΚΟΡ. α'. Ἐγὼ ἐφύτευσα, Ἀπολλὼς ἐπότισεν· ἀλλ᾿ ὁ Θεὸς ηὔξανεν.

[80.21] Ὡς οἰκοδόμους ναοῦ Θεοῦ, καταρτίζοντας τὴν ἑκάστου ψυχὴν, εἰς τὸ συναρμολογηθῆναι τῷ θεμελίῳ τῶν ἀποστόλων καὶ προφητῶν.

Κεφάλ. κα'.

ΠΡΟΣ ΚΟΡ. α'. Κατὰ τὴν χάριν τοῦ Θεοῦ, τὴν δοθεῖσάν μοι, ὡς σοφὸς ἀρχιτέκτων, θεμέλιον τέθεικα· ἄλλος δὲ ἐποικοδομεῖ. Ἕκαστος δὲ βλεπέτω πῶς ἐποικοδομεῖ. Θεμέλιον γὰρ ἄλλον οὐδεὶς δύναται θεῖναι παρὰ τὸν κείμενον, ὅς ἐστιν Ἰησοῦς Χριστός.

ΠΡΟΣ ΕΦΕΣ. Ἄρα οὖν οὐκέτι ἐστὲ ξένοι καὶ πάροικοι, ἀλλὰ συμπολῖται τῶν ἁγίων, καὶ οἰκεῖοι τοῦ Θεοῦ, ἐποικοδομηθέντες ἐπὶ τῷ θεμελίῳ τῶν ἀποστόλων καὶ προφητῶν, ὄντος ἀκρογωνιαίου [444] αὐτοῦ Χριστοῦ Ἰησοῦ, ἐν ᾧ πᾶσα οἰκοδομὴ συναρμολογουμένη αὔξει εἰς ναὸν ἅγιον ἐν Κυρίῳ, ἐν ᾧ καὶ ὑμεῖς συνοικοδομεῖσθε εἰς κατοικητήριον Θεοῦ ἐν Πνεύματι.

Κεφάλ. κβ'.

[80.22] Τί ἴδιον Χριστιανοῦ; Πίστις δι᾿ ἀγάπης ἐνεργουμένη.

Τί ἴδιον πίστεως; Ἀδιάκριτος πληροφορία τῆς ἀληθείας τῶν θεοπνεύστων ῥημάτων, οὐδενὶ λογισμῷ, οὔτε ὑπὸ φυσικῆς ἀνάγκης εἰσαγομένῳ, οὔτε πρὸς εὐσέβειαν ἐσχηματισμένῳ, διασαλευομένη.

Τί ἴδιον πιστοῦ; Τὸ ἐν τοιαύτῃ πληροφορίᾳ συνδιατίθεσθαι τῇ δυνάμει τῶν εἰρημένων, καὶ μηδὲν τολμᾶν ἀθετεῖν, ἢ ἐπιδιατάσσεσθαι. Εἰ γὰρ «πᾶν ὃ οὐκ ἐκ πίστεως, ἁμαρτία ἐστὶν,» ὥς φησιν ὁ ἀπόστολος, «ἡ δὲ πίστις ἐξ ἀκοῆς, ἡ δὲ ἀκοὴ διὰ ῥήματος Θεοῦ·» πᾶν τὸ ἐκτὸς τῆς θεοπνεύστου Γραφῆς οὐκ ἐκ πίστεως ὄν, ἁμαρτία ἐστίν.

---

[29]The attribution has been corrected.

JOHN: I am the true vine, and my Father is the vinedresser. Every branch of mine that bears no fruit he takes away, and every branch that does bear fruit he prunes that it may bear more fruit (15.1–2).

1 CORINTHIANS: I planted; Apollos watered, but God gave the growth (3.6).

80.21   As builders of God's temple, shaping the souls of each to fit well together upon the foundation of the apostles and prophets.

1 CORINTHIANS: According to the grace of God given to me, like a skilled master builder I *have* laid a foundation, and another man is building upon it. Let each man take care how he builds upon it. For no other foundation can anyone lay than that which is laid, which is Jesus Christ (3.10–11).

EPHESIANS: So then you are no longer strangers and sojourners *but* fellow citizens with the saints and members of the household of God, built upon the foundation of the apostles and prophets, Christ Jesus himself being the cornerstone, in whom the whole structure is joined together and grows into a holy temple in the Lord; in whom you also are built into it for a dwelling place of God in the Spirit (2.19–22).

80.22   What is the mark of a Christian? Faith working through love.

What is the mark of faith? Unwavering conviction of the truth of the God-breathed words, unshaken by any reasoning introduced either by physical necessity or fraudulently in the form of piety.

What is the mark of a believer? With such conviction, to be of the disposition that what is said is authoritative and to undertake not to disregard or add anything. For if "all that is not from faith is sin,"[38] as the Apostle says, and "faith is from hearing, and hearing is through God's Word,"[39] then everything outside the God-breathed Scripture, being not from faith, is sin.

[38]Rom 14.23
[39]Rom 10.17

Τί ἴδιον τῆς πρὸς Θεὸν ἀγάπης; Τὸ τηρεῖν τὰς ἐντολὰς αὐτοῦ κατὰ σκοπὸν τῆς αὐτοῦ δόξης.

Τί ἴδιον τῆς πρὸς τὸν πλησίον ἀγάπης; Τὸ μὴ ζητεῖν τὰ ἑαυτοῦ, ἀλλὰ τὰ τοῦ ἀγαπωμένου πρὸς τὸ συμφέρον τῇ τε ψυχῇ καὶ τῷ σώματι.

Τί ἴδιον Χριστιανοῦ; Τὸ διὰ τοῦ βαπτίσματος ἐξ ὕδατος καὶ Πνεύματος γεννηθῆναι ἄνωθεν.

Τί ἴδιον τοῦ γεννηθέντος ἐξ ὕδατος; Τὸ, καθὼς ὁ Χριστὸς ἀπέθανε τῇ ἁμαρτίᾳ ἐφάπαξ, οὕτω καὶ αὐτὸν νεκρὸν εἶναι καὶ ἀκίνητον πρὸς πᾶσαν ἁμαρτίαν, κατὰ τὸ γεγραμμένον. Ὅτι «ὅσοι ἐβαπτίσθημεν εἰς Χριστὸν Ἰησοῦν, εἰς τὸν θάνατον αὐτοῦ ἐβαπτίσθημεν. Συνετάφημεν οὖν αὐτῷ διὰ τοῦ βαπτίσματος εἰς τὸν θάνατον,» «τοῦτο γινώσκοντες, ὅτι ὁ παλαιὸς ἡμῶν ἄνθρωπος συνεσταυρώθη, ἵνα καταργηθῇ τὸ σῶμα τῆς ἁμαρτίας, τοῦ μηκέτι δουλεύειν ἡμᾶς τῇ ἁμαρτίᾳ.»

Τί ἴδιον τοῦ γεννηθέντος ἐκ Πνεύματος; Τὸ γενέσθαι ἐκεῖνο κατὰ τὸ διδόμενον μέτρον, ὅπερ ἐστὶ τὸ ἐξ οὗ ἐγεννήθη, καθὼς γέγραπται· ὅτι «Τὸ γεγεννημένον ἐκ τῆς σαρκὸς, σάρξ ἐστι· καὶ τὸ γεγεννημένον ἐκ τοῦ πνεύματος, πνεῦμά ἐστιν.»

Τί ἴδιον τοῦ ἄνωθεν γεννηθέντος; Τὸ «ἀπεκδύσασθαι τὸν παλαιὸν ἄνθρωπον σὺν ταῖς πράξεσιν αὐτοῦ καὶ ταῖς ἐπιθυμίαις· καὶ ἐνδύσασθαι τὸν νέον τὸν ἀνακαινούμενον εἰς ἐπίγνωσιν κατ᾽ εἰκόνα τοῦ κτίσαντος αὐτὸν,» κατὰ τὸ εἰρημένον· ὅτι «ὅσοι εἰς Χριστὸν ἐβαπτίσθητε, Χριστὸν ἐνεδύσασθε.»

Τί ἴδιον Χριστιανοῦ; Τὸ «καθαρισθῆναι μὲν ἀπὸ παντὸς μολυσμοῦ σαρκὸς καὶ πνεύματος» [445] ἐν τῷ αἵματι τοῦ Χριστοῦ· «ἐπιτελεῖν δὲ ἁγιωσύνην ἐν φόβῳ Θεοῦ» καὶ ἀγάπῃ τοῦ Χριστοῦ, καὶ «μὴ ἔχειν σπῖλον ἢ ῥυτίδα, ἤ τι τῶν τοιούτων· ἀλλ᾽ εἶναι ἅγιον καὶ ἄμωμον,» καὶ οὕτως ἐσθίειν τὸ σῶμα τοῦ Χριστοῦ, καὶ πίνειν τὸ αἷμα. «Ὁ γὰρ ἐσθίων καὶ πίνων ἀναξίως, κρῖμα ἑαυτῷ ἐσθίει καὶ πίνει.»

What is the mark of love for God? Keeping his commandments in aim of his glory.

What is the mark of love for one's neighbor? Not seeking one's own aims, but those of the beloved unto the benefit of both soul and body.

What is the mark of a Christian? Being born anew through the baptism of water and the Spirit.

What is the mark of the one born of water? Just as Christ died to sin once and for all, so also to be dead to and unmoved by all sin, according to what is written: "As many as have been baptized into Christ Jesus have been baptized into his death. Therefore we were buried with him through baptism into death,"[40] "knowing this: that our old humanity was crucified with Him in order that the body of sin might be abolished that we might no longer be slaves to sin."[41]

What is the mark of the one born of Spirit? He is to be, according to the measure given him, the very thing from which he was born, just as it is written: "That which is born of flesh is flesh, and that which is born of spirit is spirit."[42]

What is the mark of the one born anew? The "shedding of the old humanity with its deeds and lusts, and the putting on of the new, which is being renewed into knowledge according to the image of its creator,"[43] according to what is written, "As many as have been baptized into Christ have put on Christ."[44]

What is the mark of a Christian? "Being cleansed from all defilement of flesh and spirit" in the blood of Christ, "perfecting holiness in the fear of God"[45] and the love of Christ, and "having no stain or wrinkle or any such thing, but being holy and blameless,"[46] and thus to eat the body of Christ and drink His blood,[47] "for the one who eats and drinks unworthily eats and drinks condemnation upon himself."[48]

[40]Rom 6.3–4
[41]Rom 6.6
[42]Jn 3.6
[43]Col 3.9–10.
[44]Gal 3.27.
[45]2 Cor 7.1
[46]Eph 5.27
[47]Cf. Jn 6.53
[48]1 Cor 11.29

Τί ἴδιον τῶν ἐσθιόντων τὸν ἄρτον, καὶ πινόντων τὸ ποτήριον τοῦ Κυρίου; Τὸ τὴν μνήμην φυλάσσειν διηνεκῆ τοῦ ὑπὲρ ἡμῶν ἀποθανόντος καὶ ἐγερθέντος.

Τί ἴδιον τῶν φυλασσόντων τὴν τοιαύτην μνήμην; «Τὸ μηκέτι ἑαυτοῖς ζῆν, ἀλλὰ τῷ ὑπὲρ αὐτῶν ἀποθανόντι καὶ ἐγερθέντι.»

Τί ἴδιον Χριστιανοῦ; Τὸ «περισσεύειν αὐτοῦ τὴν δικαιοσύνην ἐν παντὶ, πλέον τῶν γραμματέων καὶ Φαρισαίων,» κατὰ τὸ μέτρον τῆς κατὰ τὸ εὐαγγέλιον τοῦ Κυρίου διδασκαλίας.

Τί ἴδιον Χριστιανοῦ; Τὸ ἀγαπᾶν ἀλλήλους, καθὼς καὶ ὁ Χριστὸς ἠγάπησεν ἡμᾶς.

Τί ἴδιον Χριστιανοῦ; Τὸ προορᾶσθαι τὸν Κύριον ἐνώπιον αὐτοῦ διὰ παντός.

Τί ἴδιον Χριστιανοῦ; Τὸ ἐφ᾽ ἑκάστης ἡμέρας καὶ ὥρας γρηγορεῖν, καὶ ἐν τῇ τελειότητι τῆς πρὸς Θεὸν εὐαρεστήσεως ἕτοιμον εἶναι, εἰδότα, ὅτι ᾗ ὥρᾳ οὐ δοκεῖ, ὁ Κύριος ἔρχεται.

What is the mark of those who eat the bread and drink the cup of the Lord? Keeping the unbroken memory of the one who died and rose for us.

What is the mark of those who keep such a memory? "Living no longer for themselves, but for the one who died and rose for them."[49]

What is the mark of a Christian? "Abounding in righteousness in everything more than the scribes and Pharisees," [50] according to the measure of the teaching of the Lord in the Gospel.

What is the mark of a Christian? Loving others even as Christ loved us.[51]

What is the mark of a Christian? Seeing the Lord always before him.[52]

What is the mark of a Christian? Being watchful each day and hour and being ready in the perfection of pleasing God, knowing that the Lord is coming at an hour he does not expect.[53]

[49] 2 Cor 5.15
[50] Mt 5.20
[51] Cf. Jn 13.34; Eph 5.2
[52] Cf. Acts 2.25; Ps 16.8 (LXX 15.8)
[53] Cf. Mt 25.13

Index of Scriptural Citations[1]

[1] Plain type indicates that the verses are quoted. Verses in *italic* are referenced but not quoted directly.

[2] First entry is the Masoretic numbering. LXX is in parentheses.

POPULAR PATRISTICS SERIES

ST VLADIMIR'S SEMINARY PRESS
1-800-204-2665 • www.svspress.com